Techniques in Equine Reproc

MW01687490

6th Edition

For over 30 years, Animal Reproduction Systems has been dedicated to the field of equine reproduction, establishing itself as an industry leader in innovation, product quality, and education. To this end, we published the first edition of this publication (previously referred to as the 'Black Book') in 1996. Since then it has gone through several enhancements, most recently in 2014 with the release of the 5th edition. The present (6th) edition has been extensively updated and expanded with several new chapters, photographs, and tables.

Since first published, the goal of this book has remained the same – to provide education for horse owners, breeders, and equine students. It is hoped that the 6th edition will serve as a valuable resource for reproductive equipment as well as clinical techniques.

Horse breeders are encouraged to work with their veterinarian to optimize success, which is ultimately achieved by the birth of a live, healthy foal. An essential component of a successful relationship includes a conversation between owners and veterinary professionals to outline a strategy for stallion and mare breeding management, preventive medicine, emergency situations, and foal care.

Procedures and equipment outlined in this publication have been evaluated and recommended by the Equine Reproduction Laboratory at Colorado State University.

Portions of this 6th edition have appeared in previous editions or in Animal Reproduction and Biotechnology Laboratory Bulletins 9 and 10, published by Colorado State University, and are used herein with permission. We gratefully acknowledge the significant contributions of Drs. James Voss, BW Pickett and Ed Squires over the past 3 decades to the information contained in this book.

ISBN 978-0-692-04294-6

Printed in China

Table of Contents

Table of Contents

Table of Contents

Table of Contents

Table of Contents

Table of Contents

Table of Contents

Chapter 1 Reproductive Anatomy of the Stallion

A fundamental understanding of stallion anatomy is necessary to identify reproductive abnormalities, optimize breeding management, and perform an evaluation for potential fertility. The normal male reproductive tract consists of paired scrotal testes, epididymides, spermatic cords, deferent ducts (or vas deferens), ampullae, vesicular glands, bulbourethral glands, plus a bilobed prostate gland and a penis (Figure 1-1). Spermatozoa are produced within seminiferous tubules of the testes and mature in the epididymides. Spermatozoa are ejaculated by coordinated contractions of the deferent ducts, accessory sex glands and muscles associated with the penis.

1.1 The Scrotum

The scrotum is an outpouching of skin which contains the testes, epididymides and spermatic cords. It is situated high between the hind limbs and is slightly pendulous. The scrotum is divided into two lateral pouches by a septum which is evident externally as the median raphe (Figure 1-2). The pouches lie ventrally on either side of the penis (Figure 1-3). The scrotum serves to cover and protect the testes, but its primary function is regulation of temperature in the testis and tail of the epididymis. The testes must be maintained below body temperature for normal spermatogenesis to occur. In cold weather the testes are raised closer to the abdominal wall to minimize heat loss. In warm weather, the testes descend further from the body into the scrotum.

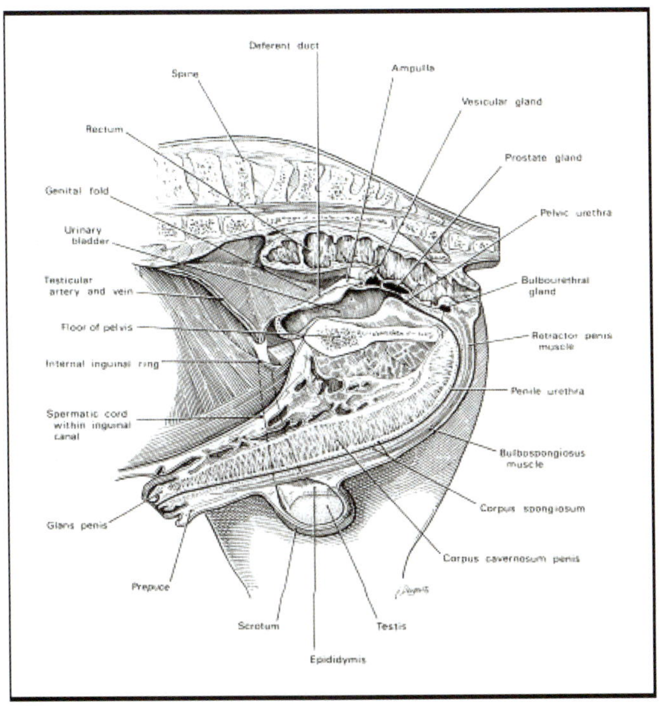

Figure 1-1 Reproductive tract of the stallion as seen in a left lateral dissection. (From: Pickett BW et al. Management of the Stallion for Maximum Reproductive Efficiency II. Animal Reproduction Laboratory Bulletin No. 05. Colorado State University, 1989).

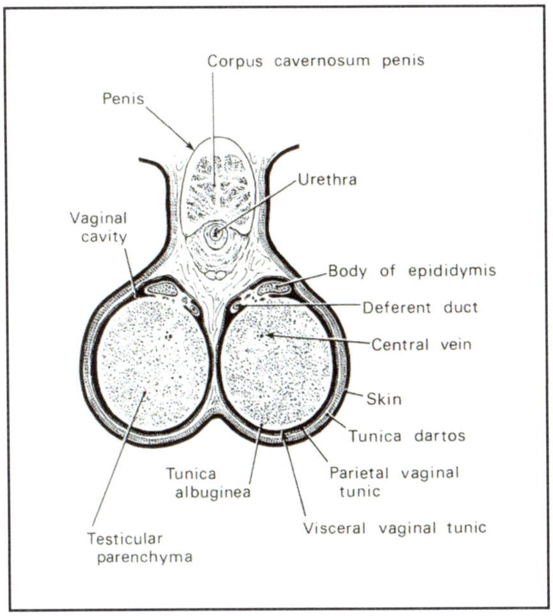

Figure 1-2 Drawing of the penis, scrotum and testes of the stallion in cross-section (from Pickett et al., 1989).

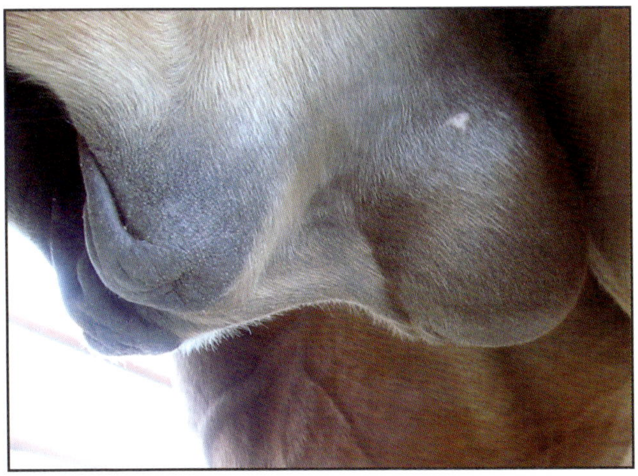

Figure 1-3 Photograph of the sheath and scrotum of a stallion.

Cooling of the testis is also accomplished by evaporation of moisture produced by numerous sweat glands within the scrotal skin and a 'counter-current heat exchange' system involving blood flow within the pampiniform plexus of the spermatic cord. Cooler venous blood from the testis enters the pampiniform plexus, an anastomosing complex of veins which surround the highly coiled testicular artery bringing warmer arterial blood from the body. Heat is transferred from the warmer arterial blood to the cooler venous blood in a counter-current heat exchange mechanism. As a consequence, arterial blood leaving the pampiniform plexus traveling toward the testes is several degrees cooler than the same arterial blood as it first enters the plexus.

1.2 The Testes

The testes are oval in shape and slightly compressed laterally. The primary functions of the testes are production of spermatozoa and androgenic hormones (i.e. testosterone) that are important in spermatogenesis, sexual differentiation, development of secondary sexual characteristics, and libido.

Palpation of the testes should reveal a smooth, regular outline and a slightly turgid, resilient texture. The size, consistency, and position of both testes should be similar. Testicular dimensions can be measured by calipers or ultrasonography; size of stallion testicles varies with age, season, and breed.

The orientation of a testis within the scrotum can be evaluated by palpation of the tail of the epididymis and the caudal ligament of the epididymis which are both located at the caudal pole of the testis and the spermatic cord, which is attached to the craniodorsal aspect of the testis.

The parenchyma of the testis contains seminiferous tubules and interstitial tissue between the tubules. Seminiferous tubules are the site of sperm production (Figure 1-4 and Figure 1-5). Sertoli cells within the seminiferous tubules support development and maturation of germ cells into spermatozoa. Tight junctions between Sertoli cells form the blood-testis barrier.

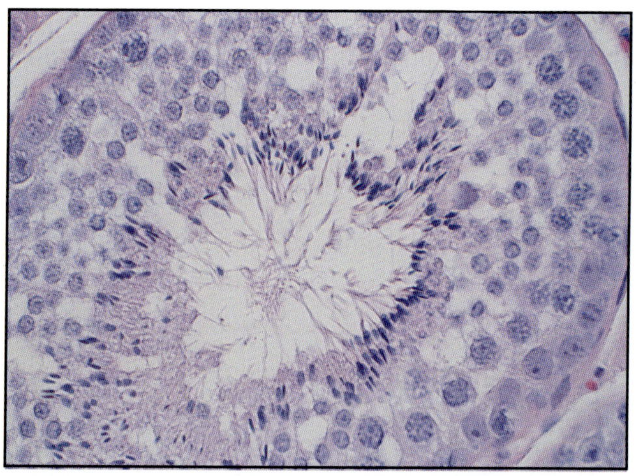

Figure 1-4 Histology photograph of a seminiferous tubule of a stallion. Note the mature spermatids adjacent to the tubule lumen.

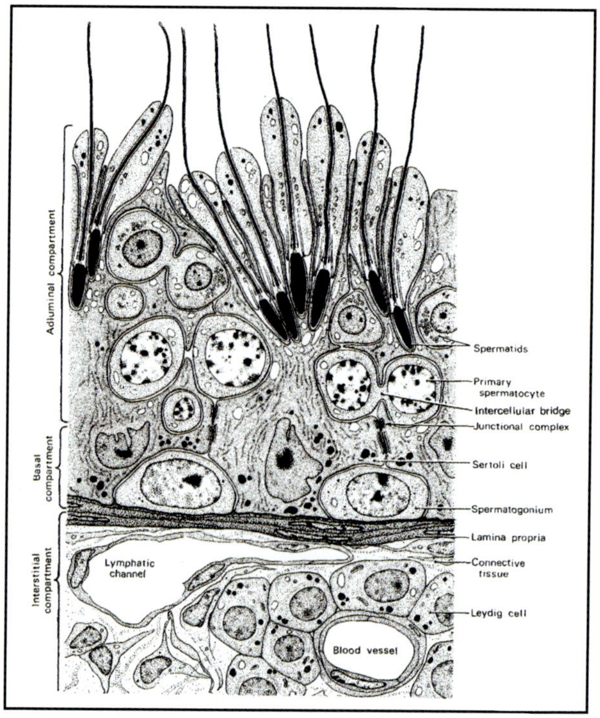

Figure 1-5 Drawing of the seminiferous tubule of a stallion testis (from Pickett et al., 1989).

Interstitial tissue contains Leydig cells, fibroblasts, lymphocytes, blood vessels, and lymphatics (Figure 1-7 and Figure 1-6). Leydig cells are responsible for production of the male sex hormone testosterone, which is important in support of spermatogenesis, maintenance of secondary sex characteristics and libido.

As noted, sperm production occurs within the seminiferous tubule. Spermatozoa are released from the seminiferous epithelium, and fluid secreted by Sertoli cells carries sperm down the lumen of the semi-

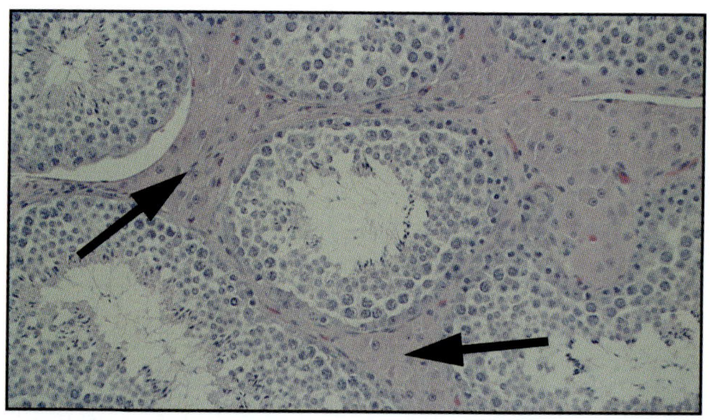

Figure 1-6 Histology photograph of a stallion testis. Note the pink staining Leydig cells surrounding the seminiferous tubules (arrows).

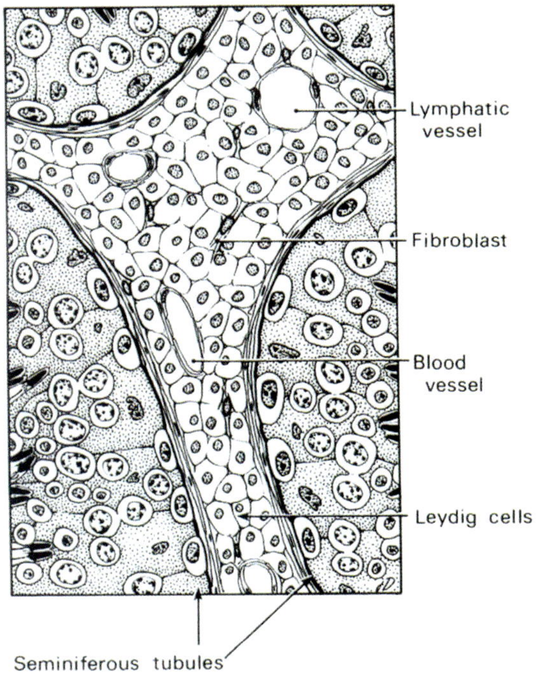

Figure 1-7 Drawing of the histology of the stallion testis showing the relationship between seminiferous tubules and interstitial tissue containing Leyding cells (from Pickett et al., 1989).

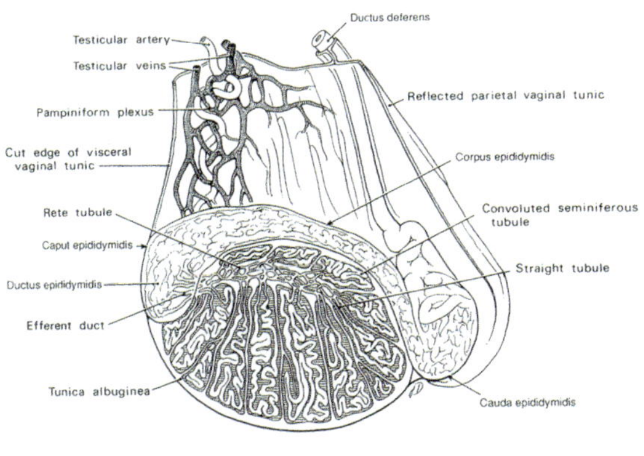

Figure 1-8 Drawing showing the relationship of the convoluted and straight seminiferous tubules, rete testis, efferent ducts, and epididymal ducts in the stallion testis (from Pickett et al., 1989).

niferous tubules, through the rete testis and efferent ducts into the epididymides (Figure 1-8).

1.3 The Epididymis

The epididymis of the stallion is a single, highly convoluted duct approximately 70 to 80 meters in length. It can be anatomically divided into head (caput), body (corpus), and tail (cauda) segments (Figure 1-9).

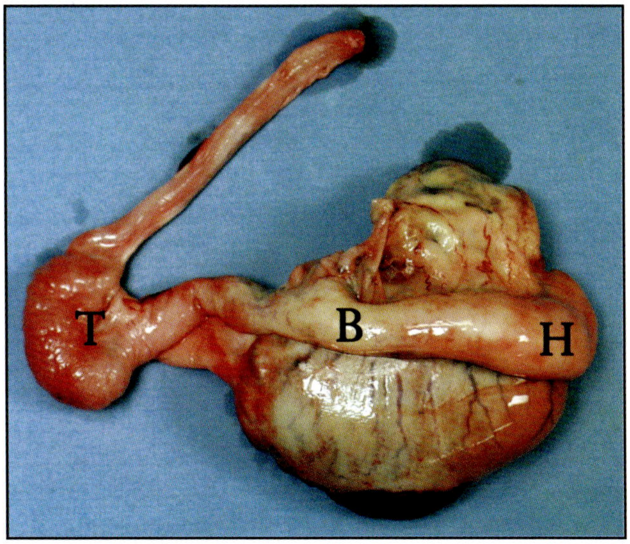

Figure 1-9 Photograph of a castrated testis with the head (H), body (B) and tail (T) of the epididymis evident.

The epididymal tail serves as a landmark for determination of the orientation of the testes within the scrotum. The tail of the epididymis is normally located caudally within the scrotum. Identification of the tail of the epididymis in the cranial scrotum indicates that the spermatic cord has rotated either 180 degrees or 540 degrees.

Maturation of spermatozoa occurs during passage through the epididymis. Spermatozoa are stored within the tail of the epididymis and proximal deferent duct. Each epididymal tail of a mature stallion often contains over 25 billion spermatozoa (Figure 1-10).

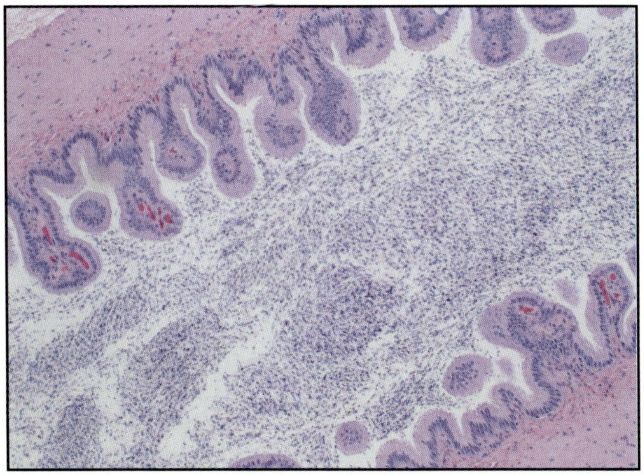

Figure 1-10 Histological image of spermatozoa within the tail of the epididymis (10x). The lumen is packed with spermatozoa.

Spermatozoa entering the epididymis are immotile and incapable of fertilization. Spermatozoa acquire the ability to move and to fertilize an oocyte during their transit through the epididymis. Equine sperm are maintained in a quiescent state during storage in

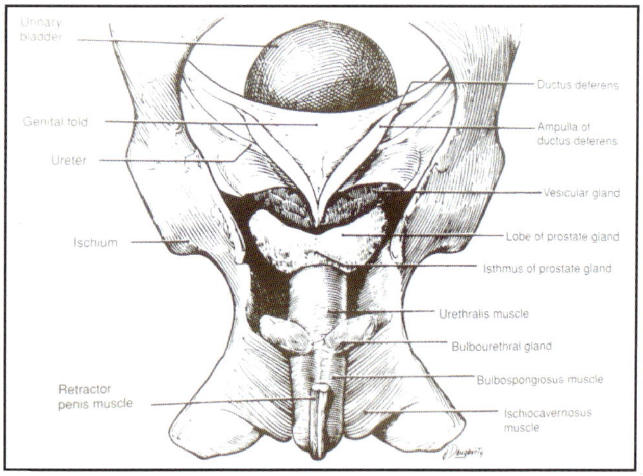

Figure 1-11 Drawing of the reproductive anatomy of a stallion (dorsal view) showing the main accessory sex glands (from Pickett et al., 1989).

the tail of the epididymis. Contact with seminal plasma at the time of ejaculation results in changes in the sperm plasma membrane and enhancement of motility.

The overall duration of stallion sperm transit through the epididymis is approximately 7.5 to 11 days. Transit of spermatozoa through just the head and body averages approximately 4 days and is not influenced by frequency of ejaculation. Transit time through the tail of the epididymis is approximately 4 to 7 days and may be influenced by ejaculation frequency. Repeated ejaculations will reduce the total number of spermatozoa stored in the tail of the epididymis.

Resorption of spermatozoa does not occur within the epididymis. It is hypothesized that spermatozoa normally pass from the deferent duct into the urethra intermittently and are voided during urination.

1.4 The Accessory Sex Glands

Stallions have four accessory sex glands, including paired ampullae, vesicular glands (seminal vesicles), bulbourethral glands, and a prostate (Figure 1-11 and Figure 1-12). Secretions from the accessory sex glands comprise a majority of the fluid portion of the ejaculate (i.e. the seminal plasma). Equine vesicular glands expand greatly during sexual stimulation and produce the gel fraction of the ejaculate. Prostatic fluid is thin and watery and may help to cleanse the urethra during ejaculation and also contributes to the seminal plasma. Secretions from the bulbourethral glands produce a majority of the pre-seminal fluid and contribute to the seminal plasma.

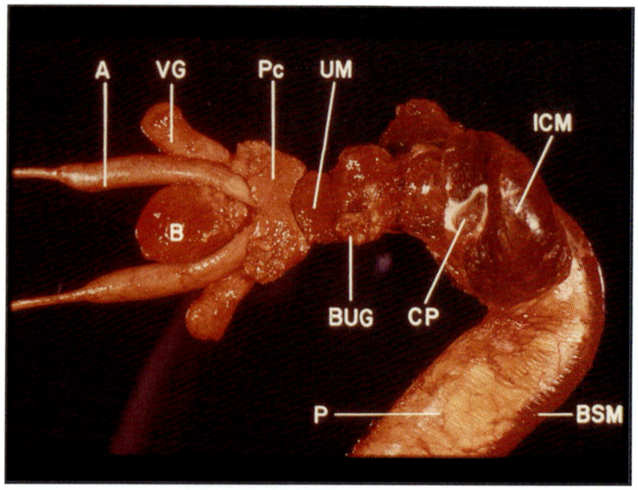

Figure 1-12 Accessory sex glands of the stallion. A-ampulla, B-urinary bladder, VG-vesicular glands or seminal vesicles, Pc-body of the prostate, UM-urethralis muscle, BUG-bulbourethral gland, CP-corpus or body of the penis, ICM-ischiocavernosus muscle, BSM-bulbospongiosus muscle, P-penis.

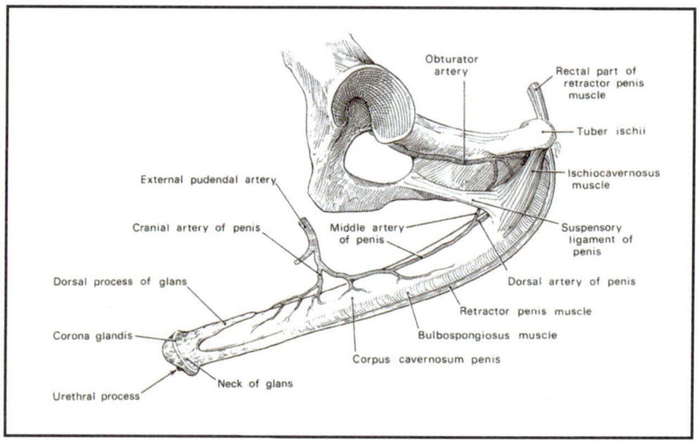

Figure 1-13 Drawing of a stallion penis and its attachment to the ischium (from Pickett et al., 1989).

1.5 The Penis and the Prepuce

The body or shaft of the penis is comprised primarily of the corpus cavernosum penis which engorges with blood during erection and the penis undergoes considerable enlargement in length and diameter (Figure 1-13, Figure 1-14 and Figure 1-15).

The corpus spongiosum, another region of spongy, erectile tissue, immediately surrounds the penile urethra. The corpus spongiosum is continuous into the corona glandis of the glans penis. The glans penis is the enlarged free end of the penis. The corpus spongiosum and corona glandis also become engorged with blood during sexual excitement and the glans may become markedly enlarged (commonly referred to as "belling" or "flowering") (Figure 1-16). The enlarged glans may seal the cervix during ejaculation and may aid in the intrauterine

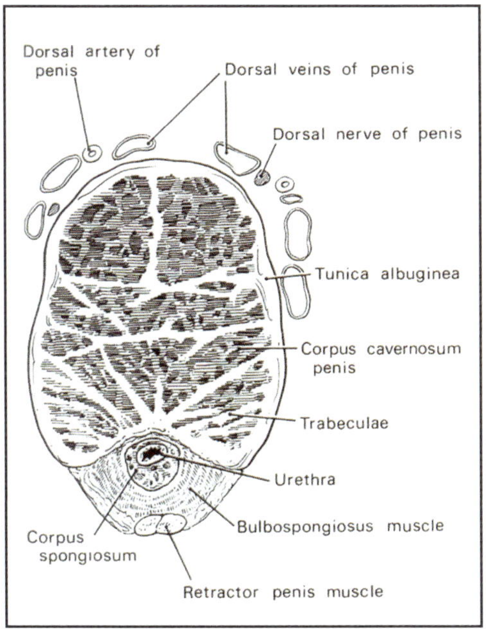

***Figure 1-14** Drawing of a cross-section of the body of a stallion penis (from Pickett et al., 1989).*

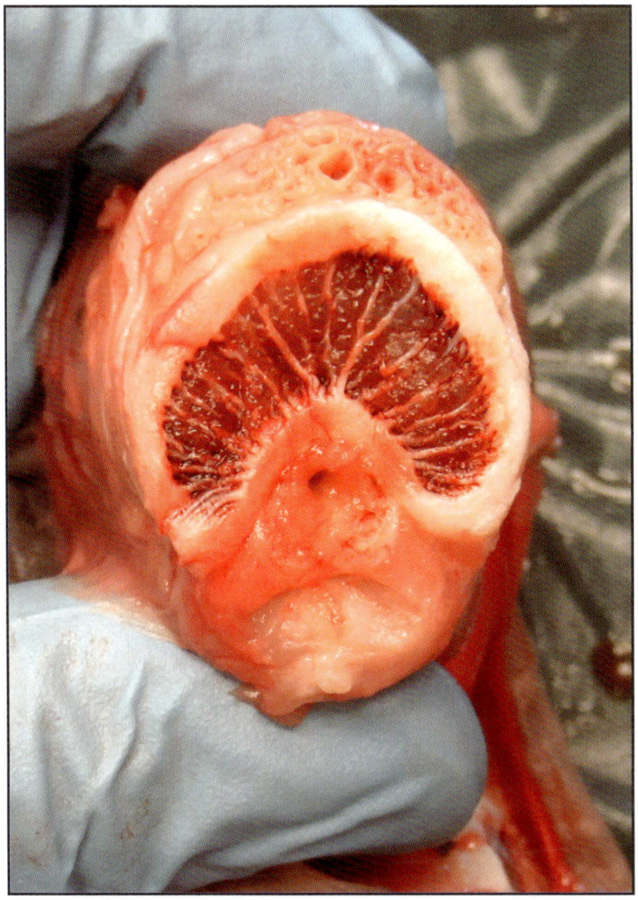

***Figure 1-15** Photograph of the cross-section of the body of a stallion penis.*

deposition of the ejaculate. A fossa glandis surrounds the urethral process on the end of the glans penis (Figure 1-17 and Figure 1-18).

A small opening in the dorsal fossa leads to a large diverticulum of the fossa glandis called the urethral

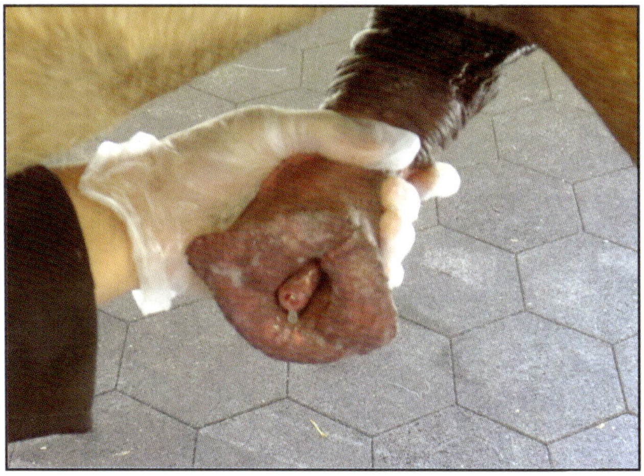

***Figure 1-16** Distal end of a stallion penis that has 'belled' during semen collection. Note the prominent urethral process surrounded by the urethral sinus in the center of the glans penis.*

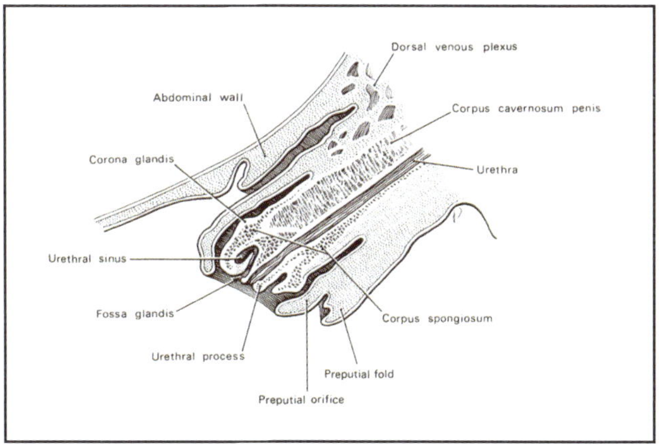

***Figure 1-17** Drawing of the distal end of the penis of a stallion (from Pickett et al., 1989).*

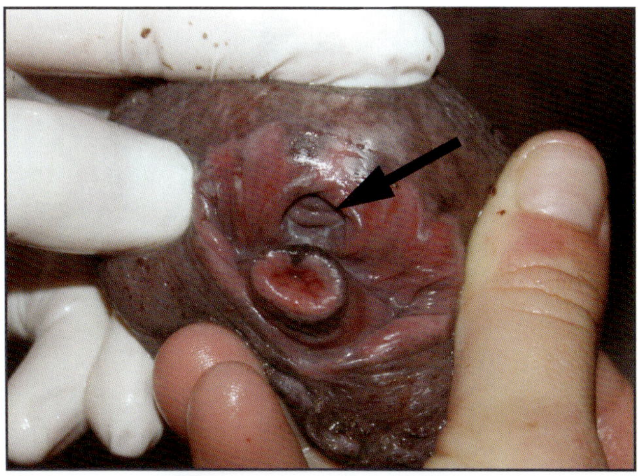

***Figure 1-18** Urethral sinus (arrow) visible within the urethral fossa surrounding the urethral process.*

sinus. Smegma, a combination of sebaceous secretions and epithelial cells, may accumulate in the urethral sinus forming "beans" (Figure 1-19). Excess accumulation of smegma may cause dis-

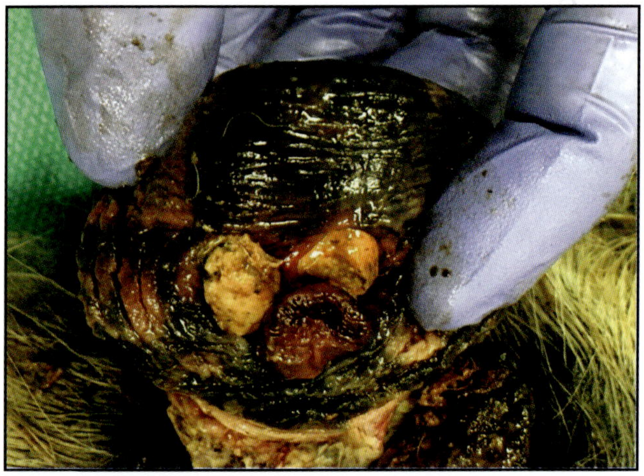

Figure 1-19 Photograph of the urethral fossa and urethral sinus filled with dried smegma ('beans').

comfort during urination or ejaculation.

The bulbospongiosus muscle is located on the caudal or ventral surface of the penile urethra. This skeletal muscle evacuates the penile urethral contents during ejaculation and urination. Rhythmic pulsations of the bulbospongiosus muscle is an indicator of ejaculation during semen collection or natural service.

1.6 Anatomy of a Spermatozoon

Although a spermatozoon contains only the essential components to carry out fertilization, it is a complex cell.

To fertilize an ovum, spermatozoa must retain:

- Metabolic processes for energy production
- Progressive motility
- Proteins necessary for survival in the female reproductive tract
- Enzymes (within the acrosome) essential for sperm penetration through the outer structures of the oocyte
- Proper plasma membrane lipid and protein distributions to permit a timely acrosomal reaction, as well as binding to and fusion with the oocyte

To accommodate these functions, a spermatozoon is compartmentalized into a head (containing an acrosome as well as the nucleus), neck, middle piece, principal piece and end piece (Figure 1-20 and Figure 1-21). Covering all of these structures is a plasma membrane composed of lipids and proteins.

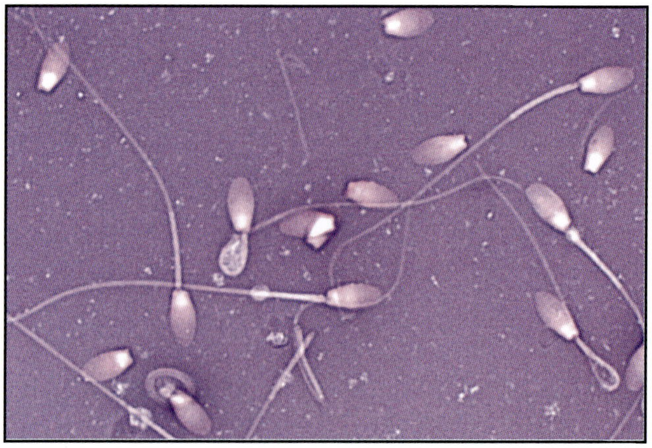

Figure 1-20 Photograph of stallion spermatozoa with a variety of morphologic abnormalities (Eosin-Nigrosin stain, 100x).

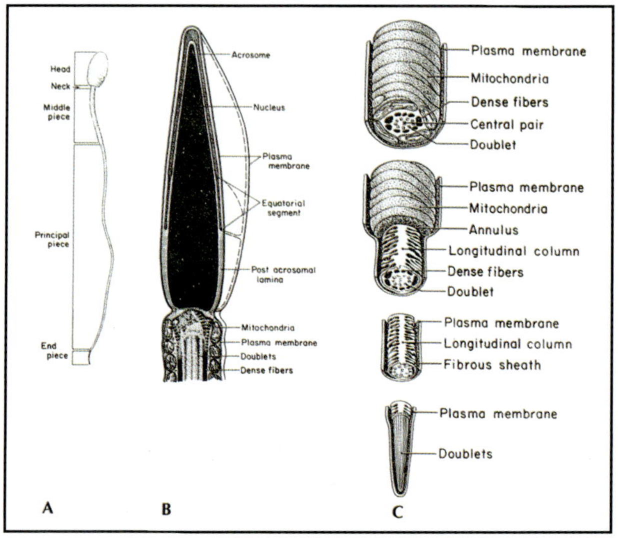

Figure 1-21 Drawing of stallion spermatozoa showing the associated parts.

Chapter 2 Reproductive Physiology of the Stallion

Testicular function is regulated by a complex interaction between endocrine (hormonal), paracrine and autocrine signals. The hypothalamic-pituitary-testicular axis is controlled by an interplay between stimulatory and inhibitory endocrine events (Figure 2-1).

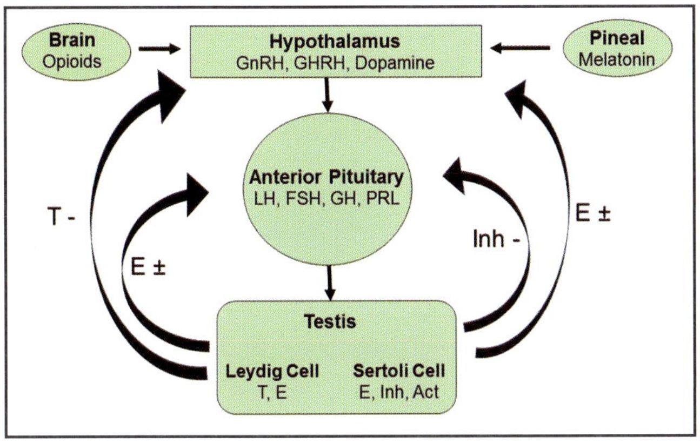

Figure 2-1 Hypothalamic-Pituitary-Testicular (HPT) axis in the stallion. A plus sign (+) indicates stimulation, a minus sign (-) indicates inhibition, a plus/minus sign (±) indicates variable stimulation or inhibition (modified from Roser, Anim Reprod Sci 2008;107:179-196).

Pulsatile secretion of gonadotropin releasing hormone from the hypothalamus results in stimulation of the anterior pituitary gland to produce and secrete gonadotropins (follicle stimulatory hormone and luteinizing hormone) in a corresponding pulsatile manner. Luteinizing hormone (LH) binds to receptors on Leydig cells of the testis and stimulates production and secretion of testosterone and estrogens. Follicle stimulating hormone (FSH) binds to receptors on Sertoli cells and stimulates production of inhibin, activin, androgen-binding protein (ABP) and other paracrine and autocrine factors needed for spermatogenesis.

Normal spermatogenesis requires high concentrations of testosterone within the testes. Concentrations of testosterone within the testes are 100 to 500 times higher than in peripheral blood. High intratesticular concentrations of testosterone are maintained, in part, by androgen-binding protein produced by Sertoli cells. ABP also functions as a carrier of androgens from the testis to the epididymis within testicular fluid.

Additional regulation of gonadotropin and gonadal steroid hormone secretion is accomplished by negative feedback suppression of GnRH and LH secretion by testosterone and estradiol, and suppression of FSH secretion by inhibin.

Males of most domestic animal species exhibit distinct pulses of LH and FSH throughout the day and corresponding pulses of testosterone secretion from the testes. Several studies have reported that stallions exhibit pulsatile release of gonadotropins (LH and FSH) and a corresponding increase in testosterone levels, while other studies have suggested that secretion of gonadotropins in stallions is more episodic and less pulsatile in nature.

Concentrations of LH and testosterone in peripheral blood of stallions are affected by season, with highest levels present in May and June (Northern Hemisphere). Levels of FSH are also affected by season, albeit to a lesser degree. Changes in gonadotropin and testosterone concentrations are photo-inducible, as exposure to an increase day length following a period of short days result in enhanced secretion.

2.1 Puberty

Puberty is the attainment of the ability for sexual reproduction or the production of offspring. Puberty results from a combination of physiological, anatomical and psychological maturation of the male reproductive system. Unfortunately, there is not a uniformly accepted definition of the onset of puberty in stallions. Attainment of puberty has been characterized based on histological development of testicular tissue, endocrine (testosterone) levels, and presence of spermatozoa in an ejaculate. The latter definition of puberty in stallions is the age at which an ejaculate first contains at least 50 million spermatozoa with a motility of at least 10 %. However defined, the age at which a male horse reaches puberty varies between individuals, breeds, season, body weight, and other factors.

Stallions reach puberty at approximately 14 to 24 months of age (20 to 21 months on average) based on sperm production. In contrast, sexual maturity, as defined by attainment of maximum testicular size and maximum numbers of spermatozoa in an ejaculate is achieved in stallions at 4 to 5 years of age.

Histologically, the testis of a male horse prior to puberty consists of 'quiescent' seminiferous tubules

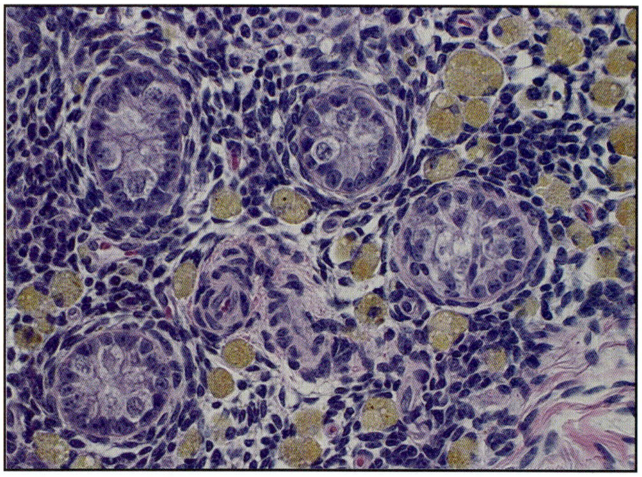

Figure 2-2 Histology of the testis of a 4.5 month old colt.

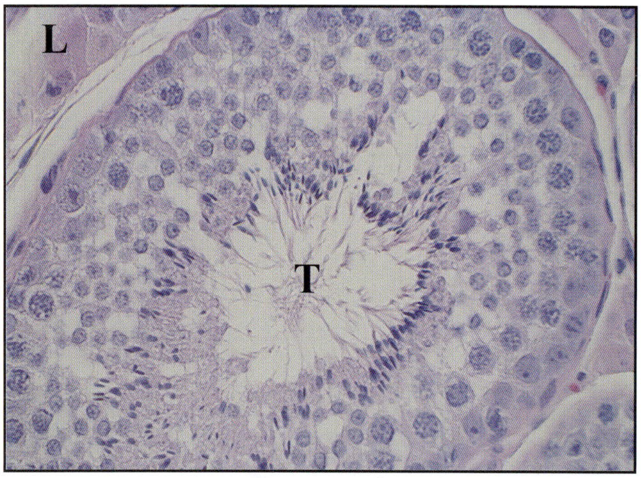

Figure 2-3 Histology of the testis of an adult (10 year old) stallion. Note the presence of Leydig cells (L) outside of the seminiferous tubule and mature spermatozoa about to be released into the lumen of the tubule (T).

with no evidence of spermatogenesis and an absence of a lumen within the tubules (Figure 2-2) as compared to a testis from an adult stallion (Figure 2-3).

A young stallion has the potential for mating and impregnating mares once puberty is reached and spermatozoa are produced. Consequently, it is common practice to either castrate or separate young stallions from fillies and mares prior to the onset of puberty.

2.2 Spermatogenesis

Spermatogenesis refers to the production of spermatozoa within seminiferous tubules of the testis by way of mitosis and meiosis (Figure 2-4 and Figure 2-5). Spermatogenesis can be divided into three stages - spermatocytogenesis, spermatidogenesis (meiosis) and spermiogenesis. Throughout spermatogenesis, developing cells are connected by intercellular bridges of cytoplasm which allows for communication between cells and synchronized development of cohorts of spermatozoa. The total time required to produce a mature spermatozoon from a spermatogonium (i.e. the duration of spermatogenesis) is approximately 57 days in the stallion.

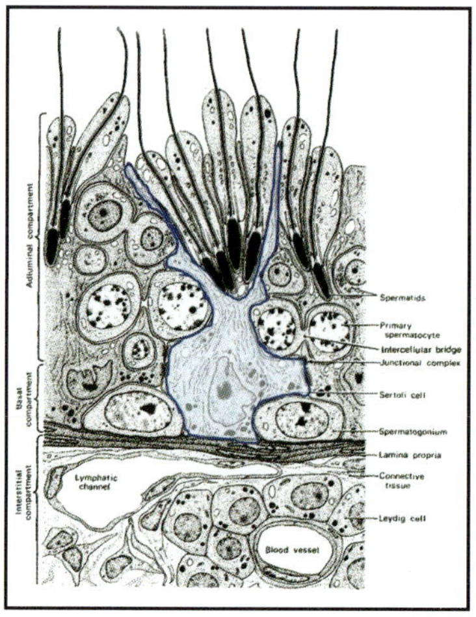

Figure 2-4 Drawing of the seminiferous tubule of a stallion testis (from Picket et al., Colorado State University, Animal Reproduction Laboratory Bulletin, 1989). A Sertoli cell which nurtures and facilitates spermatogenesis is highlighted in blue.

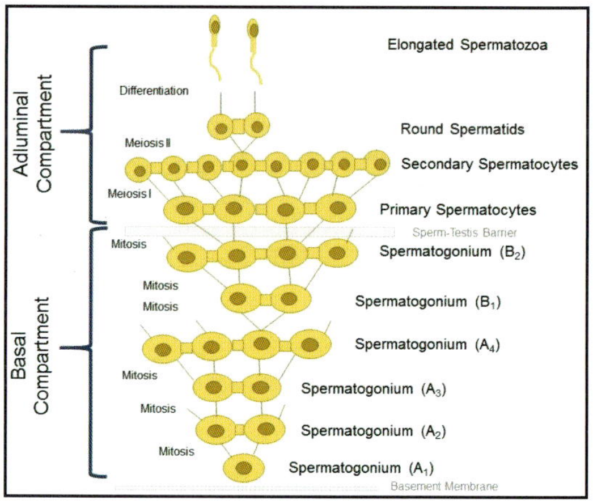

Figure 2-5 Stages of spermatogenesis. The basement membrane that surrounds the seminiferous tubule is at the bottom (grey bar) and the tight junctional complexes between Sertoli cells that constitute the Blood-Testis Barrier is indicated by the horizontal grey bar near the middle. Note that spermatogonia divide by mitosis within the basal compartment and primary spermatocytes traverse through the Blood-Testis Barrier and undergo two meiotic divisions in the adluminal compartment resulting in formation of round spermatids and eventually elongated spermatozoa.

A transient adverse medical condition, such as systemic fever leading to an increase in testicular temperature, may lead to a disruption of normal spermatogenesis. A minimum of 2 months (plus 7 to 10 days of epididymal transit time) may be required before a normal number of progressively motile, morphologically normal spermatozoa are present in an ejaculate.

Spermatocytogenesis. Spermatogonia, which are undifferentiated germ stem cells containing a diploid number of chromosomes (2N), line the basement membrane of the seminiferous tubule and the process of spermatocytogenesis occurs in the basal compartment of the seminiferous tubule. Spermatogonial stem cells undergo a sequential series of mitotic divisions (A1 to A4, then B1 to B2) during spermatocytogenesis to eventually produce primary spermatocytes (2N) and additional spermatogonia stem cells. Each spermatogonial stem cell can ultimately produce hundreds of spermatozoa. In the stallion, individual spermatogonia enter initial stages of spermatocytogenesis at approximately 12.2 day intervals.

Spermatidogenesis. Primary spermatocytes move from the basal compartment through the tight junctions between adjacent Sertoli cells into the adluminal compartment of the seminiferous tubules where they duplicate their DNA and divide meiotically (Meiosis I) into two secondary spermatocytes, each containing a haploid number of chromosomes (1N). Each secondary spermatocyte subsequently undergoes a second meiotic division (Meiosis II) to produce two round spermatids (1N). Genetic variation occurs during spermatidogenesis by chromosomal crossover, so that no two spermatids are identical.

Spermiogenesis. The final phase of spermatogenesis is called spermiogenesis, in which round spermatids are transformed into fully differentiated elongated spermatozoa consisting of a head (containing DNA) with an acrosomal cap, neck, midpiece (containing mitochondria) and a principle piece (tail).

Spermiation. Mature spermatozoa are released from their nurturing Sertoli cells into the lumen of the seminiferous tubule in a process called spermiation. Spermatozoa exit the seminiferous tubules through a closed tubular system (rete testis and efferent ducts) and eventually enter the head of the epididymis.

Cytoplasmic Droplets

Excess cytoplasm contained within a spermatid is usually phagocytosed by the Sertoli cell prior to spermiation. However, in some instances a remnant of cytoplasm may remain adherent to the proximal or distal midpiece region and is referred to as a cytoplasmic droplet. Retained cytoplasmic droplets may be shed during transit through the epididymis or may be present on spermatozoa in ejaculated semen (Figure 2-6). It has been suggested that excess residual cytoplasm may be due to an aberration in spermatogenesis and potentially associated with decreased fertility in some species. Centrifugation of stallion semen through a density gradient or a single layer of silica colloid can reduce the population of sperm with retained cytoplasmic droplets prior to artificial insemination or intracytoplasmic sperm injection (ICSI).

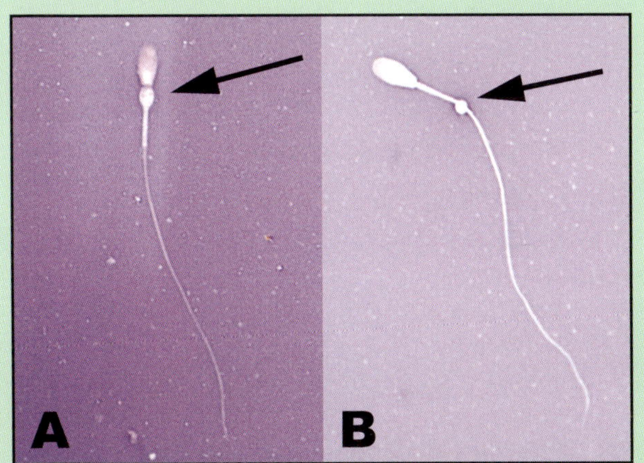

***Figure 2-6** Proximal (A) and distal (B) cytoplasmic droplets in the ejaculate of a stallion.*

2.3 Sperm Motility

Spermatozoa are non-motile and incapable of fertilization when released into the seminiferous tubules to begin their journey through the epididymis. Sperm transport through the tubular system is facilitated by a combination of fluid movement (fluid produced by Sertoli cells within the testes) and peristaltic contractions of the tubular tract.

Sperm continue to mature during passage through the head, body and the tail of the epididymis. Sperm acquire the potential to fertilize oocytes and to swim progressively on arrival into the tail of the epididymis, but true motility is not acquired until ejaculation occurs and sperm are in contact with fluid from the accessory sex glands. Acquisition of motility during transit through the epididymis and after ejaculation is facilitated by a combination of alterations in calcium, pH, and $HCO_3(-)$ concentrations (pH in epididymal fluid is very low), alteration in sperm plasma membrane proteins, dilution out of a purported 'sperm quiescence factor' present in epididymal fluid, and exposure to a purported 'forward motility protein' present in seminal plasma. The effect on sperm motility for most or all of these factors is mediated through changes in intracellular cyclic AMP levels and protein phosphorylation.

2.4 Cryptorchids, Hemi-Castrates and Geldings

A cryptorchid horse is a stallion in which one or both testes are not fully descended into the scrotum. A hemi-castrate is a stallion in which one testis has been surgically removed and the other testis remains in the horse. A gelding is a male horse in which both testes have been surgically removed. Additional comments regarding cryptorchids and hemi-castrated horses:

- Cryptorchid testes produce testosterone, but do not produce spermatozoa.
- Bilaterally cryptorchid stallions may exhibit stallion-like behavior due to continued testosterone production, but are infertile due to lack of spermatogenesis.
- Unilateral cryptorchid stallions are potentially fertile as normal sperm production should occur in the descended testis.
- Hemi-castration (removal of one testis) results in a compensatory increase in the size of the remaining testis. Since spermatozoa are produced on a 'per gram of testicular tissue' basis, hemi-castration results in increased sperm production from the remaining testis.
- Testosterone concentration in the plasma of hemi-castrated stallions are not significantly different than concentrations in intact stallions.
- Stallions unilaterally castrated for medical reasons (i.e. a testicular tumor) typically continue to have a successful breeding career utilizing the remaining testis.

2.5 Blood-Testis Barrier

The blood-testis barrier is formed by tight, adherens, and gap junctional complexes between Sertoli cells within the seminiferous tubule (see Figure 2-4). The barrier is not the basement membrane surrounding the seminiferous tubule. The blood-testis barrier isolates haploid (1N) stage sperm cells (i.e. secondary spermatocytes and spermatids) from the immune system of the stallion. Spermatogonia and primary spermatocytes are located in the basal compartment of the seminiferous tubule between the basement membrane and the blood-testis barrier. Primary spermatocytes (2N) migrate through the blood-testis barrier into the adluminal compartment where they subsequently divide by meiosis to form secondary spermatocytes (1N) and spermatids (1N).

The blood-testis barrier is also important in prevention of cytotoxic agents from gaining access to the seminiferous tubule. The barrier also allows fluid within the seminiferous tubule to be significantly different in composition than blood plasma so that the microenvironment around the latter stages of spermatogenesis is controlled and distinct.

The barrier continues from the seminiferous tubules, through the epididymis, ductus deferens and urethra. Exposure of the immune system to spermatozoa anywhere in the tubular tract could result in an adverse immune response and development of anti-sperm antibodies or aggregations of spermatozoa with inflammatory cells, such as a sperm granuloma within epididymal tissue.

The immune system of stallions is not exposed to the unique antigens on the surface of spermatozoa. Disruption of the blood-testis barrier (i.e. by blunt trauma, testicular biopsy, etc.) can potentially allow sperm to be exposed to the immune system of the stallion, leading to an autoimmune response and subsequent development of anti-sperm antibodies (ASA) of IgG, IgA, and/or IgM classes. Antisperm antibodies can cause a reduction in fertility in affected stallions.

2.6 Seasonal Aspects of Stallion Physiology

Stallions produce spermatozoa throughout the year (i.e. they do not become azoospermic), but there is a definite seasonal aspect to sperm production. The highest number of spermatozoa are produced in the summer (peak is June in the Northern Hemisphere) and the lowest number are produced in the winter (i.e. the nadir of sperm production is in December in the Northern Hemisphere).

Seasonal variation in sperm production is due to the influences of ambient photoperiod and melatonin secreted by the pineal gland. Light is detected by the retina of the eye and the photo information is translated through a complex signaling pathway to the pineal gland. Melatonin is secreted during the hours of darkness. The prolonged duration of melatonin secretion during long winter nights suppresses production of gonadotropin releasing hormone (GnRH) from the hypothalamus. Lower GnRH secretion results in decreased stimulation of the anterior pituitary gland and reduced production of follicle stimulating hormone (FSH) and luteinizing hormone (LH) which results in decreased support of testicular function.

The slow progressive increase in day length in the spring, or more appropriately stated 'the slow progressive decrease in the duration of night-time melatonin secretion', results in a ramping up of hypothalamic GnRH secretion and subsequently an increase in FSH and LH production by the pituitary and ultimately stimulation of both testosterone production and spermatogenesis. Steroid hormone levels peak between April and July in the Northern Hemisphere.

Testicular size, gonadal hormone production and spermatogenesis can also be enhanced by exposure to a stimulatory artificial photoperiod (a ratio of 16h light:8h dark). However, stallions eventually exhibit refractoriness to photoperiod stimulation in that testicular size and semen parameters are not maintained during a constant long-day artificial photoperiod.

2.7 Age Effects on Sperm Production

Stallions will produce spermatozoa throughout their lifetime. Overall semen quality is generally lower for stallions less than 3 years of age and greater than 14 years of age. Old stallions produce a lower number of progressively motile, morphologically normal spermatozoa than younger stallions and may eventually produce an insufficient number of sperm to impregnate mares with a reasonable chance of success. Consequently, aged stallions with significant testicular degeneration are generally retired from active breeding.

2.8 Epididymal Physiology and Sperm Transit

Spermatozoa are washed out of seminiferous tubules into a duct system called the rete testis and pass through efferent ducts into the head of the epididymis. The highly coiled tubular epididymis consists of three distinct zones, called the head (caput), body (corpus) and tail (cauda) (Figure 2-7) which is contiguous with the vas deferens (ductus deferens). The epididymis of a stallion is approximately 70 to 80 meters in total length.

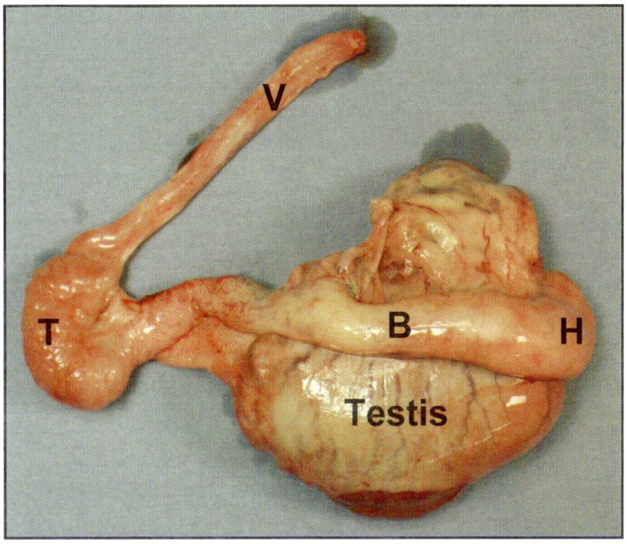

Figure 2-7 Stallion testis plus the head (H), body (B) and tail (T) of the epididymis and vas deferens (V).

The total time for equine sperm to transit through the epididymides is 7.5 to 11.0 days, with an average minimum transit time of 4.9 days.

Function of the epididymis is facilitated by androgens produced by Leydig cells of the testis. Testosterone is bound to androgen-binding protein and transported to the epididymis via fluid flowing within the tubular system. Testosterone is converted by 5α-reductase to dihydrotestosterone, a more potent androgen, within the epididymis. Castration results in rapid decrease in androgen production and eventual atrophy of the epididymal tissue.

2.9 Extragonadal Sperm Reserves

Spermatozoa are produced in the testes and stored in the epididymides and ductus deferens (vas deferens). One study indicated that the total extragonadal sperm reserves in the stallion is approximately 58.6 billion, of which 88 % were located within the epididymides (Table 1). A significant number of spermatozoa were also located in the ductus deferens (vas deferens) and ampullae. The same study noted that the extragonadal sperm reserves and epididymal content of spermatozoa were correlated with total testis weight, daily sperm production and daily sperm output. In addition, it was suggested that the extragonadal sperm reserves represented 7.3 days of sperm production.

Table 2-1 Extragonadal sperm reserves in stallions (modified from Gebauer et al., 1974;39:737-742). The ductuli efferentes (efferent ducts) refer to the tubular duct system that connects the rete testis to the head of the epididymis; the ductuli deferentia are the ductus deferens (vas deferens).

Structure	Total Number of Spermatozoa (x 10^9)	Percentage of Total Sperm (%)
Ductuli efferentes	0.2 ± 0.1	0.3
Epididymal head	8.1 ± 5.4	13.4
Epididymal body	11.4 ± 3.3	21.0
Epididymal tail	32.0 ± 8.9	53.3
Ductuli deferentia	3.1 ± 1.6	5.3
Ampullae	3.9 ± 1.9	6.7

The tail of the epididymis is the primary region for storage of sperm in the stallion and most other mammalian species. The extragonadal sperm reserves, specifically the number of spermatozoa in the tail of the epididymides, are affected by the frequency of ejaculation. The number of sperm stored in the tail of the epididymis decreases as ejaculation frequency increases. In contrast, the number of spermatozoa in the head and body of the epididymis are not affected by ejaculation frequency.

There are sufficient spermatozoa in the ductus deferens and ampullary regions to account for one ejaculate of semen. It is likely that sperm from the tail of the epididymis mixes with sperm stored within the ductus deferens and ampullae during ejaculation.

2.10 Thermoregulation of the Testis

The testes of a stallion need to be maintained at a temperature that is 2° to 6° C cooler than core body temperature for normal spermatogenesis. An increase in testicular temperature from any cause (systemic fever, local trauma, hydrocele, etc.) can reduce sperm quality and result in decreased fertility potential.

Factors important in regulation of testicular temperature include:

- Scrotal skin - heat loss by sweating and evaporative cooling
- Tunica dartos muscle - relaxes during warm temperatures allowing testes to descent further into the scrotum and contracts during cold weather to draw testes closer to the body
- Cremaster muscle - also has the ability to relax or contract in response to environmental temperature
- Pampininform plexus - a complex vascular network which serves as a counter-current heat exchanger, transferring heat from the warmer testicular artery (heading toward the testis) to the cooler testicular vein (heading away from the testis), ultimately resulting in cooler blood arriving to the testis

2.11 Ejaculation Physiology

Ejaculation is the discharge or ejection of semen from the male reproductive tract. The ejaculation process is divided into two phases - emission and expulsion.

Emission refers to the release of spermatozoa from the caudal epididymides and vas deferens plus fluids from the accessory sex glands into the pelvic urethra. This is accomplished by contraction of smooth muscle surrounding the epididymides, vas deferens and accessory sex glands (ampullae, seminal vesicles, prostate and bulbourethral glands). Emission is accompanied by closure of the bladder neck to prevent retrograde flow of semen into the urinary bladder.

Expulsion is the forceful ejection of the combined fluids (now referred to as semen) out of the urethra due to rhythmic contractions of the ischiocavernosus, bulbospongiosus, urethralis and other striated pelvic muscles. Semen is expelled in 5 to 10 jets in stallions. Each ejaculatory pulse is accompanied by a rhythmic contraction of the stallion's tail, known as 'flagging'. Flagging is used clinically as a visible sign that ejaculation is occurring during a live cover or semen collection procedure.

Sympathetic, parasympathetic and somatic nervous systems are all important in the ejaculatory process. The sympathetic nervous system regulates emission, while the somatic nervous system modulates expulsion. Injuries to the spinal cord, lesions to critical peripheral nerves (i.e. the pudendal nerve) or neurologic diseases may adversely affect nerve function and consequently interfere with the ejaculatory process.

2.12 Fractions of Equine Semen

Semen is comprised of spermatozoa produced by the testes and a fluid component originating from the testes, epididymides and vas deferens plus seminal plasma from the accessory sex glands (ampullae, seminal vesicles, prostate and bulbourethral glands and possibly some minor contribution from the urethral glands, also called Littre glands).

Stallion semen can be divided into 3 main fractions - presperm, sperm-rich, and gel fractions.

- Presperm fraction is watery in consistency and does not contain any spermatozoa. The presperm fraction originates from the bulbourethral gland with possible contribution from the prostate and is commonly emitted from the urethra when a stallion is stimulated or excited during teasing or washing prior to mating or collection. The presperm fraction serves to cleanse the urethra prior to expulsion of semen during ejaculation.
- Sperm-rich fraction is milky in appearance and consists of the first 3 jets of semen containing a high concentration of spermatozoa with secretions from the epididymides, ampullae and prostate. Approximately 70 % of sperm are contained within the first 3 ejaculatory jets.
- Gel fraction is the final fraction of semen to exit the urethra during ejaculation. The gel fraction can vary from a thin, watery secretion to a thick gelatinous mass originating from the seminal vesicles that serves to wash out any spermatozoa remaining in the urethra. Some stallions have very little gel in their semen while other stallions have a copious quantity. An in-line filter is commonly used to remove the gel fraction during semen collection.

2.13 Seminal Plasma

Seminal plasma is a combination of fluids from the testes, epididymides, vas deferens and the accessory sex glands. Testosterone is important for normal function of the accessory sex glands as well as libido and spermatogenesis. Castration results in a rapid decline in testosterone and eventual atrophy of the accessory sex glands.

Stallion seminal plasma consists of a proteins, lipids, enzymes, electrolytes, hormones (i.e. prostaglandins), trace elements and other substances. Wide variation exists between stallions in the components of seminal plasma.

Stallion seminal plasma contains high levels of glucose and very low levels of fructose, unlike bull or ram semen. The pH of normal stallion semen is 6.2 to 7.8 and the osmolality ranges from 300 to 336 mOsm. Significant alterations of pH or osmolality may be associated with a reduction in sperm motility and potentially a reduction in fertility.

Alkaline phosphatase (AP) is a dephosphorylating enzyme present in multiple tissues in the body and in seminal plasma of many animal species. In the stallion, AP activity originates in the testes and epididymides and is concentrated to very high levels in the epididymal tail. Measurement of seminal AP activity may be used as a sperm-independent marker for ejaculation in stallions. High levels of AP in the presence of spermatozoa indicate that ejaculation occurred. A high level of AP activity in seminal fluid in the absence of spermatozoa is indicative of azoospermia. In contrast, low levels of AP and the absence of spermatozoa suggest either failure of ejaculation or bilateral blockage of the ampullae.

Chapter 3 Reproductive Evaluation of the Stallion

Table 3-0 List and Part Number of ARS products used in this chapter.

Item	Part Number	Use/Comments
Scrotal Calipers	549A-101	Measurement of total scrotal width or measurement of length, width and height of individual testes

The ultimate measures of fertility of a stallion are pregnancy rate per cycle and per season and foaling rate. Although one would like every mare to become pregnant each season, a per season pregnancy rate of 90% and foaling rate of 80% are considered satisfactory. Unfortunately, fertility data are not available on many stallions and 'test breeding' to a sufficient number of mares to accurately assess fertility is expensive and often not practical.

A stallion reproductive evaluation, often termed a breeding soundness examination (BSE), may be performed to:

- Estimate future reproductive potential of a stallion
- Provide a routine evaluation prior to purchase
- Determine cause(s) of poor reproductive performance

The BSE should encompass general health of the horse, behavior, mating ability, genital examination, semen evaluation, and other parameters. In most cases, a BSE can be performed in one day. It is generally recommended that a stallion be evaluated after a period of sexual rest. In addition to the standard BSE, a test cool, and/or test freeze should be performed if a stallion is to be used in a cooled-transported semen or a frozen semen breeding program.

3.1 Identification

Each stallion should be properly and positively identified prior to evaluation. Registration name and number, age, and breed are recorded. Coat color and markings, lip tattoos, microchip information (if used), body brands, hair whorls, permanent scars, and any other identifying features should all be noted. A digital photograph may be valuable as part of the permanent medical record. The goal is to be able to accurately connect the results of a BSE to a specific stallion at a later date if necessary.

3.2 Reproductive History

A complete breeding history should be obtained, as past breeding results (conception and foaling rates) are the best indicators of a stallion's potential future fertility level. The number and type of mares bred per season (i.e. maiden, open, barren and foaling mares) and the breeding method used (i.e., hand breeding, pasture breeding or artificial insemination with fresh, cooled or frozen semen) are recorded. Results of previous reproductive evaluations, medical conditions, vaccination history (especially vaccination against equine arteritis virus), and other significant information are noted. It is also important to record the intended future use of the stallion and the number of mares anticipated for the next season, as it will be important for breeding management recommendations.

3.3 Physical Examination

A general physical examination should be performed on each stallion. To be considered fertile, a stallion must be able to mount a mare in estrus, insert his penis into the vagina, thrust appropriately, and ejaculate completely. Musculoskeletal abnormalities that may interfere with mating ability, such as back, hock, or lameness issues, or neurologic problems should be identified along with other medical conditions. Additional medical tests may be warranted in some situations. Any evidence of heritable or congenital conditions should be reported. Serum of stallions should be tested for presence of antibodies against equine arteritis virus, the agent that causes equine viral arteritis. In general, all stallions should be tested for natural exposure to the equine arteritis virus and then vaccinated if negative. Please check with your equine veterinarian for specific state regulations regarding vaccination against equine arteritis virus.

3.4 Examination of External Genitalia

The penis, prepuce, sheath, scrotum, and scrotal contents are routinely evaluated during a BSE.

Inspection of the penis and prepuce is often performed after the stallion has either 'dropped' his penis or gained an erection after teasing a mare in estrus. The penis should be of normal size, shape and be free of lesions. Palpation of the testes and epididymides are often performed after semen collection, as the stallion will be less excited and will allow for a more complete and safe examination. There should be two testes fully descended into the scrotum. Each testis should be smooth, slightly turgid and resilient on palpation, and freely movable within the scrotum. The tail of the epididymis should be easily palpated at the caudal pole of each testis. The spermatic cord should be identified on the cranial dorsal aspect of each testis.

Testes of mature stallions are normally capable of producing approximately 18 to 20 million sperm per gram of testicular tissue per day. Since testicular weight cannot be obtained in a live, intact stallion, daily sperm production potential is estimated from total testicular volume. Measurement of testicular size is performed to estimate potential daily sperm production.

Two types of testicular measurements may be obtained. Total scrotal width (TSW) can be determined with Scrotal Calipers (Figure 3-1). The testes are gently and evenly held in the ventral scrotum as the calipers are used to determine the widest measurement across both testes. The average of three measurements should be calculated. Total scrotal width is correlated with both testis weight and daily sperm production. The minimum acceptable total scrotal width for light horse stallions is 8.0 cm. Actual minimal total scrotal width is age dependent (8.1 cm for 2 to 3 year olds, 8.5 cm for 4 to 6 year olds, and 9.5 cm for stallions > 7 years old). It should be noted that determination of testicular volume is considered to be a more accurate method of predicting sperm production potential than measurement of total scrotal width.

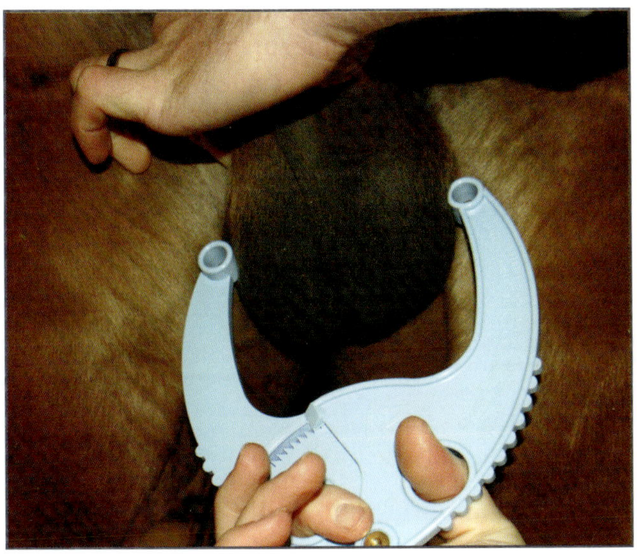

Figure 3-1 Measurement of total scrotal width using calipers.

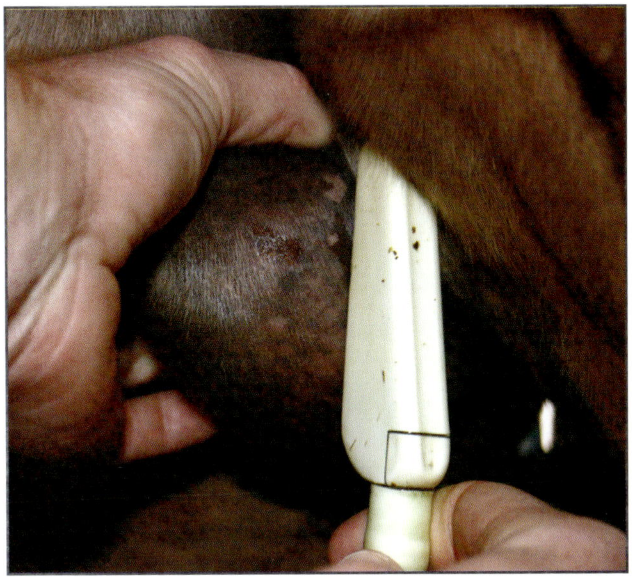

Figure 3-2 Measurement of testicular width using ultrasonography.

Alternatively, the length, width and height of each individual testis can be measured using either Scrotal Calipers or ultrasound and the data recorded in centimeters (Figure 3-2). These measurements are used to calculate testicular volume and subsequently estimate potential daily sperm production.

Testicular volume (in cubic centimeters, cm^3) of each testis can be determined using the following formula:

Testicular Volume = 0.5233 x length x width x height

The calculated volume of each testis is added together to obtain the total testicular volume (in milliliters). Expected daily sperm production (in billions of sperm per day) can subsequently be estimated using the following formulas:

Lower Range of Expected Daily Sperm Production (DSP) = (0.024 x total testicular volume) - 1.26

Upper Range of Expected Daily Sperm Production (DSP) = (0.024 x total testicular volume) - 0.76

Spermatogenic efficiency can then be determined by comparing the actual number of sperm produced each day (daily sperm output) with the calculated daily sperm production rate based on testicular volume. Stallions with an actual daily sperm output that is less than the predicted daily sperm production based on testicular volume should be evaluated for disease or dysfunction of the testes, epididymides, ductus deferens or accessory sex glands. For example, a stallion with a total testicular volume of 400 cm^3 should have a daily sperm output of approximately 5 to 11 billion. A problem may be suspected if his actual production is less than 5 billion spermatozoa per day. The relationship between testicular volume and predicted daily sperm output is presented in Figure 3-3.

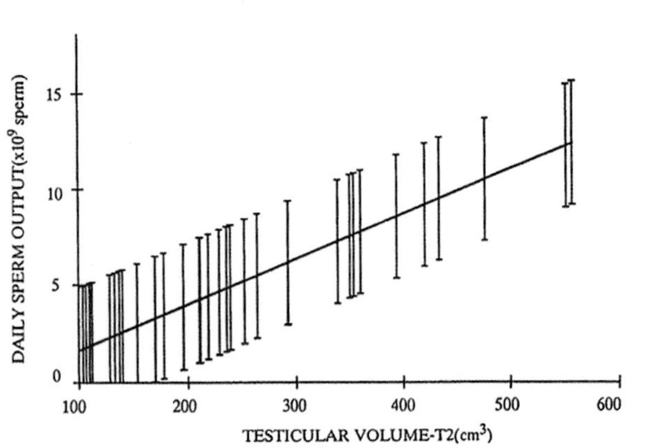

Figure 3-3 Relationship between testicular volume and daily sperm output in stallions (Love et al., Am Assoc Eq Pract 1990;36: 15-21).

Ultrasound examination of the testes and other scrotal contents may also be performed in stallions to identify lesions within the testes or characterize fluid within the scrotum.

3.5 Examination of Internal Genitalia

Examination of the internal genitalia of a stallion per rectum is not always performed as part of a reproductive evaluation, unless indicated by an abnormal history, physical examination findings, or abnormal semen parameters. Risk of injury to the stallion and personnel often outweigh potential benefits during a routine evaluation. In the event that a stallion is to be palpated per rectum, the attending veterinarian may opt to sedate the horse and administer a medication to relax the musculature of the caudal rectum. It would also be preferable to perform the examination with the stallion restrained in stocks.

3.6 Evaluation for Venereal Disease

Microbiological culture swabs are routinely collected as part of a complete BSE. Swab samples to be collected prior to washing the stallion and collection of semen include the urethral fossa, urethra, shaft of the penis and prepuce. After semen collection, a second swab from the urethra is obtained and the semen itself is often cultured. The post-ejaculate urethral swab is considered to be similar to a culture of the semen. A positive post-ejaculate urethral culture suggests an infection of the urethra, accessory sex glands or epididymis.

The two main potentially pathogenic bacteria cultured from stallions are *Pseudomonas aeruginosa* and *Klebsiella pneumoniae*. Other microbial organisms may be cultured and are often considered normal nonpathogenic bacterial flora. To determine if the organism cultured is a true pathogen, mares bred by the stallion should also be cultured. If the mares do not become pregnant and the same organism is subsequently cultured from the uterus, the organism may be considered a significant pathogen. Conversely, if mares bred to a stallion that has a positive culture for *Pseudomonas* or *Klebsiella* become pregnant and do not become infected, the organism should be considered to be a non-pathogenic bacterium.

Taylorella equigenitalis, the bacterial organism causing contagious equine metritis, and the viral agents of equine infectious anemia, coital exanthema (equine herpesvirus-3), and equine viral arteritis are also potentially venereally transmitted. It is now common to initially screen stallions for exposure to equine arteritis virus (EAV) by collection of a blood sample and serologic testing for the presence of antibodies in the blood sample. Unvaccinated stallions with antibodies against EAV (i.e. seropositive) are subsequently tested for the presence of virus in semen to determine if the horse is a chronic carrier or shedder of the virus.

3.7 Libido and Mating Ability

Libido when teased to a mare in estrus and ability to gain and maintain an erection are recorded. Sub-

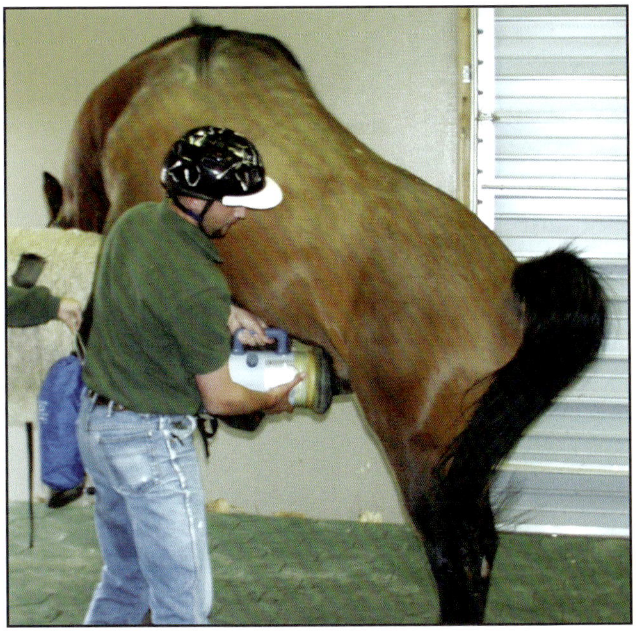

***Figure 3-4** Stallion mounting a breeding phantom.*

sequently, the ability to mount a mare or breeding phantom, insert the penis into the mare or artificial vagina, thrust, and ability to ejaculate completely are all noted (Figure 3-4).

3.8 Semen Evaluation

Techniques and equipment for collection of semen is presented in another chapter. In a breeding soundness evaluation, semen is often collected in an artificial vagina twice, one hour apart. It is anticipated that:

- Total number of spermatozoa on the second ejaculate of most horses will be approximately one-half that of the first ejaculate
- Volume of the two ejaculates will be approximately equal
- pH should remain the same or go up slightly
- Sperm motility should stay the same or increase

Each ejaculate in a breeding soundness examination should be evaluated by gross examination of the semen, measurement of pH and osmolality as well as semen volume, concentration of spermatozoa, total and progressive motility, and sperm morphology. These will be described in more detail in Chapter 4.

3.9 Test Cool

Individual stallions may have semen with high progressive motility and acceptable pregnancy rates using fresh semen, but low pregnancy rates in a cooled-transported semen program. It is advantageous to test semen for motility characteristics following cooling. Semen is collected and aliquots are extended in two or more extenders and cooled in an appropriate passive cooling system designed for equine semen. The samples are evaluated for total and progressive motility at 24 and 48 hours after cooling. A test cool can identify an optimal extender for a given stallion and identify stallions whose semen does not cool well. Adjustments in breeding management procedures or semen processing may allow some stallions with poor cooling characteristics to still be used successfully in a transported semen program. However, ultimately the only true test of fertility for a stallion in a cooled-transported semen program is pregnancy rates in mares bred.

3.10 Test Freeze

Cryopreservation may dramatically alter motility characteristics and fertility potential of sperm from some stallions. It is usually not possible to predict ahead of time which stallions will freeze well and which stallions will not freeze adequately. Consequently, a test freeze is routinely recommended to identify a freezing extender that will provide the best post-thaw motility. As with the test cool, semen is collected and aliquots are mixed with several different freezing extenders. Several straws of each sperm-extender combination are frozen and later thawed and evaluated. If it is determined that semen from the stallion has adequate post-thaw motility, subsequent freezes will be performed using the best extender identified in the test freeze. As noted previously, motility of semen after thawing is not necessarily correlated with future pregnancy rates. Some stallions have very good post thaw semen motility, but very poor pregnancy rates in mares bred with the frozen semen.

3.11 Other Tests

The presence of an adequate number of motile spermatozoa in an ejaculate is no guarantee of fertility. If results of a standard BSE do not identify a cause of subfertility or infertility, additional diagnostic tests may be indicated (Table 3-1).

A single test is often not an absolute or accurate predictor of the fertility of a stallion. Therefore, in many cases a combination of sperm function tests are used to improve the reliability of fertility estimation. Flow cytometry has become an integral technique to rapidly evaluate multiple sperm parameters on hundreds or thousands of sperm cells using fluorescent stains. Other tests, such as ultrasound and endoscopy are used to determine if pathology is present when clinical signs of scrotal swelling or hemospermia are observed.

Table 3-1 Diagnostic tests that may be performed in addition to the standard tests in a breeding soundness evaluation.

Test	Indication
Sperm Chromatin Structure Assay (SCSA)	Evaluate structural integrity of sperm chromatin by determining the susceptibility of sperm DNA to denaturation *in vitro*
Fluorescent Stains	Evaluation of plasma membrane integrity (5-CFDA and PI), viability (SYBR-14), acrosomal integrity (PSA) or mitochondrial function (JC-1 and rhodamine 123)
Hypo-osmotic Swelling Test	Evaluation to determine if sperm plasma membrane is intact and osmotically active
Sperm Capacitation Test	Determine the percentage of sperm that are capacitated and able to undergo the acrosome reaction (CTC assay and merocyanine 540)
Acrosome Reaction Tests	Determine the percentage of acrosome-intact and acrosome reacted sperm in untreated semen (FITC-PNA) and to evaluate the ability of spermatozoa to undergo the acrosome reaction *in vitro* (calcium ionophore A23187)
Progesterone Receptor Exposure	Determine the proportion of sperm with progesterone receptors and therefore capable of zona binding and ZP-mediated acrosome reaction
Sperm-Zona Binding Assay	Evaluate the ability of sperm to bind to the zona pellucida of an oocyte
Glass wool-sephadex filtration	Identify the percentage of sperm that are capacitated or have plasma membrane or acrosome damage
Transmission Electron Microscopy	Evaluation of ultrastructure detail of spermatozoa and to evaluate acrosome status of sperm
Chromosome Analysis	Evaluate numeric or structural changes in chromosomes
Testicular Biopsy	Histologic evaluation of testicular parenchyma
Hormone Analysis (baseline and provocative endocrine tests)	Evaluate pituitary and gonadal endocrine function
Ultrasound	Evaluation of the accessory sex glands, penis, testes and scrotum
Alkaline Phosphatase Test	Evaluation of ejaculatory function in azoospermic stallions
Urethral Endoscopy	Evaluate urethral integrity in stallions with hemospermia

3.12 Daily Sperm Output

Occasionally, it may be beneficial to determine daily sperm output from a stallion. Semen must be collected daily for a minimum of 5 to 7 days to deplete the extragonadal sperm reserves (epididymis and ductus deferens). After the sperm reserves are depleted and the stallion is 'cleaned out', the total number of sperm collected each day will be relatively constant and represents the number of sperm produced each day (Figure 3-5). It is expected that a normal fertile stallion will produce approximately 4 to 6 billion spermatozoa each day. Determination of daily sperm output can be used to estimate the number of mares that may be bred per day and therefore the number of mares that may be booked to a stallion for a season.

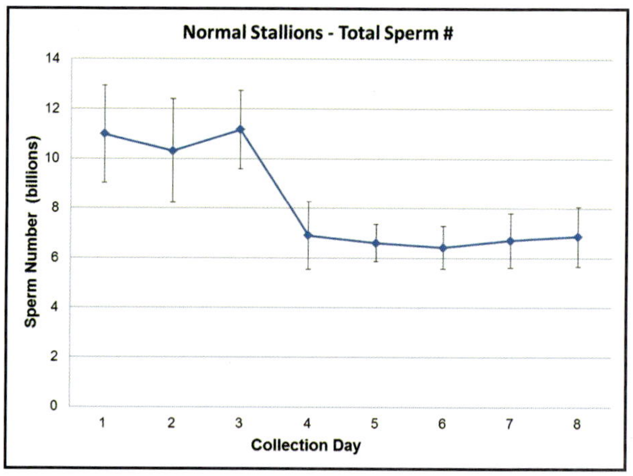

Figure 3-5 Total number of spermatozoa (mean ± s.e.m.) in the ejaculate of 8 stallions during daily collections. The extragonadal sperm reserves were depleted and the stallions were at daily sperm output (DSO) after 3 days.

3.13 Summary

Interpretation of the results of a stallion BSE should take into account the number of mares to be bred and the type of breeding program to be utilized (i.e. live cover or insemination with fresh, cooled or frozen semen). Accepted values for semen analysis are: 1) a minimum of 60 % progressively motile spermatozoa and 60 % morphologically normal spermatozoa in each ejaculate collected, and 2) a minimum of 1.0 billion progressively motile, morphologically normal spermatozoa in the second of two ejaculates collected one hour apart after sexual rest for one week at any time of the year.

The original guidelines for the BSE suggested that a satisfactory prospective breeder could expect a minimum seasonal pregnancy rate of 75 % if booked to breed 40 mares by natural service or 120 mares by artificial insemination. It is well recognized that current book sizes for many stallions are well above the original '40/120' guideline. With these stallions, it may be advantageous to evaluate semen quality at daily sperm output to determine if there are sufficient progressively motile, morphologically normal sperm available for the anticipated book size.

If the stallion has had a significant medical condition (i.e. fever, colic) recently, it is recommended that he be re-evaluated a minimum of 70 days after the conclusion of the medical condition before a final classification is assigned. The 70 day period would account for 57 to 60 days for spermatogenesis and 7 to 11 days for epididymal transit.

If the BSE identifies a stallion with a potential reproductive problem, management or therapeutic programs can be instituted to optimize future fertility. It is important to emphasize that the final criteria upon which to assess stallion fertility are ultimately the pregnancy and foaling rates in mares bred.

Chapter 4 Semen Collection

Table 4-0 List ARS products used in this chapter.

Item	Part Number	Use/Comments
CSU Model Artificial Vagina Case with Filler Cap	SAV-102	Outer plastic case of the CSU Model AV
Tubular Latex Bladder	SAVB-104	Water retention barrier inside the CSU AV case
Rubber Bands	RB-7/10	Secures bladder to AV case
Round Reusuable Latex Collection Liner	RAVL-201	Lines the inside of the AV, to be removed and cleaned between uses
Disposable Plastic Collection Liner	SAVL-101	Used in place of reusable latex liner; single use; disposable
Large (165mm) Adjustable Plastic Clamp	BPC-165	Secures the disposable collection liner to the AV case
Disposable Collection Bottle (200 ml)	SCB-200/25	Serves as receptacle for semen during collection
Disposable Nylon Mesh Gel Filter	SAVF-102/25	Separates gel and debris from sperm rich fraction of ejaculate
Small (45mm) Adjustable Plastic Clamp	BPC-118	Secures collection bottle to latex liner
Disposable Coupling Nut	SCN-101/25	Secures collection bottle to disposable liner
Surgilube® Lubricating Jelly	SSL-101	Lubrication of liner prior to collection
Collection Bottle Cover	CBC-101	Used to maintain appropriate temperature in collection bottle during semen collection
Collection Bottle Cover Warmer	562B-101	Used to pre-warm and dry bottle covers
ARS Dial Thermometer	THM-104	Measurement of temperature within AV
AV-Fill Thermometer	AVFT-101	Used to monitor temperature of water filling AV
E-Z Boy®Artificial Vagina Assembly Stand	EZB-101	Aid in assembly of the CSU Model AV
Mare Breeding Hobbles	542A-300	Used to restrain mare during breeding or collection
ARS Twitch	ET36-125	Used to restrain mare during breeding or collection
Rolled Utility Cotton	RUC-101	Used to wash penis of stallion or perineum of mare
Chlorhexidine Solution	CSD-101	Used to clean AV and other uses
Terg-A-Zyme® Detergent Powder	TAZ-101	Used to clean AV

Semen can be obtained from a stallion by collection into an artificial vagina, collection of a dismount sample after natural service, via pharmacologic ex copula ejaculation (i.e. chemical ejaculation), and by harvesting epididymal semen. This chapter will primarily review collection of semen using an artificial vagina and will provide limited comments on other semen collection techniques.

4.1 The Artificial Vagina

Several types and models of artificial vaginas (AV) are commercially available. The Colorado Model AV was initially developed in the late 1960's.

The structural 'backbone' of the CSU Model Artificial Vagina is a rigid plastic case with a handle and

Figure 4-1 CSU Model Artificial Vagina.

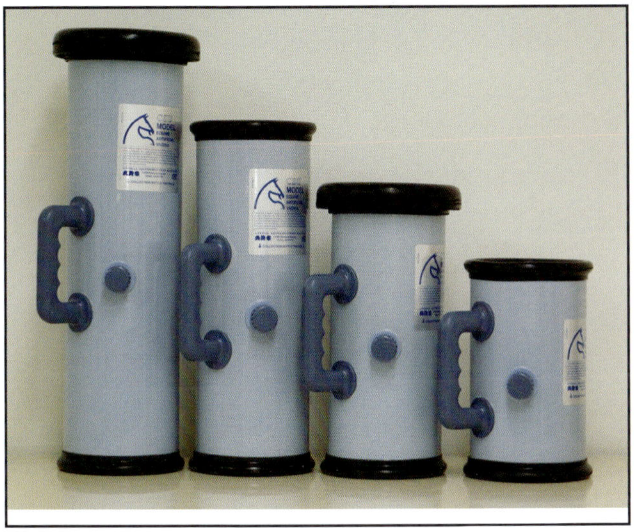

Figure 4-2 Artificial Vagina Cases for the CSU Model Artificial Vagina. From left to right, the overall lengths are 22", 19", 15" and 12" respectively.

a port for filling the system with water (Figure 4-1). A straight latex rubber tube is used to create a 'bladder' within the plastic case that can be filled with warm water. A second latex rubber tube with a coned end is used as a reusable liner during semen collection. The liner is removed and washed in between uses. Other components of the AV include a disposable collection bottle, disposable nylon mesh gel filter and an insulated cover to protect the collection bottle from sunlight and temperature fluctuations.

The primary advantages of the CSU Model AV over other types of artificial vaginas are that the CSU Model maintains its temperature for an extended period of time during cold weather, protects semen from the environment (cold, sunlight) during and after collection with a collection bottle cover, and is available in several lengths (Figure 4-2) which can be selected to accommodate individual stallions. In addition, the rigidity of the plastic AV case permits the collector an opportunity to manipulate the AV, which can provide additional stimulation for the stallion.

It is rare that a stallion cannot be trained to an artificial vagina. Many stallions will show a preference for a specific temperature, pressure, type of liner, angle at which the AV is held, etc. Further, many stallions like to have the AV pushed on them rather vigorously, while others prefer to move forward into the AV of their own volition. Individuals adept at collecting semen from stallions are acutely aware of preferences for each stallion relative to AV preparation (temperature, pressure, etc.) and how the AV is held or manipulated during collection.

An artificial vagina must possess several key characteristics to be effective for semen collection in a wide variety of conditions:

- Elicit a favorable response from the stallion
- Maintain its temperature for at least 20 minutes regardless of environmental temperature
- Adjustable to accommodate stallions of various sizes
- Constructed and cleaned in a manner that maintains semen in a viable condition
- Able to remove gel, smegma and debris from semen during collection

A lack of sensitivity on the part of the collector is commonly responsible for a stallion developing bad habits in the collection shed. Behavioral characteristics of a stallion that does not like some aspect(s) of the collection procedure or is frustrated with the procedure are listed in Table 4-1. Fortunately, most stallions that develop bad habits can be retrained, but it is a costly, time-consuming, and avoidable process.

Table 4-1 Unwanted behaviors in the stallion

Bad Habits in the Breeding Shed	Signs of a Frustrated Stallion
Numerous mounts	Savaging mares
Reluctance to be collected (slow)	Difficult to handle
Squealing while being collected	Aggression towards people
Poor sexual behavior	Disinterested

A given stallion may work an AV better and ejaculate more consistently if the AV is of the proper size, if the internal temperature and pressure are optimal, and if the liner is well lubricated and free of unwanted folds.

The length of the AV should be sufficient to accommodate the stallion's penis, at maximum thrust, without his penis entering the tapered end of the collection liner. In general, it is recommended that the AV be at least 2 inches longer than the length of the stallion's penis at the time of maximum erection. Ideally, the AV case and collection liner should allow the stallion to ejaculate as close to the end of the AV case as possible without risk of injury to the stallion. It must be remembered that each stallion is an individual and must be treated as an individual.

The temperature of the AV should not be higher than is necessary to elicit a favorable ejaculatory response. The normal temperature range inside the lumen of the AV that is adequate for most stallions is 48° to 50° C (~118° to 122° F). Increasing the internal temperature of the AV to 52° to 54° C (~126° to 129° F) can be used therapeutically if necessary to stimulate individual stallions to ejaculate without reducing sperm motility.

An artificial vagina must be able to maintain its temperature for at least 20 minutes regardless of environmental temperature. The equine breeding season begins in early to mid-February and many stallions are collected in areas where environmental temperature is sufficiently low to be detrimental to spermatozoa. In these areas, it is sometimes difficult to maintain an internal temperature sufficiently high enough in the AV during the interval from the time the AV is initially filled to when the stallion is actually collected. Furthermore, the sex drive of some stallions is low early in the season, which may prolong the collection period. In these situations, the AV should be filled to the maximum volume with hot water (57° C; 135° F) due to the necessity of maintaining an appropriate temperature for a prolonged time period. This is in case the stallion is slow to become stimulated; a full AV will maintain its temperature longer and allow additional time to properly prepare the stallion without the necessity of 're-charging' the artificial vagina with hot water.

If the AV temperature drops below an acceptable level during the collection process, the AV should be emptied and re-filled with water of the optimal temperature. Attempting to collect a stallion with a cold AV is usually unproductive, and if repeated with any degree of frequency, can be detrimental to his sexual behavior.

The stallion should be observed when he has an erection and the volume of water in the AV adjusted to optimize the internal diameter and pressure according to the size of the stallion's penis. If an adjustment is required, the collector should remove the "cap" from the AV, place an arm inside the AV, and expel only as much water as needed. The amount of water to be removed depends upon the diameter of the stallion's penis and his preference for pressure inside the artificial vagina.

An in-line filter should be used to remove gel from the ejaculate. Seminal vesicles or vesicular glands secrete a viscous, stringy, sticky, tenacious fluid commonly referred to as the gel fraction of the ejaculate. The presence and amount of gel in an ejaculate varies with season, stallion, age and sexual stimulation. Gel may prevent an accurate division of semen into aliquots for insemination as well as prevent an accurate count of spermatozoa. Consequently, the gel is usually separated from the sperm-rich portion of the ejaculate and discarded.

A stallion ejaculates in 6 to 9 "jets" with approximately 80% of the spermatozoa present in the first three jets. The gel, if any, exits in the last three jets. The CSU Model Artificial Vagina was designed with a disposable nylon mesh gel filter for the collection bottle that prevents mixing of gel with the remainder of the ejaculate. The gel filter "catches" the gel before it becomes mixed with the sperm-rich fraction.

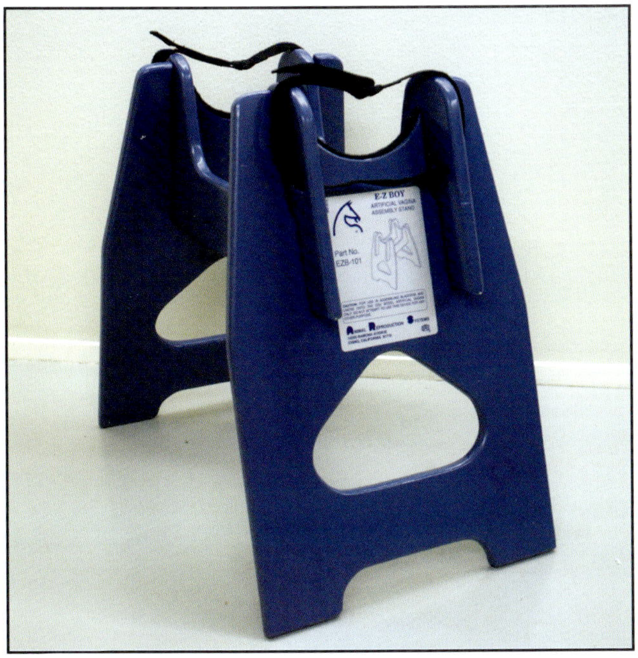

Figure 4-3 E-Z Boy® Assembly Stand.

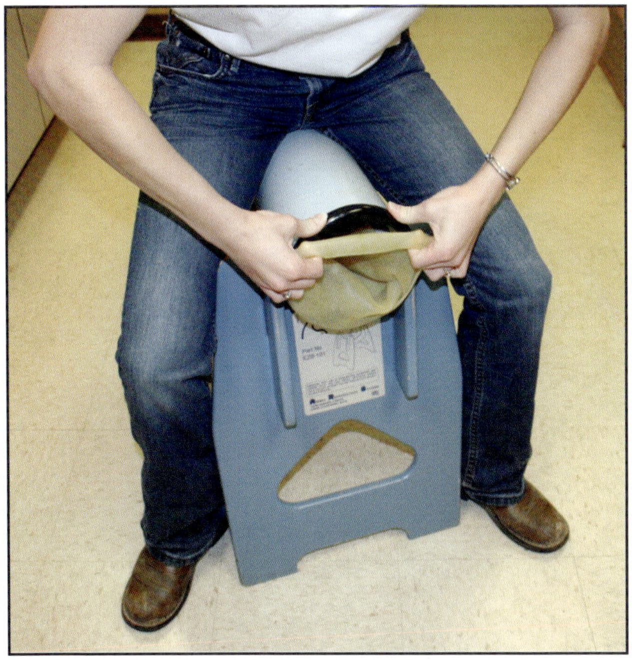

Figure 4-5 Reflecting bladder over end of AV.

4.2 Assembly of the CSU Model Artificial Vagina

The CSU Model Artificial Vagina is easiest to assemble if an assembly stand (i.e. E-Z Boy Artificial Vagina Assembly Stand) is used (Figure 4-3). The plastic AV case is placed on the assembly stand (handle down) and the Tubular Latex Bladder is passed down the center of the case (Figure 4-4). The latex bladder is first reflected over the rubber collar of the posterior end (where the penis of the stallion will enter) of the AV case (Figure 4-5 and Figure 4-6). A rubber band should be placed snugly (2 to 3 wraps) over the reflected bladder to hold it in place to prevent slippage and leakage of water (Figure 4-7). By stretching the rubber band to its maximum possible length, it is possible to get several wraps around the bladder and AV case. It is essential that this junction be tight, since the tubular latex bladder is not removed routinely, but cleaned while in the AV case.

The next step is to reflect the other end of the tubular latex bladder over the anterior end of the AV case. This is the first point in assembling the AV in

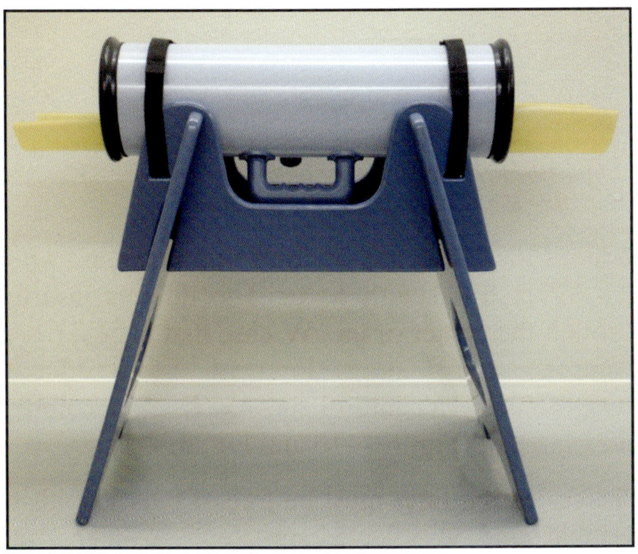

Figure 4-4 Artificial Vagina on E-Z Boy® Assembly Stand with bladder inserted through center.

Figure 4-6 Reflecting bladder over end of AV.

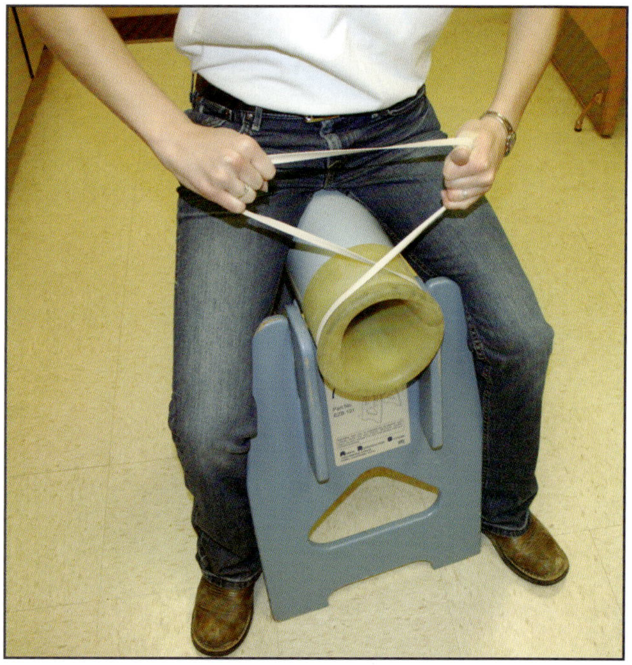

Figure 4-7 Securing bladder with rubber band.

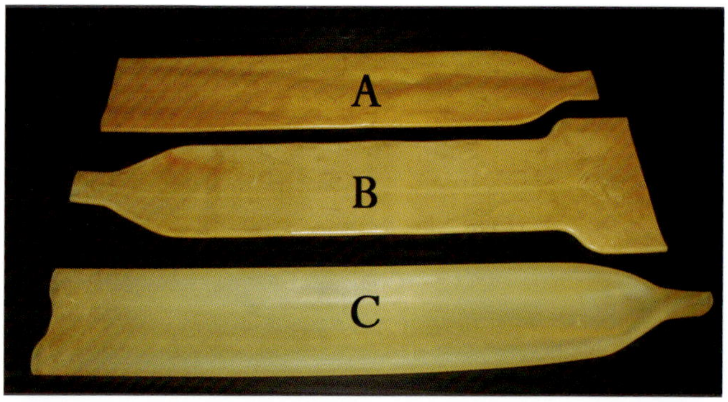

Figure 4-8 ARS Manufactures three different liner types. A) Flat, B) Flared, C) Round.

which it is possible to adjust the internal diameter, and ultimately internal pressure. Increasing the tautness, i.e., the amount that the latex bladder is stretched before it is reflected over the anterior end of the AV case reduces the amount of water that can be added. Conversely, a loose bladder will allow more water to be added and permits an increase in internal pressure. Once the bladder is appropriately positioned, a rubber band is also used on the anterior end. When the bladder is in place, the inside should resemble a smooth tube with the rubber stretched equally all the way around the inside of the AV case.

Collection liners are available in reusable latex (Figure 4-8) or disposable plastic (Figure 3-12). Colorado State University recommends that a Round Reusable Latex Collection Liner be used. These liners have a no-crease configuration which

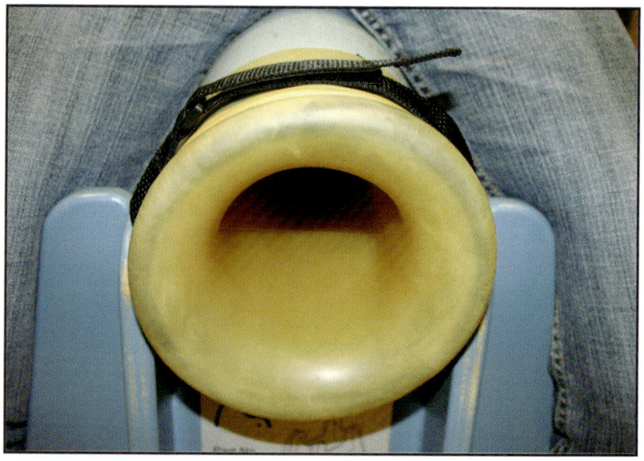

Figure 4-9 AV can be secured to E-Z Boy via Velcro® straps.

Figure 4-10 Insertion of the latex liner onto the AV case; note that the bladder is already attached.

reduces the incidence of folds and wrinkles when the AV is filled with water. The liner is inserted through the center of the AV case that is held down using the Velcro® straps (Figure 4-9), and reflected over the posterior end of the AV case and tubular latex bladder (Figure 4-10 and Figure 4-11).

The collection liner must be free of twists, folds or wrinkles and be reflected completely over the rubber collar to prevent its slipping during collection. Stretching the reusable latex collection liner over

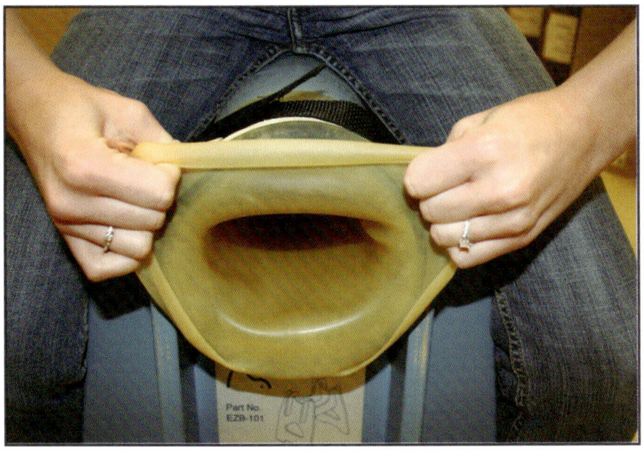

Figure 4-11 Reflecting AV Liner over AV.

the posterior end of the AV case is an art. The rubber is relatively thick and is smaller in diameter than the flared, posterior end of the AV case. Consequently, considerable stretching is necessary to reflect the rubber over the posterior end. Thus, a rubber band is not necessary to hold this liner in place. Unfortunately, if the stretching and reflecting is not done in one smooth, fluid movement, the rubber may tear, especially if excessive force is used. Care must be taken when placing the liner, as the reusable latex collection liners are relatively expensive and it is time-consuming to start over.

A Disposable Plastic Collection Liner is more likely to become twisted or wrinkled within the AV than a reusable latex collection liner. Therefore, more precautions are necessary to position a disposable plastic liner properly than for a reusable latex collection liner. Stallions generally object to creases and wrinkles in a collection liner, particularly a disposable plastic liner. However, disposable liners can be convenient and effective and many stallions can be collected successfully with these liners. Once the disposable plastic collection liner is appropriately positioned, the flared end is reflected over the posterior end of the AV case. Since the plastic has little or no stretch, a Large (165mm) Adjustable Plastic Clamp must be used to hold the disposable plastic collection liner in place (Figure 4-12).

The AV is now ready to be filled with water at 57°C (~135° F) (Figure 4-13). It is advisable to pull on the tapered end of the liner during filling to assure that wrinkles and twists do not develop, particularly when a disposable liner is being used.

After the AV is filled with water, the ARS Dial

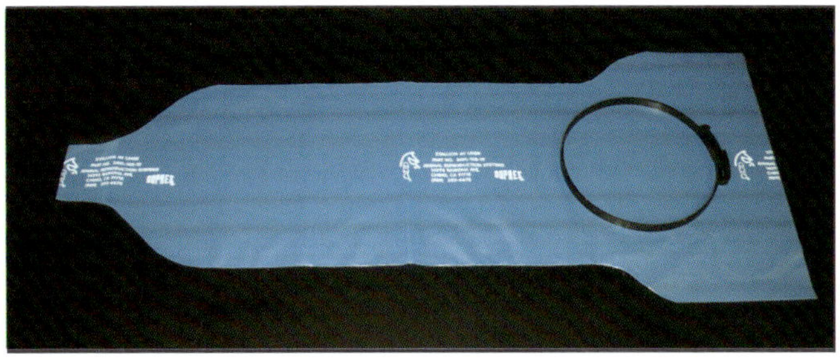

Figure 4-12 Disposable Plastic Collection Liner with Plastic Clamp.

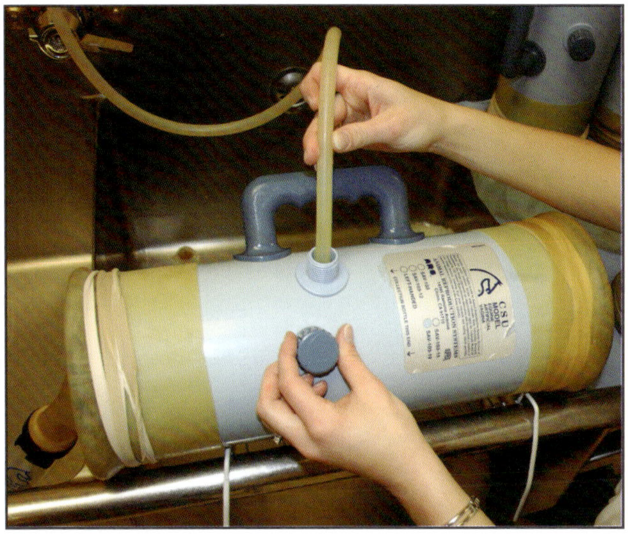

Figure 4-13 Filling AV with warm water.

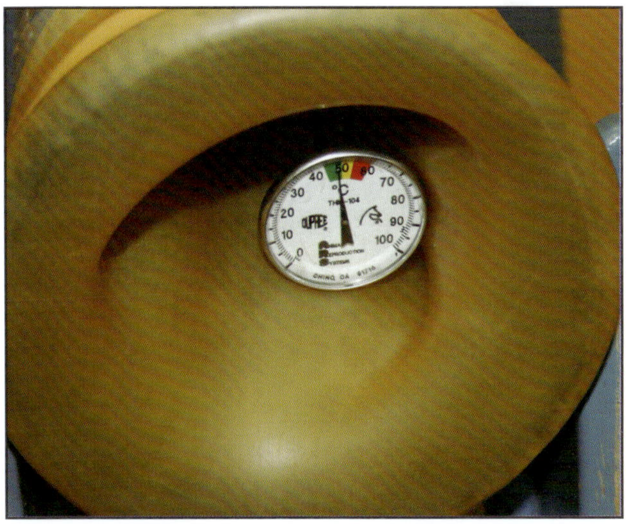

Figure 4-14 Thermometer within the Colorado Model artificial vagina.

Thermometer is placed inside to monitor the temperature (Figure 4-14). It may require several minutes for the temperature within the AV to stabilize. If the AV is used before the temperature has risen to the maximum, it can become so hot that it may injure the stallion, as well as damage the spermatozoa. Many stallions have been "burned" by someone filling an AV and using it as soon as the thermometer registered the desired temperature, but was still rising. Only when the internal temperature has stabilized at 48 to 50° C (~118 to 122° F) is the AV ready for lubrication and use.

If a stallion becomes reluctant to work the AV or fails to ejaculate, the internal temperature of the AV can be increased to 52 to 54° C (~126 to 129° F) without injuring the stallion or damaging the spermatozoa, provided certain precautions are taken during collection. Regardless of how accurate the collector may be in estimating the internal temperature with his or her hand, a thermometer should always be used.

An AV-Fill Thermometer can be installed in the plumbing system to aid in filling the AV with water of the appropriate temperature (Figure 4-15). This will conserve time and water, and heighten the awareness of laboratory personnel to the necessity of temperature control.

When the AV has reached the proper, stable temperature, a 200ml Disposable Collection Bottle is removed from an incubator, which is maintained at 37° C (98.6° F), and fitted with a Disposable Nylon Mesh Gel Filter (Figure 4-16). The lip on the plastic ring, to which the filter is attached, prevents the filter assembly from falling into the collection bottle. The collection bottle, with gel filter assembly, is placed into the tapered end of the latex collection liner (Figure 4-17), and held in place with a Small (45mm) Adjustable Plastic Clamp (Figure 4-18).

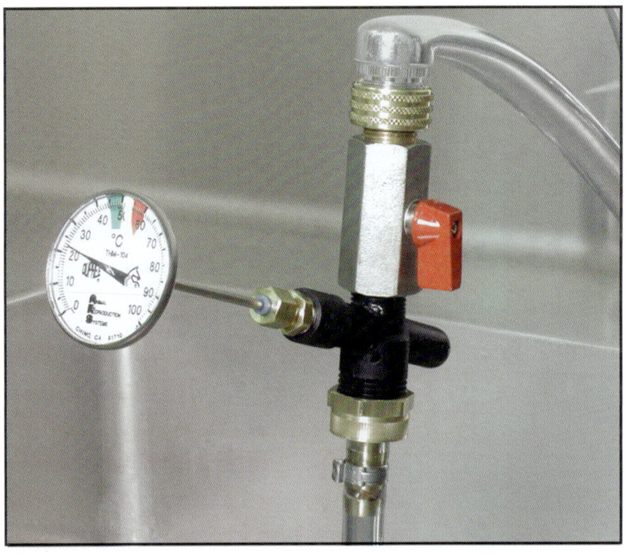

Figure 4-15 In-line thermometer for monitoring temperature of water used to fill an AV.

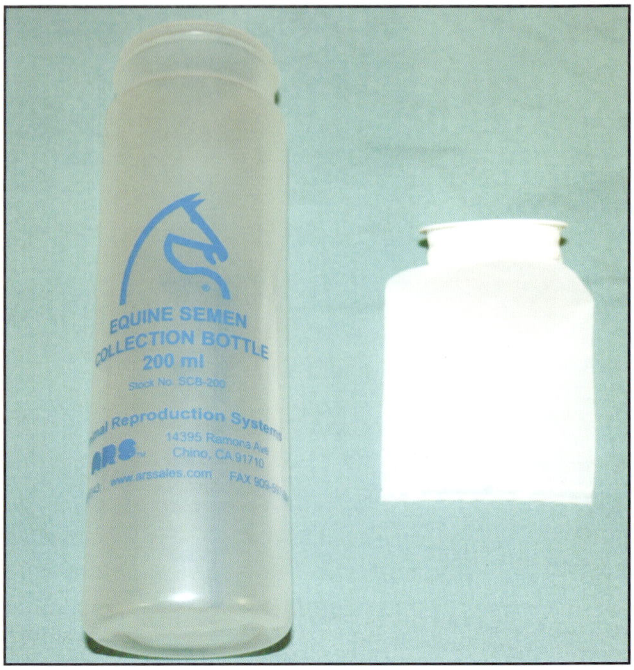

Figure 4-16 Disposable collection bottle and nylon mesh gel filter.

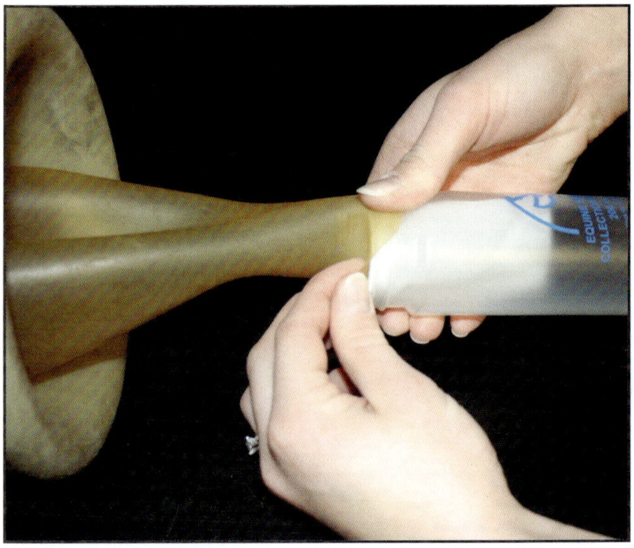

Figure 4-17 Attaching assembled disposable collection liner and mesh filter to latex AV liner.

In the event that a disposable plastic collection liner is to be used, the tapered end is attached to the collection bottle with a disposable coupling nut (Figure 4-19). The tapered end of the disposable plastic liner is threaded through the hole in the center of the coupling nut, and then the coupling nut is screwed onto the collection bottle, attaching the tapered end of the plastic liner to the collection bottle. Once the collection bottle is attached to the collection liner, regardless of whether the liner is latex or plastic, a collection bottle cover is removed from the Collection Bottle Cover Warmer (Figure 4-20), placed over the collection bottle, and attached to the AV case (Figure 4-21).

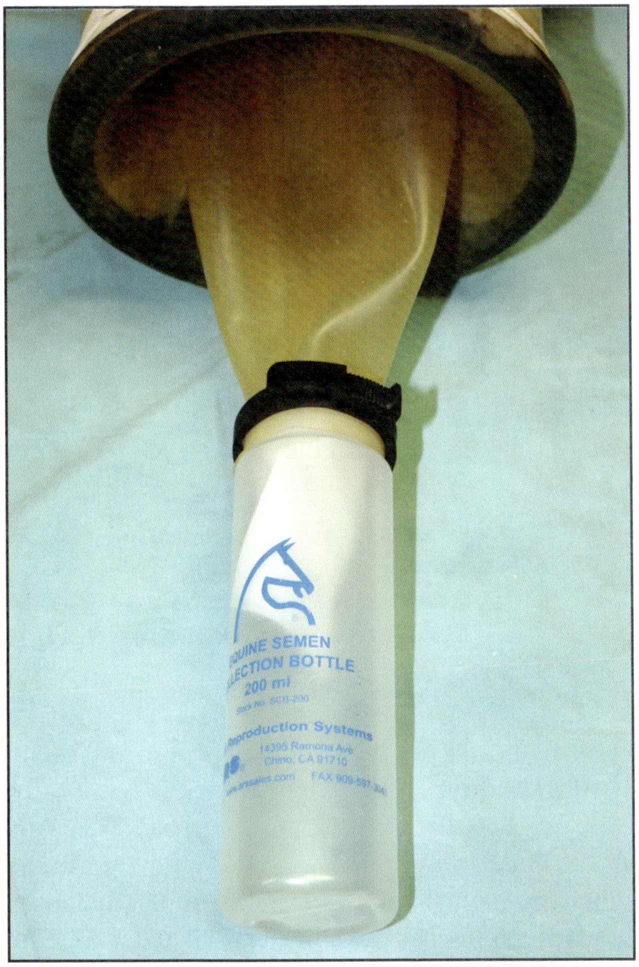

Figure 4-18 Collection bottle attached to the latex liner.

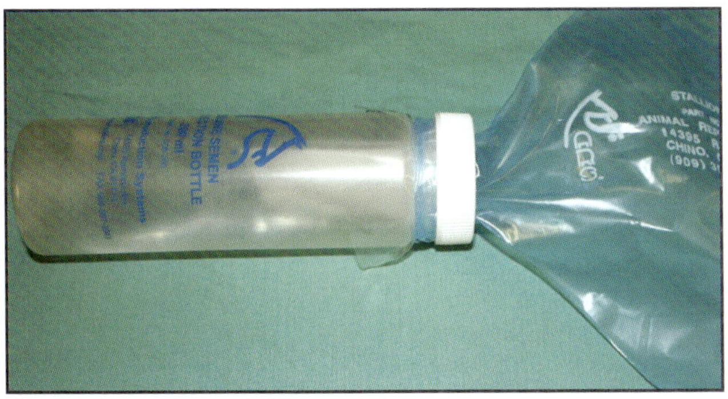

Figure 4-19 Connecting a collection bottle to a disposable collection liner with a coupling nut.

All areas of the AV, except around the anterior end, have more than one layer of material. Therefore, this is the area where most of the heat escapes. When the Collection Bottle Cover is in place, heat that escapes is trapped by the cover; thus, the disposable collection bottle remains at an acceptable temperature regardless of environmental temperature. As previously stated, all AV's, regardless of type or model, area of the world, warm or cold, should be fitted with an insulated cover to protect the semen from excessive heat and/or cold and

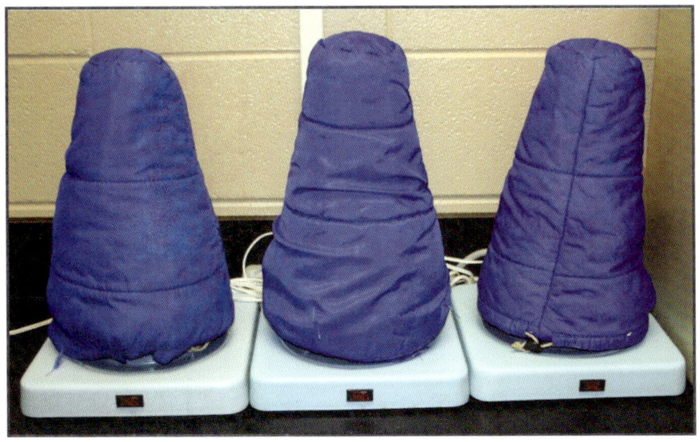

Figure 4-20 Collection bottle covers on warmers.

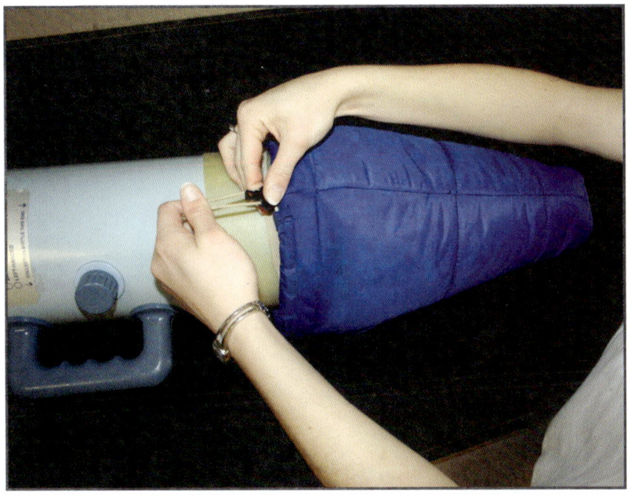

Figure 4-21 Attaching collection bottle cover to AV.

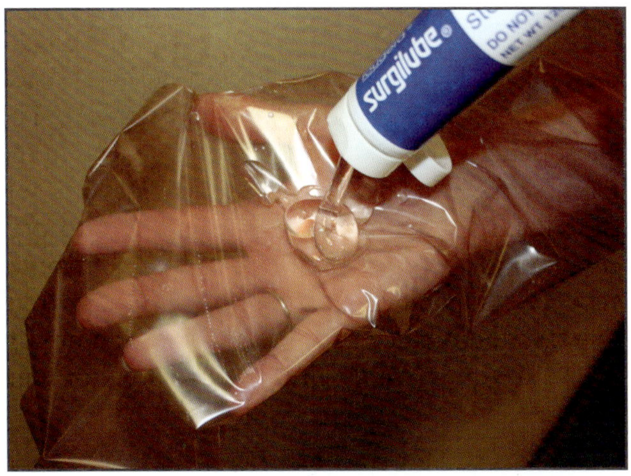

Figure 4-22 Applying lube to the palm of the hand.

light.

The next step is to lubricate the inside of the artificial vagina. A water soluble, non-spermicidal lubricant such as Surgilube® Lubricating Jelly should be used. It is recommended that AV lubricant be kept in an incubator at 37° C (98.6° F). Place approximately 1/4 to 1/3 a tube of jelly (4 oz. tube) into the palm of the hand (Figure 4-22), which is covered

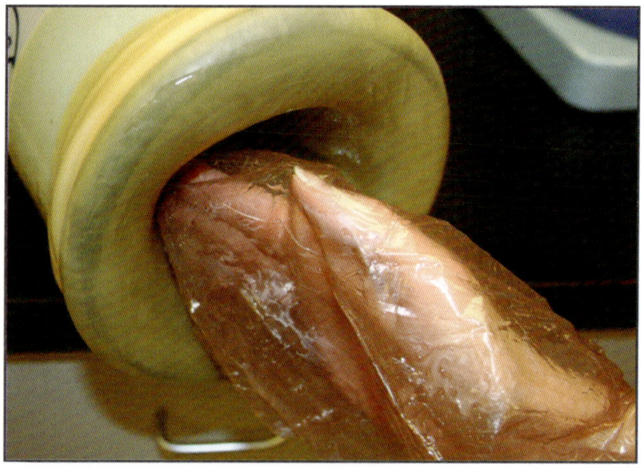

Figure 4-23 Applying lubricant to the AV.

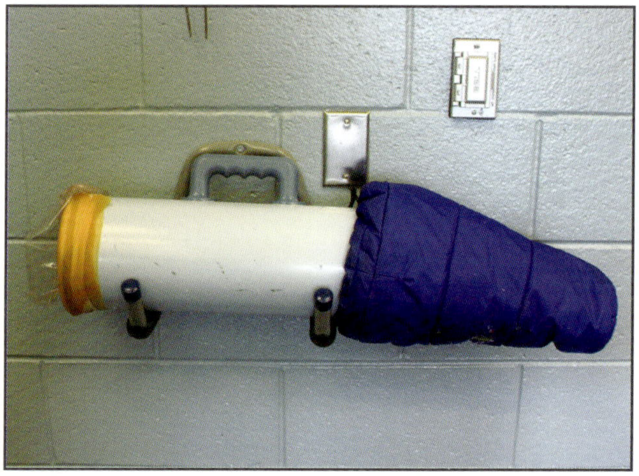

Figure 4-24 A prepared CSU model AV hanging on a wall rack ready for use.

by an obstetrical sleeve, and apply the lube inside the AV along 2/3 of its length (Figure 4-23). The largest quantity of lubricant should be placed in the first 1/3 of the artificial vagina. The sleeve is left inside the AV after the hand is withdrawn to prevent entry of foreign material, to aid in the maintenance of temperature and prevent the lube from drying. A thermometer is placed within the obstetrical sleeve in the lumen of the AV to monitor temperature.

If a twist or wrinkle is noted in the collection liner when the AV is being lubricated, it must be removed. With a reusable latex collection liner, the problem can often be corrected without removing the water, if someone pulls on the tapered end of the collection liner while another person pushes with his or her hand from inside the artificial vagina. Unfortunately, twists or wrinkles in a disposable plastic collection liner are virtually impossible to straighten without removing water from the

Figure 4-25 Clean, warm water in stainless steel bucket.

artificial vagina.

After the AV is lubricated, it is taken to the breeding shed and placed on a clean rack (Figure 4-24) while waiting for the stallion to arrive. When the time is right, the thermometer is removed and the person collecting the semen places the palpation sleeve over his/her arm. Details of the collection process will be described in a later section.

4.3 Preparation of the Stallion for Semen Collection

The ability to handle a stallion in a manner that will elicit a maximal positive sexual response, with a minimum of difficulty, is an art. In general, there are some basic rules, but each stallion handler is different, as is each stallion. Therefore, what may work in one situation may not apply in another. The amount of restraint necessary for a stallion to react favorably and still ensure safety of the mare, handler, and collector should be applied. Some stallions respond to voice commands and need only a minimum of restraint to be under complete control. Others need a chain through the mouth plus physical barriers. Every farm should have facilities that will permit a stallion to tease a mare safely so that he may become sufficiently sexually stimulated for his penis to be washed. Also, the washing procedure should constitute a sexually-stimulating experience.

Warm water [(42° C) (~108° F)] is placed into a cleanable bucket (Figure 4-25) or a bucket pro-

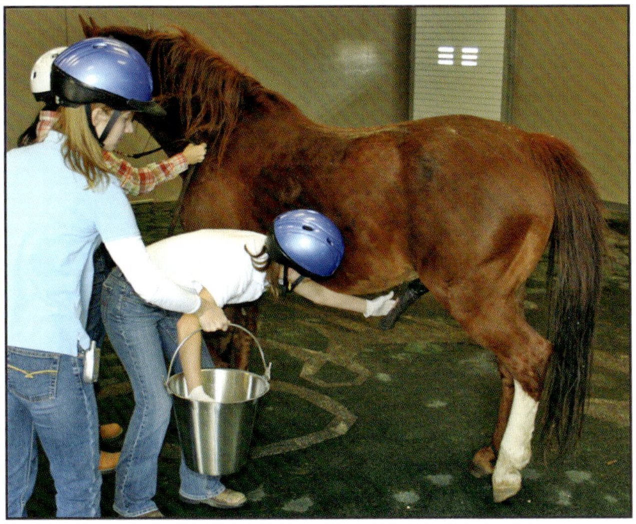

Figure 4-26 Cleaning the stallion's penis with water.

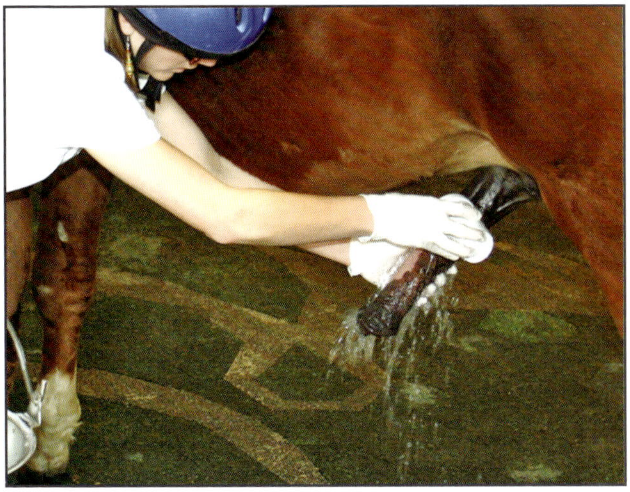

Figure 4-27 Washing stallion's penis with clean, warm water.

tected with a clean plastic liner secured with a stout rubber band. Again, measure the water temperature in the bucket, do not estimate. A container for rinsing the stallion's penis is placed into the bucket. The container used to rinse the stallion's penis should either be disposable or easily cleaned, such as stainless steel. In general, use of disposable material reduces the chance of spreading disease and reuse of unclean equipment.

The stallion is brought from his stall and presented to a mare in estrus positioned behind a well-padded barrier. He should be allowed to tease the mare with as much freedom and enthusiasm as possible without endangering himself, the mare or personnel. When a full erection is attained, the handler backs the stallion away from the mare and applies some restraint to the stallion to permit quick, effective washing.

The individual who washes the stallion should wear plastic, disposable gloves. It is generally easier, quicker and safer with most stallions if someone holds the bucket while the stallion is being washed (Figure 4-26). The stallion's erect penis should be deflected, not grasped, rinsed with water, and massaged gently, but thoroughly (Figure 4-27). More water is applied as necessary. The penis should be observed closely during the washing procedure for lesions. The urethral fossa is checked for the presence of smegma (i.e. a 'bean'). Soaps are not to be used routinely when cleaning the penis of a stallion. Overuse of soap can eliminate the normal bacterial flora on the surface of the penis and promote the overgrowth of potentially pathogenic bacteria. At the conclusion of the cleaning the penis is allowed to air dry. Drying with a clean towel may be performed, but is generally not necessary. If the stallion's penis becomes contaminated after washing, but before collection, the rinsing procedure should be repeated.

An excessive amount of debris and smegma may accumulate on the penis and prepuce if a stallion has not been washed for an extended period. If this is removed without some special precautions, a sore penis may result. A technique that is generally effective is as follows: The stallion should be presented to an estrous mare until he attains an erection, at which time the penis can be massaged gently with generous quantities of a warmed water-soluble lubricant, such as Surgilube® Lubricating Jelly. The stallion is then returned to his stall for 1 to 2 hr to permit the lubricant to penetrate and soften the smegma so that it becomes easy to remove by thoroughly washing the stallion's penis with Ivory® Liquid soap and warm water.

After a stallion's penis has been thoroughly cleansed, which may require several washings with soap and water, he should be washed only with clean, warm water for the remainder of the breeding season, provided, of course, that he is being collected on a routine basis (i.e. every other day). In a natural service program, the penis of a stallion should be washed with warm water before and after each breeding.

4.4 Preparation of the Mare for Semen Collection

Unfortunately, numerous stallions are injured each year by mares during attempts at collection of semen or during natural service. Many breeding

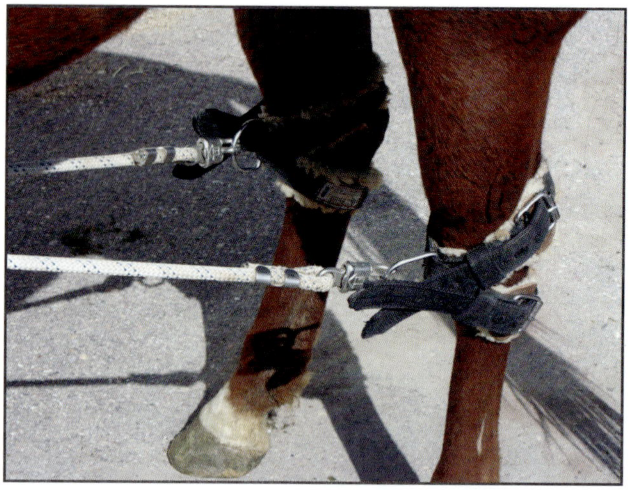

Figure 4-29 Properly fitted hock straps on Mare Breeding Hobbles.

managers do not feel it is necessary to "hobble" or appropriately restrain the mare. Failure to adequately restrain the mare can result in serious physical and/or psychological injury to the stallion, from which he may not fully recover. Numerous cases of abnormal sexual behavior are treated each year, many of which are the result of stallions having been kicked during breeding or collection of semen, which could easily have been avoided. In the event that the scrotum or penis is kicked, the stallion may become subfertile or even sterile.

Mare Breeding Hobbles (Figure 4-28 through Fig-Figure 4-30) have been designed that fit snugly over the hocks without sliding down and allow the mare to move and be moved. The hobbles effectively restrain the mare with minimal stress and can be removed quickly in case of an emergency.

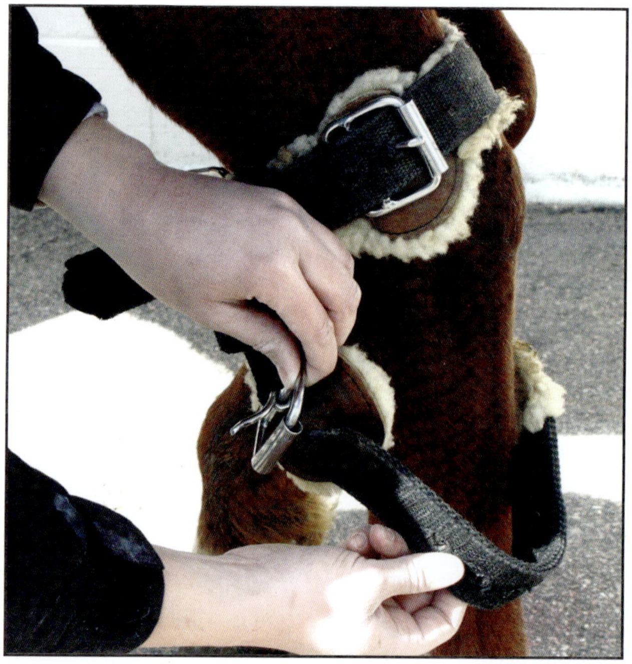

Figure 4-28 Fastening straps on mare breeding hobbles.

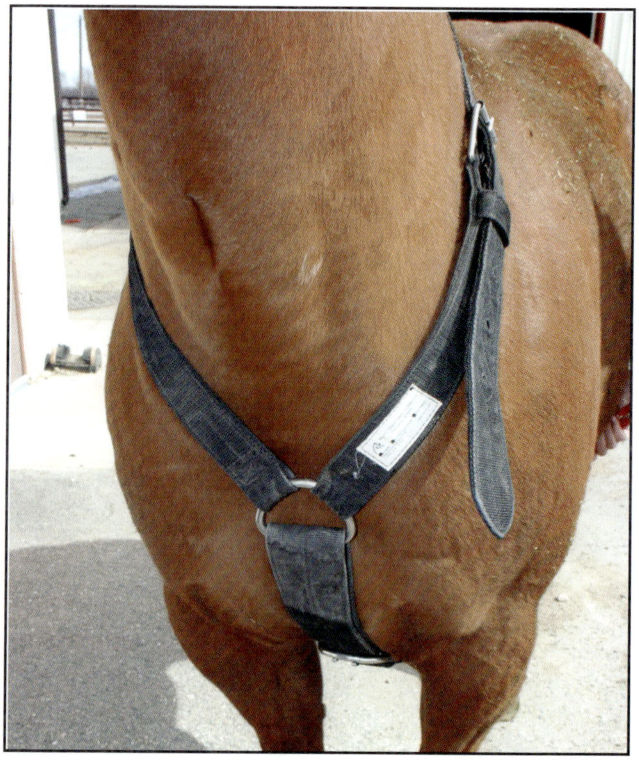

Figure 4-30 Properly fitted hobble breastplate.

The Mare Breeding Hobbles have a large nylon strap that buckles around the mare's neck. This strap can be adjusted to fit mares of almost any size. There is also a large adjustable nylon strap that goes between the mare's front legs with a buckle that permits further adjustment. Fleece is sewn inside the nylon straps that go around the hocks to provide a comfortable fit and keep the hobbles from sliding down. Attached to each end is a nylon rope with a quick-release. A rope passes through a connecting link that is attached to a "D" ring in the nylon strap between the mare's front legs. The quick-releases at the ends of the rope are attached to "D" rings on the hock straps.

The tease mare should be in estrus and readily allow the stallion to mount. The mare is usually twitched (ARS Twitch) in addition to wearing the breeding hobbles (Figure 4-31). There are numerous other methods of protecting the stallion during breeding, such as tying up one front leg of the mare, felt boots on her rear hooves, sedation of the tease mare, etc. The purpose of any restraint in the breeding shed is to prevent injury to the mare, stallion, and breeding farm personnel.

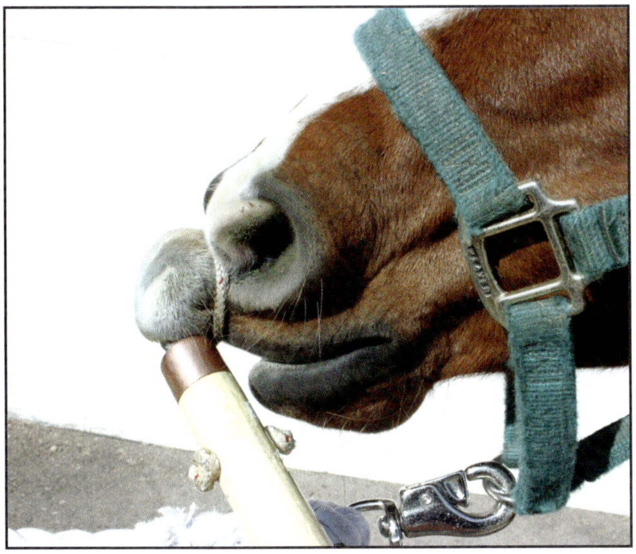

Figure 4-31 Properly applied ARS Twitch.

In further preparation for collection of semen, the mare's tail should be completely enclosed or wrapped. This may be easily done with a large sock. The sock is turned inside out over one hand. The hair on the mare's tail is formed into a ball, and clasped through the sock. The opposite hand is used to pull the sock up over the mare's tail. The sock is then taped into place at the base of the tail (Figure 4-32). When a mare's tail is so "wrapped", it permits sanitary control, and minimizes the chance of injury to the stallion's penis from loose hair across the opening of the artificial vagina, or vulva during natural service.

On many farms, there are sufficient personnel in the breeding shed for one person to hold the mare's tail to the opposite side during collection of semen or natural service. In that case, the base of the mare's tail can be wrapped for 8 to 12" with gauze, other disposable material or a washable neoprene sleeve.

The back end of the tease mare must be washed wherever the stallion's penis is likely to come into contact with hair or skin before allowing the stallion to mount. A non-residual soap such as Ivory® Liquid is adequate. The individual doing the washing should wear disposable gloves to prevent contamination. If pledgets of Rolled Utility Cotton are used to cleanse the mare, they should be used once and discarded and should not be put back into the bucket, since this contaminates the clean water. When finished, the area should be rinsed thoroughly to prevent soap from coming into contact with the penis of the stallion and potentially gaining access into the AV where it could adversely affect spermatozoa.

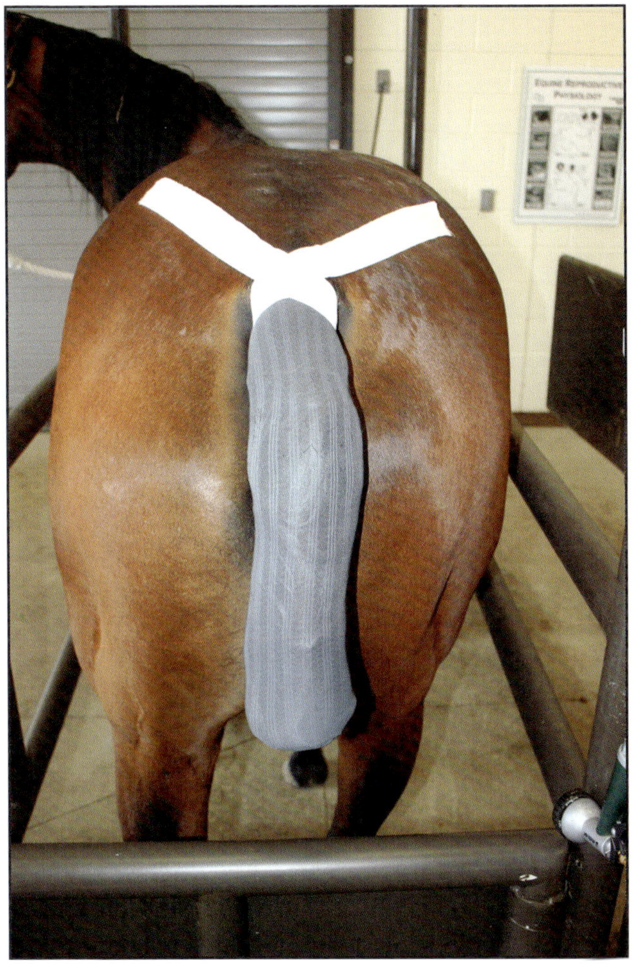

Figure 4-32 Mare with tail wrapped prior to use as a jump mare.

Stallions with good libido can be easily trained to mount a phantom, particularly during the physiologic breeding season. There are several advantages in having stallions trained to a phantom. The first is convenience. After the stallion has been trained properly, a tease mare or a mare in estrus is not always necessary. A phantom is particularly convenient when one needs to evaluate a stallion for breeding soundness, but a mare in estrus is not available. A second advantage is safety. There is less chance of injury to the stallion and personnel when collecting a stallion off a phantom.

It is important that good hygiene practices be used when collecting stallions off a phantom. The phantom must be washed between collections for disease prevention and cleanliness of the sample of semen, just as the mare must be cleaned. It is now common to wrap the working end of the phantom with disposable plastic wrap prior to each collection and replace the wrap in between stallions (Fig-

Figure 4-33 End of the phantom wrapped with disposable plastic wrap as a biosecurity precaution.

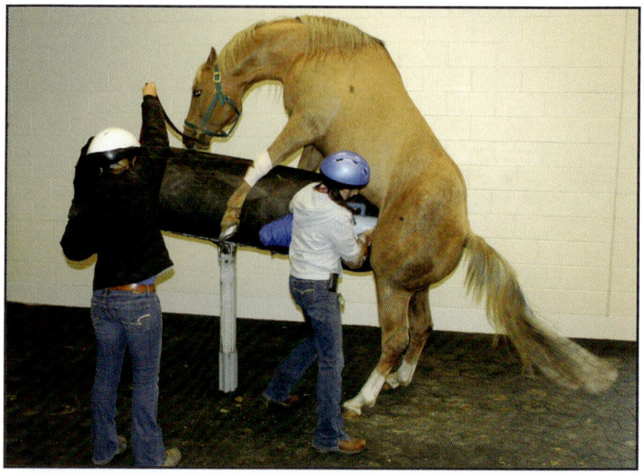

Figure 4-34 Collection of semen with the CSU Model artificial vagina.

ure 4-33). The goal is to minimize the possibility of transmission of infectious microorganisms from one stallion to another via contamination of the surface of the phantom.

4.5 Collection of Semen using the CSU Model Artificial Vagina

When the washing procedure is completed, everything should be ready so that the stallion can be immediately presented to the mare or taken to the phantom. Excessive restraint of the stallion at this time, particularly if it is done frequently, can make him frustrated and difficult to handle. The mare should be positioned in a location that has good footing, particularly for the stallion. Extreme caution should be taken to ensure that conditions are ideal before collection is attempted. If conditions are not completely satisfactory, return the stallion to his stall and correct the deficiencies. Failure to follow this procedure is the most common cause of avoidable accidents during collection of semen or breeding.

The collector should have proper footwear and attire for working around horses and should wear a safety helmet. The collector should be positioned on the near (left) side and slightly behind the stallion handler where he or she can observe both the mare and stallion. The collector should direct the mare and stallion handlers, just as the breeding shed manager does when natural service is being practiced.

The handler should make sure that the stallion has plenty of slack in the shank while he is mounted on the mare or phantom. The collector then steps forward and deflects the stallion's penis into the AV. The AV should be held at an angle that is comfortable for the stallion. As the stallion thrusts, the collector should manipulate the AV to provide maximal sexual stimulation. The left hand remains on the handle of the AV, and the right hand supports the AV from the bottom (Figure 4-34). The right hand can also be used to apply manual pressure on the base of the penis, which may help stimulate some stallions. The weight of the AV is partially supported by pushing it against the mare or phantom with the hip or body of the collector. Lifting the AV upward against the stallion's abdomen is usually more stimulating than pushing it down on the penis.

When the stallion begins to ejaculate, jets of semen (pulsations) through the urethra can be felt if the collector slides their right hand from the AV to the ventral (bottom) portion of the penis. These pulsations are usually associated with a characteristic pumping movement of the tail called “flagging”. After several pulsations, the anterior end of the AV should be gradually lowered (Figure 4-35). At this point, the collector should continue to lower the anterior end of the AV until it is almost vertical as the stallion loses his erection. If the AV is lowered too rapidly, it will cause discomfort to the stallion, and may interfere with ejaculation. Lowering the front of the AV allows semen to drain into the collection bottle.

The collector should then immediately back away from the stallion to a safe location. The AV should be held in a vertical position, and the filler cap

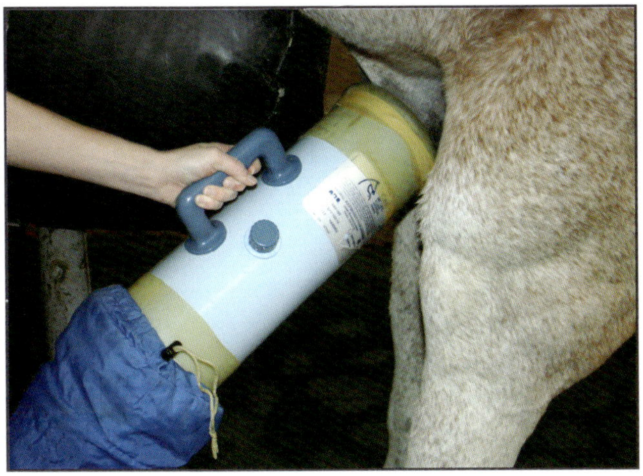

Figure 4-35 Lowering the anterior end of the AV aids the semen in reaching the collection bottle.

removed to allow water in the bladder to run out and reduce the internal pressure (Figure 4-36). This permits semen that may be present in the middle of the AV to drain into the collection bottle. Ideally, however, the collection procedure was such that semen was deposited directly into the tapered end of the collection liner. The collector should subsequently proceed to the laboratory.

Immediately after the stallion dismounts, the mare handler should pull the head and front of the mare to the left and forward. The stallion handler should back the stallion a few steps and also turn him to the left. This minimizes the risk of injury from kicking. However, the mare handler should not

Figure 4-36 Draining water from the AV after use.

move the mare before the stallion's forefeet have touched the ground, lest they become tangled in the hobbles.

4.6 Care and Cleaning the CSU Model Artificial Vagina

Ready-to-Use Reusable Latex Collection Liners (RTU) are pre-conditioned and do not require "conditioning" prior to use. All standard liners must be "conditioned" prior to their first use.

A procedure that appears to be satisfactory for "conditioning" latex collection liners is as follows:

- Turn the reusable latex collection liner inside out, i.e., so that the side that comes into contact with the semen is exposed.
- Place it in a washing machine (not the washing machine in the barn). Set the water on warm/warm and the dial on heavy load. Use the longest cycle with an extra rinse, if available.
- Put the liner through five complete cycles using a detergent that contains no dyes or fragrances.
- Using the same settings as before, repeat for five cycles, but do not use a detergent. This is in essence tap water rinses.
- Place the collection liner lengthwise in a plastic container that can be covered. Add 3 to 5 gallons of distilled or deionized water, depending upon the number of liners being "conditioned".
- The latex liners should be completely submerged. This can be done by placing heavy objects, such as bricks in individual zip-lock bags, on top of the liners.
- After the liners have remained submerged in distilled or deionized water at least 24 hr, rinse thoroughly.
- Rinse at least two additional times in distilled or deionized water.
- Hang in a dust-free cabinet to dry.

Ideally, all objects that come into contact with semen, such as the collection liner, nylon mesh gel filter, and collection bottle, should be clean and sterile. Unfortunately, this is not always possible under practical farm conditions. Dust, dirt and residues from soap and/or other cleaning agents, semen, smegma, lubricants, etc., that were not removed after the previous collections can result in poor quality semen, particularly when spermatozoa from the animal being collected is already marginal with respect to fertility.

The following method should be used to clean liners after they have been used.

- Remove the latex collection liner from the Artificial Vagina. This can be done by placing the AV upside down in a sink, after the disposable collection bottle has been removed. (Note: The water in the AV should have been removed immediately after collecting semen from the stallion). Put water into the top (open) end until approximately 2/3 full. When the AV case is raised quickly, the pressure of the water will invert the liner so that the "dirty" side is outside. Then remove from the cuff on the posterior end.
- Clean the collection liner with cold, running water until the rubber is "squeaky" clean of smegma, semen, lubricant, hair, etc. Rubber is somewhat porous; therefore only cold water should be used during the first cleaning step. Hot water is likely to "set" the proteinaceous material onto the latex rubber.
- The latex liner is then placed into a container of dilute Chlorhexidine Solution in water (1:49 ratio) and rinsed. The liner can remain in the Chlorhexidine Solution for up to 24 hours. The liner should be completely submerged. If not, drying at the junction of the air and solution will result in deposition of residue, which is exceedingly difficult to remove. The dilute Chlorhexidine Solution can be prepared by mixing 26 ounces of Chlorhexidine Solution to 20 gallons of distilled water.
- Remove collection liners from the Chlorhexidine Solution and place them in a sink. An ideal sink would have three large compartments with coved corners. The first compartment should contain hot water and Terg-A-Zyme® Detergent Powder. In this compartment, the latex liner is scrubbed with a brush.
- The second compartment contains warm tap water. The liner is rinsed in this compartment four times, changing the water each time. The water should be sufficiently warm to dissolve all the detergent, but not hot enough to make the liner "sticky".
- The third compartment contains cool, distilled or deionized water. The liner is rinsed four times, changing the water between rinses.
- The liner is then hung in a dust-free cabinet to dry.

When thoroughly dry the collection liner should be inverted, so it will be ready to use.

Remember, water and all soaps and detergents are spermicidal. Therefore, all material that comes into contact with the semen should be free of chemicals and residues; thus, the reason for numerous rinses (the final rinse with distilled or deionized water) and thorough drying.

When the breeding season is over, all rubber ware should be thoroughly cleaned, dried, placed into zip-lock bags and stored in a freezer at -20° C (-4° F) until the next year. They will stay clean under these conditions, and, most important, the rubber will not age. As rubber ages, it becomes more porous (cracked), and more difficult to clean.

To reduce microbes, dust and any chemical contaminants, it is recommended that laboratory work surfaces be washed regularly as follows: soapy water, then a clear water rinse, followed by a mild disinfectant that is relatively non-toxic. Surfaces must be allowed to dry thoroughly before use.

No effort has been made to describe methods for cleaning glassware or plastic ware. Unfortunately, these items are as difficult to clean and keep clean as rubber ware. Consequently, Animal Reproduction Systems recommends that breeding farms use disposable material whenever possible, the exception being the reusable latex collection liners for collection of semen.

Disposable plastic collection liners offer superior sanitation, and have labor-saving advantages. However, disposable liners are not tolerated by all stallions. Consequently, reusable latex liners must be used for collection of semen in those stallions.

4.7 Collection and Evaluation of a Semen Dismount Sample

In a live cover breeding program, when the stallion dismounts from the mare a sample of fluid that drips from his penis may be collected. A clean disposable plastic cup is inexpensive and effective for the purpose. The sample is evaluated under a microscope to determine the presence of spermatozoa and confirm that ejaculation occurred. The mare should be re-covered if no spermatozoa are present. The dismount sample may also be evaluated for motility, morphology and concentration of spermatozoa if deemed necessary. There is often enough debris in the sample that a hemacytometer count is required for accurate assessment of sperm concentration.

4.8 Collection of Semen by Chemical Ejaculation

Semen may be collected from stallions with severe physical disabilities by a procedure known as 'pharmacologically induced ex-copula ejaculation' or more commonly referred to as 'chemical ejaculation'. Stallions for which this procedure may be beneficial include horses with severe musculoskeletal issues, neurologic defects, penile paralysis, or other problems. The most commonly used protocol involves oral administration of imipramine followed 1 to 2 hours later by intravenous administration of xylazine. Passive emission of semen usually occurs within 1 to 3 minutes after administration of xylazine or less commonly 15 to 25 minutes after xylazine administration as the sedation effect is wearing off. Approximately 30 % to 75 % of horses ejaculate in response to imipramine/xylazine treatment. Semen may be collected into a funnel held below the prepuce (Figure 4-37) or a collection device may be placed over the prepuce and held by a strap or surcingle over the back of the stallion (Figure 4-38).

Ejaculates obtained are typically low in volume and high in sperm concentration. Semen collected by chemical ejaculation can be used to inseminate mares immediately or can be cryopreserved for future use.

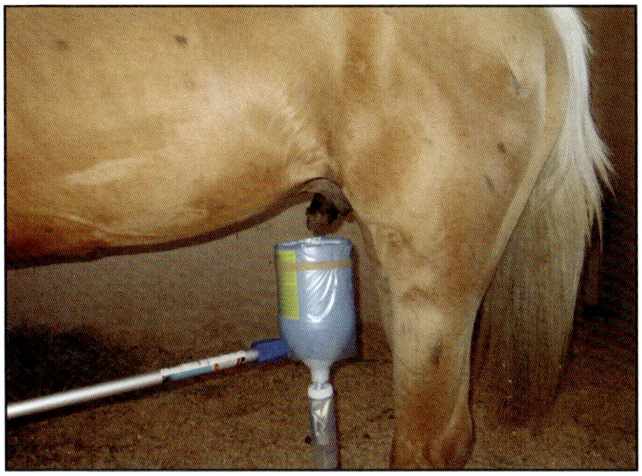

Figure 4-37 Hand-held collection device for chemical ejaculation.

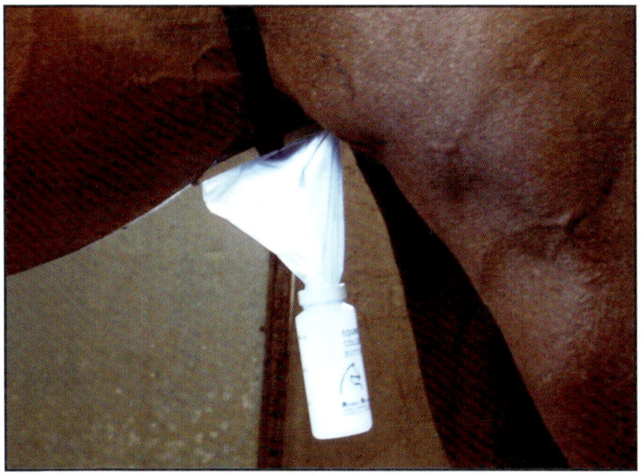

Figure 4-38 Collection bag covering sheath.

4.9 Harvesting Epididymal Semen

Spermatozoa can be harvested from the tail of the epididymis and vas deferens in the event of an unfortunate and unpredicted catastrophic injury to a stallion. Approximately 50 billion spermatozoa are stored in the two epididymides (combined) of normal stallions. Semen collected from the epididymides can be used to inseminate mares directly or can be frozen for future use.

The technique for collection of epididymal sperm is as follows: each testes, epididymis, and vas deferens is removed by standard castration techniques. The tissues are rinsed with sterile saline, placed in a clean plastic bag, and shipped overnight in a passive cooling device to a reproductive referral center. The epididymides and vas deferens are dissected free of the testes. The vas deferens is cannulated and the tubular system is flushed with seminal plasma, semen extender or air (Figure 4-39). Typically a total of 5 to 25 breeding doses, consisting of 800 million sperm each, are obtained. Harvesting epididymal sperm allows for preservation of genetic material that would otherwise have been lost.

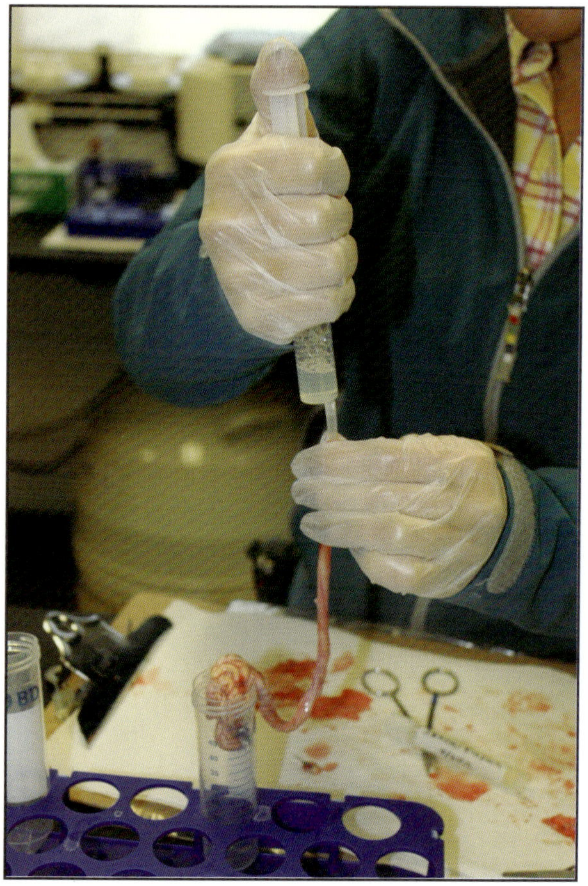

Figure 4-39 Flushing seminal plasma through the vas deferens and epididymal tail to collect epididymal sperm.

Additional Comments

- Complete Equine Artificial Vagina kits (Standard or Deluxe Models) are available through Animal Reproduction Systems; the Deluxe Kit includes the E-Z Boy AV Assembly Stand.
- Flared, Round and Straight Reusable Latex Collection Liners are available for the CSU Model™ Artificial Vaginas. The Flared version is the most popular due to the easy placement onto the AV case.
- Pre-assembled Disposable Artificial Vagina Liner Kits are also available from ARS. Each kit contains a disposable liner, nylon mesh gel filter, collection bottle and a coupling nut.

Chapter 5 Handling and Evaluation of Semen After Collection

Table 5-0 List and Part Number of ARS products used in this chapter.

Item	Part Number	Use/Comments
50mL Graduated Cylinder	537-510	Use to measure the volume of raw semen collected
100mL Graduated Cylinder	537-511	Use to measure the volume of raw semen collected
200mL Disposable Collection Bottle	SCB-200/25	Bottle to collect semen with graduations to measure collection volume
Hemacytometer Kit	537-850	Use to manually determine sperm concentration
Hemacytometer	537-686	Use to manually determine sperm concentration
Hemacytometer Re-Supply Kit	537-840/8	Used to properly dilute semen for the hemacytometer
591B Stallion Sperm Counter Kit	DENK-901	Calculate sperm concentration of raw semen
590B Stallion Sperm Counter Kit	DENK-1001	Calculate sperm concentration of raw semen
Formalin 10 Solution	FRM-101	Dilution of raw semen for sperm concentration measurement in the Densimeter or preparation of a wet mount for morphologic evaluation
Disposable Plastic Cuvette	537-204/100	Hold the sample for concentration analysis using the Densimeter
Disposable Cuvette Caps	537-205/100	Prevent sample in cuvette from spilling inside Densimeter
ARS 180µl Positive Displacement Pipette	594KR-1800	Transfer semen sample to cuvette for concentration analysis in Densimeter
EZ Mixin® -"CST"	EZM-CST	Dilution of raw semen for motility evaluation
EZ Mixin® -"BFT"	EZM-TD-BF	Dilution of raw semen for motility evaluation
ARS BLUE with Amikacin	BLU-AS	Dilution of raw semen for motility evaluation
ARS BLUE Basic Formula with Ticarcillin	BLU-BF-TD	Dilution of raw semen for motility evaluation
Disposable Plastic Transfer Pipette (1 ml)	537-665/400	Transfer of a small volume of semen for motility evaluation
Slide Warmer kit	581A-201	Maintain slides, cover slips, etc. at 37° C
Glass Slides	569A-243	Evaluation of sperm motility and/or morphology
Cover Slips	569A-244	Evaluation of sperm motility and/or morphology
Hancock Stain	HCS-101	Evaluation of sperm morphology
Video Microscope Kit	VMK-300	Evaluation of sperm motility

The goal of this chapter is to review techniques for evaluation of raw semen after collection. The artificial vagina (AV) should be held upright after collection and water in the AV bladder removed. This will allow all of the semen to drain into the collection bottle. The AV should then be taken directly into a clean laboratory for semen processing and evaluation. The AV is placed on a counter-top or in a rack designed to prevent it from rolling. The collection bottle cover is removed and the collection liner stretched to ensure that all semen has drained into the collection bottle. The small clamp is released, and the collection bottle removed from the tapered end of the liner. The disposable nylon mesh gel filter is removed and discarded, after the volume of gel has been estimated.

Each ejaculate collected during the breeding season should, at a minimum, be evaluated for volume, concentration and motility in order to determine optimal insemination doses. Additional measurements and tests may also be performed and are presented in the chapter on Reproductive Evaluation of the Stallion.

Semen should be processed quickly and efficiently once collected. It is critical that raw semen be extended as soon as possible to optimize preservation of sperm motility and viability. If any significant time is to lapse during the initial evaluation, an aliquot (i.e. 2 mls) of raw semen should be saved and the remainder of the ejaculate diluted 1:1 with warm semen extender (i.e. E-Z Mixin®- CST).

5.1 Gross Evaluation of Semen Quality

The gel-free semen is transferred into a warm graduated cylinder and initially evaluated for color and consistency. Color changes may be associated with the presence of debris, blood, urine, or purulent material (i.e. infection of the reproductive tract) (Figure 5-1 and Figure 5-2). Clarity or consistency of the sample can often be used as an initial assessment of sperm concentration.

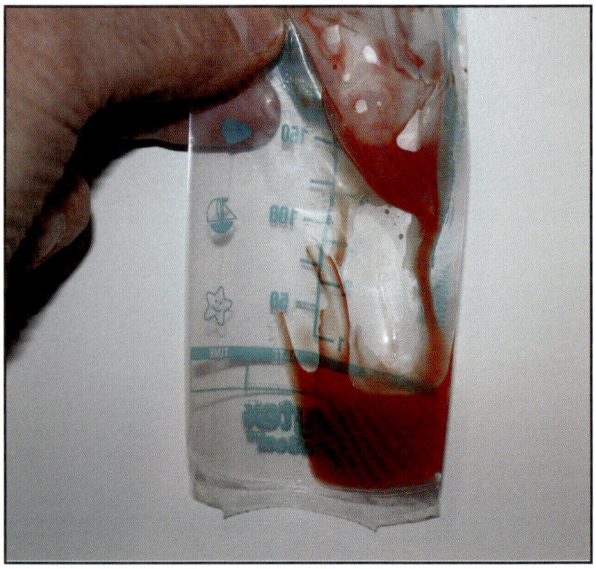

Figure 5-1 Blood in an ejaculate of a stallion (hemospermia).

Figure 5-2 Urine in an ejaculate of a stallion (urospermia).

5.2 pH

A pH meter should ideally be used to determine the pH of raw semen (Figure 5-3). The normal pH of equine semen ranges from 7.2 to 7.7. The pH of normal stallion semen can be affected by season, frequency of ejaculation, and sperm concentration. Inflammation of the reproductive tract or contamination of the ejaculate with soap or urine can lead to an abnormally high pH.

5.3 Volume Determination

The volume (ml) of gel-free semen is determined using a 50ml Graduated Cylinder or 100ml Graduated Cylinder (Figure 5-4). An accurate assessment of volume is critical for determination of total number of spermatozoa in an ejaculate. Volume of the ejaculate may be increased following excessive teasing of a stallion to a mare in estrus prior to collection. However, the concentration of sperm per

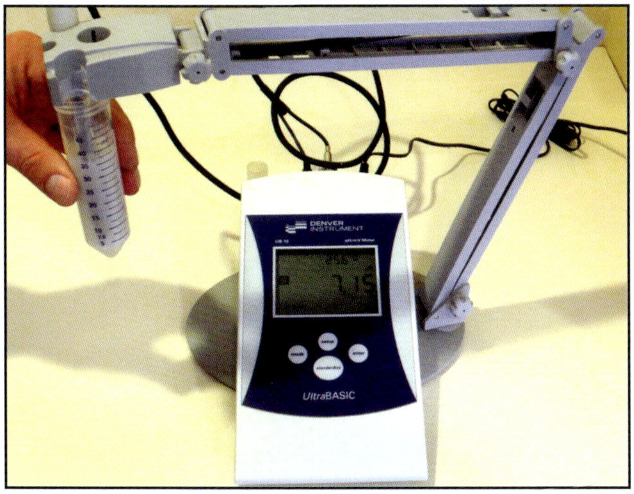

Figure 5-3 Measuring pH of stallion semen.

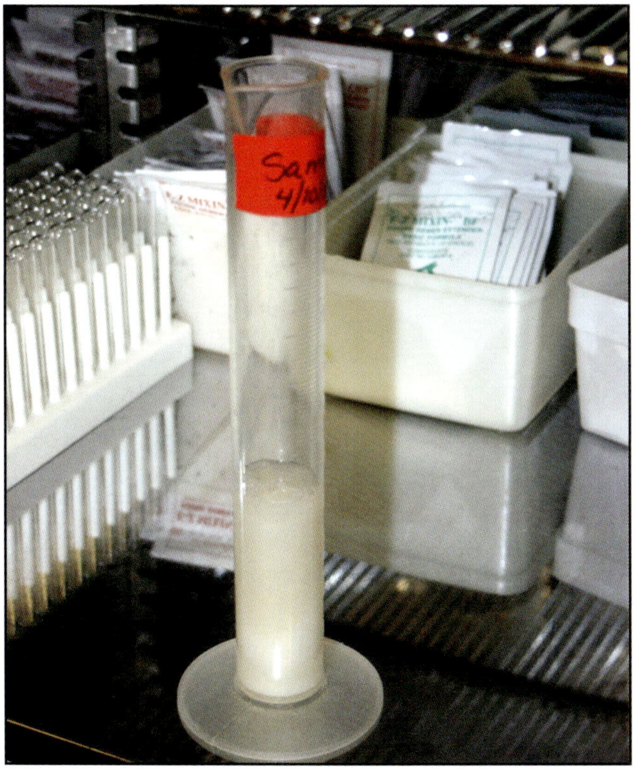

Figure 5-4 Semen sample in a graduated cylinder.

ml will be reduced in this circumstance and as a consequence the overall number of sperm in the ejaculate is not affected.

A warm 50ml or 100ml graduated cylinder is removed from an incubator maintained at 37°C (98.6°F), and tilted to about a 30° angle so that the raw semen can be poured from the collection bottle slowly down the side. Once semen is in the graduated cylinder, it should be labeled with the name of the stallion, date and time collected, and the volume recorded. A 200ml Disposable Collection Bottle accurately graduated in increments of 2.0 ml is also available, which makes transfer of semen for volume measurements to a graduated cylinder an unnecessary step.

Figure 5-5 Hemacytometer Re-Supply kit that includes the Thrombo-TIC system for counting equine spermatozoa.

5.4 Sperm Concentration

Concentration of spermatozoa per ml in the ejaculate may be manually counted using a Hemacytometer Kit, estimated using a Densimeter, or determined using a DNA cell counter. An accurate assessment of sperm concentration is a critical parameter in the calculation of the total number of sperm in an ejaculate.

The manual method involves counting individual sperm cells using a light-microscope and Hemacytometer. Precise dilution of a well-mixed semen sample is critical for accuracy of counts. A 1:100 dilution of semen is generally appropriate, and can be readily prepared using the Thrombo-TIC diluting system that is included in the Hemacytometer Re-Supply Kit (Figure 5-5). The system was initially designed for counting platelets in blood. A 10 µl capillary pipette (Figure 5-6) is filled with semen and transferred into a vial containing 990 µl of buffer (Figure 5-7). The vial is thoroughly mixed. This will provide a 1:100 dilution of semen. A larger capillary tube is filled part way with the diluted semen (Figure 5-8) and used to load the hemacytometer chamber (Figure 5-9). The sperm are allowed to settle onto the hemacytometer grid for a few minutes prior to counting. If a significant length of time is anticipated before counting the sperm number, it is recommended the hemacytometer be placed into a covered petri dish above a moist paper towel to maintain the humidity and prevent

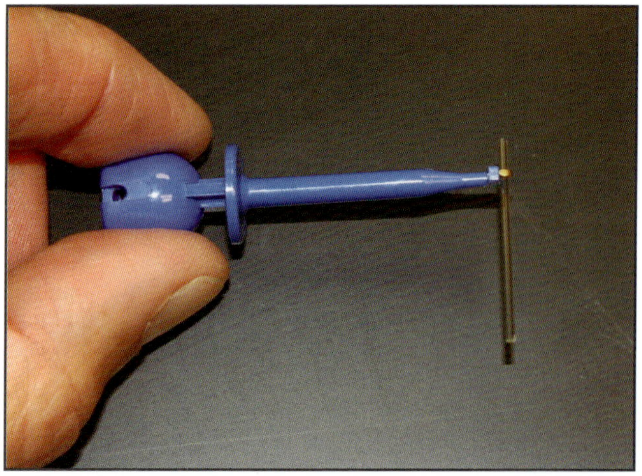

Figure 5-6 Handling the small (10 μl) capillary tube using the ARS Capillary Holder.

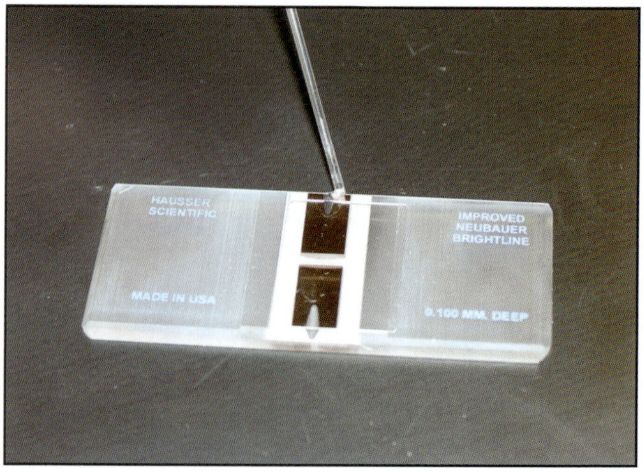

Figure 5-9 Loading a hemacytometer with diluted semen from the Thrombo-TIC system.

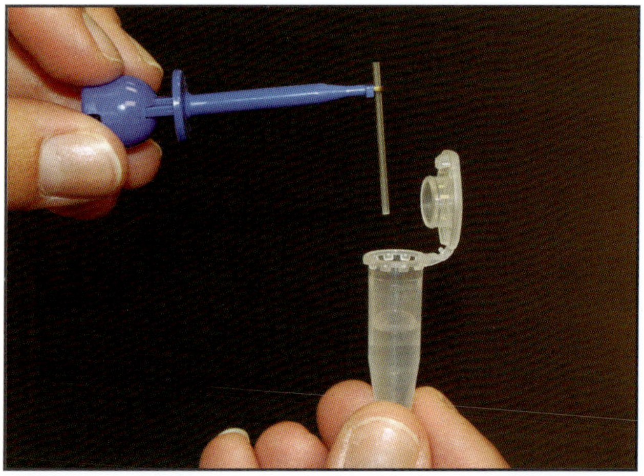

Figure 5-7 Placing the small capillary tube into the buffer diluent.

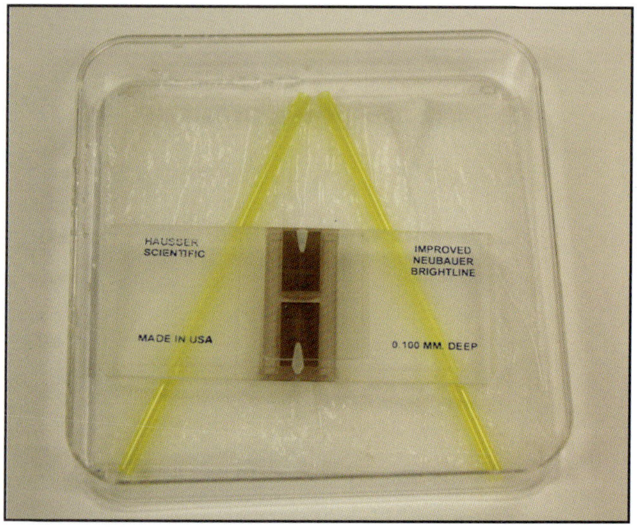

Figure 5-10 Humidified chamber for a loaded hemacytometer.

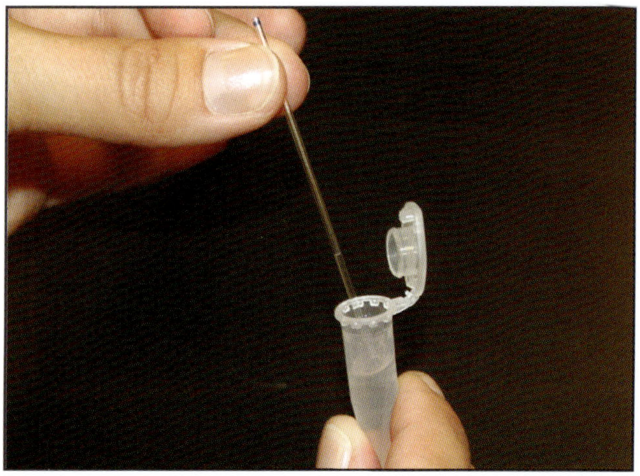

Figure 5-8 Loading the larger capillary tube with diluted semen.

the sample from drying out (Figure 5-10). The total number of sperm present in one of the nine large squares (each comprised of 25 smaller squares) is counted. Most commonly, one counts the number of sperm (or more specifically sperm heads) in the 25 squares within the central larger square of the hemacytometer (Figure 5-11, left).

The number of sperm counted correlates to the sperm concentration in millions per ml. Alternatively, one can count the number of sperm within any 5 of the 25 squares within the larger central square and multiply the results by 5 to yield the sperm concentration in millions per ml (Figure 5-11, right).

In order to prevent over-estimation, only sperm heads lying on the left and upper lines are recorded. Both sides of the hemacytometer chamber are

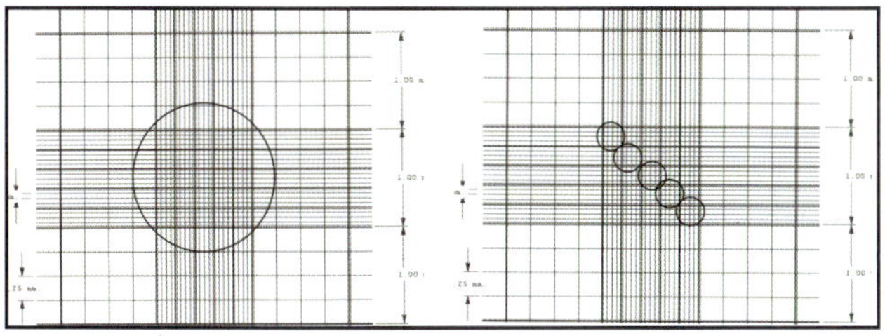

Figure 5-11 Options for estimating sperm concentration using a hemacytometer. The example on the left shows all 25 squares within the large circle; the example on the right shows 5 small squares, each within a small circle.

counted, and the values averaged. If the values differ by more than 10%, the chamber should be refilled and re-counted.

Advantages of the manual counting method are that it is inexpensive, can be performed on extended semen samples, and the equipment can be easily transported from one location to another. The principal disadvantage of the manual counting method is that it requires more technical skill and time than a spectrophotometer and is not suited for situations where large numbers of semen samples must be counted rapidly.

A calibrated spectrophotometer is a quick, accurate alternative to the hemacytometer for estimating the concentration of sperm cells in equine semen. Spectrophotometers rely on the principle that, when a beam of light of known wavelength is focused on a tube containing a suspension of particles (i.e., sperm cells), part of the light will be absorbed, scattered, or transmitted, depending upon the number, size, shape, and opacity of the particles. Since the size and shape of sperm cells is consistent from sample to sample within a species, the change in light transmitted from sample to sample is largely due to differences in sperm cell concentration.

The 534A Densimeter from Animal Reproduction Systems was the first spectrophotometric device designed specifically for estimating sperm concentration in equine semen. Two versions, the 591B Stallion Sperm Counter Kit, and 590B Stallion Sperm Counter Kit are now available, (Figure 5-12 and Figure 5-13). All ARS Densimeters are calibrated at the factory using data from hemacytometer counts of stallion semen. The 591B Densimeter is capable of estimating sperm concentration and can perform all calculations required to create appropriate insemination doses. The basic information about the ejaculate (gel-free volume and sperm

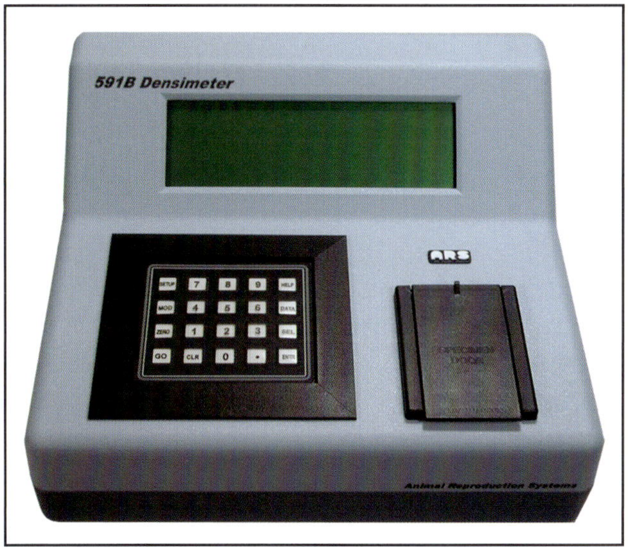

Figure 5-12 The 591B Equine Densimeter.

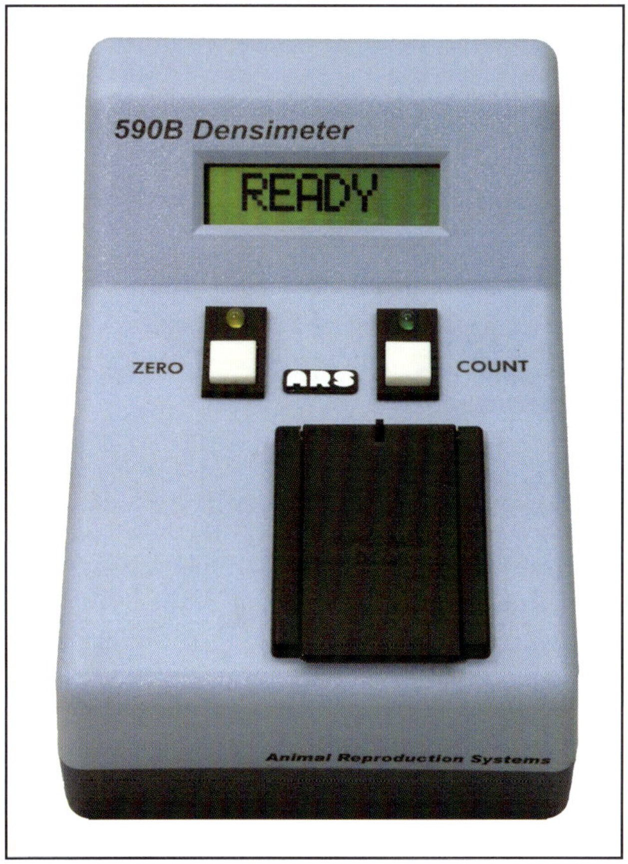

Figure 5-13 The 590B Equine Densimeter.

motility) is entered via a keypad, and the software uses this information to calculate the appropriate volumes of raw semen and extender to prepare doses for fresh or cooled insemination. The 590B Densimeter is a portable, 2-button version with the same accuracy of the larger units. Both the 591B and 590B Densimeters can be connected to a computer running E-Z Records^{TM} Equine software to provide reports on each collection, stallion summaries and other information. Densimeters cannot be used to count semen samples extended with an opaque extender and it may overestimate sperm concentration in samples contaminated with debris.

Steps needed to obtain a semen count are as follows. First, 3.42 ml of Formalin 10 Solution is dispensed into a new clean Disposable Plastic Cuvette. The cuvette is inserted into the Densimeter and the system is 'zeroed'. The cuvette is removed and 180 µl of raw semen is added using the ARS 180µl Positive Displacement Pipette. A Disposable Cuvette Cap is placed on the cuvette and the semen and diluent solution are gently, but thoroughly mixed. The cuvette is placed back into the Densimeter and the COUNT or GO button is pressed. The Densimeter will evaluate the light transmission through the diluted semen sample and provide a digital read-out of sperm concentration in millions/ml. A detailed description of the procedure is presented in Chapter 6 Step-by-Step Guide for Use of the Densimeter on page 46.

5.5 Motility Estimation

An accurate evaluation of sperm motility is one of the most important components of a semen evaluation. Unfortunately, sperm motility is not always highly correlated with fertility of a stallion.

The motility of raw, gel-free semen may be difficult to evaluate accurately since the concentration is often too high to examine individual cells and sperm cells in raw semen tend to clump or agglutinate. Consequently, raw semen is usually diluted with warm extender to aid in the evaluation of sperm motility. Semen may be diluted to a concentration of 25 million sperm per ml by adding 180 µl of raw semen measured with the ARS 180µl Positive Displacement Pipette to the volume of extender noted in Table 5-1, provided the initial sperm concentration is known.

Alternatively, a simple method is to use a dilution of 1 part semen to 20 parts extender (i.e. E-Z Mixin® - CST) prior to evaluation. This can be achieved by adding 0.25 ml of raw semen to 4.75 ml of extender that has been pre-warmed to 37° C.

Table 5-1 Volume of semen extender required to add to a standard volume of raw semen (180 µl) to provide a final concentration of approximately 25 million sperm per ml, when the original sperm concentration in the ejaculate is known.

Sperm Concentration (Millions per mL)	Extender Volume (mls)
100	0.5
150	1.0
200	1.5
250	2.0
300	2.0
350	2.5
400	3.0
450	3.5
500	3.5
550	4.0
600	4.5
650	4.5
700	5.0
750	5.5
800	6.0
850	6.0
900	6.5
850	7.0
1000	7.5

Using a Disposable Plastic Transfer Pipette, one drop of extended semen is placed onto each end of a clean Glass Slide and covered with a clean Cover Slip. The quality of the examination is enhanced if the glass slides and coverslips are maintained at 37° C using the Slide Warmer Kit. After each slide is prepared, it is examined microscopically at a magnification of 200X to 400X. The most accurate manual evaluations are performed using a phase-contrast microscope equipped with a heated stage warmer maintained at 37° C like the ARS Video Microscope Kit.

Generally, two motility estimates are determined when examining a semen sample. The percentage of sperm that are moving in any manner is recorded as the total motility, and the percentage of sperm that are moving in a forward manner is recorded as the progressive motility.

Several computer-assisted semen analysis (CASA) systems are commercially available that provide automated objective estimates of total motility, progressive motility, sperm velocity, and other motion characteristics. CASA units provide rapid unbiased motility estimates of large numbers of sperm, but may be cost prohibitive for many equine breeding operations.

Longevity of sperm motility can be used as a crude indicator of ejaculate quality. Longevity can be determined by evaluation of motion characteristics over time for raw and extended semen samples maintained at either room temperature (20° to 25° C; 68° to 77° F) or cooled to refrigerator temperature (4° to 6° C; 39° to 43° F).

5.6 Morphology

Examination of sperm morphology (or physical characteristics of individual spermatozoa) is an important component of a complete Breeding Soundness Evaluation. ARS Hancock Stain, a simple, one-step vital dye containing eosin and nigrosin stains, is one of the most common stains used to evaluate sperm morphology. A drop of stain (approximately 50 µl) is placed adjacent to a similar sized drop of raw semen on one end of a Glass Slide (Figure 5-14). The stain and semen are mixed (Figure 5-15) and then smeared along the length of the slide using a Cover Slip or another glass slide (Figure 5-16). The test slide is allowed to dry and then examined under oil immersion at 1000x magnification using a standard light microscope (Figure 5-17).

Morphological characteristics are evaluated for a minimum of 100 spermatozoa in each of two slides

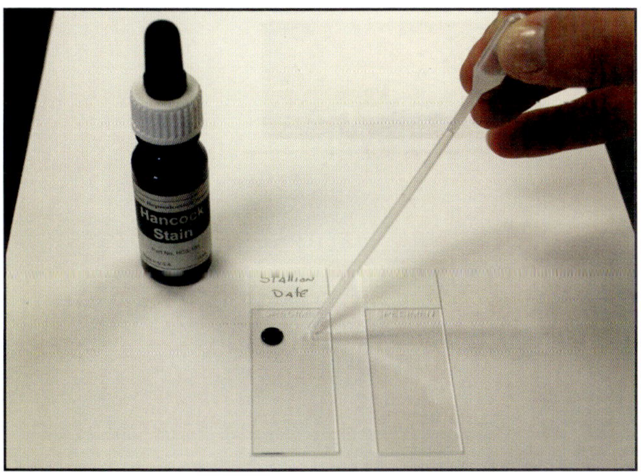

Figure 5-14 Adding a drop of semen adjacent to a drop of Hancock stain.

Figure 5-15 Mixing a drop of semen with a drop of Hancock stain to prepare a slide for sperm morphology evaluation.

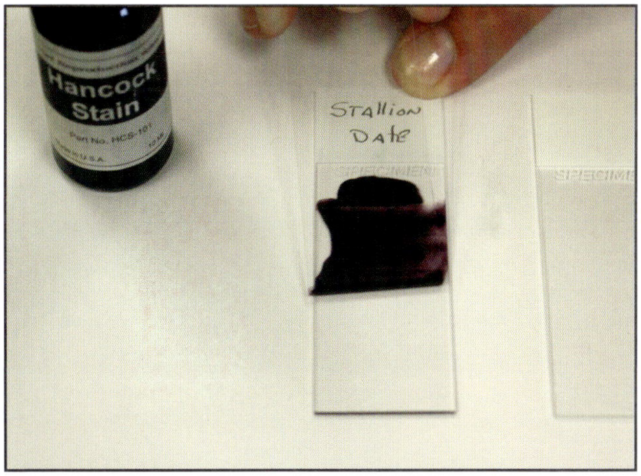

Figure 5-16 Preparation of a morphology slide after mixing semen and Hancock stain.

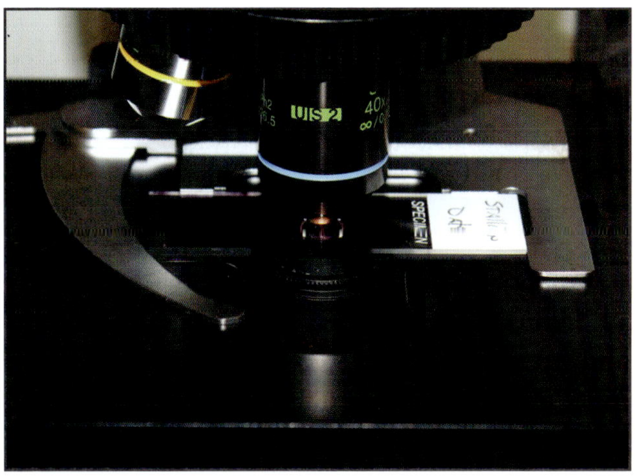

Figure 5-17 Evaluation of stallion sperm morphology.

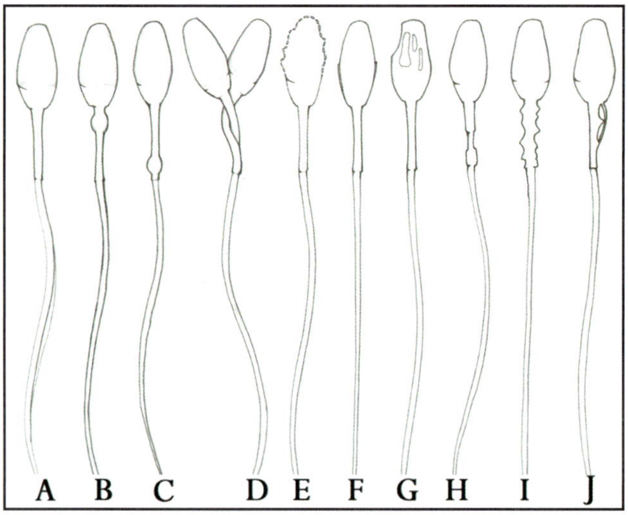

Figure 5-18 Drawing of equine spermatozoa, showing a normal spermatozoon (A), sperm with proximal (B) and distal (C) protoplasmic or cytoplasmic droplets, a sperm with two heads (D), a sperm undergoing the acrosome reaction (E), a sperm missing the acrosomal cap following the acrosome reaction (F), a sperm with a head defect (G), and sperm with midpiece defects (H, I, J).

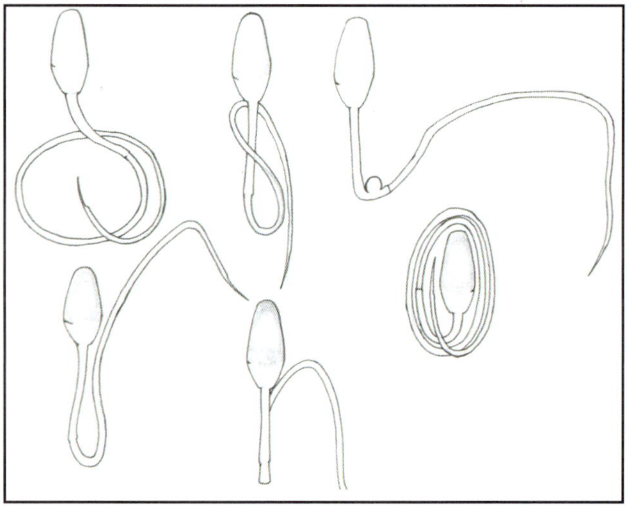

Figure 5-19 Drawing of equine spermatozoa with coiled tails.

and the results averaged. The number of normal sperm and the number of sperm with specific morphologic defects are recorded (Figure 5-18). The most common defects observed in stallion spermatozoa are abnormal head, detached head, abnormal/broken neck, abnormal midpiece, proximal droplet, distal droplets, coiled tail (Figure 5-19), and kinked tail. Studies have reported that fertility in stallions is positively correlated with the percentage of morphologically normal sperm and inversely correlated with the percentage of sperm with abnormal heads, proximal droplets and abnormal midpieces. ARS Hancock Stain has also been used as a 'live-dead' stain. Live sperm, with intact plasma membranes do not take up eosin and will appear white against a dark background, while dead sperm with damaged plasma membranes will take up eosin and appear red, pink or light purple against the dark nigrosin background (i.e. 'red is dead', Figure 5-20). In most stallions, the percentage of live cells as determined by vital dye exclusion is highly correlated with sperm motility. A discrepancy may suggest that a population of live but immotile sperm is present in an ejaculate.

A better, but more expensive alternative to the eosin-nigrosin stain for sperm morphology evaluation is to preserve semen in buffered formal-saline (i.e. Formalin 10 Solution), prepare a wet mount slide, and examine the semen sample using a phase-contrast microscope or a differential interference contrast (DIC) microscope (Figure 5-21).

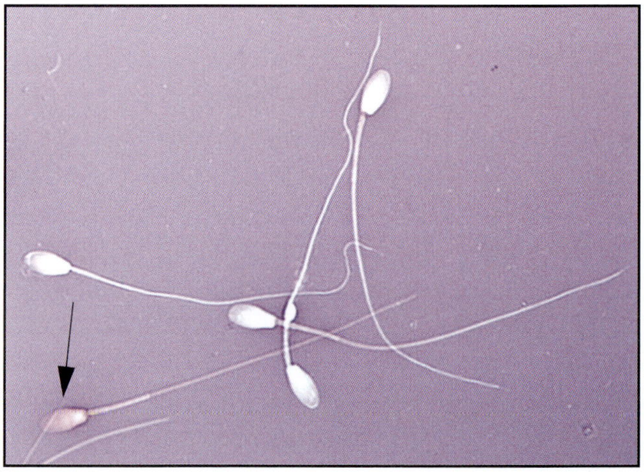

Figure 5-20 Stallion spermatozoa stained with ARS Hancock stain for evaluation of morphology. Sperm with a damaged plasma membrane stain pink/red (arrow).

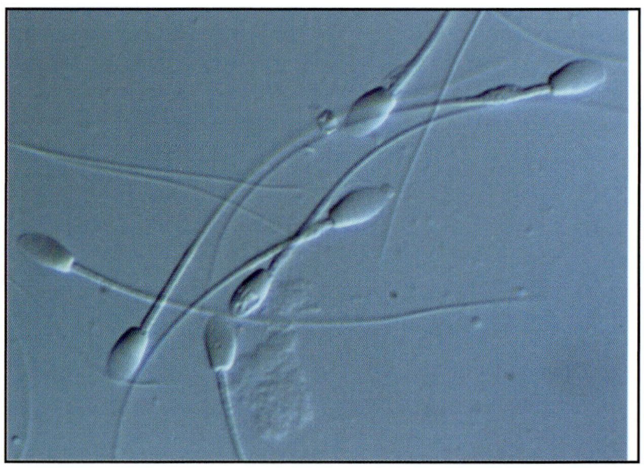

Figure 5-21 Stallion spermatozoa evaluated using a DIC microscope.

5.7 Calculations

Once the volume and concentration have been determined, the total number of sperm in the ejaculate can be calculated:

Total sperm number (millions) =

volume (mls) x concentration (millions per ml)

With the additional knowledge of progressive motility, the total number of progressively motile sperm (PMS) in the ejaculate can be calculated:

Total number PMS (millions) =

total sperm # (millions) x progressive motility (%)

The total number of progressively motile sperm in the ejaculate can subsequently be used to determine the number of fresh and cooled doses available, and/or the number of straws of frozen semen that can be obtained. Preparation of semen for fresh insemination, preparation of cooled-transported semen, and semen freezing and storage are discussed in subsequent chapters.

Chapter 6 Step-by-Step Guide for Use of the Densimeter

Table 6-0 List and Part Number of ARS products used in this chapter.

Item	Part Number	Use/Comments
591B Stallion Sperm Counter Kit	DENK-901	Calculate sperm concentration of raw semen and automatic calculation of breeding doses.
590B Stallion Sperm Counter Kit	DENK-1001	Calculate sperm concentration of raw semen
Formalin Dispenser	537-215-01	Pump to accurately dispense 3.42 ml
Formal 10 Solution	FRM-101	Dilution media used for Stallion Sperm Concentration measurements
Disposable Plastic Cuvettes & Caps (100/box)	537-204-205C/100	Square container to hold sample for use in Densimeter
180 µl Positive Displacement Pipette	594KR-1800	Positive displacement pipette for measuring raw semen
Disposable Pipette Tips (100/rack)	594TR-R/100	Disposable tip used with ARS Pipette
Kimwipes®	537-669	Clean lint free tissue for wiping sides of pipette

One of the most important factors in evaluation of a stallion for potential fertility is accurate determination of sperm number. The 590 and 591 series Densimeters are both highly accurate and repeatable in estimating sperm concentrations per ml of gel-free semen. Further, the 591 series Densimeters have a built-in program that permits easy, accurate calculation of the number of spermatozoa needed for a fresh insemination dose or amount of raw semen and extender required for a cooled dose.

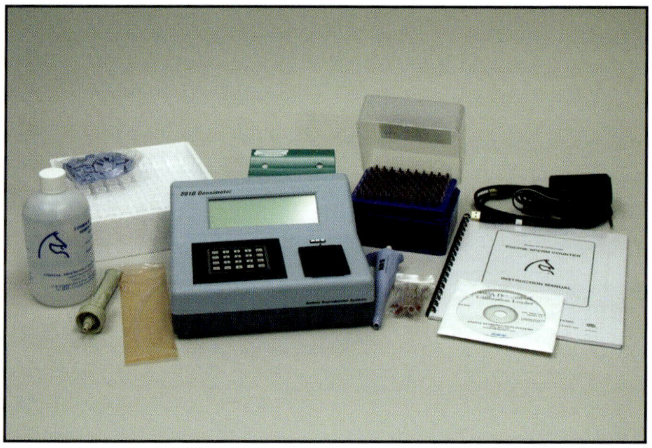

Figure 6-1 The Model 591B Stallion Sperm Counter Kit (DENK-901).

6.1 Model 591 Series Densimeter

The 591 series has a built in expert system with the ability to calculate both Immediate Use and Cooled and Shipped insemination doses. The program provides step-by-step instructions for processing semen according to Colorado State University's recommendations.

The 591B Densimeter is part of the 591B Stallion Sperm Counter Kit, which contains all supplies necessary for 100 semen concentration measurements (Figure 6-1). This device is also capable of performing Foal IgG concentration measurements when the appropriate optional software and supplies are purchased.

To begin operation, the unit should be turned on using the power switch on the back at least 5 minutes prior to use. This allows the machine to warm up. A longer warm up period is recommended if the temperature is below 20° C.

An introductory screen will display the animated ARS logo along with the device manufacturer, model, version, and serial number. After a short pause, the following Main Screen will appear.

The Stallion calibrations for the 591 series Densimeters offers two different operations: 'Immediate Use' and 'Cooled and Shipped'. The Immediate Use calibration performs all of the calculations required for on-farm breeding. The Cooled and Shipped calibration calculates all dose information that is needed for stored and/or transported semen doses. The currently selected operation is shown on the Main Screen. When purchased, the Densimeter is initially set to use the Immediate Use calibration.

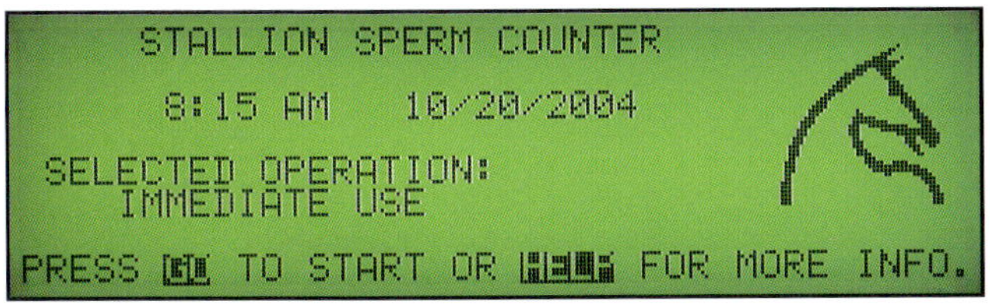

Figure 6-2 Main Densimeter Screen.

6.2 Immediate Use Calibration

From the Main Screen (Figure 6-2) press the GO button on the keypad. The Densimeter screen will provide step-by-step instructions on how to prepare the Densimeter and the semen sample for analysis. As the screen below shows (Figure 6-3), dispense 3.42 ml of Formalin 10 Solution into a fresh clean Disposable Plastic Cuvette (Figure 6-4). Take care to only touch the cuvette on the ribbed sides. Place the cuvette in the specimen compartment with a ribbed side facing forward (Figure 6-5). Close the specimen compartment and press ZERO.

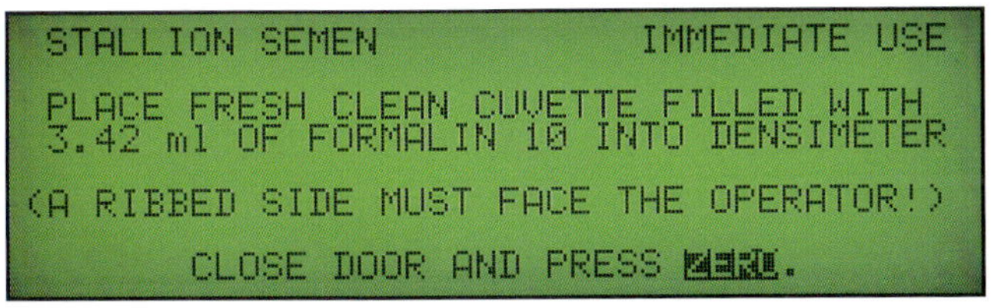

Figure 6-3 Instruction screen.

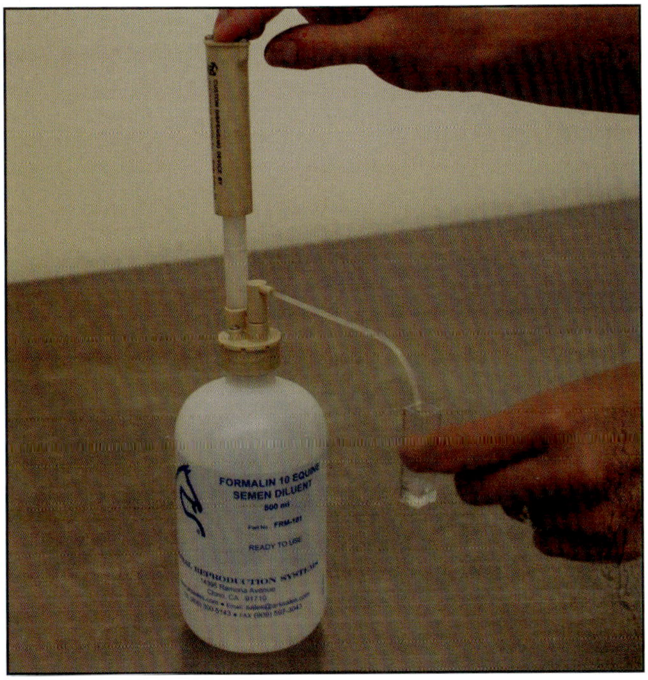

Figure 6-4 Dispensing Formalin solution into cuvette.

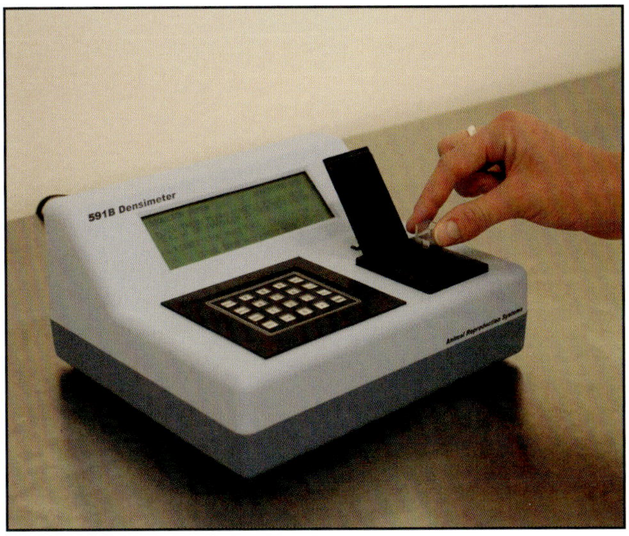

Figure 6-5 Loading cuvette into 591B Densimeter.

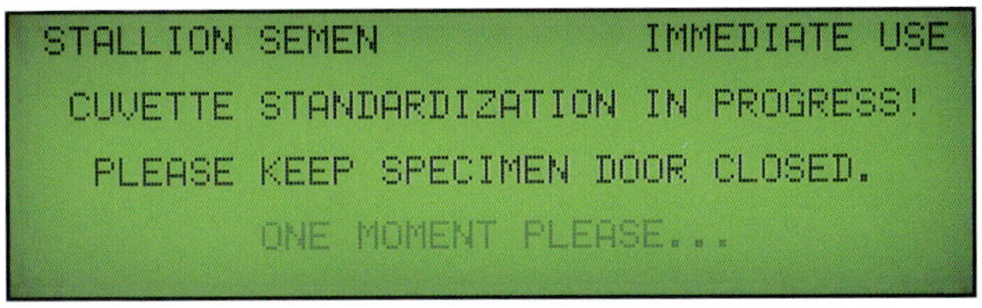

Figure 6-6 591B Densimeter display during standardiz-ing.

The Densimeter is now "zeroing" or standardizing the cuvette filled with Formalin 10 Solution (Figure 6-6).

DO NOT OPEN THE SPECIMEN COMPARTMENT WHILE STANDARDIZATION IS IN PROGRESS!

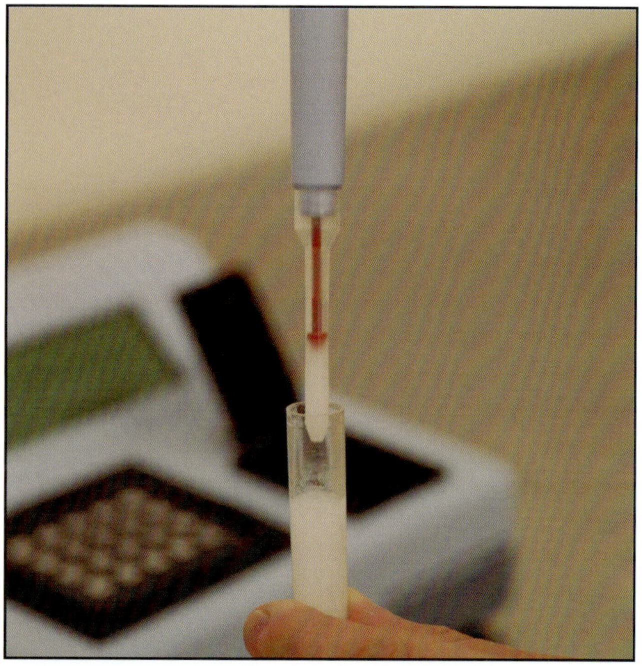

Figure 6-7 Drawing raw semen into pipette.

Figure 6-8 591B Densimeter display requesting semen to be added to cuvette.

Once the standardization is complete, the Densimeter screen will instruct the operator to add 180 µl (0.18 ml) of raw semen to the cuvette(Figure 6-7).

1. Draw up 180 µl of semen into a new 180 µl pipette tip using the 180 µl Positive Displacement Pipette (Figure 6-8).
2. Wipe the outside of the pipette tip with a Kimwipe® (Figure 6-9).
3. Dispense the semen in to the cuvette containing 3.42 ml of Formalin 10 solution (Figure 6-10).
4. A Cuvette Cap should be placed on the cuvette before gently inverting the cuvette several times to fully mix the semen with the Formalin 10 solution.

Once the solution is mixed, place the cuvette in the Densimeter specimen compartment with a ribbed side facing forward. Close the compartment and press GO.

DO NOT OPEN THE SPECIMEN DOOR WHILE THE SPERM COUNT IS IN PROGRESS.

Figure 6-9 Wiping sides of pipette to remove excess semen.

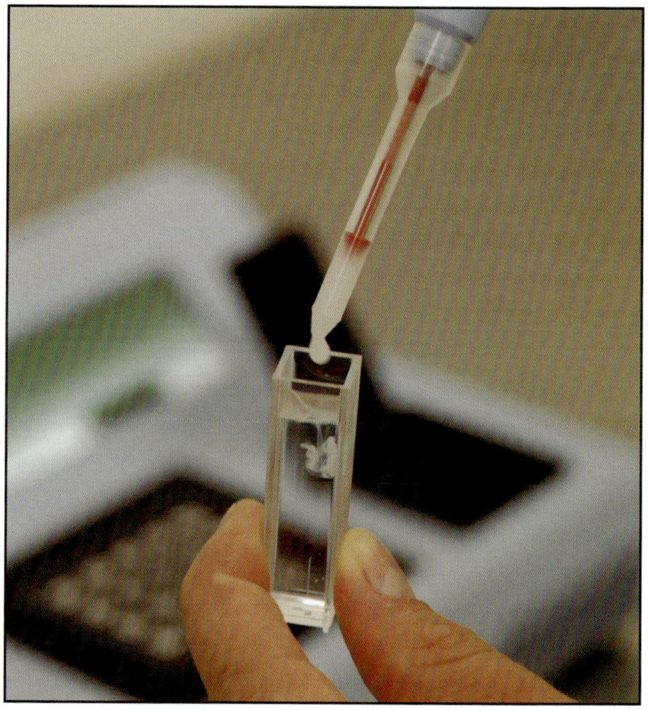

Figure 6-10 Adding semen into cuvette filled with Formalin 10 solution.

Figure 6-11 591B Densimeter display during counting process.

The sperm concentration measurement will take about 25 seconds (Figure 6-11). When done, the concentration, in millions of sperm per ml, will be displayed in large numbers on the screen (Figure 6-12).

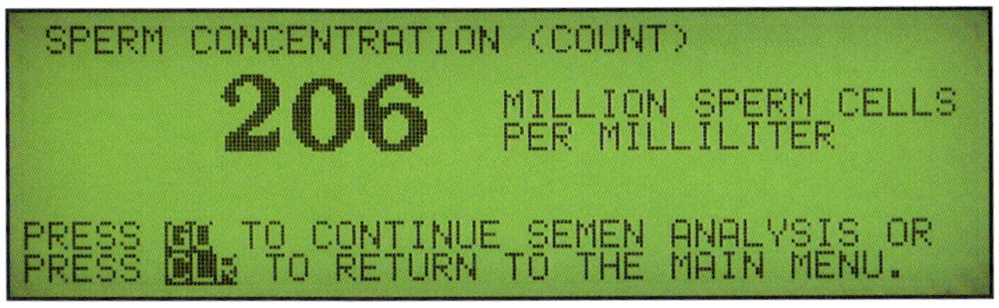

Figure 6-12 591B Densimeter display showing sperm concentration.

The following screen will then appear:

Figure 6-13 591B Densimeter initial input screen.

The Densimeter needs three entries from the user to complete the dose calculations (Figure 6-13). The first entry is the volume of gel-free semen collected from the stallion. The second two entries are the number of motile sperm desired in a dose and the percentage of motile sperm cells in the sample. The Densimeter enters a standard value into these two fields that can be changed by the operator. To change the values, press MOD. A flashing cursor will appear in the TOTAL GEL-FREE VOLUME line. Enter the gel-free volume of the ejaculate (mls) (Figure 6-14). The volume should be measured with a graduated cylinder or a 200 ml collection bottle.

Figure 6-14 Entering semen volume into 591B Densimeter.

When the correct volume has been entered, press ENTR. The TOTAL SPERM/EJACULATE will immediately be calculated and displayed by the Densimeter. The cursor will jump to the next parameter that can be modified: MOTILE SPERM/DOSE (Figure 6-15). This value represents the desired number of motile sperm in each insemination dose.

Figure 6-15 591B Densimeter display with motile sperm per dose selected.

Figure 6-16 591B Densimeter display with motility

To modify this value, simply key in the number desired and press ENTR. If the displayed default value of 500 million motile sperm per ml is to be used, press SEL. The cursor will then jump to the MOTILITY field (Figure 6-16).

The default value of 50% motility is already displayed. This can be changed by keying in the percent motile spermatozoa estimated for the ejaculate and then pressing ENTR. Once all parameters display the appropriate values for the ejaculate, press the GO key. The results of the dose calculations will be shown (Figure 6-17).

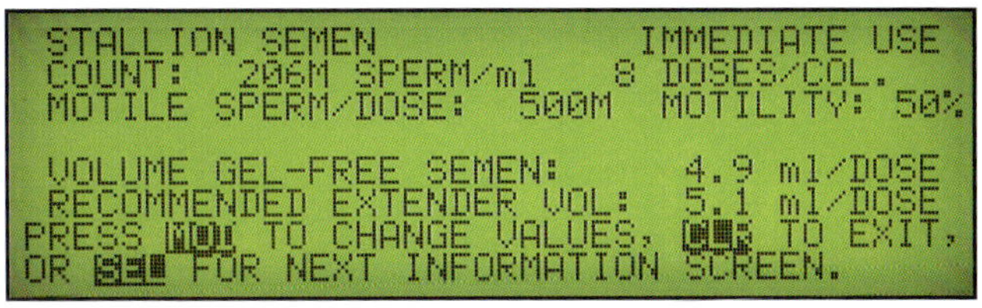

Figure 6-17 591B Densimeter displaying dose information.

At the top of the screen, a summary of the collection is displayed. This summary provides the sperm concentration (COUNT), the number of doses available in the entire collection (DOSES/COL.), the number of motile sperm per dose (MOTILE SPERM/DOSE) and the motility percentage (MOTILITY). The bottom half of the screen displays the recommended volumes of gel-free semen and extender needed for preparation of one fresh insemination dose. The values shown on this screen can be modified by the operator by pressing the MOD key. Changes made to these parameters will be immediately reflected on the screen.

6.3 Cooled and Shipped Calibration

The Cooled and Shipped calibration is similar to using the Immediate Use calibration. From the Main Screen, with Cooled and Shipped as the selected operation, press the GO key to begin the analysis. The Densimeter will prompt the user to dispense 3.42 ml of Formalin 10 solution into a fresh clean disposable cuvette. The cuvette should then be placed in the specimen compartment with a ribbed side facing forward. Once the lid is closed, press ZERO to begin the zeroing process.

After the Densimeter has been zeroed, the user should add 180 µl of raw semen using a fresh clean pipette tip. As with the Immediate Use calibration, the pipette tip should not touch the Formalin 10 solution in the cuvette when the semen is added. A cuvette cap should be placed on the cuvette before gently inverting the cuvette several times to fully mix the semen with the Formalin 10 solution. Replace the cuvette into the specimen compartment and close the door. Press the Go key to start the sperm concentration measurement. This process will take approximately 25 seconds and the concentration in millions of spermatozoa per ml will be displayed in large numbers when the measurement is complete (Figure 6-18).

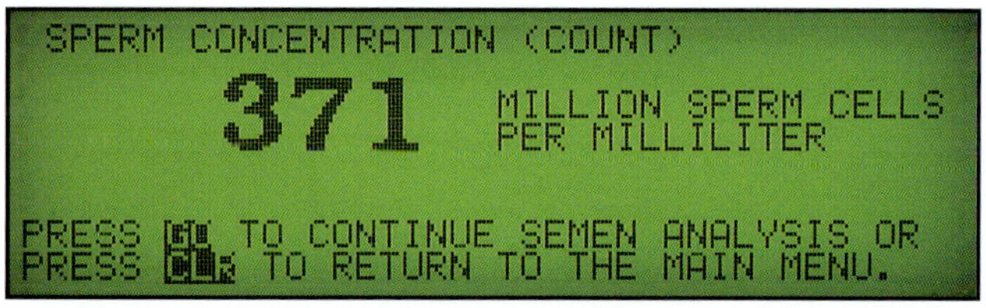

Figure 6-18 591B Densimeter displaying sperm concentration.

Press the GO key to continue the semen analysis. The next phase will recommend and calculate a Cooled and Shipped insemination dose (Figure 6-19).

Figure 6-19 591B Densimeter initial input screen for cooled and shipped dose.

In the same fashion as for the Immediate Use calibration, the user can input the appropriate values for the current collection by pressing MOD and keying in the numbers. When finished, press the GO key to continue. This will bring up the first of three results screens (Figure 6-20).

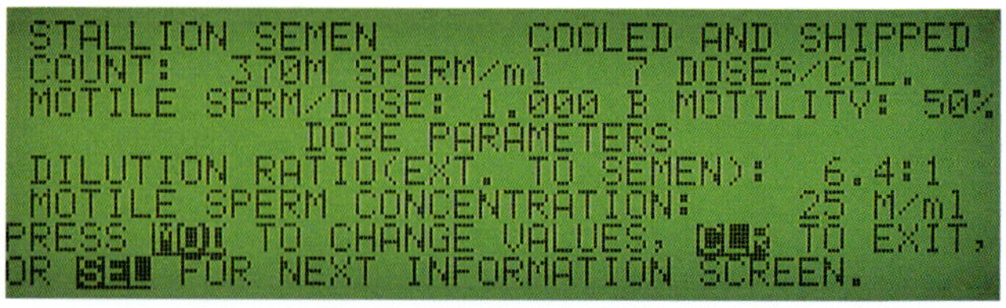

Figure 6-20 591B Densimeter cooled and shipped initial result screen.

The screen displays a summary of the collection at the top. This summary includes the concentration (COUNT), the number of doses available in the entire collection (DOSES/COL.), the number of motile sperm per dose (MOTILE SPRM/DOSE) and the motility percentage (MOTILITY). Below that are listed the DOSE PARAMETERS. This includes the ratio of extender to semen for the dose (DILUTION RATIO) and the motile sperm concentration of the dose. By pressing the MOD key, the user can modify any of these values other than the COUNT. The affected fields will automatically adjust to any modifications the user makes. Once all (if any) changes are in place, the user can press SEL to view the next screen. This screen displays the rest of the dose parameters (Figure 6-21) which include the volume of gel-free semen for one dose, the recommended volume of extender per dose, and the total insemination dose volume.

Figure 6-21 591B Densimeter cooled and shipped dose information screen.

If desired, the user can modify the total volume of the insemination dose. However, changing the total volume may alter other dose parameters, such as the volume of extender to add, or the motile sperm concentration of the dose. The Densimeter will automatically calculate any of these changes. The user can view these changes by cycling through all of the results screens (pressing SEL).

Pressing SEL from the above screen will display the final results (Figure 6-22). This screen provides recommendations for extending the entire collection at once to the desired concentration. The screen also displays how much of the extended semen is to be used for one dose and the total number of motile spermatozoa in each dose if the recommended extender and dose volumes are used.

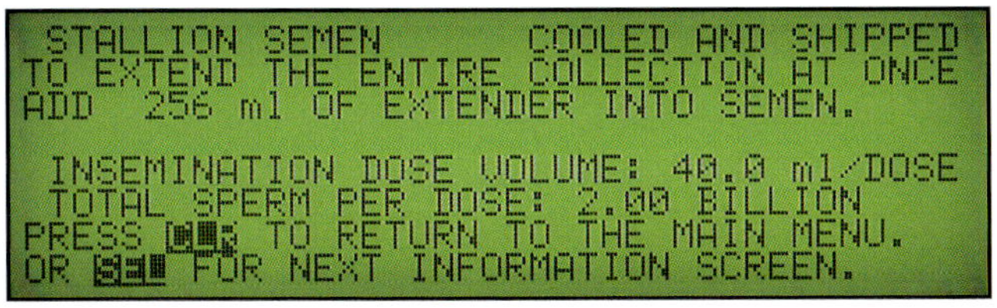

Figure 6-22 Final results screen for Cooled and Shipped dose.

Once the user has completed the sperm concentration analysis, the test cuvette may be removed from the Densimeter and discarded.

6.4 Model 590 Series Densimeter

The Model 590B Densimeter is lightweight and can be operated cordless, making it portable. The model is manufactured with rechargeable batteries that can be recharged anywhere in the world.

The Model 590 Densimeter is simple to use for estimating sperm concentration. However, the 590 does not have the built-in calculation capability of the 591B Densimeter. The 590B Densimeter is part of the 590B Stallion Sperm Counter Kit, which contains all supplies necessary for 100 sperm concentration measurements. The Model 590 is also capable of performing foal IgG concentrations measurements with the appropriate optional software and equipment.

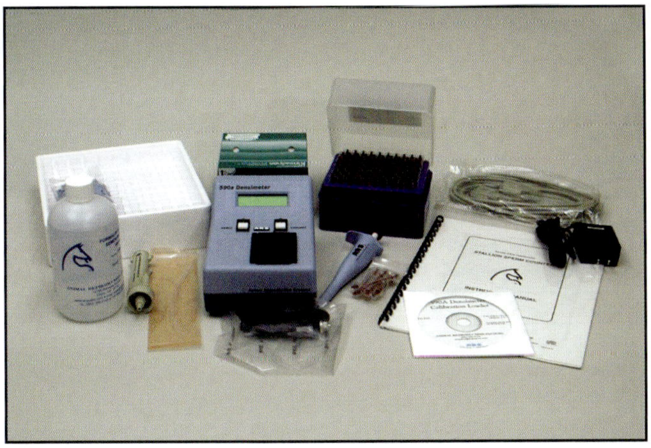

Figure 6-23 The Model 590 Stallion Sperm Counter Kit components for estimating the number of spermatozoa per ml.

To begin operating the 590 Densimeter it must be turned on using the power switch on the back of the unit. It is recommended that the unit be allowed to warm-up for at least five minutes prior to use. For temperatures below 20° C a longer warm-up period is recommended.

The 590 Densimeter will display a series of screens when initially switched on. These screens will provide the device manufacturer, model, version, and serial number. Once the introductory sequence is finished, the display will read:

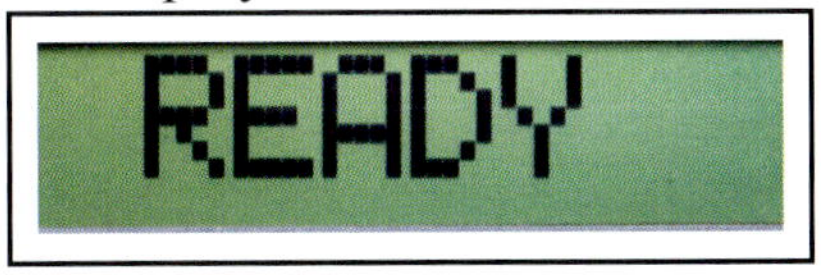

To begin a sperm concentration analysis, the user will first need to fill a fresh clean disposable plastic cuvette with 3.42 mL of Formalin 10 solution using the supplied pump. The cuvette is placed in the specimen compartment and the lid closed. Press the white button marked ZERO to start the standardization (Zeroing) of the instrument. The following series of screens will be displayed during this process. The yellow LED light above the ZERO button will flash as the unit zeros.

When this step is complete, the yellow LED will remain lit and the Densimeter will display the following series of screens.

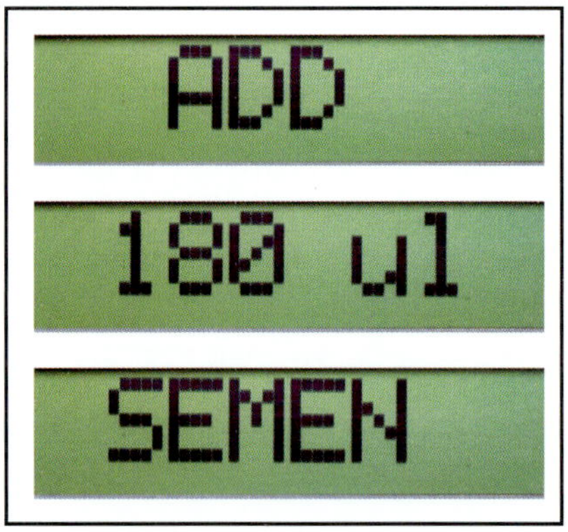

The user is instructed to add 180 µl of raw semen to the cuvette containing the Formalin 10 solution. The cuvette should then be capped, inverted gently several times to mix the semen and formalin solution, then replaced into the Densimeter. The COUNT button is pressed to start the concentration analysis. This step takes approximately 25 seconds. While measuring the semen, the following series of screens will be displayed:

DO NOT open the specimen compartment while the sperm count is in progress. Once the counting process is complete, the concentration in millions of sperm per ml will be displayed as follows:

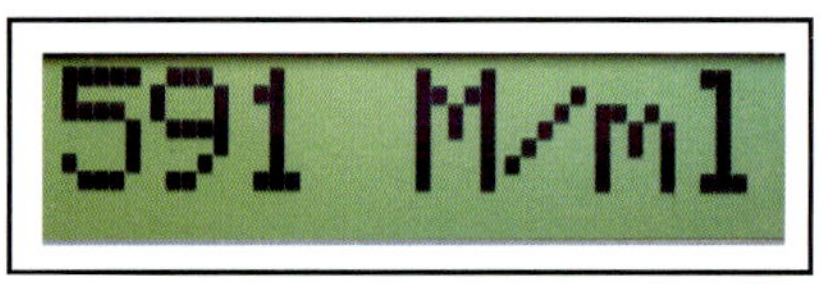

The sperm concentration analysis is complete. The cuvette should be removed from the Densimeter and discarded.

Chapter 7 Preparation of Fresh Semen for Insemination

Table 7-0 List and Part Number of ARS products used in this chapter.

Item	Part Number	Use/Comments
EZ Mixin® -"BF"	EZM-BF	Semen extender that does not contain antibiotics
EZ Mixin® -"CST"	EZM-CST	Semen extender that contains amikacin for fresh and cooling semen
EZ Mixin® -"BFT"	EZMTD-BF	Semen extender that contains ticarcillin
50ml Graduated cylinder	537-510	Used to measure volume of raw semen in the ejaculate
100ml Graduated cylinder	537-511	Used to measure volume of semen extender to use for dose.
Conical Centrifuge Tube	537-742/25	Used to hold extended semen during centrifugation
E-Z Cushion	EZC-101	Used to recover a higher percentage of spermatozoa during centrifugation
Sink Vacuum Aspirator Pump	537-785	Kit used after centrifugation to remove supernatant from sperm pellet

Equine semen should always be evaluated and processed as soon as possible after collection and prior to insemination. Gel-free volume, concentration, and motility parameters should be measured immediately after each collection. Failure to measure these basic parameters may lead to an inability to quickly recognize potential problems with a stallion. The resulting delay in instituting a management or therapeutic plan could lead to decreased pregnancy rates.

All semen should be labeled with the name of the stallion, collection date, and collection time. Labels should be placed on all containers and syringes holding semen until the mare is inseminated. Positive identification of the mare and verification of the stallion should always be made prior to insemination.

It is generally not recommended to use raw (unextended) semen for artificial insemination. Sperm motility, viability, and longevity are all rapidly lost in raw semen. Addition of semen extender 'protects' spermatozoa from cold shock, provides an energy source, reduces the potential detrimental effects of seminal plasma, and results in prolongation of motility, viability and longevity. Also, dilution of semen may reduce or eliminate bacterial contamination if the extender contains an appropriate antibiotic.

Extender should be added to raw semen after determination of the gel-free volume and sperm concentration. Semen should be extended as soon as possible and certainly within 15 minutes after collection.

Any of the E-Z Mixin® semen extenders can be used to dilute fresh semen to be used immediately. E-Z Mixin® - BF does not contain an antibiotic while E-Z Mixin® - CST, and E-Z Mixin® - BFT contain amikacin and ticarcillin, respectively. E-Z Mixin® extenders consist of Component A (125 ml of USP purified water in a plastic bottle), and Component B (powdered ingredients contained in a

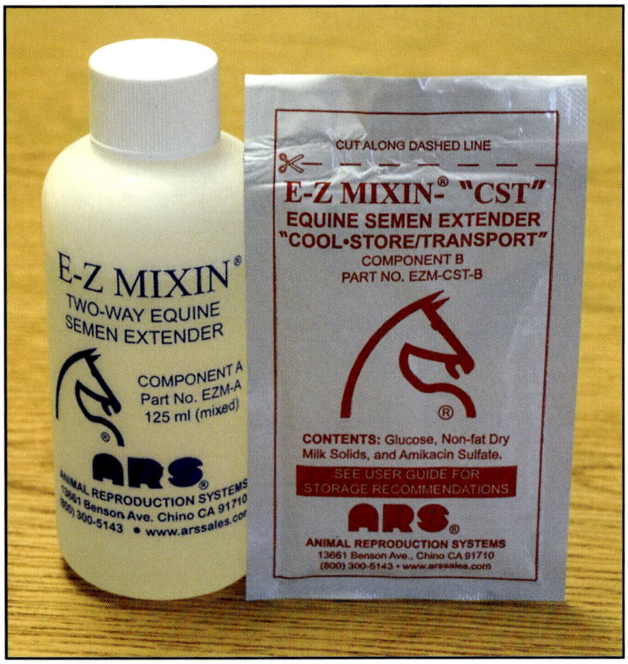

Figure 7-1 ARS EZ Mixin®-CST semen components A (Liquid) and B (Powder).

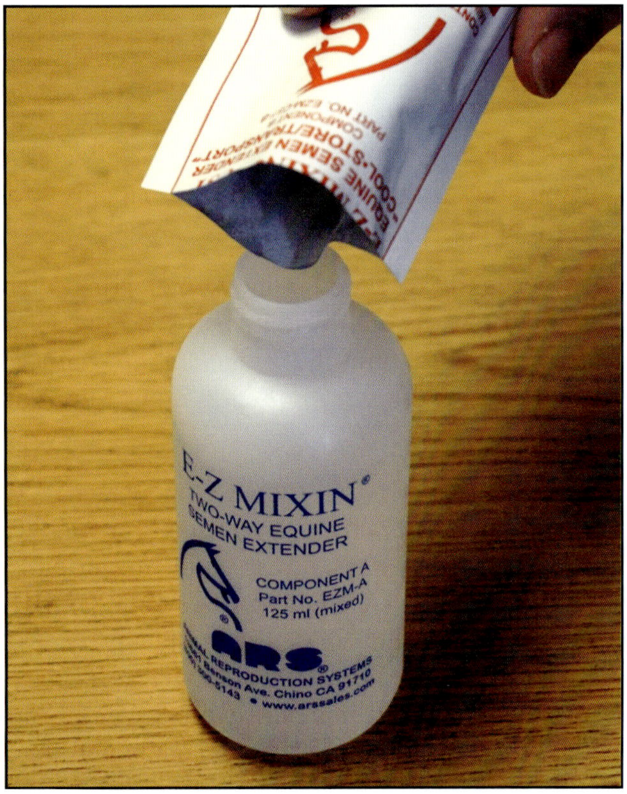

Figure 7-2 Adding component B to component A.

sealed, foil-lined packet) (Figure 7-1). The extender is prepared for use by placing the powdered ingredients from the foil packet into the bottle of water (Figure 7-2). After addition of the powdered ingredients, the two components should be gently and thoroughly mixed. The extender must be warmed to 37°C (98.6°F) prior to use. One can place the anticipated number of component A (water) bottles needed for the next day in an incubator the night before. It is not recommended that the water bottles be stored in an incubator indefinitely. Once reconstituted, any unused extender should be discarded.

After mixing raw semen with warm extender, the extended semen should be allowed to cool and then held at room temperature, approximately 20-22°C (68-72°F), until it is used for fresh insemination. Spermatozoa stored in an incubator at body temperature lose their mobility/viability more rapidly than when held at room temperature after extension. Extended semen should also be protected from the harmful effects of light. Extended semen from most stallions can be stored for up to 6 hours at room temperature in a dark environment. However, it is strongly recommended that semen be inseminated as soon as possible after collection and processing. If semen must be stored for more than 6 hours, it should be processed appropriately and cooled to approximately 5°C (41°F) as described in Chapter 8.

7.1 Preparation of a Single Breeding Dose

If there is only one mare to breed and the number of progressively motile sperm in the freshly collected semen is not a limiting factor, the number of sperm in each insemination dose may be increased substantially (i.e. consider inseminating 1 to 2 billion progressively motile spermatozoa, PMS). No one wants to 'waste' extra spermatozoa. However, it is still recommended that the final volume of fluid inseminated (raw semen plus extender) not exceed 50 ml. The mare is going to have to eliminate excess fluid and clean up residual dead sperm infused into her uterus. A more important consideration, however, is sperm concentration. It is recommended that the concentration of sperm in an insemination dose be ≥ 25 million PMS per ml. Pregnancy rates may be reduced if sperm concentration is too dilute.

A simple technique to prepare a single breeding dose for fresh insemination is described below, under the following circumstances:

- Sperm concentration is ≥ 100 million sperm per ml
- Progressive motility is ≥ 50%

Example 7-1

Calculation to determine the volumes of raw semen and semen extender required for preparation of a single breeding dose containing 500 million progressively motile spermatozoa using fresh semen.

Semen parameters utilized in this example:

- Volume = 37 ml
- Concentration = 245 million sperm per ml
- Progressive Motility = 65%

Parameter	Calculation
Raw semen volume/dose	$= \frac{\text{Desired \# PMS}}{(\text{Concentration} \times \text{PM*})}$
Example	
Raw semen volume/dose	$= \frac{\text{500 Million PMS}}{(\text{245 Million/ml} \times 0.65)}$
	$= \frac{\text{500 Million PMS}}{(\text{159.25 Million/ml})}$
	$= 3.14ml$
Extender Volume/dose	Final AI volume desired – volume of raw semen
Example Volume of Extender	$= 20ml - 3.14ml$
	$= 16.86ml$

* PMS = Progressively Motile Sperm

If the above parameters are both met, raw gel-free semen can be added to semen extender in a ratio of 1:1 (semen:extender). If the concentration is ≥ 100 million sperm per ml and the progressive motility is > 50%, using 10 ml of raw semen with an equal volume of extender will provide a minimum of 500 million progressively motile sperm in each insemination dose. It is recommended that the maximum final insemination volume does not exceed 50 mls.

7.2 Preparation of a Single Breeding Dose When Sperm Numbers Are Not Limited

The 591 series Densimeter is capable of calculating insemination doses automatically (See "Model 591 Series Densimeter" on page 46). A consistent and accurate calculation of the optimal insemination dose is often required. An accepted standard for a minimum insemination dose of fresh semen is:

- 500 million progressively motile sperm (PMS)
- Diluted with semen extender to a concentration of 25 million PMS per ml
- Total volume of 20 ml (raw semen plus extender)

An accurate calculation of the volume of raw semen and semen extender used to produce an insemination dose containing 500 million progressively motile sperm (PMS) can be obtained using the formula below (see Example 7-1).

Raw Semen Volume/Dose (mls)

$$RawSemenVolumePerDose = \frac{\text{Desired \# PMS}}{Concentration \times PM^*}$$

*PM = Progressive Motility

Determination of the amount of semen extender to be added to the raw semen can be made by subtracting the volume of raw semen required from the final desired volume of the insemination dose (FinalVol.) (i.e. 20 mls) as follows:

Extender Volume/Dose (mls)

$$ExtenderVolumePerDose = FinalVolume - VolRaw^*$$

*VolRaw = Volume of Raw Semen

The actual insemination dose can be prepared by first pouring the required volume of extender into a warmed 50ml Graduated Cylinder or 100ml Graduated Cylinder. The graduated cylinder should be clean and ideally maintained in an incubator at 37° C (98.6°F). Next, add the required volume of raw semen to the graduated cylinder containing the semen extender. Cover the top of the graduated cylinder with a small amount of Parafilm® and gently mix the contents. The insemination dose is now complete and can be drawn up into a pipette attached to a syringe.

Example 7-2

Calculation to determine the number of breeding doses in an ejaculate.

Parameter	Calculation
# Breeding Doses in Ejaculate	$= \dfrac{\text{Total \# PMS*}}{\text{Standard Breeding Dose}}$
Example	
# Breeding Doses in Ejaculate	$= \dfrac{\text{5,892 Million PMS}}{\text{500 Million PMS}}$
	= 11.8 doses

*Total # PMS = volume (mls) x concentration (millions) x progressive motility (%)

* PMS = Progressively Motile Sperm

7.3 Calculation of the Number of Breeding Doses in an Ejaculate

The total number of breeding doses available in the ejaculate can subsequently be determined using the following formula (see Example 7-2), presuming a standard breeding dose of 500 million progressively motile sperm is to be used for fresh semen artifical insemination:

$$\text{\# Breeding Doses} = \frac{\text{Total PMS in Ejaculate}}{\text{500 Million PMS}}$$

Alternatively, the number of breeding doses per ejaculate can easily be determined using the following formula (see Example 7-3), if the volume of raw semen per dose has been calculated:

$$\text{\# Breeding Doses in Ejaculate} = \frac{\text{Gel-free Volume}}{\text{Vol. Raw Semen/dose}}$$

7.4 Preparation of Multiple Breeding Doses from a Single Ejaculate

Multiple breeding doses of fresh semen can easily be prepared for insemination by mixing the volume of raw semen required for all doses with the appropriate volume of extender. Individual breeding doses can then be partitioned into individual aliquots (i.e. graduated cylinders or 50 ml conical centrifuge tubes, etc.) for subsequent use or individual breeding doses can be removed from a single large graduated cylinder holding all of the extended semen. The advantage of initially partitioning the extended semen into separate aliquots is that one can quickly prepare individual doses and not 'run out of semen' for the last mare to be bred. If doses are removed from one common graduated cylinder, there is a risk that the volume of extended semen will be 'short' for the last mare. Also, when a single large volume of extended semen is prepared, it is important to gently mix the bulk volume prior to removing each insemination dose, so that each dose contains a uniform number of spermatozoa.

Example 7-3

Alternative calculation to determine the number of breeding doses in an ejaculate.

Semen parameters utilized in this example:

- Volume = 37 mls
- Concentration = 245 million sperm per ml
- Progressive Motility = 65 %

Parameter	Calculation
# Breeding Doses in Ejaculate	$= \dfrac{\text{Gel-free volume (ml)}}{\text{Volume Raw Semen/Dose*}}$
Example	
# Breeding Doses in Ejaculate	$= \dfrac{\text{37 ml}}{[\text{500 million PMS} \div (245 \times 0.65)]}$
	$= \dfrac{\text{37ml}}{3.14}$
	= 11.8 doses

$$\textbf{*Volume raw semen/dose} = \frac{\textbf{Desired \# PMS}}{(\textbf{Concentration} \times \textbf{PM})}$$

Note: it may be beneficial to prepare a slightly larger amount of extended semen than required in case some of the extended semen is lost during preparation or distribution into individual breeding doses.

Multiple breeding doses can be prepared using the technique outlined below (see Example 7-4).

Example 7-4

Calculations to prepare multiple breeding doses from a single ejaculate.

Semen parameters utilized in this example:

- Volume = 37 ml
- Concentration = 245 million sperm per ml
- Progressive Motility = 65 %

Parameter		Calculation
Volume of raw semen needed	=	# mares to be bred x volume raw semen per dose*
Example		
Volume of raw semen needed	=	6 mares x 3.14 ml
	=	18.84 mls
Volume of extender required	=	(# mares x 20 ml per dose) – volume of raw semen
Example		
Volume of extender required	=	(6 mares x 20 ml per dose) – 18.84 ml raw semen
	=	120 ml – 18.84 ml raw semen
	=	101.86 ml semen extender

$$^{*}VolumeRawSemenPerDose = \frac{\text{Desired \# PMS}}{(\text{Concentration} \times \text{PM})}$$

Steps:

1. Calculate the *amount of raw semen required* for a single breeding dose of fresh semen (at 500 million PMS/dose).
2. Determine the *number of mares to be bred* with fresh semen that day.
3. Multiply the number of doses required by the volume of raw semen required for each dose
4. Calculate the *final total volume* required to provide an insemination volume of 20 mls per dose for each mare. This is performed by multiplying the number of mares to be bred by the volume per dose (20 mls).
5. Subtract the volume of raw semen required from the final total volume to yield the *volume of semen extender required.*
6. Add the calculated volume of extender to a warmed graduated cylinder.
7. Then add the calculated volume of raw semen required.
8. Cover graduated cylinder with Parafilm® and gently mix.
9. Each mare should be inseminated with a volume of 20 mls of extended semen containing 500 million PMS.

7.5 Cooling 'Extra' Doses

Once the initial doses of semen for fresh inseminations have been prepared, consider cooling several doses of semen from the initial ejaculate in case you want to breed the mare(s) again the next day or in case other mares that need to be bred to the stallion are identified later in the day. The latter scenario unfortunately occurs somewhat frequently during the breeding season. A common circumstance that leads to this situation is collection of the stallion early in the day (i.e. to avoid excessive environmental heat) and evaluation of mares later in the morning or early afternoon (often on outside breeding farms).

Note that if additional insemination doses are to be cooled, it is recommended to use a semen extender that is designed for cooled storage of equine semen (i.e. E-Z Mixin® - CST). Also note that the total number of progressively motile sperm initially prepared in a cooled dose is higher than that of a fresh insemination dose. Each cooled dose should contain 1 billion progressively motile sperm when initially packaged (See "Guidelines for Preparing Cooled Semen" on page 68).

7.6 Centrifugation of Semen for Preparation of a Fresh Insemination Dose

It is generally not necessary to centrifuge semen for fresh insemination. However, centrifugation may be necessary for some individual stallions. Specific guidelines as to when to centrifuge semen are:

1. A high volume, low sperm concentration and/or low motility ejaculate

   If the initial sperm concentration is less than 100 million per ml and the progressive motility is ≤ 50%. At an initial concentration of < 100 million sperm per ml, a simple dilution of 1:1 (semen:extender) would yield a final concentration of less than 50 million sperm per ml. Factoring in a progressive motility of ≤ 50%, the final concentration of progressively motile sperm would be < 25 million per ml. For some stallions, the concentration of progressively motile sperm per ml is low enough that a 1:1 dilution (raw semen: extender) will yield a potential insemination dose of > 50 mls. Centrifugation will concentrate spermatozoa into a soft pellet that can be resuspended in a smaller volume that is more concentrated.

2. 'Toxic' seminal plasma.

   Semen from some individual stallions does not maintain adequate motility and/or viability with prolonged exposure to their own seminal plasma. Centrifugation would remove the majority of seminal plasma from the ejaculate and semen extender could subsequently be added.

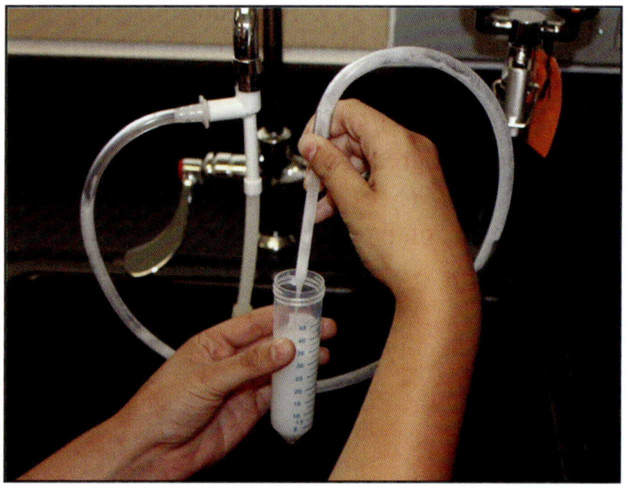

Figure 7-3 Aspiration of supernatant following centrifugation using a sink vacuum aspiration set.

7.7 Cushion Centrifugation for Preparation of a Fresh Semen Dose

Is is recommended that a cushion be used when centrifuging stallion semen. The technique for centrifugation of semen to prepare a fresh insemination dose consists of the following steps when using a **cushion**:

1. Collect semen and evaluate (gel-free volume, concentration, progressive motility).
2. Extend semen 1:1 with extender (i.e. E-Z Mixin® - BF).
3. Transfer the extended semen into one to six (as needed) 50ml Centrifuge Tubes.
4. Draw up the appropriate volume (i.e. 0.5 to 3.0 mls) of E-Z Cushion™ into a sterile pipette.
5. Pass the pipette gently through the extended semen to the bottom of the conical tube.
6. Gently deposit the cushion on the bottom of the tube, beneath the extended semen.
7. Centrifuge at 1,000 x gravity (x *g*) for 20 to 25 minutes. (The method used to calculate the relative centrifugal force or gravitational force (x *g*) for any centrifuge is presented in Appendix 1).
8. At the end of centrifugation, the sperm will be compacted into a soft pellet at the bottom of each conical tube below a supernatant of seminal plasma/extender and above the cushion. Aspirate off and discard the supernatant leaving a total volume of approximately 10 mls. This may be easily accomplished using a Sink Vacuum Aspirator Pump Kit (Figure 7-3).
9. Gently aspirate the cushion from beneath the sperm pellet after removal of the supernatant is optional (Figure 7-4).
10. Resuspend the sperm pellet in the seminal plasma/extender that remained in the conical tube.
11. Combine the resuspended semen from all centrifuge tubes.
12. Measure of volume of the recombined sample.
13. Determine the Sperm Concentration in the combined sample.

Figure 7-4 Aspiration of cushion from below the sperm pellet.

14. Calculate the volumes of a) resuspended semen and b) fresh semen extender to be added to the resuspended semen to produce one or more insemination dose(s) of 25 million progressively motile sperm per ml. Note: if only one mare is to be bred with the centrifuged semen, the entire volume of resuspended semen could be used.
15. Add the required volume of resuspended semen to the fresh semen extender and gently mix.
16. Draw up the required volume into a syringe attached to an insemination pipette and inseminate the mare.

7.8 Standard Centrifugation for Preparation of a Fresh Semen Dose

The technique for centrifugation of semen to prepare a fresh insemination dose consists of the following steps when **not** using a cushion:

1. Collect semen and evaluate (gel-free volume, concentration, progressive motility).
2. Extend semen 1:1 with extender (i.e. E-Z Mixin® - BF).
3. Centrifuge at 400 x gravity (x *g*) for 13-15 minutes. (The method used to calculate the relative centrifugal force or gravitational force (x *g*) for any centrifuge is presented in Appendix 1).
4. At the end of centrifugation, the sperm will be compacted into a pellet at the bottom of each conical tube below a supernatant of seminal plasma/extender. Aspirate off and discard the supernatant leaving a total volume of approximately 10 mls. This may be easily accomplished using a Sink Vacuum Aspirator Pump.
5. Resuspend the sperm pellet in the seminal plasma/extender that remained in the conical tube.
6. Combine the resuspended semen from all centrifuge tubes.
7. Measure of volume of the recombined sample.
8. Determine the Sperm Concentration in the combined sample.
9. Calculate the volumes of a) resuspended semen and b) fresh semen extender to be added to the resuspended semen to produce one or more insemination dose(s) of 25 million progressively motile sperm per ml. Note: if only one mare is to be bred with the centrifuged semen, the entire volume of resuspended semen could be used.
10. Add the required volume of resuspended semen to the fresh semen extender and gently mix.
11. Draw up the required volume into a syringe attached to an insemination pipette and inseminate the mare.

The volume of semen extender to be combined with the resuspended semen can be determined by simple subtraction.

Note:

- Sperm recovery when **not** using a cushion is approximately 75%.
- Sperm recovery when using a cushion is approximately 95%.

Example 7-5

Determination of the volume of centrifuged semen required for a single breeding dose. A cushioned centrifugation technique was used in this example. Extended semen was placed into two 50ml Centrifuge tubes and centrifuged. The volume of the two combined pellets after removing the supernatant and cushion was 10 mls.

Semen parameters utilized:

- Volume = 40 mls
- Concentration = 47 million sperm per ml
- Progressive Motility = 35 %

Parameter	Calculation
Volume of centrifuged semen	$= \frac{\text{Desired \# PMS}}{\left[\frac{[(\text{Total \# Sperm in Ejaculate} \times \text{Progressive Motility})]}{\text{10 ml resuspended volume}}\right]}$
Example	
Volume of centrifuged semen	$= \frac{\text{500 Million PMS}}{\left[\frac{(\text{40 ml} \times \text{47 million sperm/ml} \times 0.35)}{\text{10 ml}}\right]}$
	$= \frac{\text{500 Million PMS}}{\left[\frac{(\text{1, 880 million sperm/ml} \times 0.35)}{\text{10 ml}}\right]}$
	$= \frac{\text{500 million PMS}}{\left[\frac{\text{658 million PMS}}{\text{10 ml}}\right]}$
	$= \frac{\text{500 million PMS}}{65.8}$
	=7.6 mls resuspended semen needed for one dose*

* Assumes recovery of ~100% of the sperm after centrifugation

In the example above, a total of 658 million progressively motile sperm was available after centrifugation. In practical terms, this ejaculate contained a sufficient number of PMS to inseminate only one mare. The volume of resuspended semen (combining the 2 pellets) needed to provide 500 million PMS would be 7.6 mls. If only 7.6 mls of resuspended semen were to be used, one would need 13.4 mls of extender to comprise an insemination volume of 20 mls (Example 7-6). However, in most cases the entire 10 mls volume of resuspended semen, a combination of the two 5ml pellets, (containing all 658 million PMS) should be added to 10 mls of fresh extender and the entire 20 ml extended dose inseminated into a single mare. There would not be enough spermatozoa to breed a second mare, and it would be a waste to throw away the additional 158 million PMS if a dose of only 500 million PMS was used.

Example 7-6

Determination of the volume of semen extender required to provide a 20 ml insemination dose

Semen parameters utilized:

- Total Volume Insemination Dose Desired = 20 mls
- Volume of Resuspended Semen = 7.6 mls (see Example 7-5 above)

Parameter		Calculation
Volume of extender	=	Final insemination volume desired – volume of resuspended centrifuged semen required
Example		
Volume of extender	=	20 mls – 7.6 mls
Volume of extender	=	13.4 mls

Chapter 8 Preparation of Semen for Cooled Storage and Transportation

Table 8-0 List and Part Number of ARS products used in this chapter.

Item	Part Number	Use/Comments
ARS BLUE with Amikacin	BLU-AS	Casein based extender that contains Amikacin.
ARS BLUE Basic Formula with Ticarcillin	BLU-BF-TD	Casein based extender that contains Ticarcillin.
E-Z Mixin® -"CST"	EZM-CST	Modified Kenney semen extender that contains Amikacin.
E-Z Mixin® -"BFT"	EZMTD-BF	Modified Kenney semen extender that contains Ticarcillin.
E-Z Mixin10® -"CST"	EZM10-CST	Alternative semen extender that contains Amikacin.
E-Z Mixin10® -"BFT"	EZM10TD-BF	Alternative semen extender that contains Ticarcillin
50ml Graduated cylinder	537-510	Used to measure volume of raw semen and/or extender
Centrifuge Tubes and Caps	537-742/25	Used to hold extended semen during centrifugation and/or to ship cooled semen
E-Z Cushion	EZC-101	Used to recover a higher percentage of spermatozoa during centrifugation
Sink Vacuum Aspirator Pump Kit	537-785	Kit used after centrifugation to remove supernatant from sperm pellet
50ml All Plastic Syringe, sterile	544S-00007/25	Used to ship cooled semen in
Equitainer I Shipper, Tube Style	EQSH-TUBE-101	Cooled semen transport system
Equitainer I Shipper, Cup Style	EQSH-CUP-101	Cooled semen transport system

A majority of equine breed registries accept the use of cooled-transported semen for artificial insemination.

Stallion semen may be cooled for transport to a distant location or to hold semen on the breeding farm until the next day. In addition, 'extra' doses of semen may be available after all on-farm mares booked to the stallion have been bred and the required number of cooled doses has been shipped. It may be prudent to cool one or two 'extra' doses in case another mare on the farm needs to be bred or a late phone call requesting shipped semen is received.

Techniques for semen collection and preparation of semen for fresh insemination were presented in chapters 4 to 7. The goal of this chapter is to review preparation of semen for cooled storage and transportation.

8.1 Advantages and Disadvantages of Cooled Semen

There are numerous advantages to a system that permits semen to be shipped and/or stored. These advantages include:

- Elimination of the cost and stress of shipping a mare and/or foal to a breeding farm
- Reduction in the risk of disease exposure to mare and/or foal by keeping them at home
- Reduction in the cost of mare care by maintaining the mare at home

- Reproductive management of the mare can be performed at home
- Access to a wider genetic pool and to superior stallions

In spite of these important advantages, there are some disadvantages of utilizing cooled-transported semen. Disadvantages include:

- Cost involved in the collection, packaging and shipment of semen to the mare owner and shipment of the container back to the stallion station. The cost of container shipment may be reduced by use of a disposable semen shipment container.
- Increased veterinary costs for mare management. Mares in a shipped semen program need to be examined more frequently to determine the optimal day to order semen and hormone therapy is usually required to induce ovulation in a controlled and predicted time period. The ultimate goal is to ship semen once during a given cycle and inseminate the mare with an adequate number of progressively motile spermatozoa within 24 hours prior to ovulation.
- Increased technological skill is required to properly prepare semen for shipment.
- Not all stallions produce semen that is suitable for cooled storage and shipment.
- Personnel receiving shipped semen require increased knowledge to properly handle and evaluate the semen.

In most instances, the advantages of cooled-transported semen far outweigh the disadvantages. Some of the disadvantages can be overcome by proper training of farm personnel.

8.2 Physiology of Cooling Equine Spermatozoa

Spermatozoa are specialized cells with a single function, which is to fertilize an ovum (egg). Since they have only one function, spermatozoa possess characteristics necessary to carry out that function, but have lost many other cellular components and attributes. Spermatozoa have efficient mechanisms for movement, but limited biosynthetic and repair capabilities and contain only half (haploid) the number of chromosomes as other cells in the body.

Another characteristic of spermatozoa is that ejaculated spermatozoa are programmed to undergo sequential cellular changes termed capacitation and the acrosome reaction, the timing of which are critical for a spermatozoon to fertilize an ovum. Spermatozoa that undergo capacitation and the acrosome reaction prematurely (i.e. during handling or processing), will not survive for an extended time period and will not be capable of fertilization. Factors that delay or prevent capacitation and the acrosome reaction will also render a spermatozoon incapable of fertilizing an ovum. In general, stallion spermatozoa undergo these changes during a time frame consistent with the interval between natural breeding and ovulation. This provides a high proportion of spermatozoa prepared to fertilize an ovum at a time when the ovum is most capable of being fertilized. Handling and cooling of spermatozoa, particularly if done improperly, can affect the timing or capability of spermatozoa to capacitate, acrosome react, and fertilize an ovum.

Cooling stallion spermatozoa to 5°C (41°F) induces a transition in sperm membranes from the liquid-crystalline to a gel state. Since damage can arise due to these changes, why would anyone want to cool semen? At body temperature, sperm metabolism is maximal and at room temperature it is not much lower. Waste products (lactic acid and/or CO_2) can increase the acidity of semen, causing permanent cellular damage; peroxidation of membrane lipids occurs, resulting in membrane damage; and cells, in general, wear out. All of these processes render stallion spermatozoa maintained at body temperature post ejaculate essentially sterile within 12 to 24 hours. For each 10°C (18°F) reduction in temperature of cells, cellular metabolism is reduced by 50% from what it was at the higher temperature. Therefore, if spermatozoa are stored at 5°C (41°F), their metabolic needs are only about 10% of what they would be at 38°C (~100°F). Consequently, spermatozoa stored at 5°C (41°F) do not produce as many waste products, lipid peroxidation occurs more slowly, and the cells do not wear out as quickly. All of these factors tend to lengthen the fertile life of cooled spermatozoa, compared to spermatozoa stored at body or room temperature.

Certain steps can be taken to minimize damage to spermatozoa resulting from cooling, but such damage cannot be eliminated completely. By extending stallion spermatozoa in a medium containing membrane-protecting additives and carefully controlling the rate of cooling, the harmful effects of cooling can be minimized. When these steps are taken, spermatozoa of many stallions can be maintained for at least 24 hours without reducing their fertilizing potential.

Cellular injury can be caused directly by rupturing membranes or indirectly by altering cellular functions. Rapid cooling of stallion spermatozoa from room temperature to 5°C (41°F) induces damage characterized by an abnormal pattern of motility (i.e. a tight forward or backward circular pattern), rapid loss of motility, acrosomal damage, plasma membrane damage, reduced metabolism, and loss of intracellular components. Collectively, this damage is referred to as 'cold shock'. Indirect and/or latent cooling damage is more difficult to discern. It may not be evident for some time (i.e. hours) after spermatozoa have reached 5°C (41°F), or may not even be detectable until after spermatozoa are rewarmed to 38°C (~100°F), or after mares are bred.

Some of the damage to spermatozoa during cooling is due to changes that occur in the plasma membrane as it goes through transition from the liquid-crystalline to a gel state. This damage can be reduced by including additives in the extender and also by careful, slow cooling through the temperature zone where transition from the fluid phase to the solid phase occurs.

Most protective additives contain either lipids or lipophilic molecules. These compounds likely affect the plasma membrane directly, although the exact mechanism by which this occurs is unknown. Other additives can bind calcium and magnesium. These additives likely protect spermatozoa by binding ions and reducing ion leakage into spermatozoa during membrane transitions.

Extenders containing skim milk are commonly used to protect stallion spermatozoa from cold shock. The specific mechanism by which milk protects spermatozoa is unknown.

8.3 Cooling Rate, Storage Temperature and Optimal Sperm Concentration

The purpose of cooling spermatozoa is to slow cellular metabolism and prevent deterioration. Therefore, the more rapidly cooling can be accomplished, while avoiding cold shock and/or other damage, the better.

Cooling rate of extended semen is dependent upon volume (larger volumes cool more slowly than smaller volumes) and initial temperature of the sperm suspension. The optimal system would cool spermatozoa in a curvilinear fashion, with semen cooling at the greatest rate initially and progressing to slower rates as the spermatozoa near final temperature.

Properly extended stallion semen can be rapidly cooled from 37° to 19°C (98.6° to ~66°F) without incurring cold shock damage. A slower rate of cooling (approximately -0.3°C per minute) should be provided from 19° to 8°C (~66° to ~46°F) to prevent cold shock. A rapid rate of cooling can be resumed from 8°C (~46°F) to a final storage temperature of 5°C (41°F).

The critical temperature window between 19 and 8°C (~66 and ~46°F), most likely corresponds to the transition temperatures of the different lipids in the plasma membrane compartments of stallion spermatozoa when membranes change from the liquid-crystalline state to a gel state. The slow cooling rate may allow time for movement of lipids and/or proteins within the membranes to prevent whole-scale membrane damage. Once these lipids and/or proteins have reached their final destinations within the gel-state membrane, rapid cooling can resume without further membrane damage.

Stallion semen should be stored at 5°C (41 °F) to preserve motility if the anticipated storage time is greater than 6 to 12 hours.

One of the common mistakes in shipping cooled semen is failure to dilute or extend the semen properly. As described earlier, for insemination of fresh semen, semen may be diluted 1:1 (semen:extender). However, for shipment of cooled semen, the ejaculate should be diluted at least 1:3 with an appropriate extender like E-Z Mixin® - CST or E-Z Mixin® - BFT. More importantly, the ejaculate should be diluted to a concentration of approximately 25 million motile spermatozoa per milliliter. This is because a high concentration of seminal plasma has been shown to be deleterious to cooling and storage of extended stallion semen. The effect of seminal plasma can be reduced by diluting the seminal plasma with extender. However, if semen is diluted with too much extender, such that the concentration becomes less than 25 million motile spermatozoa per ml, fertility will be reduced.

8.4 Centrifugation of Semen for Cooled Storage

Centrifugation of semen and removal of seminal plasma may be an alternative to extensive dilution of seminal plasma with extender for stallions whose semen does not maintain favorable sperm motility after cooling in the presence of seminal plasma. In addition, centrifugation is a means of concentrating the spermatozoa for stallions with a very low sperm concentration.

If centrifugation is used as a method of concentrating spermatozoa, 5 to 20% of the seminal plasma should remain in the sample prior to addition of semen extender and cooling. Removal of all seminal plasma after centrifugation is associated with a decrease in sperm motility after cooled storage compared to samples that contain 5 to 20% seminal plasma.

Care must be used when centrifuging semen as high centrifugal forces have been associated with a reduction in sperm motility and a loss of spermatozoa during removal of the supernatant. If detrimental effects of centrifugation of semen can be minimized, removal of 80 to 95% of the seminal plasma may be beneficial for maintenance of sperm motility during cooled storage.

The technique for centrifugation of semen to prepare a cooled insemination dose consists of the following steps when using a cushion:

a. Collect semen and evaluate (gel-free volume, concentration, progressive motility).

b. Extend semen 1:1 with extender (i.e. E-Z Mixin® - CST).

c. Transfer the extended semen into one to six (as needed) 50ml Centrifuge Tubes.

d. Draw up the appropriate volume (i.e. 0.5 to 3.0 mls) of E-Z Cushion™ into a sterile pipette.

e. Pass the pipette through the extended semen to the bottom of the conical tube.

f. Gently deposit the cushion material on the bottom of the tube, beneath the extended semen.

g. Centrifuge at 1,000 x gravity (x *g*) for 20-25 minutes. (The method used to calculate the relative centrifugal force or gravitational force (x *g*) for any centrifuge is presented in Appendix 1).

h. At the end of centrifugation, the sperm will be compacted into a soft pellet at the bottom of each conical tube below a supernatant of seminal plasma/extender. Aspirate off and discard all of the supernatant leaving a total volume of approximately 10 mls. This may be easily accomplished using a Sink Vacuum Aspirator Pump Kit.

i. Gently aspirate the cushion from beneath the sperm pellet after removal of the supernatant (optional).

j. Resuspend the sperm pellet in the seminal plasma/extender that remained in the conical tube.

k. Combine the resuspended semen from all centrifuge tubes.

l. Measure of volume of the combined sample.

m. Determine the sperm concentration in the combined sample.

n. Calculate the volumes of a) resuspended semen and b) fresh semen extender (i.e. E-Z Mixin® - CST) to be added to the resuspended semen to produce each insemination dose, consisting of 1.0 billion progressively motile sperm (40 ml volume at 25 million PMS per ml).

o. Add the required volume of resuspended semen to the semen extender and gently mix.

p. Place the extended semen dose in a storage container (i.e. Whirl-Pak® bag, baby bottle liner, 50 ml syringe, centrifuge tube) and place the container into a passive cooling device along with the proper paperwork.

8.5 Antibiotics in the Semen Extender

Inclusion of antibiotics in a semen extender is important for reducing or eliminating bacterial growth. However, some antibiotics are more appropriate for use in cooled stored semen than others. Extenders routinely used for cooled semen should contain either amikacin sulfate, ticarcillin, or amikacin sulfate plus potassium penicillin G.

Table 8-1 ARS Extenders and antibiotics.

ARS Extender	Antibiotic
EZM-BF	None
EZM-CST / BLU-AS	Amikacin
EZM-CST+ / BLU-AS-KPG	Amikacin / Potassium Penicillin G
EZM-BF+ / BLU-BF-KPG	Potassium Penicillin G
EZM-BFT / BLU-BF-TD	Ticarcillin

8.6 Extenders for Storage of Cooled Semen

As noted previously, spermatozoa from most stallions deteriorate quickly unless they are extended immediately after collection. It is therefore recommended that semen destined for cooled-storage be evaluated and extended as soon as possible after collection. If some portion of the ejaculate is to be used for fresh insemination, that aliquot may be extended and maintained at room temperature (i.e. 20° to 22°C; 68° to 71.6°F) for up to 6 hours. If the duration from collection to insemination is to be longer than 6 hours, it is recommended that the semen be extended and cooled appropriately.

Dilution of seminal plasma is absolutely essential for maintaining viability of stallion spermatozoa. Although seminal plasma acts as a transport medium for spermatozoa during natural mating, the seminal plasma is quickly dispersed once it is in the uterus. In general, seminal plasma is not a good extender for stallion spermatozoa; spermatozoa die more quickly when maintained in seminal plasma than when extended with an appropriate diluent. There are numerous valid reasons to extend stallion semen even when it is to be used immediately on the farm. However, extension is absolutely essential when semen is to be cooled and shipped.

The following are reasons to extend stallion semen prior to insemination or cooling:

- To permit effective antibiotic treatment of semen and minimize the possibility of transmission of pathogenic organisms. The antibiotics should be in the extender before semen is added.
- To extend the life of spermatozoa. Even semen from a highly fertile stallion should be extended.
- To protect spermatozoa from unfavorable environmental conditions.
- To increase the volume of the inseminate.

To enable proper evaluation of sperm motility.

An appropriate extender should provide:

- Compatible osmotic pressure (300 to 400 mOsm).
- A stable pH of 6.8 to 7.0.
- Proper balance of mineral elements (i.e., electrolytes, non-electrolytes).
- Proper combination of nutrients.
- Neutralization of toxic products produced by spermatozoa.
- Protection against changes in temperature.
- Stabilization of enzyme systems and integrity of membranes.

Numerous extenders have been developed for stallion semen. These have included egg yolk, milk, milk by-products and additives to regulate osmolarity and/or pH. Several semen extenders designed for use with cooled-transported equine semen are commercially available.

An extender composed of nonfat, dried milk solids, glucose, and antibiotics may be routinely used for a majority of stallions. The extender of this category that has been tested and used most extensively in the equine breeding industry is E-Z Mixin® - CST, which contains the antibiotic amikacin sulfate (Figure 8-1).

8.7 Test Cool

It is recommended that a 'test cool' be performed on semen from a stallion for which no cooled semen data is available. A test cool compares semen extenders and evaluates sperm motility following cooled storage of semen at a standardized sperm dilution (25 to 50 million spermatozoa per ml) in the storage-shipping container to be used during the breeding season. The goal is to determine if semen from the stallion cools well and to identify the semen extender that optimizes motility during cooled storage.

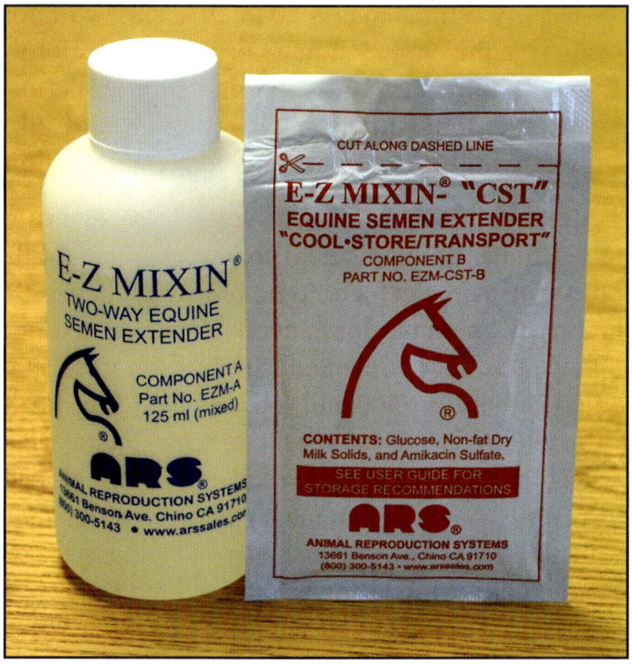

Figure 8-1 E-Z Mixin® - CST semen extender.

It should be noted that, unfortunately, evaluation of the motility of cooled semen is not always a good indicator of true fertility. The only measure of true fertility is the pregnancy rate of mares bred. There are stallions that have good fertility with fresh semen and good motility characteristics after cooling, but have poor pregnancy rates with cooled semen. In general, it is estimated that 70 to 80% of stallions will have semen that cools adequately. It is also anticipated that sperm motility will decrease approximately 20 to 30% after 24 hours of cooled storage for most stallions.

A test cool may consist of the following procedures:

a. Collect semen from the stallion to be evaluated
b. Perform a standard semen evaluation (gel-free volume, concentration, motility)
c. Dilute gel-free semen to a concentration of 25 million progressively motile sperm per ml in each semen extender to be tested
d. Transfer 40 mls of each type of extended semen into the same kind of storage container that is to be used during the breeding season (i.e. Whirl-Pak bag, baby bottle liner, 50-ml syringe, centrifuge tube)
e. Place the storage containers in the same type of passive cooling device that will used during the breeding season
f. Cool for 24 hours
g. Open the passive cooling device, gently mix the storage containers and remove a small aliquot of extended semen for evaluation
h. Immediately place the storage containers back into the passive cooling system, if the temperature can be maintained at 5° to 8°C (41° to 46.4°F), or place into an insulated container within a refrigerator set at 5° to 8°C (41° to 46.4°F)
i. Warm up each aliquot of semen in a 37°C (98.6° F) incubator for 10 minutes
j. Evaluate motility characteristics (i.e. total and progressive motility) after warming and record
k. Repeat evaluation procedure at 48 hours after collection
l. Compare motility characteristics between the semen extenders tested at the time of initial collection and after 24 and 48 hours of cooled storage
m. Determine if semen from the stallion 'qualifies' for use in a cooled-transported program and which extender was most suitable for preserving motility
n. Determine if additional tests, such as evaluation of different extenders, passive cooling systems, or removal of seminal plasma (centrifugation) are necessary

8.8 Management of 'Poor Coolers'

Semen from some stallions may not tolerate cooled storage and overnight transport in a traditional semen extender. Options for breeding management of 'poor coolers' may include:

- Test cool and selection of a more optimal semen extender
- Centrifugation and removal of seminal plasma
- Use of same day delivery service only (i.e. counter-to-counter and not overnight courier)
- Only breeding mares with fresh semen on-farm

If semen from an individual stallion does not cool well in a traditional extender made of nonfat, dried milk solids and glucose, selection and testing of an alternative extender with other base ingredients, such as EZ-Mixin 10 or ARS Blue should be considered.

Stallions that are determined to be 'poor coolers' may benefit from removal of a majority of seminal plasma in the ejaculate by centrifugation. However, removal of all seminal plasma after centrifugation results in poor motility after cooled storage. Therefore, it is generally recommended that 5 to 20% of the seminal plasma should remain with the sperm pellet after centrifugation. The remainder of the seminal plasma supernatant is removed using a Sink Aspirator Pump Kit and discarded. An appropriate semen extender (i.e. E-Z Mixin® - CST) is then added and the spermatozoa are resuspended.

In addition, during the breeding season it may be advantageous for a stallion owner or manager to periodically hold back a dose of semen, store it in a passive cooling system, and evaluate the semen 24 hours later. In this way the stallion owner or manager can keep track of motility characteristics of the shipped semen in case a potential problem arises. This may help differentiate between problems with the stallion, problems encountered during shipment, and problems on the mare breeding farm.

8.9 Guidelines for Preparing Cooled Semen

The recommended guidelines for preparation of a cooled semen dose are as follows:

- A minimum of 1 billion progressively motile spermatozoa (PMS) should be packaged in each cooled dose
- A semen-to-extender ratio of at least 1:3 should be used
- The final concentration in the extended dose should be 25 million PMS per ml
- The volume of extended semen should be 40 mls in most instances. However, a final volume > 40 mls may be necessary in some circumstances to provide a 1:3 dilution ratio and a minimum concentration of 25 million PMS per ml. The final insemination volume, however, should not exceed 60 mls. If so, consider centrifugation of the ejaculate
- A billion progressively motile sperm are included in the initial dose prepared because it is anticipated that a significant number of sperm (usually estimated at a 20 to 30% loss) will not survive the cooled-storage process. Therefore even if only 50% of the original motile sperm are still motile after 24 hours, there would still be 500 million PMS available for insemination

The total number of progressively motile sperm in the ejaculate, the number of mares on-site, and the number of mares off-site to be bred will dictate the number of breeding doses available. As noted previously the recommended doses for fresh and cooled semen are 500 million and 1 billion PMS, respectively. Mare owners or managers may request that two doses of cooled semen be shipped. However, the stallion manager and/or owner must ultimately make the decision as to how many doses of semen are shipped for each mare and the breeding priority if confronted with a situation in which there are more mares to be bred than breeding doses available. It should be noted that reducing the number of sperm per breeding dose may result in decreased pregnancy rates. Therefore, it may be better to provide fewer doses and maximize the probability of obtaining pregnancies from mares that are inseminated. Obviously, it is recognized that multiple factors, some practical and some political, need to be considered when determining the final breeding strategy when the number of mares to be bred is greater than the number of doses available.

8.10 Calculation of the Number of Cooled Breeding Doses in an Ejaculate

The 591 series Densimeters is designed to automatically perform all required calculations for cool transported doses. The total number of cooled breeding doses available in the ejaculate can be determined using the following formula, presuming a standard breeding dose of 1 billion (1,000 million) progressively motile sperm is to be used:

 # Cooled Doses in Ejaculate = Total # PMS ÷ 1,000 million PMS

Example 8-1

Calculations to determine the number of cooled breeding doses in an ejaculate.
Cooled Dose = 1 billion PMS (or 1,000 million PMS)
Semen parameters utilized:

- Volume = 37 mls
- Concentration = 245 million sperm per ml
- Progressive Motility = 65%.

Parameter	Calculation
# Cooled Doses in Ejaculate	$= \frac{\text{Total \# PMS}}{\text{1,000 million PMS}}$
Example	
# Doses in Ejaculate	$= \frac{\text{5,892 PMS}}{\text{1,000 million PMS}}$
	5.89 cooled doses

Alternatively, the number of cooled breeding doses per ejaculate can be determined using the following formula (if the volume of raw semen per dose has been calculated):

 # Cooled Doses in Ejaculate = Gel-free volume (ml) ÷ volume raw semen/dose

Example 8-2

Calculation of the number of cooled breeding doses in an ejaculate (based on volume of raw semen per dose)
Cooled Dose = 1 billion PMS (or 1,000 million PMS)
Semen parameters utilized:

- Volume = 37 mls
- Concentration = 245 million sperm per ml
- Progressive Motility = 65 %

Parameter	Calculation
# Cooled Doses in Ejaculate	$= \frac{\text{Gel-fee volume (ml)}}{\text{Volume raw semen/dose*}}$
Example	
# Doses in Ejaculate	$= \frac{\text{37 mls}}{\left[\frac{\text{1,000 million PMS}}{(245 \times 0.65)}\right]}$
	= 5.89 cooled doses

*Volume raw semen/dose = Desired # PMS / (Conc. x Progressive Motility)

8.11 Preparation of a Single Cooled Semen Dose

A simple technique that can be used to prepare a cooled semen dose is described in this section, based on an ejaculate with a sperm concentration of > 100 million sperm per ml and a progressive motility of > 50%. If the sperm concentration is < 100 million sperm per ml and the progressive motility is < 50%, the ejaculate should be centrifuged to remove seminal plasma and concentrate the spermatozoa.

An accurate calculation of the volume of raw semen used to produce each cooled insemination dose can be obtained using the following formula:

Volume of raw semen (mls) = Desired # PMS ÷ (Concentration x Progressive Motility)

Determination of the amount of semen extender to be added to the raw semen can be made by subtracting the volume of raw semen required from the final desired volume of the insemination dose (i.e. 40 mls) as follows:

Extender Volume (mls) = Final AI volume desired – volume of raw semen required

The actual insemination dose can be prepared by first pouring the required volume of extender into a warmed 50ml Graduated Cylinder. The graduated cylinder should be clean and ideally maintained in an incubator at 37° C (98.6°F). Next, add the required amount of raw semen to the graduated cylinder containing the semen extender. Cover the top of the graduated cylinder with a small amount of Parafilm® and gently mix the contents. The insemination dose is now complete and can be packaged and placed into a passive cooling system.

Note: Additional guidelines for preparation of a cooled dose are as follows:

1. If the volume of raw semen needed to make up a cooled dose is less than 10 mls, sufficient extender can be added to make up a total volume of 40 mls.
2. If the volume of raw semen needed is between 10 and 15 mls, add 3 times as much extender as semen to make up the final cooled dose. The final volume is never to exceed 60 mls.
3. If the volume of raw semen needed is greater than 15 mls, the ejaculate should be centrifuged.

Example 8-3

Calculations to determine the volumes of raw semen and semen extender required for preparation of a single cooled insemination dose.

Cooled Dose = 1 billion PMS (or 1,000 million PMS)\

Semen parameters utilized:

- Volume = 37 mls
- Concentration = 245 million sperm per ml
- Progressive Motility = 65 %

Parameter		Calculation
Volume of raw semen needed	=	$\frac{\text{Desired \# PMS}}{(\text{Conc} \times \text{Progressive Motility})}$
Example		
Volume of raw semen needed	=	1,000 million PMS ÷ (245 million per ml x 0.65)
	=	1,000 million PMS ÷ 159.25 million PMS per ml
	=	6.28 mls*
Volume of Extender	=	**Final insemination volume – volume of raw semen**
Example		
Volume of Extender	=	40 mls – 6.28 mls
	=	33.72 mls

8.12 Preparation of Multiple Cooled Doses from a Single Ejaculate

Multiple cooled doses can easily be prepared for insemination by mixing the volume of raw semen required for all doses with the appropriate volume of extender using the technique outlined below.

Steps:

1. Calculate the amount of raw semen required for a single cooled dose (at 1 billion or 1,000 million PMS).
2. Determine the number of cooled doses required that day.
3. Multiply the number of doses required by the volume of raw semen required for each dose
4. Calculate the final total volume required to provide a total volume of 40 mls per cooled dose. This is performed by multiplying the number of cooled doses by the volume per dose (40 mls)
5. Subtract the volume of raw semen required from the final total volume to yield the volume of semen extender required.
6. Add the calculated volume of extender to a warmed graduated cylinder.
7. Then add the calculated volume of raw semen required.
8. Cover graduated cylinder with Parafilm® and gently mix.
9. Each cooled dose should consist of a volume of 40 mls of extended semen containing 1 billion (1,000 million) PMS.

Example 8-4

Calculations to prepare multiple cooled doses from a single ejaculate.

Cooled Dose = 1 billion PMS (or 1,000 million PMS)

Semen parameters utilized:

- Volume = 37 mls
- Concentration = 245 million sperm per ml
- Progressive Motility = 65 %

A total of 4 cooled doses are to be prepared from this ejaculate.

Parameter		Calculation
Volume of raw semen needed	=	# cooled doses needed x volume raw semen per dose
Example		
Volume of raw semen needed	=	4 cooled doses x 6.28 mls
	=	25.12 mls
Volume of extender required	=	(# cooled doses needed x 40 mls per dose) – total volume of raw semen required
Example		
Volume of extender required	=	(4 doses x 40 mls per dose) – 25.12 mls raw semen
	=	160 mls – 25.12 mls raw semen
	=	134.12 mls semen extender

8.13 Packaging Semen for Cooling

Options for packaging semen, which include Whirl-Pak® bags, baby bottle liners, 50-ml syringes, and centrifuge tubes, often are dictated by the type of passive cooling system used. No matter which packaging system is used, the package should be labeled, at a minimum, with the name of the stallion and collection date. In addition to labeling the package containing the extended semen, good management practice indicates that a note be placed in the storage-transport container with the name of the stallion, name of the mare, date and time semen was collected, volume of raw semen, volume and type of extender, initial motility scores, and the total number of progressively motile sperm per dose.

The Whirl-Pak® is a common short-term storage package for cooled equine semen. The appropriate volume of extended semen is poured into a labeled Whirl-Pak® bag (Figure 8-2) and the excess air is expressed out (Figure 8-4). The bag is then closed by rolling the top and folding in the tabs (Figure 8-3). The filled bag is then placed inside a second Whirl-Pak® bag, which is closed in a similar manner (Figure 8-5). The dual-bag system is designed to minimize and contain loss of semen (i.e. leakage) during storage and transport. The Whirl-Pak® bags are then placed inside a passive cooling system.

Baby bottle liners may also be used to package semen for short-term cooled storage. Extended semen is poured into a liner and the air is expelled. The upper portion of the liner is then twisted repeatedly, folded over, and a small rubber band is applied over the twisted portion. Alternatively, a heat seal may be used to seal the open end of the liner. The filled liner is often placed inside a second

Figure 8-2 Adding semen to a labeled Whirl-Pak® bag filled with equine semen.

Figure 8-3 Expressing air out of the Whirl-Pak® bag.

liner to contain any leakage. The filled liners are subsequently placed in the passive cooling system.

Several passive cooling systems use syringes to store extended semen during cooled transport. The

Figure 8-4 Closing Whirl-Pak® bag.

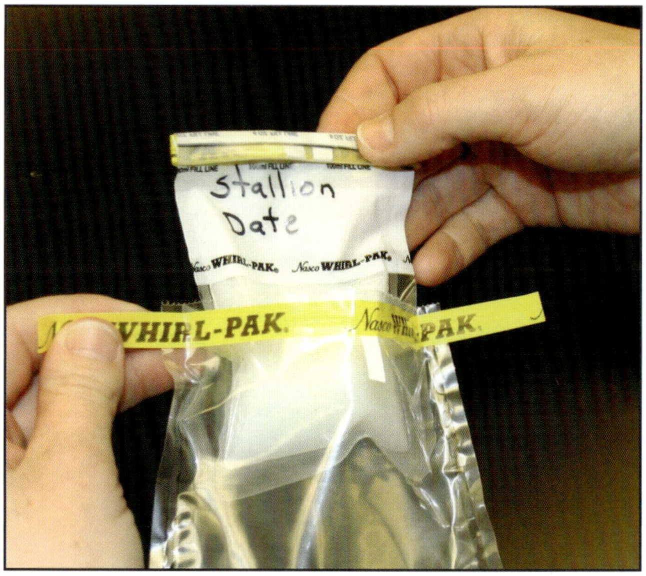

Figure 8-5 Placing filled Whirl-Pak® bag inside a second bag to prevent leakage.

appropriate volume of extended semen is aspirated into a 50ml All-Plastic Syringe. Any residual air is expelled and a cap is placed on the tip of the syringe as a seal to prevent leakage of semen and entry of air during storage. The syringe is labeled and placed directly into pre-manufactured slots within a passive cooling container.

Sterile 50-ml conical centrifuge tubes may also be used to store equine semen in a passive cooling sys-

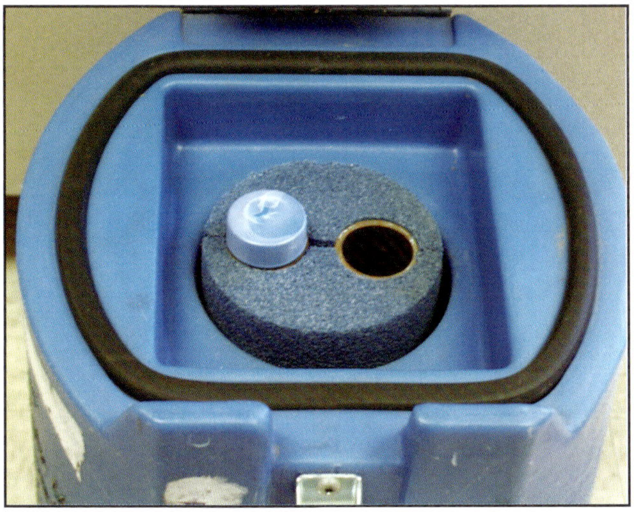

Figure 8-6 Examples of passive cooling system the Equitainer®

tem. One such system (Equitainer® Shipper, Tube Style) (Figure 8-6) has a special insert specifically designed to hold two 50ml Centrifuge Tubes. The appropriate volume of extended semen is poured into a conical tube. The top of the tube is screwed shut, sealing the tube. The tube is then placed within the passive cooling container. If only one tube is filled with extended semen, a second tube containing water is often placed in the other reservoir within the special insert. One potential issue with use of centrifuge tubes for storage of semen is that a volume of air remains within the centrifuge tube. It is the opinion of some that a prolonged exposure to air is detrimental to semen. This may be overcome by filling the entire centrifuge tube with extended semen.

8.14 Cooling Containers for Storage and Shipment of Cooled Semen

Several passive cooling systems for short-term storage and transport of extended equine semen are commercially available. All can be re-used multiple times, although some are designed and priced to be single-use and disposable.

Passive cooling systems consist of an insulated container, with designated spaces for extended semen and frozen packs. The various cooling systems have been evaluated and compared for the ability to maintain semen motility and viability at 5° to 8° C (41° to 46.4° F). The Equitainer® Shipper, Cup Style system has been reported to maintain an internal temperature of 5° to 8° C (41° to 46.4° F) and maintain sperm viability longer than the disposable containers. In general, disposable containers have a decreased ability to maintain a constant low temperature, especially when environmental conditions are extreme. However, disposable containers may be used effectively when the duration of shipment is expected to be less than 24 hours.

8.15 Shipment of Cooled Semen

A majority of cooled equine semen is shipped by commercial overnight courier service (i.e. Federal Express or United Parcel Service) or by counter-to-counter commercial airline service. On limited occasions, cooled semen may be transported by private courier, commercial bus service, or other means of transportation.

The method of shipment depends on a combination of factors, including the semen collection schedule of the stallion, day of the week, how close the mare is to ovulating, the ability of the stallion's semen to survive cooled storage, and other factors (i.e. cost, proximity of an airport, weather conditions, etc.). Many stallions are collected on a set schedule, such as every-other-day (i.e. even or odd days of the month) or Monday-Wednesday-Friday (± Saturday). The day of the week semen is to be collected is critical for shipment options, because overnight courier services do not routinely pick up on Saturday, or deliver on Sundays. Consequently, semen collected on Saturdays or Sundays must be shipped by counter-to-counter airline service. If a mare is judged to be close to ovulation when examined early in the morning on the day semen collection is scheduled, a counter-to-counter semen shipment will often be requested. Otherwise, an overnight shipment is most commonly requested. Note that with any overnight courier service, the 'Saturday Delivery Option' will need to be requested for semen collected and picked up on a Friday. Otherwise, the semen container will be delivered on the next business day (Monday).

Spermatozoa from some stallions do not survive a prolonged period of cooled storage. Semen shipments from these stallions are primarily counter-to-counter to decrease the interval from collection to insemination.

In general, overnight courier delivery is significantly less expensive than counter-to-counter airline service. This is due to the fact that additional costs are often part of the same-day delivery option, including handling fees at the collection center, a courier charge for transport of the semen to the airport of origin, the airline cargo fee, and potentially another courier or transport charge from the destination airport to the breeding farm where the mare is located.

8.16 Receipt of Cooled Semen

Semen shipped by overnight courier usually arrives in the late morning, whereas semen delivered by counter-to-counter airline service usually arrives in the late afternoon, evening or the middle of the night. The semen container should be opened and examined immediately to confirm that it contains the correct semen. The container should be labeled with the appropriate mare and stallion information. This is especially critical if multiple semen containers arrive on the breeding farm at the same time.

The mare is subsequently brought into the breeding area and prepared for insemination. The package (Whirl-Pak®, baby bottle liner, syringe, or centrifuge tube) is removed from the shipping container and gently mixed to resuspend the spermatozoa. A small aliquot of semen (i.e. 0.5 ml) is added to a small pre-warmed test tube or vial which is then placed into an incubator at 37° C (98.6° F). The semen is allowed to warm for approximately 10 minutes before being evaluated under a microscope for motility characteristics. If a problem is identified (i.e. all the sperm are immotile or dead), the stallion owner or manager should be contacted and the status of the semen reported. It would not be appropriate to wait until a pregnancy examination is performed and then call the stallion owner to inform him or her that the reason the mare did not become pregnant was poor semen quality.

Personnel on the receiving end may obtain additional data on the shipped semen, such as volume of semen shipped and sperm concentration may also be obtained. The concentration would have to be determined with a hemacytometer or DNA based cell counters, since spectrophotometric techniques (i.e. the Densimeter) are not accurate in the presence of an opaque semen extender. One may subsequently calculate the total number of progressively motile sperm in the dose received (i.e. volume x concentration x progressive motility).

In the meantime, as the aliquot of semen is warming in the incubator the mare is usually inseminated and returned to her stall, paddock or pasture. It is not necessary to pre-warm the semen that is to be inseminated as it will be warmed sufficiently by the uterus of the mare.

If two doses of semen are shipped, a decision has to be made as to when and if the second dose of semen is to be inseminated. The decision is usually based on individual stallion characteristics (i.e. does he cool well), and the age, parity status (i.e. maiden vs. multiparous mare), and uterine health of the mare. If the stallion does not cool well, it is pointless to hold onto the second dose until the following day. If the mare is a young maiden and her uterus cannot hold two doses of semen, it is pointless to inseminate both doses at the same time. Conversely, if the mare is older and has a history of fluid accumulation after breeding, one or both doses should be inseminated at once, since it is likely that significant effort will have to be made to clean up her uterus after the single insemination. A second insemination into this type of mare may actually be detrimental.

If the second dose is to be retained for insemination the next day, it can be placed back into the same passive cooling container, if the temperature can be maintained at 5° to 8° C (41° to 46.4° F) for up to 48 hours (i.e. the Equitainer®) or placed in an insulated container within a traditional refrigerator set at 5° to 8° C (41° to 46.4° F) if a disposable container was used.

8.17 Fertility of Cooled Semen

Several factors may affect the fertility of cooled-transported semen. These include:

- Inherent fertility of the stallion and mare
- Semen characteristics prior to cooling
- Cooling rate (affected by storage container)
- Storage temperature
- Duration of cooled storage
- Semen extender and antibiotic used
- Sperm concentration and insemination volume
- Sperm motility after cooling
- Timing of insemination
- Individual stallion variability

Pregnancy rates using cooled-transported semen are often slightly lower than pregnancy rates using fresh semen. In general, it is anticipated that the pregnancy rate for mares bred with fresh semen will be 50 to 60% per cycle and that the pregnancy rate using cooled semen will be 45 to 55% per cycle. If the stallion is fertile and the mares are young and reproductively normal, a first-cycle pregnancy rate of 65 to 75% may be achieved using cooled transported semen.

One may expect a 5 to 10% reduction in pregnancy rate using cooled-transported semen. There is obviously a great deal of variation between inherent fertility of individual stallions, ability of spermatozoa of individual stallions to withstand the cooling process, types of mares being bred in various breeding programs (i.e. percentage of maiden, foaling, open and barren mares), and management of both stallions and mares.

8.18 Problems Associated with a Shipped Cooled Semen Program

Problems encountered in shipped semen programs are largely due to poor communication between the mare owner/manager and the stallion owner/manager. Mare owners may complain about the inability to order semen or reorder semen if the mare does not ovulate. Complaints arise when no one at the stallion farm answers the phone, if there is no answering machine, or if no one calls back in a timely manner. Mare owners may also be concerned if there is a complete lack of identification or information (i.e. stallion name, date of collection) on the individual packages of semen or in the shipping container. An additional topic of concern for the mare owner is if their mare gets 'bumped' from the daily breeding list by another mare booked to the same stallion and semen is not shipped. Mare owners may also be frustrated if the stallion is only collected on a Monday, Wednesday, Friday basis (and not on weekends), if there is no counter-to-counter option, and if the stallion is unavailable due to show or performance events scheduled during the breeding season.

Stallion owners complain that mare owners order semen too early in the cycle or too late on a collection day, or want to ship semen more than once during an estrous cycle. Stallion owners are concerned that the semen is occasionally handled improperly on the mare end. Stallion owners also lament that they do not receive feedback from mare owners regarding quality (i.e. motility) of shipped semen or pregnancy status of mares that were bred to their stallion. Another complaint is that they often receive orders for shipped semen even though they do not yet have a contract for the mare.

A potential problem with shipped semen that does not exist if the mare is on the same farm as the stallion is that a semen shipment is occasionally 'lost' or 'misplaced' during transport. The mare may ovulate before the semen is located and delivered and/or the sperm may not survive the additional time period.

Semen that is shipped counter-to-counter by commercial airline carrier may be exposed to x-rays used for security screening at airports. However, research results have indicated that there is no significant adverse effect of such irradiation on the viability or fertility of stallion spermatozoa. In addition, semen transport containers may be opened for inspection during shipment.

These issues aside, the use of cooled-transported semen has dramatically altered the way horses are managed and bred throughout the world. In general, the system works remarkably well and problems may be minimized or eliminated by education of farm personnel, good communication between personnel involved with mare and stallion management, attention to detail, and care and diligence during semen collection, handling, and insemination.

Chapter 9 Semen Freezing and Storage

Table 9-0 List and Part Number of ARS products used in this chapter.

Item	Part Number	Use/Comments
E-Z Mixin® - "BF"	EZM-BF	Semen extender used as a centrifugation media when processing frozen semen
Centrifuge Tubes and Caps	537-742/25	Used to hold semen during centrifugation
E-Z Cushion	EZC-101	Used to recover a higher percentage of spermatozoa during centrifuga-tion
Sink Vacuum Aspirator Pump Kit	537-785-Kit	Used after centrifugation to remove supernatant from sperm pellet
Disposable 5 ¾ Inch Glass Pasteur Pipette	537-506/250	Disposable tip connected to aspirator pump to remove supernatant
Hemacytometer Kit	537-850	Used to estimate sperm concentration in extended semen samples
Freezing Straws, 0.5ml	537-670-CLE/100	0.5 ml polyvinyl chloride straws used to store frozen semen
ARS Custom Printed Freezing Straws, 0.5ml	537-670-CLE-PS/100	0.5 ml polyvinyl chloride straws for frozen semen custom printed with any desired text
Bubbler Comb	BC-101/25	Used to insert airspace into 0.5ml straws of extended semen prior to seal-ing and freezing
Sealing Powder for Freezing Straws	537-671	Polyvinyl alcohol powder used to seal straws of semen prior to freezing
ARS Freezing Rack	FSR-101	Floating rack used to suspend freezing straws over liquid nitrogen
E-Z Freezin® Packet Stand	EZF-PS	Convenient stand to hold E-Z Freezin® packets
ARS Freezing Straw Filler	FSF-101-KIT	0.5ml freezing straw filling system
E-Z Freezin® - "LE"	EZF-LE	Semen freezing extender (lactose EDTA and egg yolk based)
E-Z Freezin® - "MFR5"	EZF-MFR5	Semen freezing extender (skim-milk and egg yolk based)
CryoMax™- "LE"	EZF-CM-LE	A new generation semen freezing extender (lactose EDTA and egg yolk based)
CryoMax™ - "MFR5"	EZF-MFR5	A new generation semen freezing extender (modified French formula)
E-Z Freezin® Test Freeze Kit	EZF-TEST-KIT	Kit containing two packets of the E-Z Freezin® Original and CryoMax freezing extender formulas for preforming a test freeze on a stallion
Goblets (10mm 5 straws capacity) Goblets (13mm 11 straws capacity)	537-731/200 537-733/150	Polyethylene storage units designed to hold straws of frozen semen; attached to canes for storage within a canister of a liquid nitrogen Dewar
Aluminum canes (10mm Goblets) Aluminum canes (13mm Goblets)	537-732/100 537-734/75	Used to hold goblets containing straws of frozen semen within a canister of a liquid nitrogen Dewar
Storage Dewar (Model MVE/XC 20)	537-701	Liquid nitrogen tank that holds 20.5 liters
Storage Dewar (Model XC 47/11-6)	537-711	Liquid nitrogen tank that holds 47.4 liters
Vapor Shipper (Model SC 4/3V)	537-721	'Dry' shipper used to transport straws of frozen semen in liquid nitrogen vapor
Thermoregulated Water Bath	586A-201	Used to thaw straws of frozen semen
Disposable Insemination Tube	544 Series	Used to inseminate frozen semen
20ml Disposable Weigh Boat	537-814/500	Used to hold sealing powder

The first 'frozen-semen' foal was born in 1957 to a mare inseminated with frozen-thawed epididymal spermatozoa. Subsequently, significant progress has been made on the use and success of frozen semen in the equine industry. Unfortunately, success with frozen semen in the stallion has not paralleled the success in bulls. The primary reason for this is that bulls which do not freeze well are not maintained as breeding animals, whereas there is little selection in the equine industry based on freezing traits of stallions.

Most major breed registries allow the registration of foals conceived with frozen semen, with the notable exception of the Jockey Club (Thoroughbred horses). If unsure, it would be prudent to check with the appropriate breed registry to confirm whether the use of frozen semen is approved prior to collecting and freezing semen.

The goal of this chapter is to review general concepts of cryopreservation of stallion semen and present techniques used for freezing stallion semen at Colorado State University.

9.1 Advantages and Disadvantages of Frozen Semen

Advantages of incorporating semen freezing into an equine breeding program include:

- Long-term preservation of genetic material for future use
- Insurance against unanticipated loss of a stallion
- Semen can be collected from a young horse prior to castration
- Mares can be bred while the stallion is at a show, is unable to be collected, or is deceased
- Mares can still be bred if the stallion provides insufficient spermatozoa to inseminate all required mares on a given day
- The mare can remain at the home farm; reducing costs, stress of hauling, and potential exposure to infectious diseases; it is much less expensive to ship a container of frozen semen than transporting a mare across the country
- Frozen semen can be shipped to the mare farm in advance of the breeding season or in advance of the estrous cycle; sufficient semen could be shipped in one container to cover multiple mares for an entire breeding season
- Semen can be shipped world-wide, giving mare owners greater access to valuable genetics
- Frozen semen can be stored indefinitely in liquid nitrogen
- Semen can be collected and frozen in the non-breeding season

However, there are also some distinct disadvantages of frozen equine semen, including:

- Not all stallions freeze well; post-thaw motility and/or pregnancy rates may be unacceptable in individual stallions; there is no selection of stallions for fertility with frozen semen
- There is no laboratory test for predicting fertility of frozen semen
- Mare management and breeding expenses are often increased
- Pregnancy rates per cycle are generally lower with frozen semen than with fresh or cooled semen from most stallions
- Training is required for processing, packaging, and freezing semen; stallions are often shipped to a specialized facility for collection and freezing
- Costs associated with the storage of frozen semen
- Lack of industry standards for frozen semen (i.e. post-thaw motility, number of sperm inseminated, number of doses used per cycle, timing of insemination, etc.)

In most instances, the advantages of frozen semen outweigh the disadvantages. Some of the disadvantages can be overcome by proper training of farm personnel.

Clinical Comment

The AQHA has amended Registration Rules REG111 and REG112 to the following: *Sperm, embryos and oocytes from foals born in 2015 or after will not be able to be used beyond two calendar years following that animal's death or sterilization.* Semen frozen from AQHA registered stallions born prior to 2015 can still be used indefinitely to register foals with the AQHA.

9.2 Principles of Freezing Equine Semen

The general steps for cryopreservation of equine semen include mixing freshly collected semen with a basic skim milk extender, centrifugation to remove seminal plasma and concentrate the spermatozoa into a pellet, resuspension of the semen in a freezing extender containing a cryoprotectant, cooling to -120° C (-184° F) over liquid nitrogen vapor, and subsequent storage in liquid nitrogen at -196° C (-320° F) (Table 9-1).

Important parameters for semen frozen using the above technique include:

- Total number of sperm/straw = 100 million
- Number of straws per insemination dose = 8
- Total number of sperm per insemination dose = 800 million
- Post-thaw motility should be ≥ 30 %

In order for a frozen-thawed sperm to fertilize an oocyte, it must retain the following attributes:

- Metabolism for production of energy
- Progressive motility
- Intact acrosome
- Normal plasma membrane
- Normal DNA

Table 9-1 Guidelines for preparation of frozen stallion semen.

Step	Procedure
1	Select the optimal freezing extender for an individual stallion based on a test freeze
2	Collect and evaluate semen; dilute with skim milk extender (1:1 ratio)
3	Centrifuge to concentrate spermatozoa and remove seminal plasma
4	Add freezing extender to dilute sperm to 200 million sperm per ml
5	Package extended semen in labeled 0.5 ml straws
6	Pre-cool loaded straws from room temperature to 5° to 8° C in a refrigerator
7	Freeze over liquid nitrogen vapor
8	Plunge into liquid nitrogen
9	Transfer into LN2 tank for storage

The acrosome contains enzymes required for penetration of the sperm through structures that surround the oocyte. Proteins on the plasma membrane of the sperm are important for attachment to the plasma membrane of the oocyte during fertilization.

Damage to spermatozoa during the freezing and thawing processes results from intracellular or extracellular ice crystal formation, osmotic shock, dehydration, toxicity of salts or cryoprotectants, and alterations in acrosomal or plasma membrane structure or function. Successful cryopreservation is dependent on a complex series of interactions between extender, cryoprotectants, cooling rate, and warming/thawing rate. Glycerol is the most common cryoprotective agent used for stallion semen, although several other agents (i.e. amides) have been incorporated into the new generation freezing extenders (i.e. CryoMax™ LE and CryoMax™ MFR5). The amount of cryoprotectant(s) added to semen is a balance between the minimum amount necessary to provide protection during freezing/thawing and the maximum amount that is not detrimental to sperm survival or fertility.

ARS CryoMax™ Freezing Extenders

CryoMax™ freezing extenders are successfully being used to freeze semen from multiple species.

- Available for poor freezer stallions
- Available for non-domestic animals
- Available for dogs

Two custom formulas of each CryoMax™ freezing extender are also available without glycerol for stallions that do not freeze well in an extender containing glycerol.

9.3 Test Freeze

A test freeze should be performed the first time semen from an individual stallion is frozen. It may be optimal to collect the stallion several times to deplete the extra-gonadal sperm reserves before performing the test freeze. Some freezing centers advocate a series of test freezes before the 'optimal' protocol is selected for an individual stallion.

The test freeze would compare post-thaw motility characteristics between two or more freezing extenders, centrifugation techniques, cooling rates, sperm concentrations, and possibly different straw sizes and thawing rates. The goal would be to identify a customized cryopreservation protocol for the individual stallion to maximize sperm survival after freezing and thawing. Following the test freeze, one or more straws are thawed at the recommended rate and warmed to 37° C for 10 minutes to evaluate motility of the frozen-thawed spermatozoa.

ARS Test Freeze Kit

- Compare 4 freezing extenders
- Select the extender that is best for each individual stallion
- E-Z Freezin® LE
- E-Z Freezin® MFR5
- E-Z Freezin® CryoMax™ LE
- E-Z Freezin® CryoMax™ MFR5

See Appendix 2 for more information on how to perform a test freeze.

Equine semen can be processed for cryopreservation either with or without use of a cushion in the centrifugation step. Standard centrifugation techniques without a cushion result in recovery of ~ 75 % of spermatozoa in the initial sample. The advantage of incorporating a cushion centrifugation technique is that the cushion allows for increased centrifugation speed and duration, which ultimately results in enhanced sperm recovery (≥ 90 %) without a detrimental effect on sperm motility, viability or morphology. This chapter will describe the techniques involved in freezing semen when a cushion is incorporated in the centrifugation step.

See Appendix 2 on page 214 for additional details on test freezing.

9.4 Semen Freezing Procedure (Step-by-Step)

1. Collect semen using standard techniques.
2. Perform a routine semen evaluation (volume, concentration, motility).
3. Dilute the raw semen 1:1 with a 'fresh semen' extender such as E-Z Mixin® - BF; the goal is to dilute out the potential negative effects of seminal plasma (Figure 9-1).
4. Transfer the extended semen into a series of 50 ml conical centrifuge tubes (Figure 9-2); it is critical that an even number of tubes be placed in the centrifuge and that the tubes be balanced by weight before centrifugation. Loading an uneven number of tubes or loading tubes that

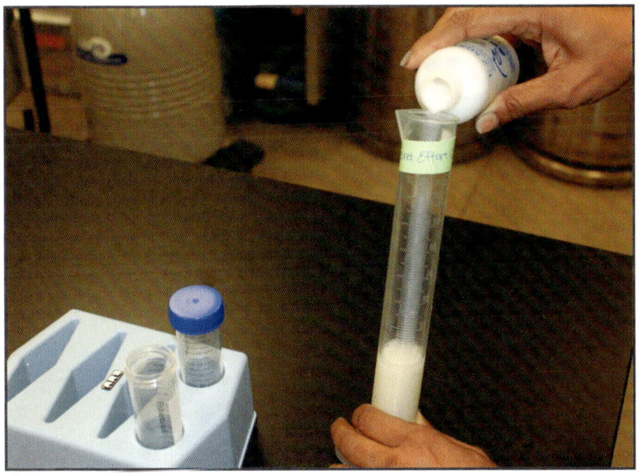

Figure 9-1 Adding semen extender into a graduated cylinder containing raw semen.

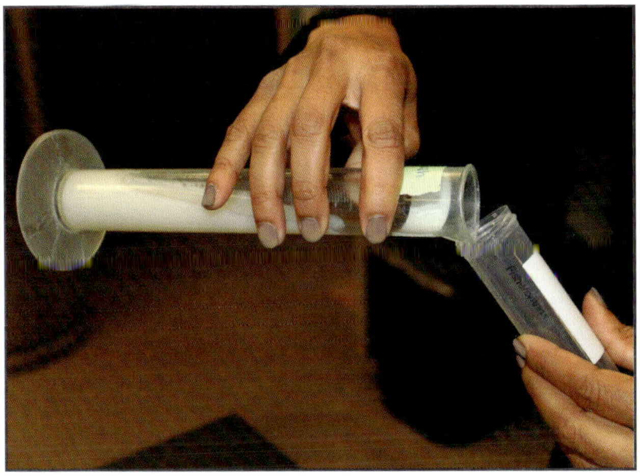

Figure 9-2 Transferring extended semen into a 50 ml conical centrifuge tube.

Figure 9-3 Dispensing a cushion (arrow) below the extended semen in a centrifuge tube. In this photograph a cushion volume of 3.0 mls was used. Currently a cushion volume of 0.5 mls is utilized for centrifugation.

are not balanced will lead to damage to the centrifuge. If an uneven number of tubes of extended semen are produced, an additional tube filled with the proper volume of water should be used to balance the centrifuge.

5. Carefully add 0.5 mls of a cushion, such as E-Z Cushion™, beneath the extended semen at the bottom of the centrifuge tube (Figure 9-3); the cushion allows for centrifugation at a greater force for a longer time period without damaging spermatozoa and provides a higher total recovery of sperm.
   - Load 0.5 mls E-Z Cushion into a pipette
   - Pass the pipette through the extended semen to the bottom of the conical tube
   - Slowly dispense the cushion below the semen
6. Balance pairs of centrifuge tubes by weight (Figure 9-4). As noted previously, centrifugation with an uneven number of tubes or unbalanced tubes will result in damage to the centrifuge.
7. Centrifuge at 1,000 x *g* for 25 minutes (Figure 9-5) using a timer. The goal is to end up with a soft pellet of sperm on top of the cushion (see Appendix 1 on page 213).

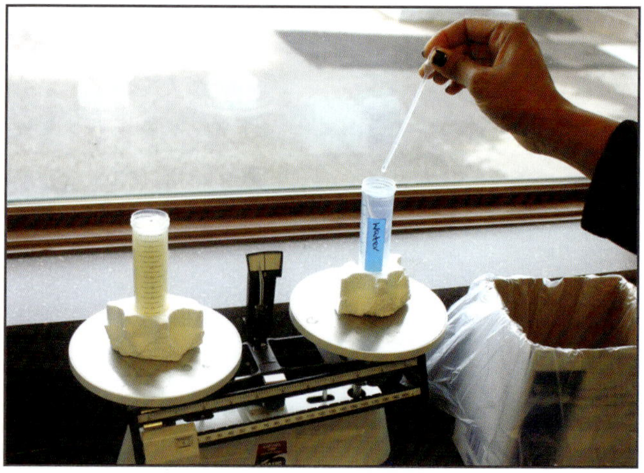

Figure 9-4 Balancing the weight of two centrifuge tubes (currently uneven). The tube on the left contains extended semen; the tube on the right contains water. Add or remove water to the tube on the right to properly balance the weight against the tube containing semen.

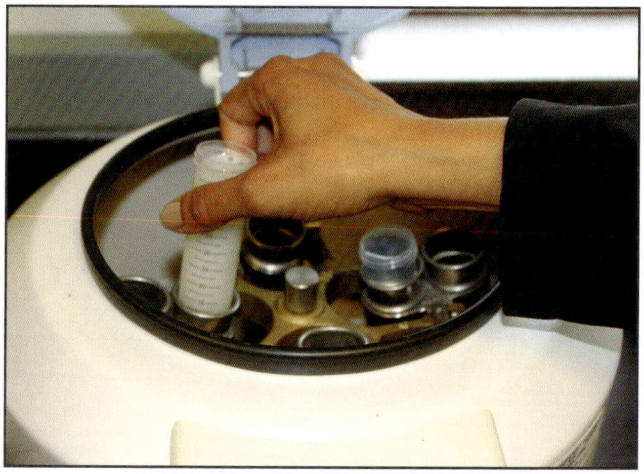

Figure 9-5 Placing a pair of centrifuge tubes into opposite buckets within a centrifuge.

Clinical Comment

Centrifugation *without* a cushion will require a slower speed and shorter duration, such as 400 x *g* for 15 minutes. The percentage of spermatozoa recovered will be significantly less than that recovered using a cushion.

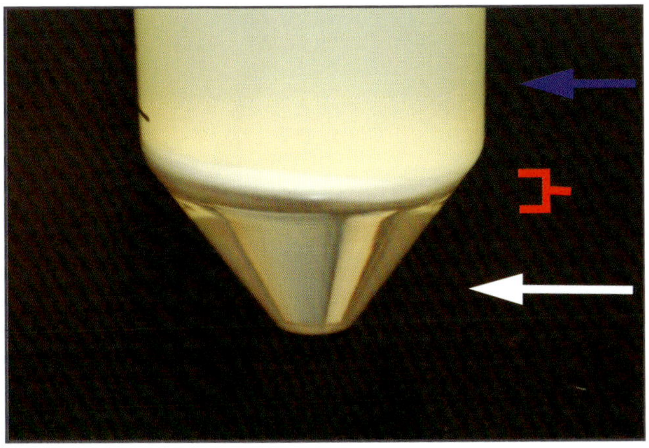

Figure 9-6 Sperm pellet (red bracket) below the supernatant (blue arrow) and cushion (white arrow). In this photo the cushion volume was 3.0 mls. Currently a cushion volume of 0.5 mls is utilized for centrifugation.

8. Remove the centrifuge tube from the centrifuge and observe the sperm pellet layered between the supernatant (seminal plasma and extender) and the cushion (Figure 9-6).

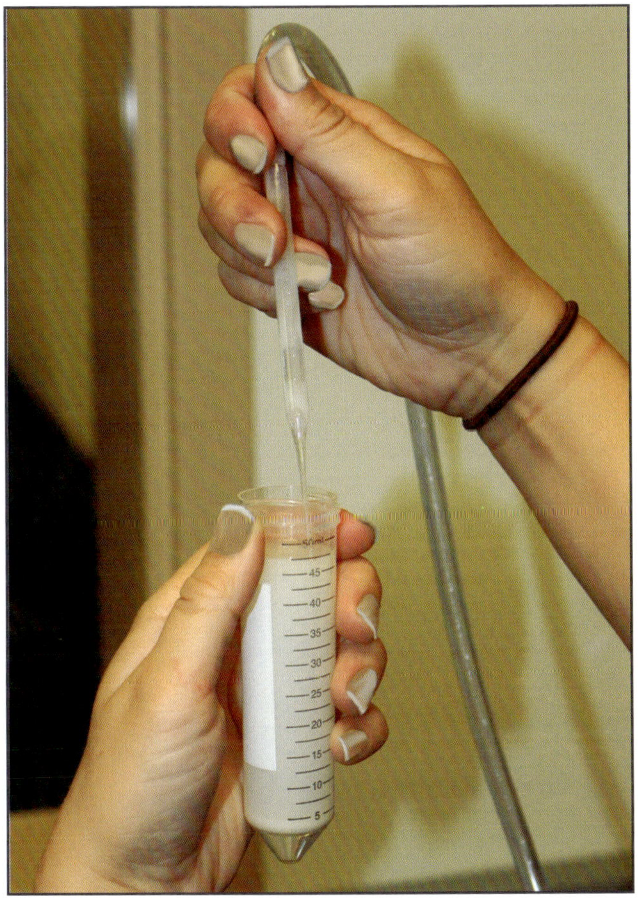

Figure 9-7 Aspiration of supernatant from above the sperm pellet using a sink aspiration unit. A clean new Disposable 5 ¾ Inch Glass Pasteur Pipette is attached to the sink aspiration unit and used to remove the supernatant.

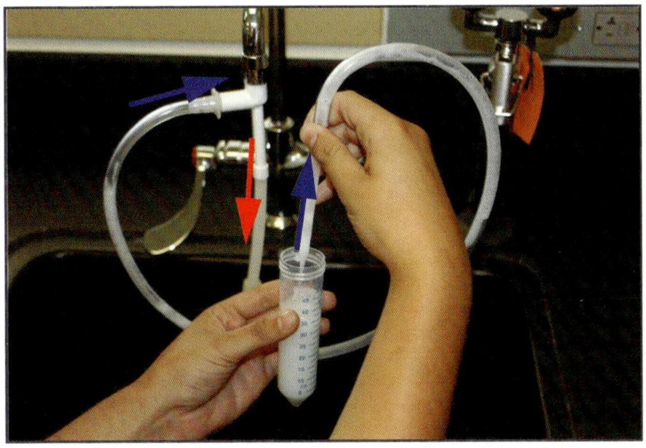

Figure 9-8 Sink aspiration unit. The unit is attached to a water faucet. Turning on the faucet will initiate water flow down the tubing into the sink drain (red arrow) which creates a suction on the inflow line (blue arrows). Note the Pasteur pipette attached to the end of the inflow line.

9. Aspirate off the supernatant (seminal plasma and extender) leaving a small amount of fluid above the sperm pellet (Figure 9-7 and 9-8); be careful not to disturb the sperm pellet. The supernatant can be aspirated using the ARS Sink Vacuum Aspirator Pump Kit. The Aspiration Pump is attached to the faucet of a sink. A Disposable 5 ¾ Inch Glass Pasteur Pipette is attached to the suction tube of the Aspiration Pump. When the faucet is opened, passage of water through the Aspiration Pump will create a suction. The Pasteur pipette should be slowly lowered until it touches the surface of the supernatant. The supernatant will be suctioned up the tubing and will be discarded through the outflow tubing into the sink. Apply a minimum amount of suction and keep the pipette at the surface of the supernatant to prevent disturbance of the sperm pellet at the bottom of the centrifuge tube.

10. The small volume of cushion (0.5 mls) does not have to be removed. It will not interfere with either cryopreservation of the semen or the fertility of mares inseminated with the frozen semen.

11. Combine sperm pellets from all of the centrifuge tubes if there are more than one tube (Figure 9-9).

12. Measure the final total volume of concentrated spermatozoa with a pipette after all pellets have been combined (Figure 9-10).

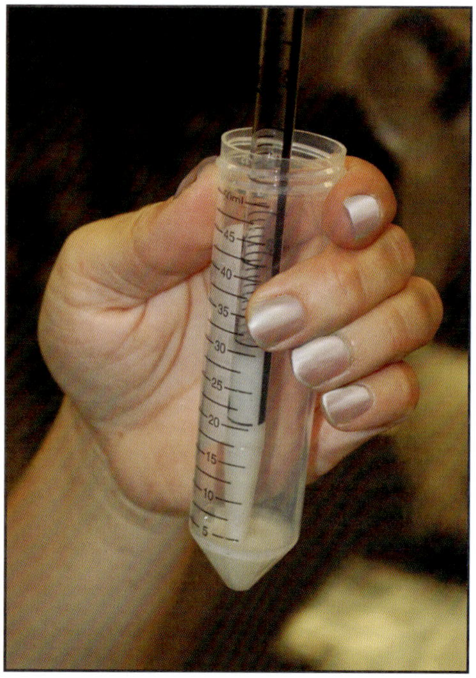

Figure 9-9 Transferring sperm pellets from multiple tubes into one tube using a pipette.

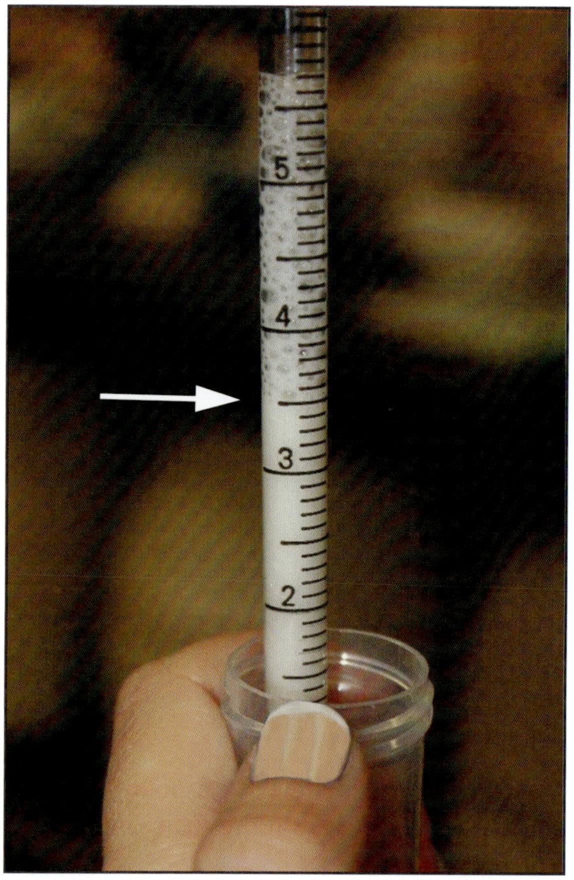

Figure 9-10 Measuring the total combined volume of all sperm pellets using a pipette. The arrow indicates the correct volume; only bubbles are present in the pipette above the arrow.

Clinical Comment

- Centrifugation using a cushion will yield (approximately) a 95 % recovery of sperm initially present in the ejaculate.
- After centrifugation, the concentration of spermatozoa is too high to accurately determine a concentration.
- Consequently, the next step is to dilute the spermatozoa with freezing extender so that an accurate assessment of concentration can be performed.

Once an accurate sperm count has been acquired, the semen is diluted further with additional freezing extender to a final concentration of 200 million sperm per ml

13. Add freezing extender (initial dilution) (Figure 9-11).

    Add a volume of freezing extender from Table 9-1 based on the original total number of spermatozoa in the ejaculate. The sperm concentration will subsequently be approximately 350 to 400 million spermatozoa per ml. Some variability in post-dilution concentration will be present due to centrifugation efficiency and volume of the sperm pellet(s) after centrifugation.

Example Calculation

Semen Volume (mls)	27
Concentration (million/ml)	524
Total Number of Sperm (billions)	14.148
Pellet Volume after Centrifugation (mls)	3.6

In the example above, a volume of 35 mls of freezing extender would be added to the combined semen pellets.

Table 9-1 Chart to aid in the initial dilution of the semen pellet after centrifugation.

Total Number of Sperm in the Original Ejaculate (billions)	Volume of Freezing Extender to add for Initial Dilution (mls)
26	65
24	60
22	55
20	50
18	45
16	40
14	35
12	30
10	25
8	20
6	15
4	10
2	5
1	2.5

Figure 9-11 Adding CryoMax^{TM} LE freezing extender to initial pellet.

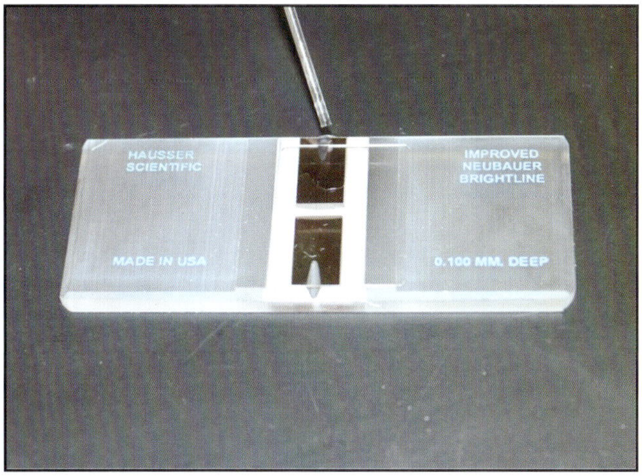

Figure 9-12 Determination of sperm concentration using a hemacytometer. Details on use of the hemacytometer are presented in 5.4 on page 39.

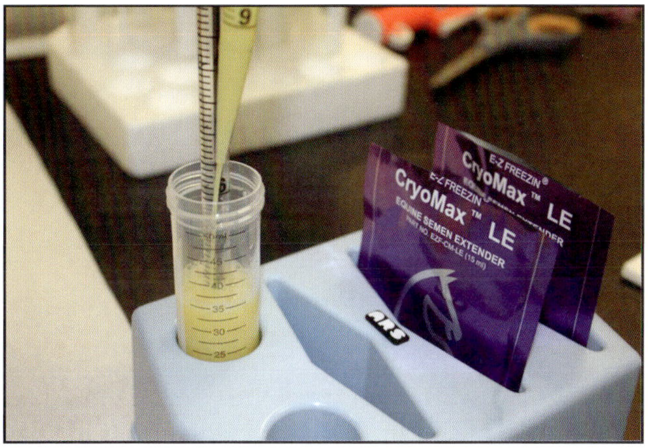

Figure 9-13 Adding the final amount of freezing extender to dilute the spermatozoa to an actual concentration of 200 million sperm per ml.

14. Determine the actual sperm concentration after the initial dilution using either a Hemacytometer (Figure 9 12) or a NucleoCounter.

15. Add more freezing extender to yield a final true concentration of 200 million sperm per ml (Figure 9-13).

16. Evaluate sperm motility again after the final addition of freezing extender and prior to packaging the sperm into straws (Figure 9-14). Often the percentage of motile sperm after addition of extender will be higher than the motility prior to the centrifugation step as some dead or damaged sperm will be retained in the supernatant.

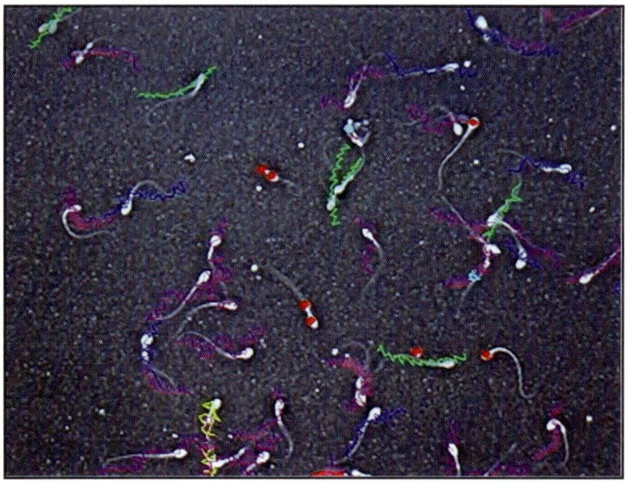

Figure 9-14 Evaluation of sperm motility using a computer assisted semen analysis (CASA) system.

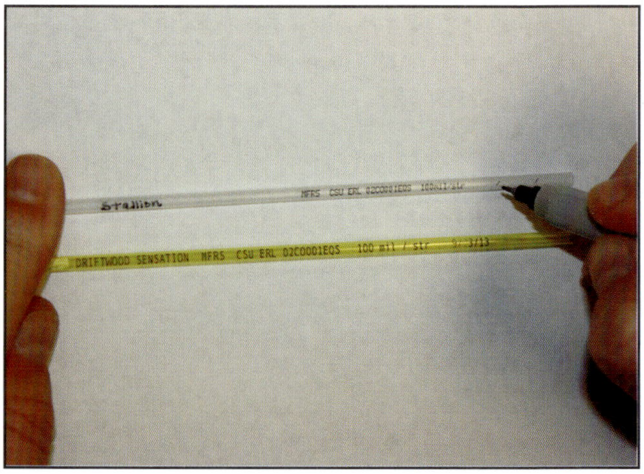

Figure 9-15 Semen straw printed with appropriate information. Straws can be hand-written or pre-printed using a computer and straw printer.

Example Calculation

Initial Extended Volume $=$ *pellet* $+$ extender added

Total # Sperm $=$ Initial Extended Volume $\times$ *Concentration*

Final Volume $=$ Total # Sperm $\div 200$

Additional extender $=$ Final Volume $-$ Initial Extended Volume

Extended concentration $= 312$ million/ml

Initial Extended Volume $= 3.6 + 35 = 38.6ml$

Total # Sperm $= 38.6 \times 312 = 12.043$ billion sperm

Final Volume $= 12,043$ million sperm $\div 200 = 60.2mls$

Additional extender needed $= 60.2 - 38.6 = 21.6$ mls

17. Label a series of 0.5 ml Freezing Straws with the following information (Figure 9-15):
    - Stallion name
    - Registration number
    - Freeze Date
    - Extender type
    - Location of Freezing Center
    - Sperm Concentration or Sperm Number per straw

Straws can be labeled by hand with an extra-fine permanent marking pen taking care that the information is neatly written and legible or straws can be custom printed (i.e. ARS Custom Printed Freezing Straws).

18. Load extended semen into the 0.5 ml labeled straws (Figure 9-16). One can use an automatic straw-filler system or a hand-held device (ARS Freezing Straw Filler) to fill straws (Figure 9-17 and Figure 9-18). Extended semen can be placed into a 50 ml conical tube to facilitate loading with the straw filler system. The extended semen should be drawn up into the straws until the cotton plug becomes wet, which will then solidify, creating a seal on that end of the straw.

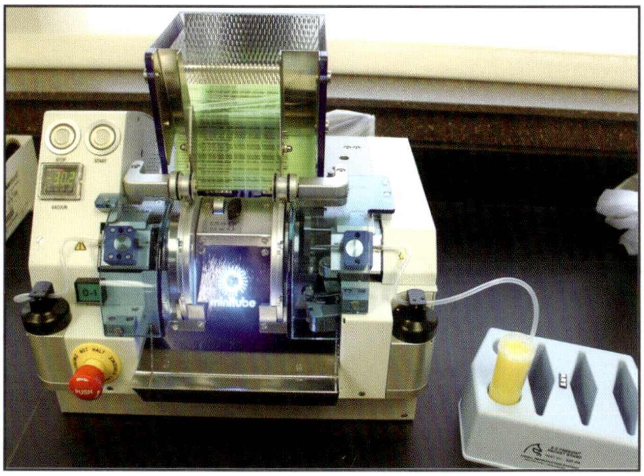

Figure 9-16 An automatic straw filling system.

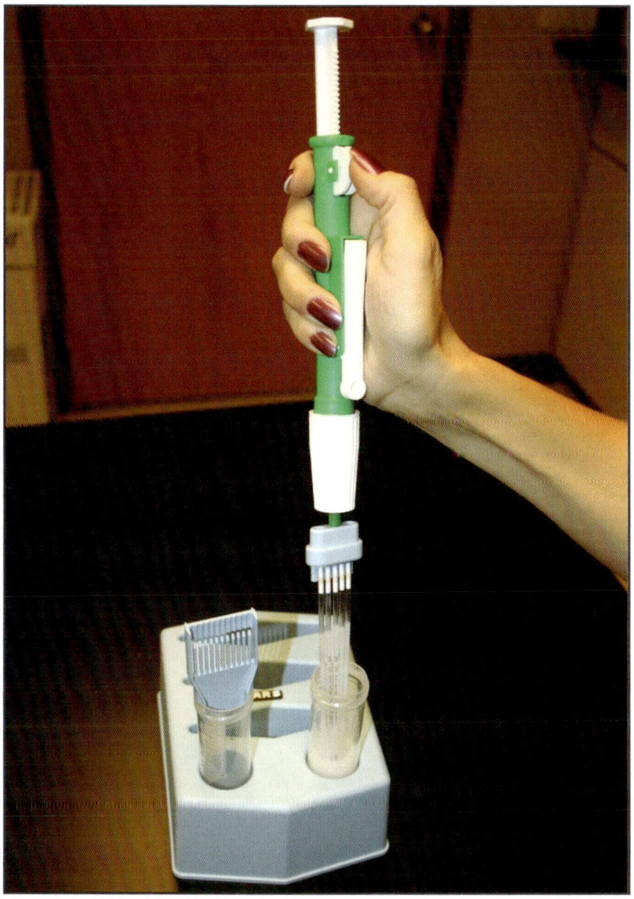

Figure 9-17 Hand held straw filling device (ARS Freezing Straw Filler) attached to a pipette. Semen is being loaded into the straws out of a 50-ml conical centrifuge tube.

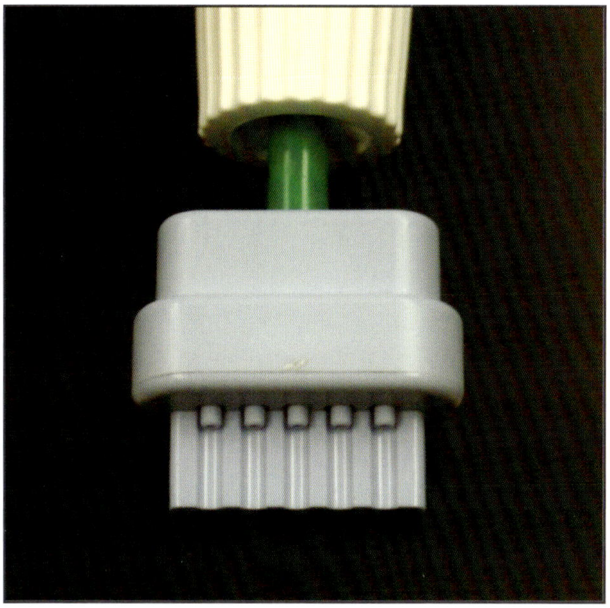

Figure 9-18 Close-up view of the hand-held straw filling device. A total of 5 straws can be filled at once using this device.

19. Create a 'bubble' within the straw using an ARS Disposable Bubbler Comb (Figure 9-19). The comb displaces a small volume of semen and creates an air pocket, which is important during the freezing and thawing processes to avoid fracturing the straw or expelling the plug.

20. The open end of the filled straws should subsequently be sealed with polyvinylchloride (PVC) Sealing Powder (Figure 9-20 and Figure 9-21), a metal ball (BB), heat sealed, etc.

21. The loaded, sealed straws are then 'flicked' to move the bubble into the center of the straw (Figure 9-22 and Figure 9-23). Theoretically, this can be used as a quality control for continued cryopreservation during storage; equine semen straws are frozen horizontally with the bubble in the center, but are stored vertically in LN2 tanks. If straws are unintentionally thawed during storage (i.e. the tank runs out of LN2), the bubble may eventually float or rise to the top of the straw. However, tests have shown that the bubble does not always change location after thawing.

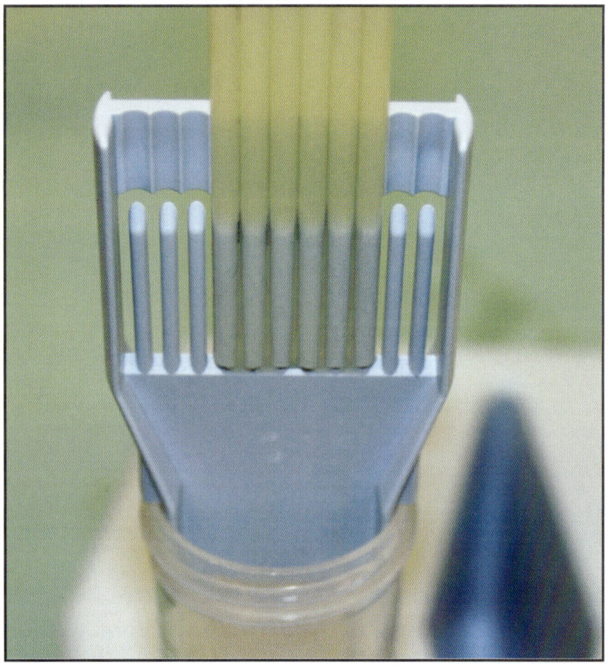

Figure 9-19 Inserting the open end of a series of 0.5 ml straw filled with extended semen onto a bubbler comb. A small consistent amount of semen will be discharged out of the straws and can be collected into a 50 ml conical tube. Extended semen that accumulates in the conical tube can be reloaded into additional straws for cryopreservation.

Figure 9-20 Sealing the ends of 0.5 ml straws of extended semen with PVC powder. A small amount of Sealing Powder for Freezing Straws is dispensed into a 20ml Disposable Weigh Boat. The open end of the straws are tamped into the powder until a plug approximately 0.25" has been created. Excess sealing powder is wiped off with a KimWipe™ or paper towel. When all straws have been loaded and sealed, the weigh boat and any remaining sealing powder are discarded.

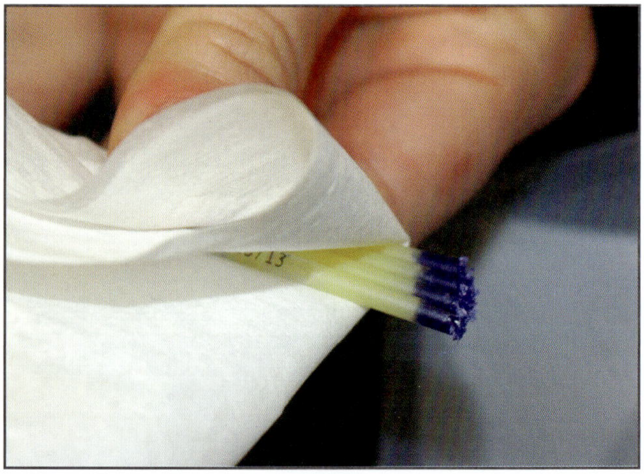

Figure 9-21 Wiping off excess sealing powder from straws using a KimWipe™.

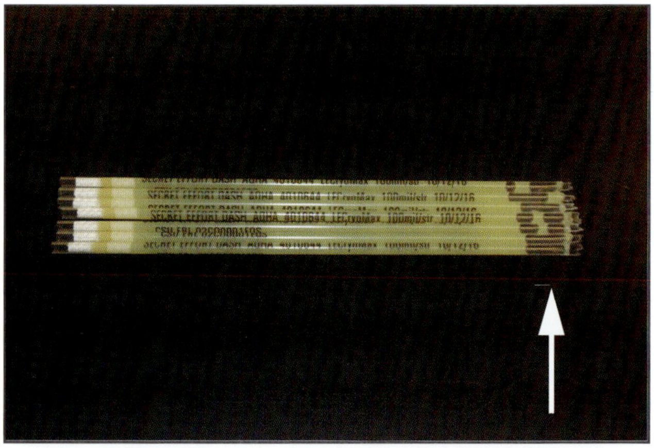

Figure 9-22 Loaded straws with the bubble at one end (arrow).

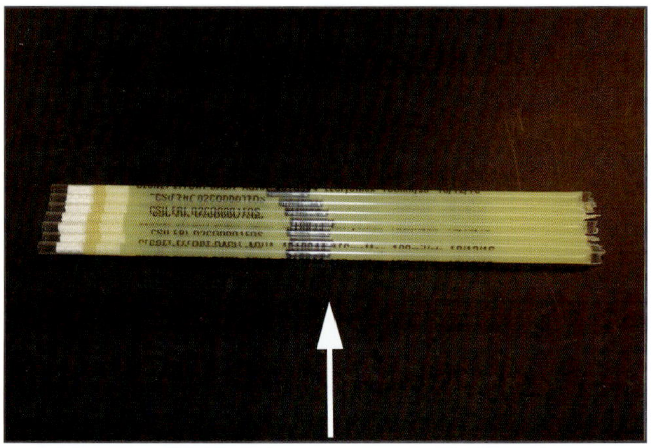

Figure 9-23 Loaded straws after the bubble has been flicked to the center (arrow).

22. Filled, sealed straws are loaded onto floating ARS Freezing Racks; each rack can hold up to 50 straws (Figure 9-24).
23. The loaded rack is placed into a refrigerator to slowly pre-cool the extended semen down to 5º to 8º C prior to cryopreservation (Figure 9-25).
    - Semen extended with CryoMax™ LE or E-Z Freezin® LE should be cooled for 30 minutes
    - Semen extended with CryoMax™ MFR5 or E-Z Freezin® MFR5 should be cooled for 60 minutes
24. After the appropriated pre-cooling period, the loaded floating racks are transferred from the refrigerator into a styrofoam container filled with approximately 2" of liquid nitrogen (Figure 9-26). The straws should be 3 cm above the surface of liquid nitrogen which will expose them to liquid nitrogen vapor. ARS Freezing Racks are designed to float so that straws are held at the correct distance above the level of liquid nitrogen.

Figure 9-24 Loading straws onto ARS Freezing Rack.

Figure 9-25 Placement of two loaded racks into a refrigerator for pre-cooling prior to cryopreservation.

Figure 9-26 Placement of a floating rack loaded with straws of extended semen into a Cooler Chest of liquid nitrogen.

Figure 9-27 Dumping straws from liquid nitrogen vapor directly into liquid nitrogen using pre-cooled semen freezing forceps.

25. Straws are allowed to remain suspended in liquid nitrogen vapor for 15 minutes or until the temperature reaches -120º C. After 15 minutes, the straws are plunged into the liquid nitrogen (Figure 9-27). To accomplish this task, the tip of Semen Freezing Forceps are submerged into liquid nitrogen for a sufficient time to allow for temperature equilibration (i.e. pre-cool the forceps). Once equilibrated, the tongs can be safely used to dump the straws off the rack directly into the liquid nitrogen.

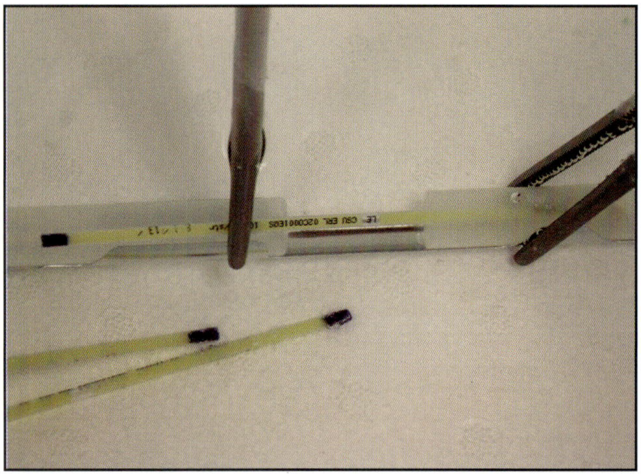

Figure 9-28 Placing straws into goblets attached to canes under liquid nitrogen. It is convenient to place one full breeding dose (8 straws) into each individual goblet.

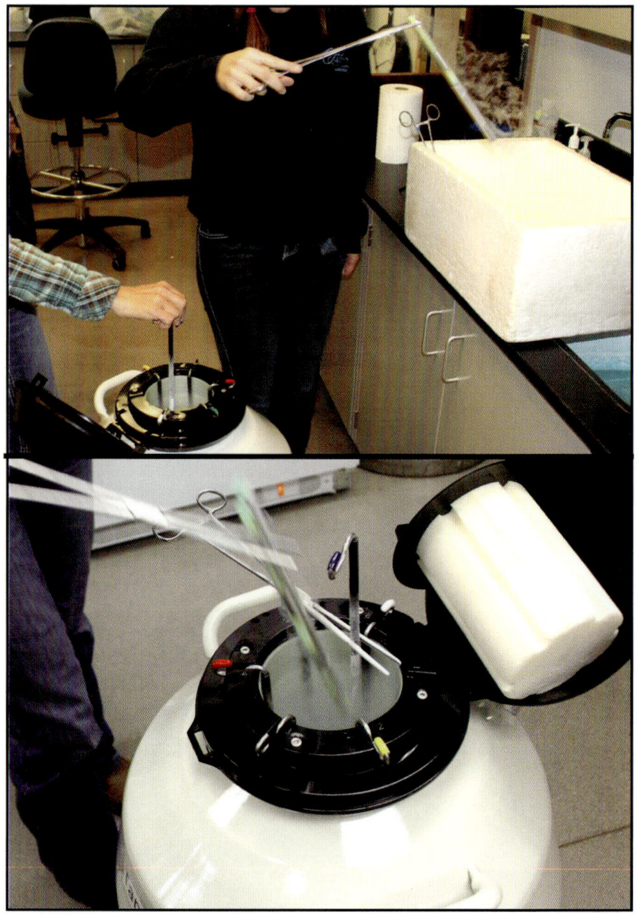

Figure 9-29 Transferring a cane/goblet of frozen semen from a styrofoam container (upper photo) into a canister within a Dewar of liquid nitrogen (lower photo).

26. Straws are allowed to remain in liquid nitrogen until they have reached final temperature (i.e. when the liquid nitrogen stops bubbling). This should only take a few seconds.

27. Straws are subsequently transferred into plastic goblets already fixed onto aluminum canes while still immersed in liquid nitrogen (Figure 9-28). The aluminum canes should be properly labeled to allow for easy identification, inventory control and removal. Different colored tabs, letters or numbers can be placed onto the end of the canes. The plastic goblets are snapped onto the canes. The open end of the goblets should face the tab on the cane, which will be stored upwards in the liquid nitrogen tank. The goblets and canes should be immersed in liquid nitrogen for sufficient time to be equilibrated to the temperature of LN2 before being loaded. Pre-cooled tongs are used to load the frozen straws into the goblets while keeping everything submerged in the liquid nitrogen.

28. Canes loaded with goblets of frozen semen straws are quickly moved from the styrofoam container of liquid nitrogen into a long-term storage tank (Storage Dewar) of liquid nitrogen (Figure 9-29). The transfer process should be accomplished as quickly as possible to avoid undue exposure to room temperature. Freezing forceps equilibrated in liquid nitrogen are used to firmly grasp the tab at the top of one aluminum cane. The cane is lifted so that the cane is vertical. The goblets will be filled with liquid nitrogen if this is performed properly. The cane is quickly placed into the desired canister within the Storage Dewar and the canister is lowered back down into the Dewar. The process is repeated until all of the canes are transferred into the Storage Dewar.

29. A record of the frozen straws should be created, including the number of straws per cane, the canister in which the canes are located, the storage tank identification number, the number of straws per breeding dose and the post-thaw motility data.

9.5 Post-Thaw Evaluation

- The post-thaw quality of spermatozoa should be evaluated on at least one straw after every freeze.
- Prepare a Thermoregulated Water Bath at 37° C (98.6° F).
- Without bringing the level of the cane above the frost-line of the storage Dewar, remove one 0.5 ml straw from the goblet and immediately submerge it into the water bath for 30 sec (Figure 9-30).
- Remove the straw from the water bath after 30 seconds and wipe the straw dry.
- Cut off one end of the straw and place the open end of the straw into a clean test tube. Cut the remaining end of the straw allowing the thawed semen to drain into the tube.
- Transfer a drop thawed semen onto a glass slide, place a cover slip over the semen drop and evaluate spermatozoal motility under a microscope immediately after thawing (0 time).
- Place the test tube in an incubator at 37° C (98.6° F) or into a warming block set on top of a slide warmer for 10 minutes.
- Evaluate semen a second time after 10 minutes of incubation. If there is any concern about the quality of a given sample, a second straw from that same freeze should be evaluated.
- For frozen-thawed semen, the percentage of progressively motile spermatozoa should be at least 30 % at 10 min after thawing to be considered commercially acceptable. If the percentage of progressively motile spermatozoa is less than 30 %, the straws from this freeze should be destroyed and another ejaculate obtained and processed in order to only maintain an inventory of high quality frozen semen. The decision to keep spermatozoa of lesser quality will depend upon such factors as stallion's age, ability to obtain and freeze additional ejaculates, value of his foals, the risk the owner is willing to assume to obtain pregnancies, and the availability of advanced assisted reproduction techniques, such as intracytoplasmic sperm injection (ICSI).

Figure 9-30 Thawing one straw of semen from a freeze for a post-thaw examination.

Figure 9-31 Storage tanks or Dewars of liquid nitrogen.

9.6 Containers for Storage and Shipment of Frozen Semen

Frozen semen may be stored indefinitely in tanks or Storage Dewars filled with liquid nitrogen at -196° C (-320° F). Storage Dewars are available in various sizes, with corresponding differences in holding capacity (i.e. number of straws), volume of liquid nitrogen, and working duration (Figure 9-31). It is important to check the level of liquid

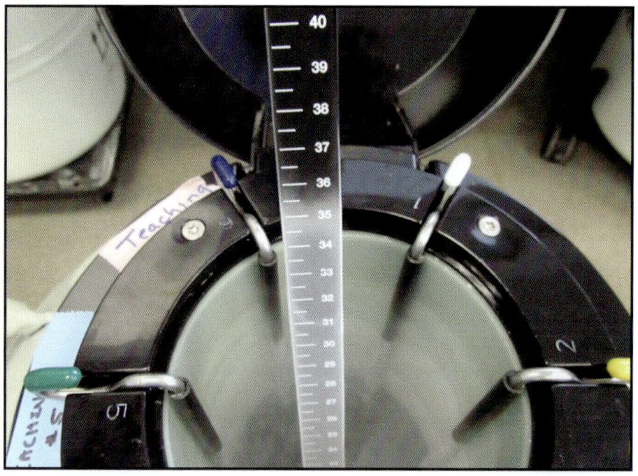

Figure 9-32 Measuring the level of liquid nitrogen in a Dewar using a calibrated plastic measuring stick. Note the frost line on the stick corresponding to the level of liquid nitrogen.

Figure 9-33 Vapor Shipper' or 'Dry Shipper' outside (left) and within a protective shipping carton (right). This shipper has a static holding time of 21 days.

nitrogen in the storage tanks on a regular basis. This may be accomplished by submerging a calibrated plastic measuring stick to the bottom of the tank, raising it and reading the liquid nitrogen level at the frost line that appears on the stick (Figure 9-32).

9.7 Shipment of Frozen Semen

Frozen semen is usually transported from one facility to another using a Vapor Shipper or 'Dry Shipper' (Figure 9-33). Vapor shippers are 'charged' by adding liquid nitrogen to the center and allowing the liquid nitrogen to be absorbed into the wall of the container. Original vapor shippers require approximately 24 hours to be fully 'charged' after which any remaining liquid nitrogen fluid is poured off. Newer vapor shippers are available that can be charged with liquid nitrogen within 2 hours. Straws of frozen semen are placed into a canister within the center of the unit which is now maintained at -196º C (-320º F) by liquid nitrogen vapor. The unit is therefore 'dry' (i.e. contains no liquid nitrogen fluid) when shipped.

The specific procedure for loading a Vapor (Dry) Shipper:

- Make sure the Vapor Shipper is 'charged' and ready to ship.
- Locate the record for the frozen semen to determine how many straws per dose and where they are stored in the Dewar.
- Fill a styrofoam container with about 2 inches of liquid nitrogen.
- Locate the cane(s) holding the desired straws in the Dewar without bringing the canisters above the frost line in the neck of the Dewar.
- Using long handled forceps that have already been precooled (i.e. dipped) in liquid nitrogen, firmly grasp the tab of the desired cane, and quickly (within 2 to 3 seconds) transfer the cane into the styrofoam container of liquid nitrogen.
- Gently lower the canister back into the Dewar and seat it in its place.
- Once the canes are in the liquid nitrogen bath within the styrofoam container, verify stallion name, date, and number of straws. Add or remove straws, depending on what needs to be shipped, as needed. Loaded all straws into goblets attached to an aluminum cane.
- Open the lid of the Vapor Shipper. With one hand, grasp the top of the cane with pre-cooled forceps, but keep the cane submerged in liquid nitrogen until the shipper canister is ready.
- With the other hand, grasp the canister within the Vapor Shipper, quickly raise it to the frost line, and drop the cane containing the frozen semen into place. This transfer process should also only take 2 to 3 seconds.
- Lower the canister into place, and replace the lid of the Vapor Shipper.
- Place the Vapor Shipper into the Protective Shipping Carton/Container along with the appropriate paperwork related to the frozen semen.

- Update the frozen semen storage log confirming the number of straws of frozen semen removed from the Dewar and where they were sent and the mare intended to be bred.
- Close the lid of the storage Dewar if not already done.

Vapor shippers may be transported by commercial overnight courier service (i.e. Federal Express or United Parcel Service) or by counter-to-counter commercial airline service. The straws of frozen semen should be removed and placed into storage Dewars of liquid nitrogen as soon as possible upon arrival at the new facility. In general, vapor shippers are to be returned to the farm or facility of origin immediately for subsequent reuse.

The amount of semen (i.e. number of straws or number of breeding doses) shipped for each mare to be bred is dependent on an agreement between the stallion owner and the mare owner, breeding manager and/or farm veterinarian. There is no industry standard regarding insemination dose or breeding frequency. Frozen semen may be bought, sold, and shipped by the straw or by the breeding dose, or semen may be marketed and sold with or without a pregnancy or live foal guarantee.

International shipment from the United States requires that semen be collected, processed, and frozen at a USDA approved collection center. Individual countries (i.e. Australia) or geo-political units (i.e. European Union) have their own regulations regarding import of frozen semen. Therefore, it is critical that these regulations be fully understood prior to freezing. Specialized blood tests, cultures, and a quarantine period are often required. The complete regulations and requirements can be accessed at:

http://www.aphis.usda.gov/regulations/vs/iregs/animals/

9.8 Thawing Frozen Semen

It is critical that straws of frozen semen be correctly identified prior to thawing. Lift the appropriate canister high enough in the tank to gain access to the correct canes. Keep all semen below the frost line within the neck of the tank. If necessary, straws may be removed from the Dewar and quickly placed in a shallow bath of liquid nitrogen to allow for proper identification.

It is recommended that frozen semen be thawed according to the guidelines provided by the facility or individual that initially froze the semen. In general, semen frozen in 0.5 ml straws may be thawed by placement into a 37º C Thermoregulated Water Bath for 30 seconds. Macro straws (5.0 mls) are usually thawed in a water bath at 50º C for 45 seconds. The outside of the straws are dried with a paper towel and the colored plugs of straw sealant are cut off with scissors. The open end of the straws is placed into a warmed test tube and the cotton plug at the other end is subsequently cut off with scissors (Figure 9-34). Semen is then allowed to drain into the warmed test tube.

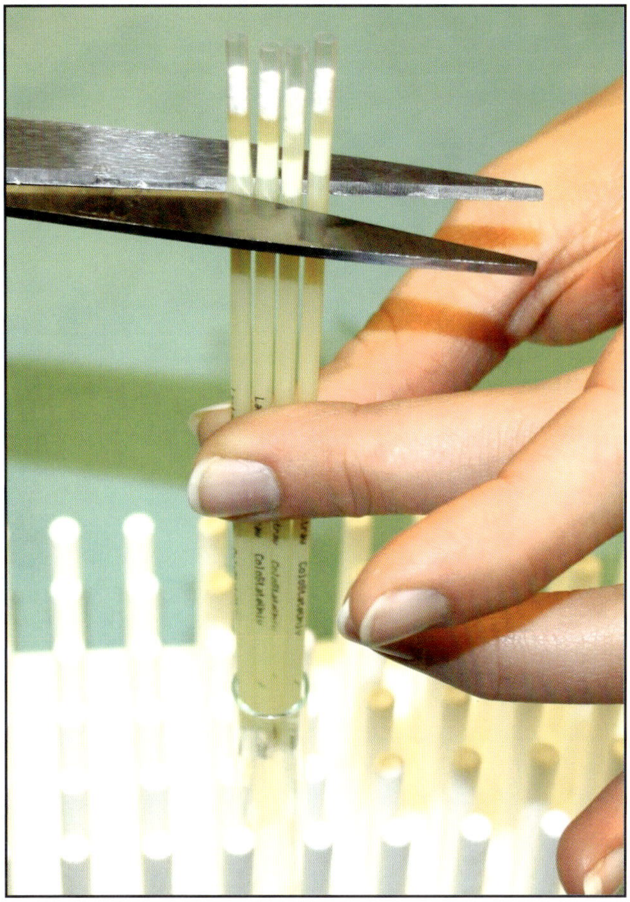

Figure 9-34 Cutting the ends off 0.5 ml straws so that thawed semen can run into a warmed glass vial.

Semen from the test tube is drawn up into an insemination pipette (Figure 9-35). Sufficient semen usually remains within the bottom of the test tube to evaluate post-thaw motility. The test tube is placed in an incubator at 37º C for 10 minutes prior to evaluation of sperm motility.

An alternative technique that is useful when inseminating a mare with a very limited number of straws (i.e. 1 to 4 straws) is to utilize a system that allows

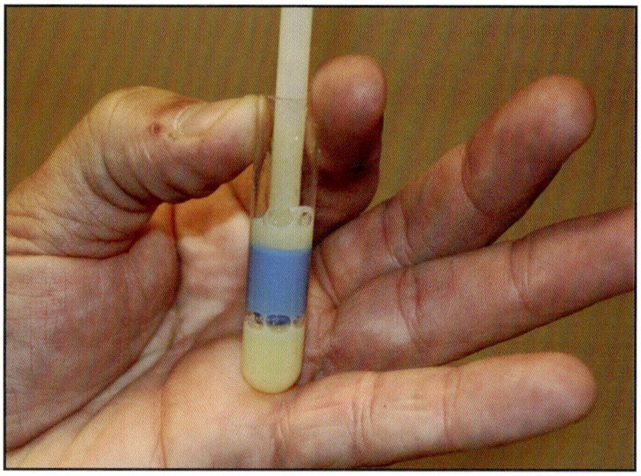

Figure 9-35 Drawing up thawed semen into an insemination pipette.

thawed straws to be loaded directly into the insemination pipette (Figure 9-36). The appropriate number of individual straws are thawed as previously described and the colored plug of sealant is snipped off with scissors. The insemination pipette is passed through the cervix and positioned within the uterus (i.e. uterine body or tip of the correct uterine horn). One straw is loaded onto a special stylet (Figure 9-37) and passed down the length of the pipette. Once seated against the end of the pipette, the stylet is advanced pushing the cotton plug to the tip which will fully discharge the semen out of the end of the pipette. The pipette is maintained within the uterus while the stylet is withdrawn, the dispensed straw affixed to the stylet removed (Figure 9-38) and the next straw loaded. The process is repeated until all of the thawed straws have been inseminated.

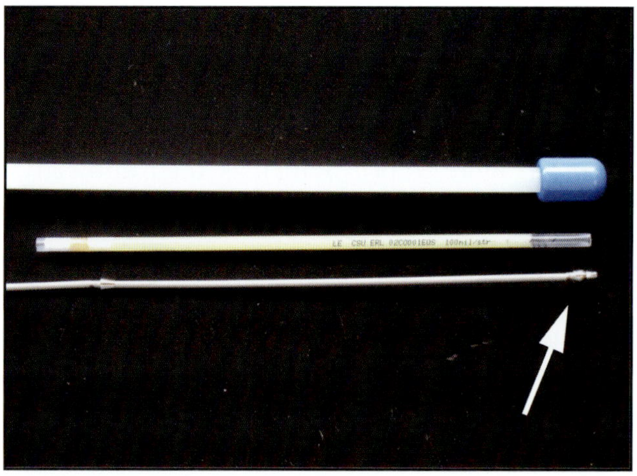

Figure 9-36 Insemination pipette with stylet system. The sealant plug has been removed from a 0.5 ml straw of frozen stallion semen. Note the bulb of the stainless steel stylet (arrow).

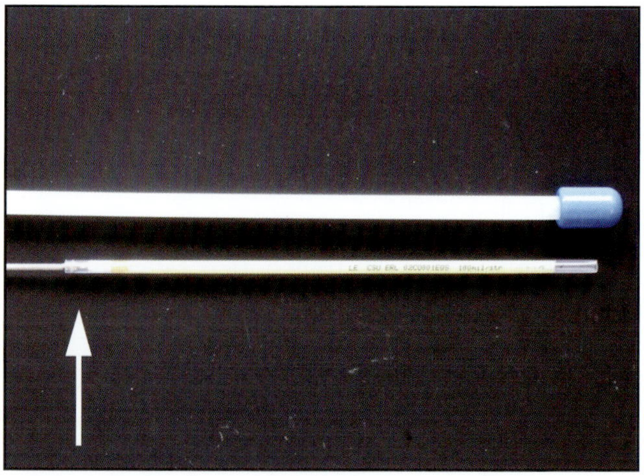

Figure 9-37 The 0.5 ml straw has been loaded onto the stylet. The bulb of the stylet (arrow) is within the straw adjacent to the cotton plug.

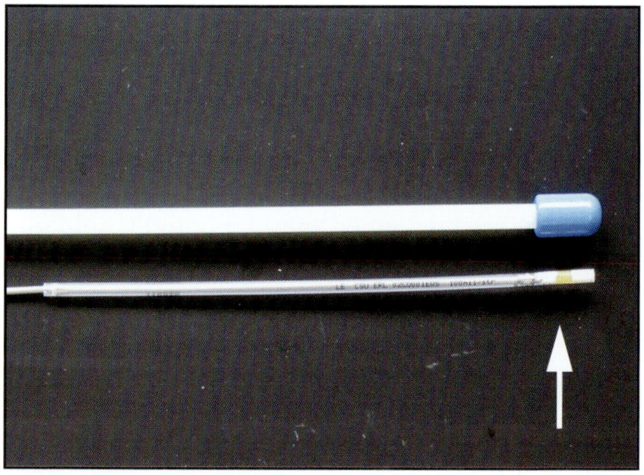

Figure 9-38 Advancement of the stylet pushes the cotton plug distally expelling the semen out of the end of the pipette. Note the position of the bulb (arrow) and cotton plug after advancement of the stylet during insemination.

9.9 Insemination of Mares with Frozen Semen

The frozen-thawed semen in the insemination pipette may be deposited into the body of the uterus using a traditional insemination technique. Alternatively, semen may be deposited at the tip of the uterine horn near the utero-tubular junction on the side of the pre-ovulatory follicle using a 'deep-horn' technique. Pregnancy rates are highest if mares are bred with frozen semen as close to ovulation as possible. In general, the goal is to inseminate within 8 to 12 hours prior to ovulation and/or within 6 hours after ovulation. As a consequence, mare management (i.e. the number of ultrasound examinations per day) usually must be increased to accomplish this goal.

A timed insemination protocol may be utilized following administration of an ovulation inducing agent such as human chorionic gonadotropin or a GnRH agonist such as deslorelin acetate to yield a predictable ovulation. If two doses of frozen semen are available, it is recommended to inseminate the mare with one dose within 8 to 12 hours prior to the anticipated ovulation and inseminate the second dose immediately after ovulation is detected. However, if only one dose of frozen semen is available, it is recommended that the mare be inseminated immediately after ovulation has been confirmed.

Clinical Comment

Administration of a GnRH agonist such as deslorelin or histrelin to a mare in estrus with a large follicle and uterine edema should induce ovulation in approximately 40 hours. Consequently, administration of the hormone at 8:00 pm should result in a timed ovulation at 12:00 (noon) 40 hours later. However, not all mares ovulate at 40 hours; some ovulate earlier and some ovulate later. Consequently, it is still recommended that mares be examined every 6 hours after GnRH agonist administration to monitor follicle status and detect ovulation.Induction of a timed ovulation is very helpful in the management of mares being bred with either a dose of frozen-thawed semen both pre- and post-ovulation or bred with a single dose of frozen thawed semen (post-ovulation only).

Chapter 10 Reproductive Problems in the Stallion

Stallions may exhibit a variety of problems that can adversely affect their reproductive performance or fertility. Some issues may be overcome by modifications of stallion management, breeding schedule, or semen collection/processing procedures, depending on the breed and owner/trainer compliance.

A list of some of the more common and less common reproductive problems in stallions is presented in the table below.

Table 10-1 Reproductive Problems in the Stallion

Common Reproductive Problems	Less Common Reproductive Problems
Behavior	**Behavior**
Aggressive breeding behavior	Ejaculatory dysfunction
Poor libido	
Testes/Epididymides/Scrotum	**Testes/Epididymides/Scrotum**
Cryptorchidism	Epididymitis
Testicular degeneration	Hydrocele
	Hematocele
	Inguinal/scrotal hernia
	Neoplasia (teratoma, seminoma, Leydig cell tumor, Sertoli cell tumor)
	Orchitis
	Spermiostasis or epididymal storage dysfunction ('sperm accumulator')
	Torsion of the spermatic cord
Accessory Sex Glands	**Accessory Sex Glands**
	Persistent infection with EAV
	Plugged or blocked ampullae
	Seminal vesiculitis
Penis and Urethra	**Penis and Urethra**
Smegma accumulation	Coital exanthema (EHV-3)
	Contagious equine metritis (CEM)
	Cutaneous habronemiasis
	Neoplasia (sarcoid, squamous cell carcinoma, melanoma)
	Penile dysfunction (phimosis, paraphimosis, and priapism)
	Trauma (laceration, hematoma)
	Urethral rent
Semen/Sperm	**Semen/Sperm**
Low sperm concentration	Abnormal acrosome
Poor sperm motility	Hemospermia
Sperm morphological abnormalities	Pyospermia
	Sperm chromatin abnormality
	Urospermia
Miscellaneous	**Miscellaneous**
	Chromosomal abnormalities
	Developmental abnormalities (i.e. male pseudohermaphroditism)

10.1 Poor Libido

Stallions may exhibit poor libido when teased to a mare in estrus. The reduced libido may be a result of adverse experiences, such as stallions disciplined for exhibiting sexual interest in mares during performance or training; showing spontaneous erection or masturbation; or mishandled during breeding under halter. In other cases the lower interest may be due to adverse environmental conditions, such as excessive heat, humidity or cold, or a preference for mares of a specific color, size, behavior, or musculoskeletal pain, etc. Stallions used primarily for pasture breeding may be somewhat reserved when exposed to a sedated, hobbled and twitched mare in a breeding shed.

Affected stallions may show little to no interest or fail to gain an erection when presented to a mare in heat. Some stallions may express anxiety or viciousness when allowed to interact with an estrual mare. Management options include reconditioning training by repeated and patient exposure to a mare in heat. Care should be taken to minimize negative reinforcement (i.e. reprimands) when handling such a stallion. In some cases simply a change in the person handling the stallion may be effective.

Medical therapies that may be beneficial in some stallions to relieve anxiety or enhance libido include diazepam, gonadotropin releasing hormone, aqueous testosterone, phenylbutazone and/or xylazine.

10.2 Ejaculatory Dysfunction

Stallions with ejaculatory dysfunction typically have good libido, ability to gain an erection, can mount a mare or breeding phantom, and exhibit normal copulatory behavior. Unfortunately, ejaculation of semen does not occur, even after multiple mounting attempts. Ejaculatory dysfunction may be due to a physiological, psychological or pathological problem.

Ejaculatory failure should be differentiated from azoospermia, bilateral blocked ampullae and retrograde ejaculation, all of which will result an absence of spermatozoa in the collection container after an apparent ejaculation. Visual observation of 'tail flagging' and manual detection of urethral pulsations at the base of the penis are suggestive of ejaculation.

Measurement of alkaline phosphatase (AP) levels in fluid recovered during a collection attempt can be used to determine if the tubular tract is patent (i.e. vas deferens and ampullae) and if fluid was contributed from the testes and epididymides. High levels of AP in the seminal fluid (i.e. > 1,000 U/L) indicate a contribution from the testes and epididymides (with or without sperm present). In contrast, low AP levels in recovered fluid (i.e. < 100 U/L) indicate either absence of ejaculation or bilateral blockage of the vas deferens or ampullae. Transrectal palpation and ultrasonography of the internal genitalia may be helpful to detect the presence of a blockage. Retrograde ejaculation can be diagnosed by catheterization of the urinary bladder after an apparent ejaculation without spermatozoa in the collection cup.

Medical treatment options for ejaculatory dysfunction depend on the primary cause. Imipramine hydrochloride can be administered to lower the ejaculation threshold for stallions in either a live cover or artificial insemination program. A combination of imipramine hydrochloride followed by xylazine hydrochloride may be successful in inducing passive emission of semen or 'chemical ejaculation' for stallions in an AI program.

Additional management considerations for stallions with ejaculatory issues include changing the type of artificial vagina, altering the temperature and pressure within the AV, application of manual pressure or stimulation to the glans penis and/or application

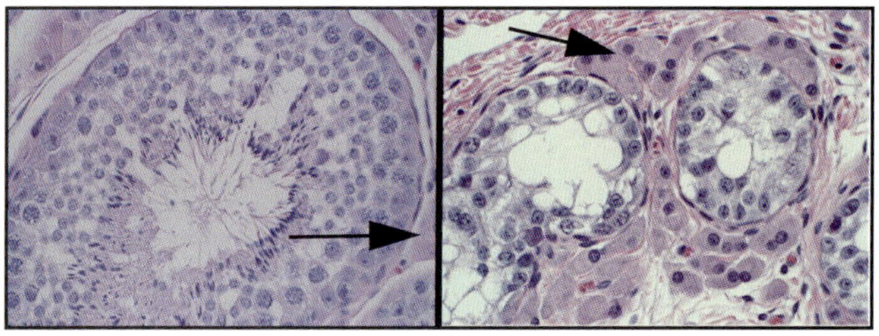

Figure 10-1 Histology of a normal testis (left) and a cryptorchid testis (right). Note the presence of mature spermatids in the normal testis and the absence of spermatids in the cryptorchid testis. Leydig cells are present outside of the seminiferous tubules in both testes (arrows).

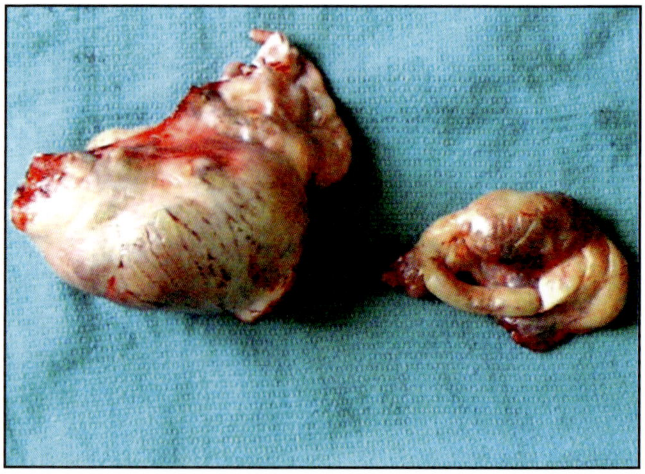

Figure 10-2 Normal (left) and cryptorchid testis (right) surgically removed from a unilaterally cryptorchid stallion.

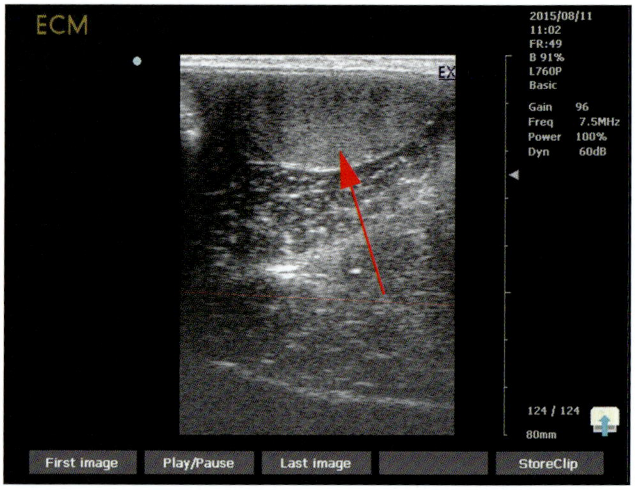

Figure 10-3 Ultrasound image of a cryptorchid testis (arrow).

of a hot wet compress to the base of the penis during a collection attempt.

10.3 Cryptorchidism

A stallion is considered to be a cryptorchid if one or both testes are not fully descended into the scrotum. Cryptorchid testes may be located outside of the inguinal canal, within the inguinal canal or inside of the abdominal cavity anywhere from the internal inguinal ring to adjacent to the kidneys. Failure of one or both testes to descend into the scrotum may be due to genetic predisposition, insufficient androgen stimulation or other unknown factors.

Testes of colts begin to pass through the inguinal canal between month 9 and 10 of fetal development and are usually fully descended into the scrotum between 30 days before to 10 days after birth in the normal colt. Although documentation is limited, inguinal retained testes have been reported to enter the scrotum in some individual horses by 2 to 3 years of age or more.

Cryptorchid testes are incapable of producing sperm due to the elevated temperature of the retained testes (Figure 10-1). Consequently, a stallion would be sterile if both testes are retained. Libido and aggressive male behavior may be exhibited by cryptorchid stallions since testosterone is still produced by the retained testes.

Stallions with one retained testis and one scrotal testis are usually fertile since an adequate number of motile sperm is produced by the descended testis to get mares pregnant. A cryptorchid testis is usually significantly smaller than the normal scrotal testis (Figure 10-2).

Accurate diagnosis of cryptorchidism is not difficult if the horse has one owner and if adequate medical records have been maintained. However, it may be less obvious if a horse purchased at auction as a gelding begins to show stallion-like behavior when exposed to mares at his new home. A veterinary examination may be required to determine if the horse is a true gelding or a bilateral cryptorchid. The horse may be sedated to allow for a more thorough examination of the external inguinal region. Often inguinal retained testes of 'high flankers' are easier to detect when the horse is more relaxed after sedation. A transrectal palpation may be performed in order to detect the presence of abdominally retained testes (Figure 10-3). Ultrasound examination of the external inguinal region and transabdominal ultrasound in the flank region may also be useful to determine the location of retained testes.

Hormonal testing may be indicated if testes cannot be located by palpation or ultrasound examination in a gelding exhibiting stallion-like behavior. Analysis of testosterone levels in a single blood sample is often sufficient to document the presence or absence of testicular tissue. Geldings have very low blood testosterone levels, whereas cryptorchid stallions have moderately elevated levels and intact stallions have very high testosterone levels. If testosterone level in a single sample is not diagnostic, an hCG-stimulation test may be performed. A blood sample is collected prior to and 1 to 2 hours after intravenous administration of 10,000 IU of human chorionic gonadotropin (hCG). If one or more testes are present, the LH-like biological activity of the hCG will cause an increase in testosterone levels in the second sample as compared to the first sample (Table 10-2).

Table 10-2 Testosterone levels in intact stallions, cryptorchid stallions and geldings prior to and after administration of hCG.

Horse	Testosterone (pg/ml)	
	Pre-hCG	Post-hCG
Gelding	< 100	No change
Cryptorchid	> 100	Increase
Intact Stallion	> 500	Increase

Estrogen levels may also be measured to help differentiate between cryptorchid stallions and geldings three or more years of age. Estrogen testing for cryptorchidism is not considered to be of diagnostic value in young horses.

It has recently been reported that serum concentrations of anti-Müllerian hormone (AMH) is higher in intact and cryptorchid stallions than in geldings.

Medical treatment (i.e. hCG or GnRH administration) to stimulate descent of retained testes in horses is controversial in regards to both effectiveness and ethical considerations. Although sporadic anecdotal reports suggest that hormone administration may have aided testicular descent in some horses, a majority opinion is that medical treatment is not effective.

It is generally recommended that cryptorchid colts and stallions be castrated. Castration should eliminate undesired aggressive or stallion-like behaviors as well as prevent potential adverse medical conditions associated with the presence of cryptorchid testes, such as testicular neoplasia and torsion of the spermatic cord.

10.4 Testicular Degeneration

Testicular degeneration (TD) refers to the process of deterioration of the structure and function of the testes which may result in decreased fertility. Testicular degeneration may be caused by an acute insult such as trauma, excessive heat or cold, toxins, etc. or may be associated with a slowly progressive degeneration of unknown origin often associated with advanced age.

Clinical signs associated with age-related testicular degeneration usually begin with decreased sperm output due to reduced spermatogenic efficiency. Spermatogenic efficiency (sperm produced per cc of testis) can be determined by comparing actual daily sperm output (DSP) to predicted daily sperm production (DSP) based on testicular measurements. A decrease occurs in the percentage of morphologically normal and progressively motile spermatozoa in the ejaculate along with a decrease in the pregnancy rate per cycle. Serum concentrations of estrogen, testosterone and inhibin decline, along with a decrease in the testosterone response to administration of GnRH. Finally, an increase in the percentage of sperm with chromatin defects, a decrease in testicular size and an increase in blood levels of FSH and LH are detected.

The testes may become softer as the condition progresses, with end-stage testicular degeneration often associated with small firm testes. An increase in the number of immature round spermatogenic cells may be present in the ejaculate in some cases of acute testicular degeneration. Testicular biopsy may provide for a definitive diagnosis of TD, but is not usually performed in valuable breeding stallions and is often not necessary to obtain a clinical diagnosis.

Identification and removal of the inciting cause may allow for restoration of testicular function and resumption of fertility in stallions affected by acute TD of known origin. Unfortunately, there are no well-substantiated treatment options for idiopathic testicular degeneration. The number of progressively motile, morphologically normal spermatozoa in the ejaculate at daily sperm output (DSO) should be determined and mare book size adjusted accordingly. Enhanced breeding management, incorporation of sperm concentration and/or separation techniques, deep horn insemination and other procedures may result in adequate pregnancy rates per cycle and per season. Assisted reproduction procedures such as intracytoplasmic sperm injection (ICSI) may be a final option. Eventually stallions with advanced testicular degeneration are retired from breeding.

10.5 Testicular Tumors

The most common neoplasia of the testis is the seminoma, which is a tumor of germ cell origin. Other primary testicular tumors, such as Leydig cell tumors or Sertoli cell tumors are less common.

A slowly progressive, non-painful enlargement of one testis is the predominant clinical sign (Figure 10-4). Manual palpation and ultrasonography of the scrotum and scrotal contents can be used to differentiate an increase in testicular mass from other causes of scrotal enlargement such as a hydrocele, hematocele or inguinal hernia.

Local and progressive extension of the tumor up the spermatic cord is not uncommon with Sertoli cell tumors in the stallion. Metastasis is not common, however. A definitive diagnosis can be made by biopsy or fine needle aspiration *in situ*. However, in most instances a histopathological diagnosis is made after surgical removal of the affected testis.

Treatment is removal of the affected testis.

10.6 Torsion of the Spermatic Cord ('Testicular Torsion')

Rotation or torsion of the spermatic cord 180° or less does not cause discomfort or clinical issues with sperm production or fertility. Although not common, a spermatic cord torsion of 180° may occasionally be detected during a routine examination of a normal stallion. In contrast, torsions of greater than 360° lead to compromised blood flow, decreased testicular function and profound pain. Complications include ischemic damage and eventually gangrene of the associate testis.

Clinical signs associated with torsion of the spermatic cord include acute colic and swelling of the scrotum. Torsion of the spermatic cord occur most commonly after exercise or breeding.

Diagnosis is made by manual palpation of the scrotum, identification of location of the tail of the epididymis and evidence of an enlarged cord. Ultrasound examination can be performed to rule out other causes of unilateral scrotal enlargement such as an inguinal or scrotal hernia.

Treatment is surgical removal of the affected testis. In most instances, diagnosis and surgical intervention is not rapid enough to salvage the affected testis.

10.7 Spermiostasis or Sperm Accumulation

Spermatozoa of some stallions accumulate in the epididymis, vas deferens and/or ampullae. A clinical syndrome of spermiostasis or 'sperm accumulation' has been described in stallions that exhibit a decrease in sperm motility in the absence of ejaculation (i.e. mating or collection) over a few days. Affected stallions may have an ejaculate with high sperm concentration and low motility. Initially, a high percentage of sperm will have morphological defects, including detached heads (Figure 10-5). The percentage of abnormal sperm will decrease over time as the stallion is collected on a regular basis.

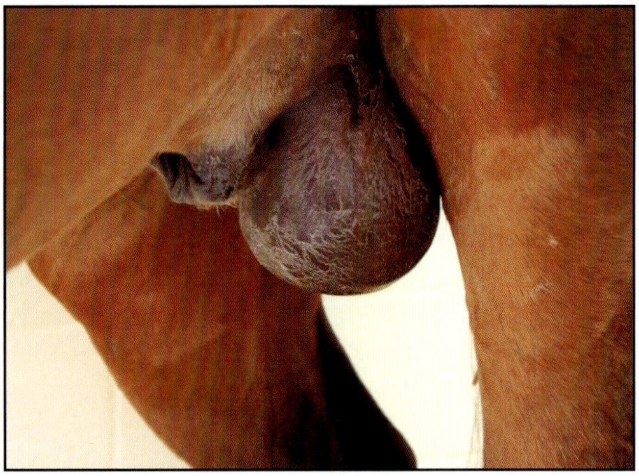

***Figure 10-4** Enlarged testis in a stallion secondary to a seminoma.*

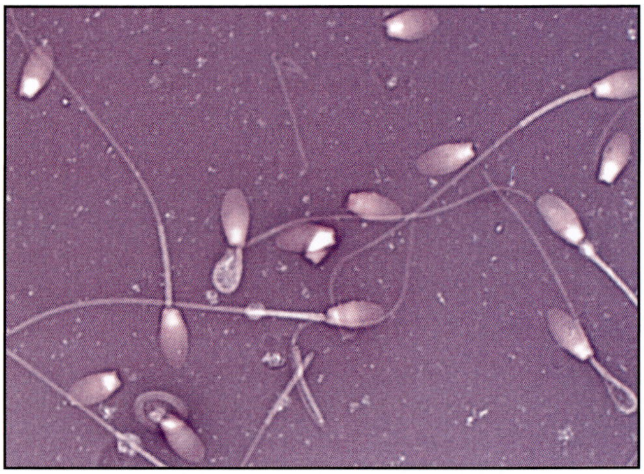

***Figure 10-5** Spermatozoa from a stallion affected by spermiostasis. Note the high percentage of detached heads.*

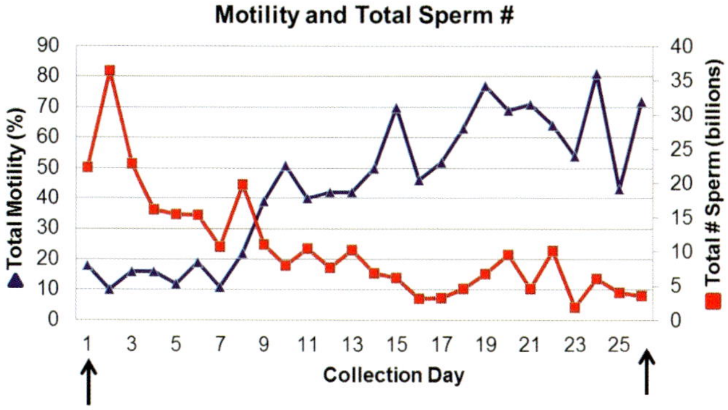

Figure 10-6 Graph of total sperm numbers and sperm motility from a stallion affected by spermiostasis.

Sperm accumulation syndrome may be a consequence of an abnormality in the sperm transport system. However, a defect in the epididymis may also be present as a rapid decline in sperm motility has been noted in some stallions with even a short duration (3 to 4 days) of sexual abstinence. In these stallions, the seminal plasma or epididymal environment may be responsible for the decreased motility. The role of 'toxic seminal plasma' in affected stallions has not been evaluated sufficiently.

Management of stallions with spermiostasis would include frequent breeding or semen collection to 'clean-out' dead sperm from the epididymides. It may take 5 to 10 days or more of repeated semen collections (1 to 3 collections per day) to remove dead accumulated spermatozoa from affected stallions, which would essentially take the stallion down to daily sperm output (DSO) (Figure 10-6). Subsequent semen analysis would typically show a pattern of normal sperm concentration, moderate progressive motility, and a majority of spermatozoa with normal morphology (i.e. very few detached heads).

Stallions affected by 'sperm accumulation' would have poor fertility potential if bred infrequently. Affected stallions could do well in a pasture breeding scheme as frequent natural mating would potentially keep the stallion cleaned out. Semen from affected stallions could also be collected and frozen for future use once the stallion has been cleaned out.

10.8 Blocked or Plugged Ampullae

The ductus deferens (vas deferens) and/or ampullae may become occluded with dead spermatozoa. Blockage of the ductus deferens may be a more severe consequence of abnormal sperm transport as described above for stallions with sperm accumulation.

Affected stallions appear to ejaculate (i.e. flag their tail, exhibit urethral pulsations, show behavioral characteristics, etc.), but no spermatozoa are present in the ejaculate if the condition is bilateral. Often stallions with bilateral blocked ampullae present with a history of infertility (pasture breeding stallions or stallions bred in hand without semen collection or evaluation) or azoospermia as determined by semen collection or evaluation of a dismount sample following a live cover.

A diagnosis of blocked ampullae can be made after a combination of tests to rule out other potential causes of azoospermia, which include advanced testicular degeneration, retrograde ejaculation and ejaculation failure. Behavior of the stallion, flagging of the tail flagging, and presence of urethral pulsations should all be monitored during semen collection to determine if physiological ejaculation actually occurred.

A fluid sample from the collection vessel should be examined for presence of spermatozoa and analyzed for concentrations of alkaline phosphatase (AP) (Table 10-3). The primary sources of alkaline phosphatase in semen are the testes and epididymides. Seminal plasma alkaline phosphatase activity < 100 U/L indicates failure of testicular and/or epididymal secretions to exit the penis. Therefore, an ejaculate with no sperm and low alkaline phosphatase activity suggests either ejaculation failure or bilateral blockage. Levels > 1000 U/L indicate a contribution of the testes and/or epididymides to the fluid collected. An ejaculate with no sperm and high AP levels suggest testicular dysfunction.

Table 10-3 Interpretation of alkaline phosphatase levels in semen from stallions.

Alkaline Phosphatase (U/L)	Interpretation
< 100	Failure of ejaculation or bilateral blockage
> 1000	Normal ejaculation

Palpation and ultrasonography of the internal genitalia should be performed on stallions suspected of bilateral blockage. Ideally, the stallion should be sedated, restrained (i.e. in examination stocks) and administered N-butylscopolammonium (Buscopan®) to relax the smooth muscle of the rectum and facilitate a more complete and safe evaluation. The normal ampullae are approximately 1 to 2 cm in diameter with a narrow lumen visible on transrectal ultrasound examination. Ampullae plugged with spermatozoa are markedly enlarged with a dilated lumen filled with echogenic fluid.

Treatment to unblock the ampullae include repeated semen collection attempts, manual massage of the ampullae during palpation per rectum, and administration of oxytocin to induce contraction of the smooth muscle of the ampullae. In a majority of cases, the sperm blockage will eventually be released, resulting in ejaculation of a very large number of dead non-motile spermatozoa with a high proportion of detached heads. Subsequent collections will eventually result in an increase in sperm motility and a decrease in the percentage of sperm with morphological abnormalities.

10.9 Seminal Vesiculitis

Bacterial infection of one or (rarely) both seminal vesicles occasionally occurs in stallions and may result in reduced fertility and uterine infections in mares bred or inseminated. *Pseudomonas aeruginosa* and *Klebsiella pneumoniae* are the most common organisms associated with seminal vesiculitis in stallions.

There are usually no external clinical signs in a stallion with infected seminal vesicles. Semen evaluation will reveal high numbers of white blood cells (PMNs) in semen and blood may be present in the gel fraction of the semen. Bacterial culture is indicated to determine the organism involved and the antimicrobial susceptibility pattern. Palpation and ultrasound examination per rectum will often reveal unilateral or bilateral enlargement of the seminal vesicle(s).

Treatment involves lavage using an endoscope passed proximally up the urethra to the level of the seminal colliculus and insertion of a cannula into the affected seminal vesicle. Antibiotics may be infused into the seminal vesicle(s) after the lavage procedure. Systemic antibiotics may have reduced efficacy due to low rate of diffusion into the affected structure. Appropriate antibiotics may be added to semen collected from the stallion to prevent infection in mares to be inseminated.

10.10 Hemospermia

Stallions may bleed during semen collection or during a live cover mating (Figure 10-7). A small laceration sustained during mating by friction against tail hairs of the mare may be present on the end of the glans penis or distal urethral process. Active bleeding from these sites may not be evident unless a full erection is present. Bleeding may also be associated with the presence of cutaneous habronemiasis lesions ('summer sores') or squamous cell carcinoma lesions.

Another site of bleeding during mating or semen collection is from a rent or tear in the proximal urethra. The presence of a urethral rent may be detected during videoendoscopic examination of the urethra (Figure 10-8). The stallion is sedated (i.e. a combination of detomidine hydrochloride and butorphanol tartrate) and the scope passed

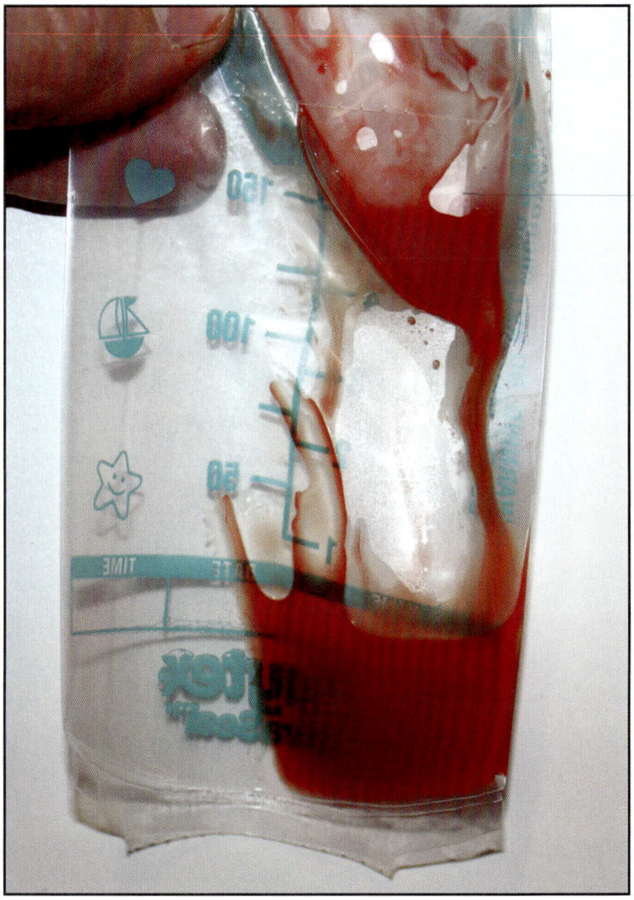

Figure 10-7 Blood in the ejaculate from a stallion with a urethral rent.

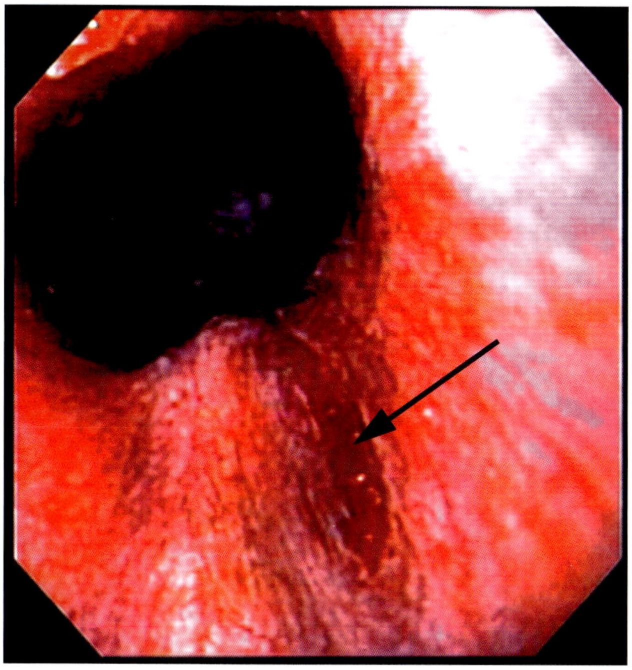

Figure 10-8 Videoendoscopic image of a urethral rent in a stallion with hemospermia (arrow).

proximally up the urethra. The rent is usually located approximately 6 to 10 cm distal to the seminal colliculus.

Management of hemospermia due to a urethral rent includes a prolonged period of sexual rest (i.e. 6 to 12 months) and potentially a perineal urethrotomy or similar surgical procedure. A perineal urethrotomy involves an incision into the urethra below the perineal region, which would allow urine to bypass the distal aspect of the penis and relieve pressure on the proximal urethral lesion.

A fourth potential site of blood loss from the penis of a stallion during mating is the seminal vesicles. Inflammation of the seminal vesicles (seminal vesiculitis), due to bacterial infection may result in the presence of blood within the gel fraction of the ejaculate.

Stallions that bleed during ejaculation generally have reduced fertility. An accurate diagnosis of the source of blood is important as the location and cause of the bleeding will determine the optimal course of management or therapy as well as the prognosis for recovery.

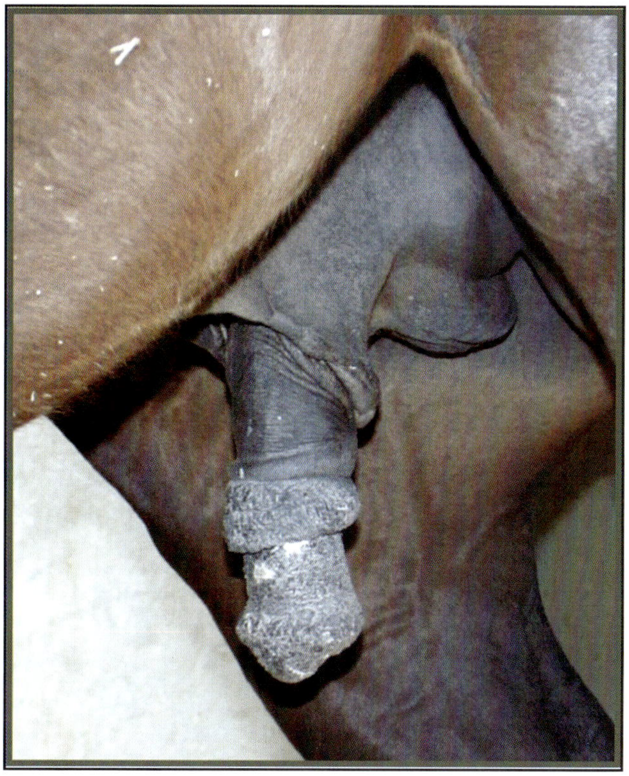

Figure 10-9 Penis of a stallion with paraphimosis secondary to colitis.

10.11 Penile Paralysis (Paraphimosis)

Flaccid paralysis of the penis can be a complication of severe penile injury, secondary to priapism (persistent penile erection), neurologic disease (i.e. rabies, EHV-1, spinal injuries), edema of purpura hemorrhagica, EVA, EIA and administration of certain phenothiazine-type tranquilizers (i.e. acepromazine). Stallions with acute paraphimosis may recover completely, depending on the cause. However, stallions with chronic paraphimosis have a poor prognosis for future fertility.

Diagnosis is made by observing prolapse of the penis and an inability to retract the penis into the prepuce (Figure 10-9). Treatment or management is dependent on the severity and duration of the paraphimosis. Underlying medical conditions that may be associated with the condition should be addressed immediately. Topical ointments may be applied to the penis and the penis may be placed in a sling to avoid further complications.

Chemical ejaculation may be required to obtain semen from the stallion if no progress is made in resolving the paraphimosis.

10.12 Coital Exanthema (EHV-3)

Equine herpesvirus 3 (coital exanthema) virus is transmitted primarily by live cover mating, but can be spread by fomites (i.e. during reproductive evaluations or artificial insemination). The virus is species specific and will not affect humans. The incubation period is approximately 6 to 10 days.

The virus will not adversely affect the ability of a mare to conceive and will not result in embryonic loss or abortion. The primary issue for the mare or stallion is local pain or discomfort.

A presumptive diagnosis can be made based on observance of numerous small, raised reddened vesicular blisters on penis of a stallion or vulva of a mare. Viral shedding is highest when active vesicles are present. The lesions resolve within 2 to 3 weeks, leaving depigmented white plaques. Laboratory confirmation of EHV-3 infection can be made by viral culture and/or PCR analysis.

Sexual rest is indicated as the virus is highly contagious to horses. Topical ointments may be applied to decrease secondary bacterial infections.

10.13 Equine Viral Arteritis (EVA)

Exposure of unvaccinated adult stallions to equine arteritis virus can lead to persistent infection (i.e. a carrier state) in approximately 30 to 60 % of horses. The virus localizes in accessory sex glands and is shed in the semen of carrier stallions.

Initial acquisition of the virus by a stallion is likely to be via respiratory route (i.e. aerosolized virus or direct horse-to-horse contact with a mare transiently shedding the virus). The virus may be subsequently be transmitted from the stallion to mares following insemination with fresh, cooled or frozen semen as well as live cover.

Clinical signs associated with acute infections include fever, anorexia, depression, nasal discharge, conjunctivitis, dependent edema and skin rash. Laboratory diagnosis includes serology for presence of antibodies, virus isolation and PCR analysis. A positive serology test indicates either exposure to the virus or that the stallion has been vaccinated. Seropositive horses should have semen analyzed for presence of virus.

There is no 100 % effective treatment to completely eliminate virus from carrier stallions. Maintenance of the virus in accessory sex glands is dependent on the presence of testosterone. Attempts have been made to reduce testosterone levels and subsequently eliminate the virus through suppression of pituitary function, either via hormone administration (i.e. altrenogest) or vaccination against GnRH.

Vaccination of seronegative stallions with an approved vaccine against equine arteritis virus (ARVAC, Ft Dodge) will prevent infection and establishment of the carrier state. It is recommended that all intact stallions greater than 12 months of age be vaccinated against EAV. Stallions should be tested to confirm that they are seronegative prior to vaccination. Evidence of seronegative status prior to development of a positive titer after vaccination may be important when considering sale of semen, sale of the stallion or international shipment of the stallion or semen (i.e. all medical records should be retained).

Chapter 11 Anatomy of the Mare

It is important to have an understanding of normal reproductive anatomy of the mare in order to perform common reproductive procedures, such as insemination, speculum examination, and collection of a uterine culture, cytology, and biopsy (Figure 11-1).

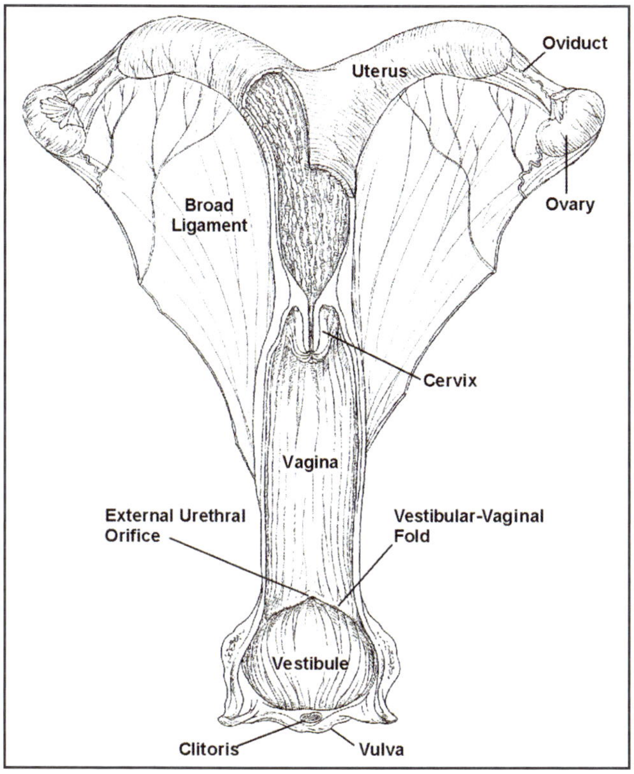

Figure 11-1 Drawing of the reproductive tract of the mare.

11.1 Ovary

Mares have two ovaries (left and right) located adjacent to the tip of each uterine horn. The ovaries of a filly foal contain all of the oocytes (eggs) that she will ever have at the time of her birth. Females do not produce new gametes during their adult lifetime, unlike the situation with sperm production in males. Each oocyte is enclosed by a specialized structure within the ovary called a follicle. As a follicle grows, a fluid-filled chamber or antrum forms within the follicle. Granulosa cells that line the follicle secrete the follicular fluid that fills the antrum.

Adult horses cycle at approximately 21 day intervals. The culmination of each estrous cycle is ovulation of a dominant follicle (Figure 11-2). During estrus, the dominant follicle increases in diameter by 3 to 5 mm per day. Preovulatory follicles in the

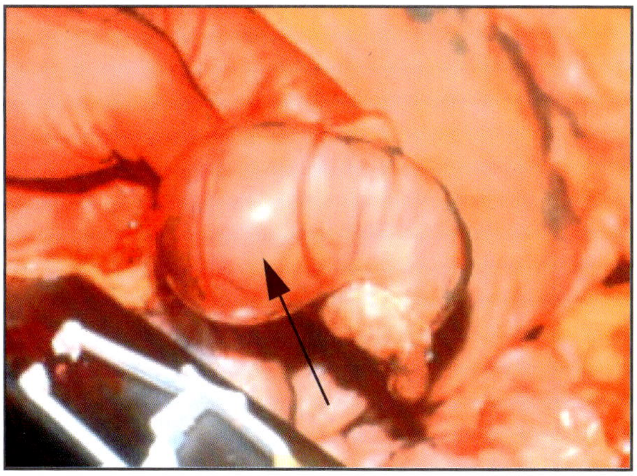

Figure 11-2 Preovulatory follicle of a mare (arrow).

mare are approximately 40 to 45 mm in diameter. The size of the preovulatory follicle is somewhat breed dependent:

- Quarter Horse and Arabian breeds ovulate follicles 35 to 45 mm in diameter
- Thoroughbred and Standardbred mares typically ovulate follicles 40 to 50 mm in diameter
- Warm-blood breed mares ovulate follicles 45 to 55 mm in diameter
- Draft breed mares ovulate follicles 50 to 60 mm in diameter

Individual mares are reasonably consistent in regards to ovulating follicles within a certain size range. However, some mares may irregularly ovulate a follicle smaller than anticipated, which can disrupt breeding plans.

At ovulation, the follicle ruptures into the ovulation fossa releasing follicular fluid and the oocyte. The follicle subsequently collapses and several hours later begins to fill with blood. The corpus hemorrhagicum (CH) is the transient blood-filled structure that forms after ovulation (Figure 11-3). The CH will develop into the corpus luteum (CL) by invasion of granulosa and theca cells from the follicular wall. Over the next few days these cells undergo a process called luteinization in which their structure and hormone production capability is altered.

The mature corpus luteum of the mare is 2 to 3 cm in diameter and is contained within the substance of the ovary (i.e. there is no crown or papilla of luteal tissue that protrudes outside of the equine ovary)

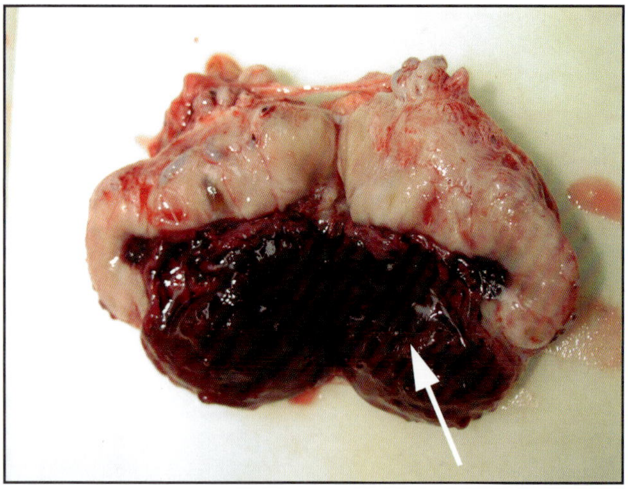

Figure 11-3 Corpus hemorrhagicum of a mare(arrow).

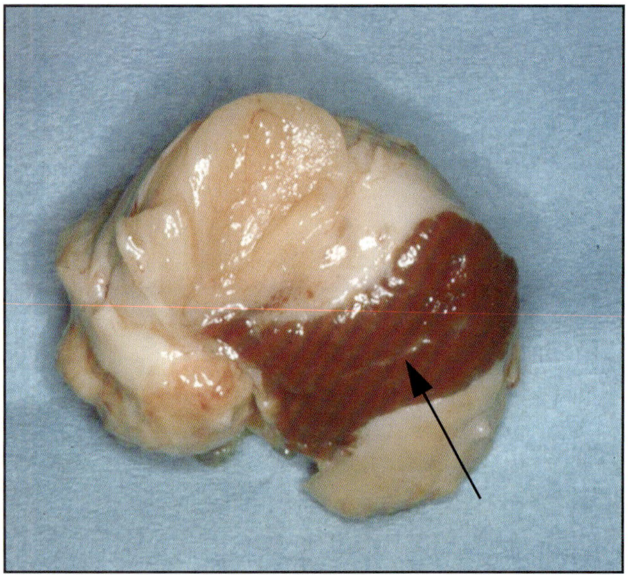

Figure 11-4 Corpus luteum of a mare(arrow).

(Figure 11-4). If the mare is not pregnant, prostaglandins are released from the uterine lining or endometrium approximately 12 to 14 days postovulation. This results in destruction of the corpus luteum or luteolysis. The corpus albicans (CA) is the connective tissue remnant of the inactive, atrophied corpus luteum.

11.2 Oviduct

The oviduct (sometimes called the uterine tube) is the tubular system which collects the oocyte after ovulation and is the site of fertilization. The oviduct is subdivided into 3 main regions, the infundibulum, ampulla and isthmus (Figure 11-5). The infundibulum is the funnel-shaped end of the oviduct adjacent to the ovaries. Irregular finger-like processes called fimbria are located at the cranial border of the infundibulum. In the mare the

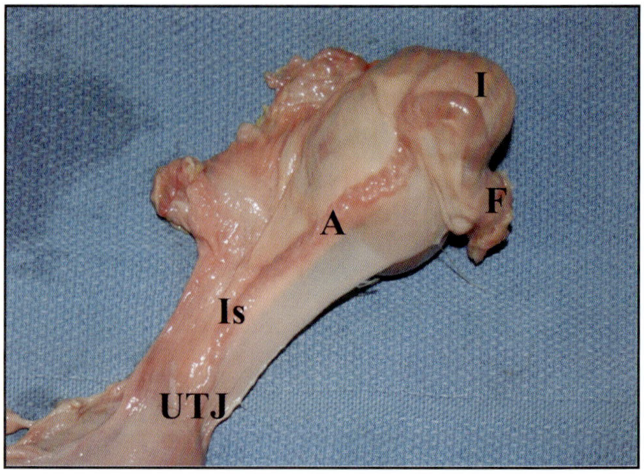

Figure 11-5 Equine oviduct. F- fimbria, I- infundibulum, A – ampulla, Is – isthmus, UTJ – utero-tubular junction.

infundibulum covers the ovulation fossa and facilitates entry of the oocyte into the oviduct. The ampulla is the major central portion of the oviduct between the infundibulum and the isthmus. The isthmus is the caudal segment of the oviduct that is attached to the tip of the uterine horn. The opening of the oviduct into the tip of the uterine horn is the utero-tubular junction (UTJ).

Spermatozoa travel from the site of ejaculation or insemination through the utero-tubular junction proximally up into the oviduct. Fertilization of the oocyte by an individual spermatozoon takes place in the ampullar segment of the oviduct. The developing equine embryo spends approximately 5 to 6 days in the oviduct before exiting the utero-tubular junction and entering the uterus. Passage through the isthmus and UTJ is facilitated by prostaglandin E_2 secretion by the embryo. Oocytes that are not fertilized are retained in the oviduct and typically do not gain access to the uterus.

11.3 Uterus

The uterus is a muscular organ designed to nourish and protect the early embryo, provide structural and functional support for the placenta, and eventually cause contractions sufficient for expulsion of the fetus at parturition. Mares have a 'Y' shaped uterus, with two uterine horns of medium length and a relatively short uterine body (Figure 11-6).

The uterus is suspended in the caudal abdomen of the mare by a portion of the broad ligament called the mesometrium. The major blood vessels supplying the uterus, called the uterine arteries and veins,

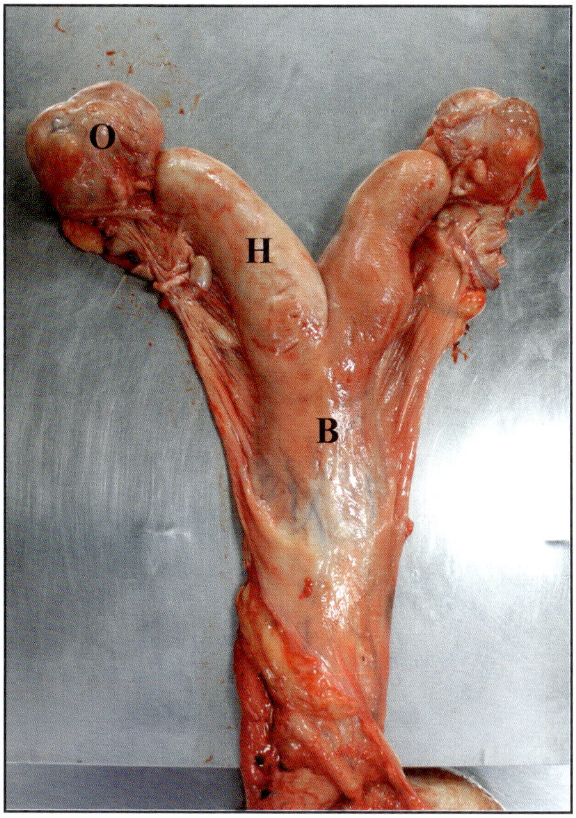

Figure 11-6 Equine uterus and adjacent structures. H- uterine horn, B – uterine body, O- ovary.

traverse through the broad ligament. The outer surface layer of the uterus is called the serosa. The myometrium, or muscular layer, is comprised of two layers of smooth muscle; an inner circular layer and an outer longitudinal layer. The endometrium refers to the internal lining of the uterus. It contains glands which produce substances, commonly referred to as 'uterine milk', which nurtures the early embryo. The endometrium is also the surface to which the placenta of the older conceptus will eventually attach via structures called microcotyledons.

11.4 Cervix

The cervix is a thick-walled tubular muscle located between the uterus and the vagina. In the mare, the cervix is approximately 7.5 to 10 cm (3" to 4") in length. The cervix protrudes about 1 to 2 cm into the vagina in the mare (Figure 11-7). Numerous small low longitudinal folds line the lumen of the cervix or cervical canal. These cervical folds are continuous with the folds of the lining of the uterus (endometrium). The tone and character of the cervix changes dramatically during different stages of the estrous cycle in response to prevailing ovarian steroid hormones. In estrus, the cervix is soft, relaxed, and open in response to elevated levels of estradiol and an absence of progesterone. This allows semen to pass through the cervical canal into the uterine lumen during natural breeding and allows for clearance of dead spermatozoa, inflammatory cells and fluid by uterine contractions after breeding.

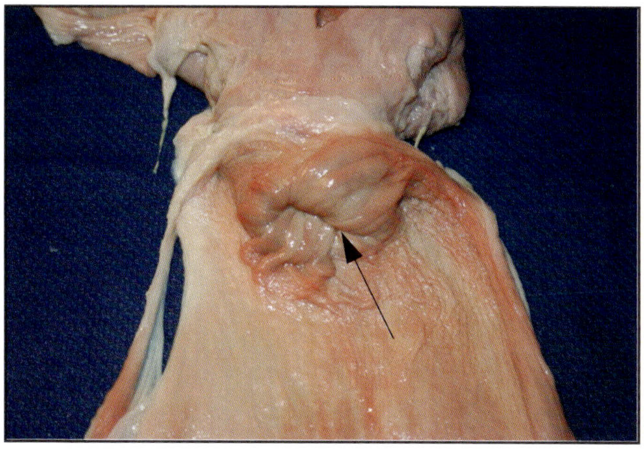

Figure 11-7 Equine cervix. Note the longitudinal folds adjacent to the cervical lumen (arrow).

When the mare goes out of heat after ovulation, an increase in progesterone causes the cervix to close and increase in tone. The cervix remains tightly closed throughout gestation and relaxes only at the time of parturition to allow passage of the foal.

The cervix functions as a major physical barrier to prevent bacteria and other microorganisms from ascending into the uterus.

11.5 Vagina

The vagina is a muscular structure that extends from the vestibular-vaginal fold cranially to the cervix. The lumen of the vagina is generally collapsed except during breeding or foaling. The hymen is a membranous fold located at the vestibular-vaginal junction. A hymen may be present in maiden mares and may vary from a thin band to a completely imperforate structure that wholly occludes the external orifice of the vagina.

11.6 Vestibule

The vestibule is the portion of the female reproductive tract that lies between the vulva and the vagina. The cranial border of the vestibule is the vestibular-vaginal fold or transverse fold. Just caudal to the transverse fold on the ventral surface of the vestibule is the external urethral orifice, which is the entrance to the urinary bladder. Care must be taken not to catheterize the bladder when performing artificial insemination (AI) in the mare due to the location and easy accessibility of the urethra.

11.7 Vulva

The vulva is the caudal termination of the genital tract and is comprised of paired labia, dorsal and ventral commissures and the clitoris. The labia or lips of the vulva are homologous to the scrotum of the male. The vulva and the area surrounding it (anus and skin) are referred to as the perineal area or perineum. The presumed ideal perineal conformation in mares has the vulva situated in a vertical position, with approximately two-thirds of the vulva located below the pelvic brim (Figure 11-8).

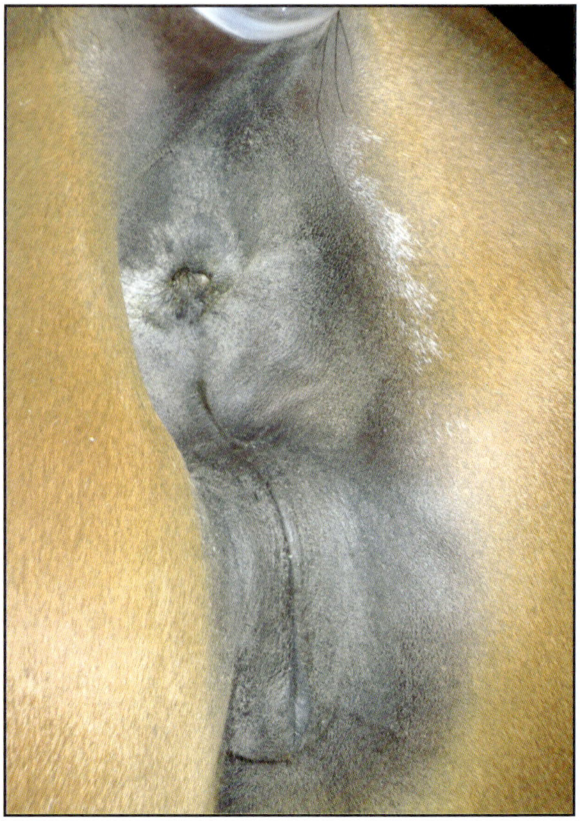

Figure 11-9 Abnormal perineal conformation in which the dorsal aspect of the vulva is tilted cranially.

This is an important consideration when performing AI in the mare; because any materials or instruments being introduced into the reproductive tract should enter the vulva at a slight upward angle, which is the natural angle of intromission of the stallion's penis, so that they pass up and over the floor of the pelvis.

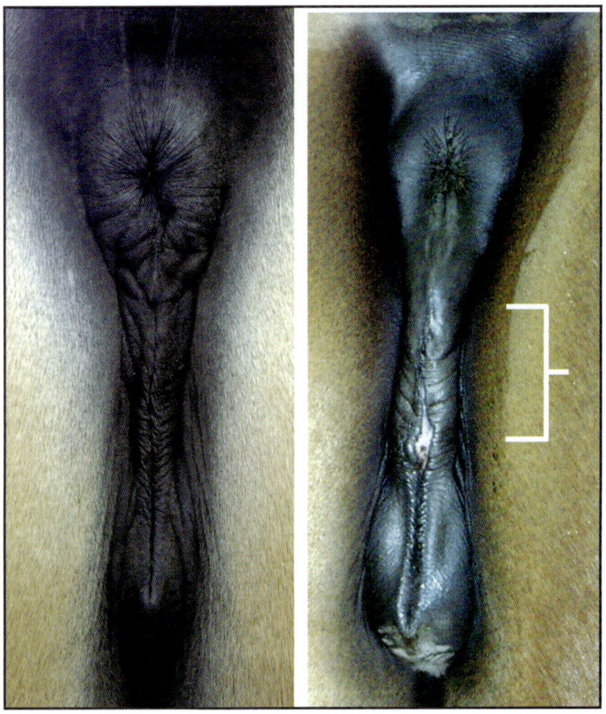

Figure 11-8 Normal perineal anatomy of a mare (left) and vulva of a mare with a Caslick procedure which closed the top portion of the vulva (right).

Tilting or angling of the dorsal aspect of the vulva cranially predisposes the mare to uterine infections (Figure 11-9). A minor surgical procedure, referred to as an episioplasty or Caslick procedure, may be used to close the dorsal aspect of the vulva and prevent aspiration of air and/or ascension of bacteria or fecal material cranially into the reproductive tract.

Chapter 12 Reproductive Physiology of the Nonpregnant Mare

12.1 Seasonality and the Transition Period

A majority of mares enter a prolonged anovulatory phase referred to as winter anestrus beginning in October or November in the Northern Hemisphere. The winter anestrus period may be preceded by a 'fall transition period' consisting of irregular waves of follicle development and regression without ovulation. Eventually the ovaries become inactive or dormant for several months.

Factors that influence seasonal reproductive activity in mares include geographic latitude, ambient photoperiod, environmental conditions (i.e. temperature, weather), nutrition, age, breed and housing. Young mares and mares that gave birth the previous season have the highest probability of becoming anestrus, whereas barren mares housed indoors have a lower probability of becoming anovulatory during the late fall and winter. Nutrition plays a role in seasonality, as mares in poor body condition going into the fall and winter months are more likely to become acyclic than mares with higher body condition scores. Increasing the plane of nutrition and allowing mares to graze on green grass pasture has been reported to stimulate ovulation earlier in the year. Mare age is also a factor in that older mares begin cycling an average of about 2 weeks later in the spring than younger mares.

Seasonal anestrus is often subdivided into deep anestrus and transition (shallow anestrus) periods characterized by the amount of follicular activity present. Deep anestrus is defined by minimal ovarian follicular development (i.e. follicles < 20 mm in diameter). The behavior of mares in deep anestrus may range from receptive (teasing in), to indifferent (passive), to unreceptive (teasing out) reflecting a general absence of influence from ovarian steroid hormones.

A progressive increase in the duration of the ambient photoperiod in the spring stimulates ovarian function. From a practical standpoint, the onset of transition in mares occurs when the first developing follicle of the season reaches 20 to 25 mm in diameter. The term 'late transition' may be used when one or more follicles are ≥ 30 mm in diameter.

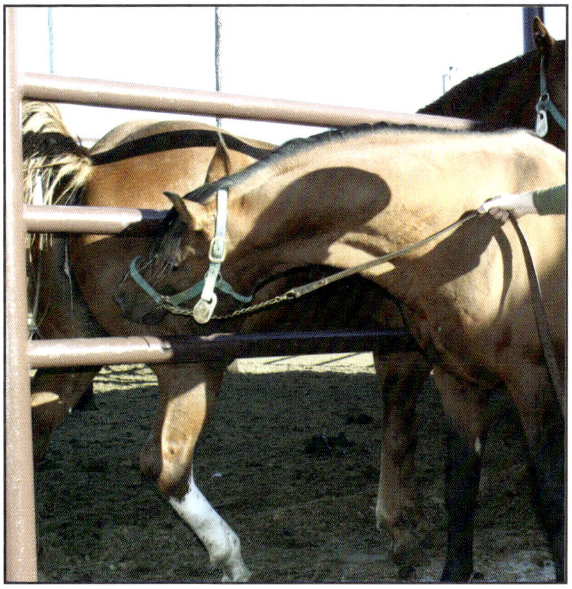

Figure 12-1 Photograph of a mare in estrus (teasing in heat).

Mares may exhibit multiple waves of follicular growth and regression during the transition period. The transition period may last for 50 to 70 days or more prior to the first ovulation of the season. Once a mare has ovulated, she will generally continue to cycle at regular intervals. Behaviorally, transitional mares may display prolonged or irregular periods of estrus in response to estrogens produced by developing follicles.

The mean calendar date of the first spontaneous ovulation of the year in anestrus mares maintained under ambient light conditions in North America ranges from the middle of March to early May.

12.2 Physiologic Breeding Season

The natural or physiologic breeding season of horses extends from April to October in the Northern Hemisphere. Mares are polyestrus in that they exhibit repeated estrous cycles during the breeding season. Mares ovulate at approximately 21 day intervals throughout the breeding season. The equine estrous cycle can be divided into 2 phases, based on sexual receptivity. Estrus refers to the period during which mares are receptive to advances of the stallion (Figure 12-1). Behavioral estrus typically lasts 5 to 7 days and is stimulated by increasing levels of the hormone estradiol produced by the developing dominant follicle and an absence of progesterone. Mares typically ovulate 1

Figure 12-2 Photograph of a mare (right) in diestrus (teasing out of heat).

to 2 days before they go out of heat.

Diestrus refers to the period during which mares reject advances of the stallion (Figure 12-2). Progesterone production by the corpus luteum controls behavioral responses of the mare during the 14-16 day diestrus period.

12.3 Follicle Selection and Control of Ovulation

Mares utilize an active process of follicular selection to limit the number of ovulations in most estrous cycles to one ovulation. The mechanism of follicle selection involves a complex interaction between pituitary gonadotropins (follicle stimulating hormone, FSH; and luteinizing hormone, LH) and ovarian hormones. The major or primary follicular wave of the equine estrous cycle, or the wave that ends with ovulation during estrus, originates in diestrus approximately 7 to 8 days after ovulation when a cohort of follicles emerge from a pool of smaller follicles over a period of several days. After emergence, follicles in the wave go through a common growth phase for approximately 6 to 7 days during which all follicles increase in size at approximately the same rate (3 mm/day). Deviation occurs at the end of the common-growth phase and represents the point at which the future dominant follicle continues to develop and smaller subordinate follicles regress.

Follicle stimulating hormone produced by the anterior pituitary gland provides the drive for emergence and initial growth. All of the follicles in the follicular wave require FSH for initial growth and development. The future dominant follicle usually emerges approximately 1 day earlier than the other follicles in the wave. Consequently, this follicle is slightly larger than the other follicles in the cohort at the end of the common-growth phase. Circulating levels of FSH peak when the largest follicle is approximately 13 mm in diameter. Levels of FSH subsequently decline as first inhibin and then estradiol are produced by the larger follicles within the wave.

Deviation takes place approximately 3 days after the FSH peak as levels of FSH are declining. Deviation occurs when the largest follicle is 22 to 25 mm in diameter. The process of deviation represents selection against future development of subordinate follicles by factors produced by the dominant follicle. The developing dominant follicle becomes increasingly responsive to FSH and luteinizing hormone as compared to other follicles in the wave, due in part to an increase in the number of gonadotropin receptors in the dominant follicle stimulated by elevated intrafollicular estradiol levels. Consequently, the larger follicle continues to develop at a rate of 3 to 5 mm per day in the face of declining circulating FSH levels while subordinate follicles begin to regress. Continued development and subsequent ovulation of the dominant follicle after deviation is stimulated by the prolonged elevation or surge of LH. Mares usually go out of heat 1 to 2 days after ovulation.

12.4 Physiology of the Estrous Cycle

Ovulation consists of the collapse of the dominant follicle accompanied by release of the follicular fluid and the oocyte (egg). The oocyte is picked up by the oviduct and transported distally down the infundibulum of the oviduct toward the ampulla, which is the site of potential fertilization.

The former follicle remains collapsed for 8 to 12 hours after ovulation. Subsequently, the lumen of the follicle fills with blood from ruptured capillaries which lined the wall of the follicle. The blood rapidly clots, resulting in formation of a temporary structure called the corpus hemorrhagicum (CH).

Granulosa and theca cells from the wall of the follicle invade into the blood clot using the fibrin strands of the clot as an architectural framework. At the same time, physiologic changes in these cells, a process called luteinization, results in a shift in steroid hormone production from estrogen and testosterone to progesterone.

Rapid multiplication of these luteinized cells leads to formation of the corpus luteum (CL). The corpus luteum produces large amounts of progesterone which is responsible for blocking the expression of behavioral estrus, altering the secretion and development of endometrial glands, closure of the cervix and a variety of other physiologic processes. Progesterone concentration at the time of ovulation is low (< 0.5 ng/ml). Levels begin to increase above 1.0 ng/ml 1 to 2 days after ovulation as the corpus luteum forms. Progesterone levels peak at approximately day 5 and remain elevated until day 12 to 14 after ovulation.

In the non-pregnant mare, pulsatile secretion of prostaglandins from the endometrium of the uterus produced 13 to 14 days after ovulation causes destruction of the corpus luteum, a process called luteolysis. The decline in progesterone to basal levels and an increase in estrogens associated with development of another dominant follicle results in a return to behavioral estrus and another opportunity for ovulation and pregnancy.

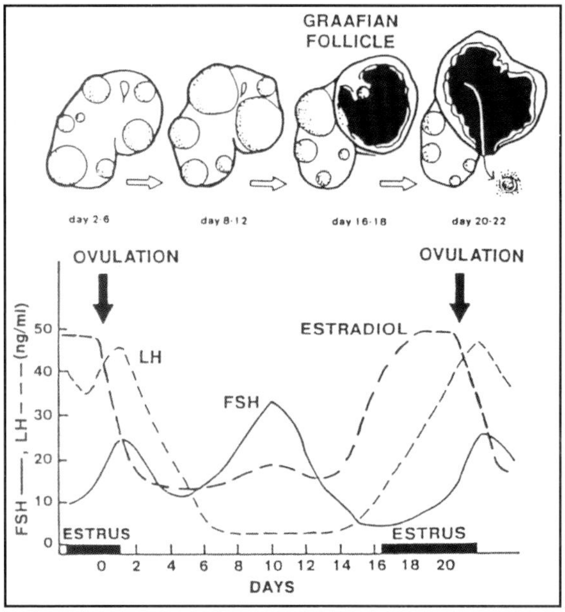

***Figure 12-3** Physiologic events of the follicular phase of the estrous cycle (from Neely et al., Equine Reproduction, Veterinary Learning Systems, Co., Inc., 1983, pp. 12-22). A wave of FSH in the middle of diestrus stimulates development of the dominant (Graafian) follicle. Estradiol produced by the dominant follicle reaches peak concentration 1 to 2 days prior to ovulation. A prolonged surge of LH induces ovulation of the dominant follicle; plasma LH concentration reaches peak concentration 1 day after ovulation.*

The physiologic events of the equine estrous cycle are shown in Figure 12-3 and Figure 12-4.

12.5 Monitoring the Estrous Cycle

Clinically, stages of the estrous cycle can be monitored by evaluation of the following:

- Estrous behavior based on teasing or other observations
- Diameter and growth patterns of the largest ovarian follicle based on palpation and ultrasonography per rectum
- Presence or absence of an ovarian corpus luteum on ultrasound examination
- Uterine edema patterns visible on ultrasound examination
- Uterine/cervical tone detected by manual palpation of the reproductive tract per rectum
- Cervical characteristics evaluated by vaginal speculum examination.

Understanding the principles of follicular development is important for predicting interval to ovulation, response to prostaglandin therapy, and response to ovulation-inducing agents. These principles are also used in the evaluation of techniques for stimulating follicular development in seasonally anestrous or transitional mares and superovulation in cycling mares.

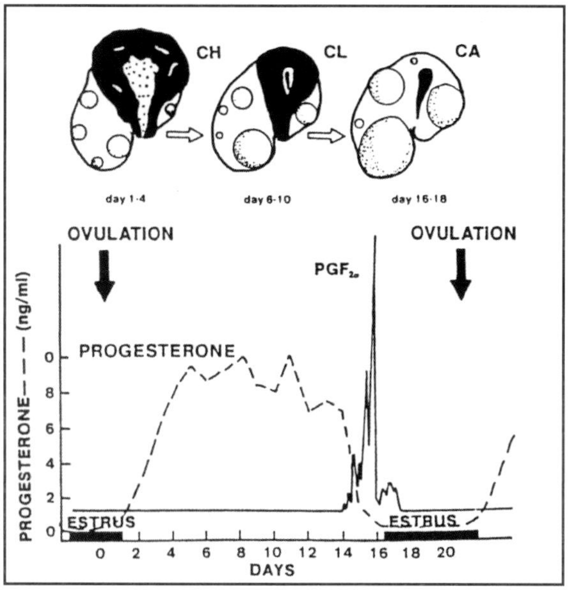

Figure 12-4 Physiologic events of the luteal phase of the estrous cycle (From Neely et al., 1983). A blood filled structure called the corpus hemorrhagicum (CH) forms within the former dominant follicle after ovulation. Subsequently, invasion of luteinized granulosa and theca cells into the CH results in formation of the corpus luteum (CL), which produces progesterone. Pulsatile release of prostaglandins ($PGF_{2\alpha}$) from the endometrium of a non-pregnant mare results in destruction of the CL. The resulting atretic structure is termed a corpus albicans (CA).

Chapter 13. Reproductive Evaluation of the Mare

Table 13-0 List and Part Number of ARS products used in this chapter.

Item	Part Number	Use/Comments
Sterile Disposable Vaginal Speculum	EDVS-102/10	Used to perform vaginal examinations
Speculum Light	537-664	Light source for speculum examinations
Sterile Obstetrical Sleeves	SLG-105/25	Sleeve used for artificial insemination and other reproductive procedures
Culture Swab	CSS-101/25	Sterile swab for uterine culture or endometrial cytology sample collection
Surgilube® Lubricating Jelly	SSL-101	Sterile lubricant for obstetrical procedures
Centrifuge Tubes and Caps	537-742/25	Hold sample of low-volume uterine lavage for centrifugation
Glass Slides	569A-243	Hold sample for cytologic evaluation under microscope

The goal of a mare reproductive evaluation or breeding soundness examination (BSE) is to identify known or potential reproductive abnormalities and to evaluate the potential for a mare to become pregnant and carry a foal successfully to term. Mare reproductive examinations are most commonly performed in the following situations:

- Prepurchase examination.
- Open mares prior to the onset of the breeding season.
- Problem mares during the breeding season.
- Barren mares at the end of a breeding season.
- Mares with a history of embryonic loss, abortion or other reproductive problems.

13.1 Reproductive History

All mares should be properly identified, and the registration name, registration number, microchip number, breed and birth date recorded. Photographs should be taken or accurate drawings of markings and tattoos recorded. A complete breeding history should be obtained, including current reproductive status (maiden, open, barren, pregnant or foaling) (Table 13-1), number of cycles bred during the last season, date of last breeding, breeding technique used (artificial insemination, natural cover or pasture breeding), date of last foal, number of previous foals and any previous history of abnormal estrous cycles, uterine infections, embryonic loss or abortion.

Table 13-1 Definition of terms describing reproductive status of mares

Term	Definition
Maiden	Mare that has never been bred, either by natural service or artificial insemination
Open	Mare that was intentionally left open or non-pregnant during the previous breeding season
Barren	Mare that was bred the previous season, but did not become pregnant or remain pregnant
Pregnant	Mare currently confirmed to be pregnant
Foaling or Wet	Mare with a nursing foal at her side

13.2 Physical Examination

A general physical examination should be performed in addition to the reproductive examination to assess whether the mare has the capacity to carry a foal to term. The evaluation should include, but is not limited to, examination of the oral cavity, eyes, and respiratory, cardiac and musculoskeletal systems. In addition, diet and body condition should be evaluated. Broodmares do not have to be fit for athletic competition, but they should not be severely overweight or underweight.

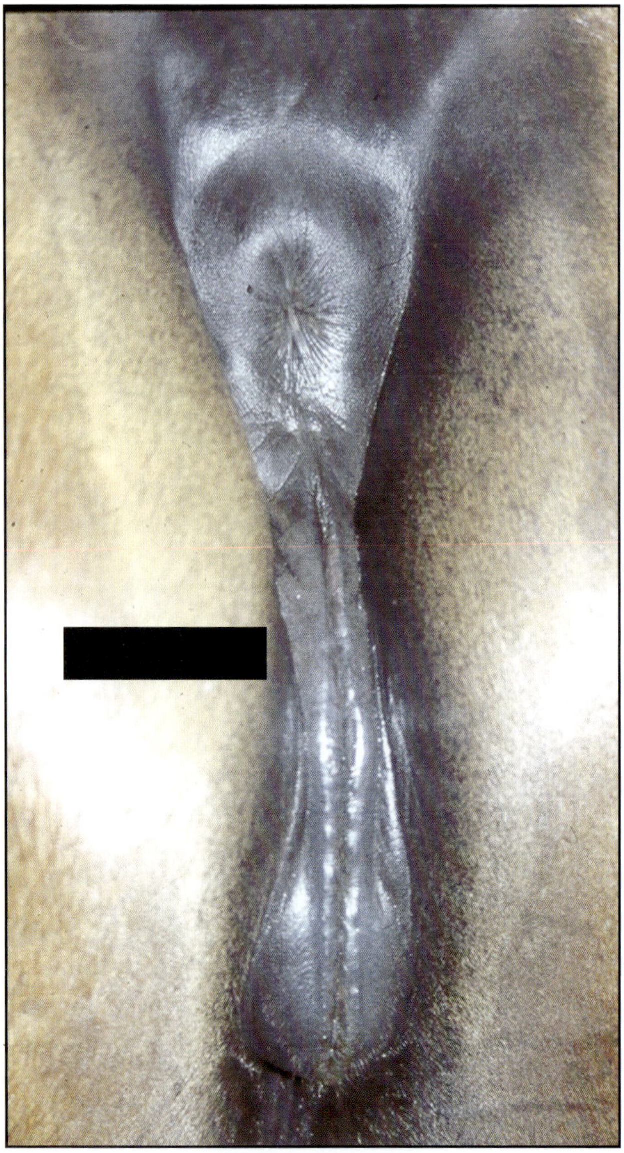

Figure 13-1 Normal perineal conformation of a mare. Bar denotes approximate location of the pelvic bone.

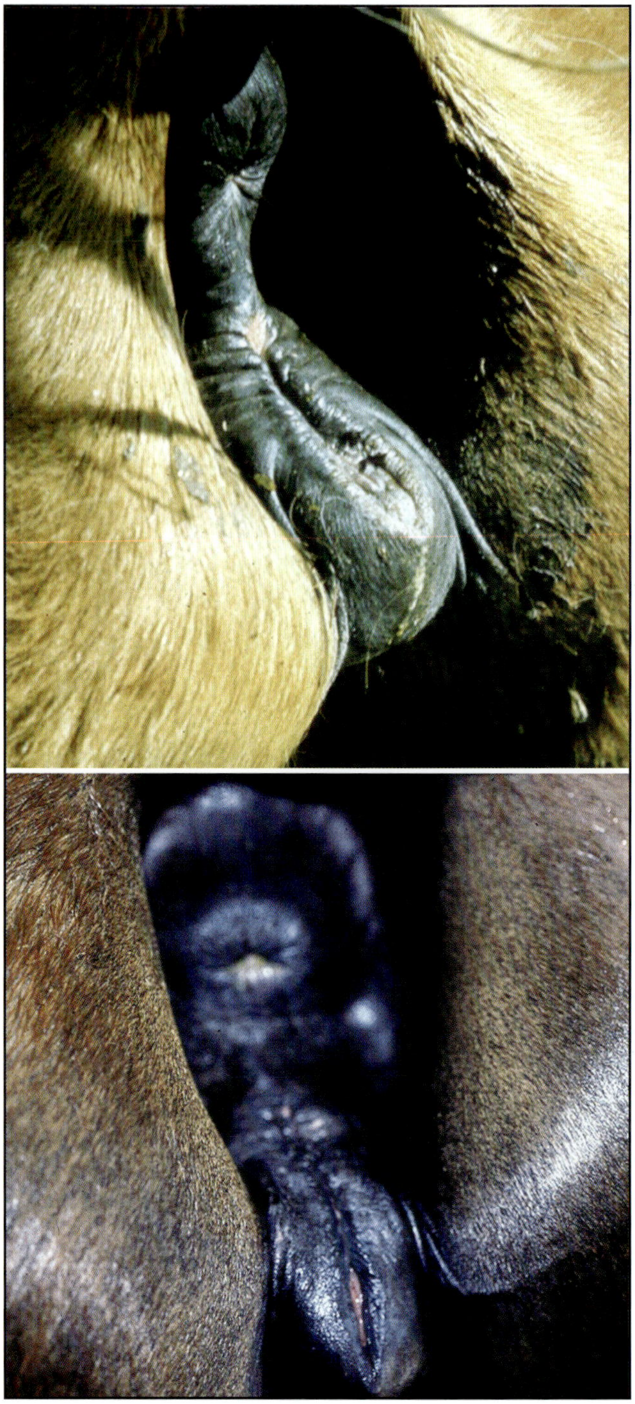

Figure 13-2 Examples of poor perineal conformation in mares.

13.3 Perineal Conformation

The external genitalia (vulva) should be evaluated for conformation and muscular tone. The vulva is the first physical barrier for prevention of contamination of the reproductive tract by pathogenic organisms. The optimal perineal conformation consists of a vulva in a nearly vertical position with at least 70% of the vulva ventral to the brim of the pelvis (Figure 13-1).

The muscular tone of the vulva should be sufficient to prevent aspiration of air into the vestibule or vagina, a condition commonly referred to as windsucking. Horizontal sloping of the vulva secondary to recession of the anus and/or poor muscular tone to the labia of the vulva may predispose the mare to an ascending infection of the uterus (Figure 13-2).

Prevention of bacterial contamination of the reproductive tract due to abnormal perineal conformation or poor muscular tone of the vulva may be attained by performing a minor surgical technique termed an episioplasty or Caslick procedure (Figure 13-3). The episioplasty must be completely opened in late gestation 1 to 2 weeks prior to foaling to avoid severe tearing of the perineum as the foal is forcefully expelled during parturition.

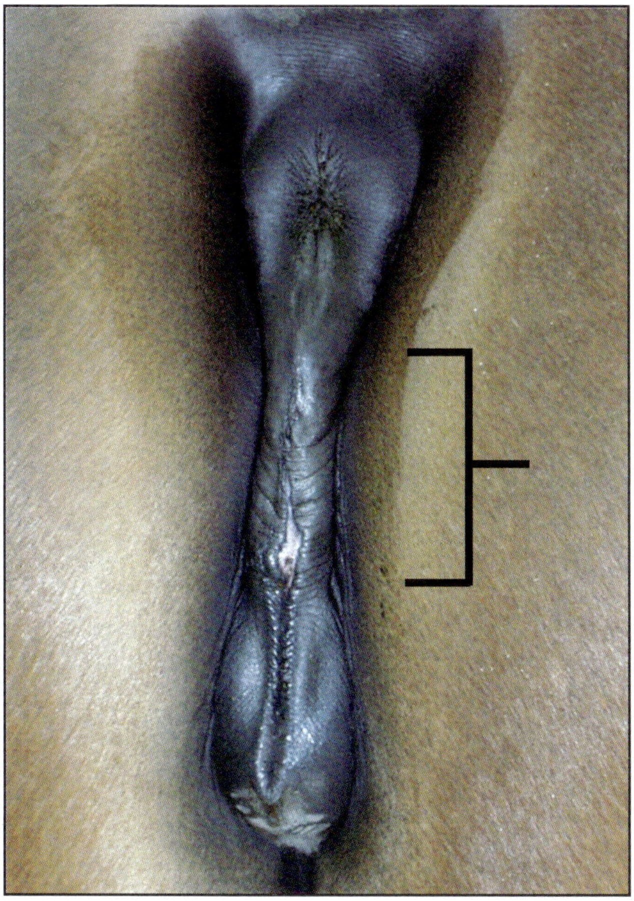

Figure 13-3 Photograph of the vulva of a mare with a Caslick. The upper half of the vulva has been sutured closed (bracket)

13.4 Estrus Detection

The mare should be teased with a stallion that exhibits good libido in order to successfully evaluate estrous cycle stage. Adequate time should be taken to allow shy or nervous mares to express behavioral estrus. Maiden mares may not show heat well and foaling mares may not show heat unless the foal is restrained and safely away from the stallion. It is often not very efficient to tease mares as a group, since often the only mares that may come to the fence or tease rail may be assertive mares in heat or mares that want to attack the stallion. One may not be able to determine the heat status of mares that remain at a distance from the stallion. It is generally more effective, but certainly more time consuming to tease mares individually. There are many systems used for teasing mares, including chutes, rails, fences, pens and paddocks. Keys to successful teasing are patience, persistence and knowing the behavioral characteristics of each mare.

Estrus refers to the period during which mares are receptive to the advances of the stallion. Estrus typically lasts 5 to 7 days and is stimulated by elevated estrogen levels produced by developing follicles. Common behavioral responses of mares in estrus when teased with a stallion include raising of the tail, passive urination, repeated eversion of the labia with exposure of the clitoris (winking), and assuming a mating posture with the hind legs spread apart.

Diestrus refers to the period during which mares reject the advances of the stallion. Progesterone production by the corpus luteum controls the behavioral responses of the mare during the 14 to 16-day diestrous period. When teased to a stallion, mares in diestrus will pin their ears back, kick, switch their tail, vocalize and attempt to either actively move away from the stallion or to aggressively attack the stallion.

13.5 Palpation

The goal of manual palpation per rectum is to identify significant features of the reproductive tract, determine stage of the estrous cycle and identify potential problems.

Ovarian structures that may be noted during palpation include developing and preovulatory follicles (Figure 13-3), a fresh or recent ovulation, and an early developing corpus hemorrhagicum. The uterus is generally large and edematous during estrus and has a characteristic 'doughy' feel. The cervix of a mare in heat is generally soft and relaxed. After ovulation, the increase in progesterone causes the uterus and cervix to increase in tone.

A mature corpus luteum is located entirely within the ovary and cannot be detected or palpated per rectum (Figure 13-4).

13.6 Ultrasonography

Ultrasound is used in broodmares to monitor the estrous cycle and visualize structures in the reproductive tract that cannot be discerned on palpation per rectum, in the early diagnosis of pregnancy, diagnosis of twins and evaluation of potential ovarian or uterine pathology (Figure 13-6 to Figure 13-11). Ultrasonography is an excellent technique for monitoring follicular development, predicting and confirming ovulation, and determining the presence or absence of a corpus luteum.

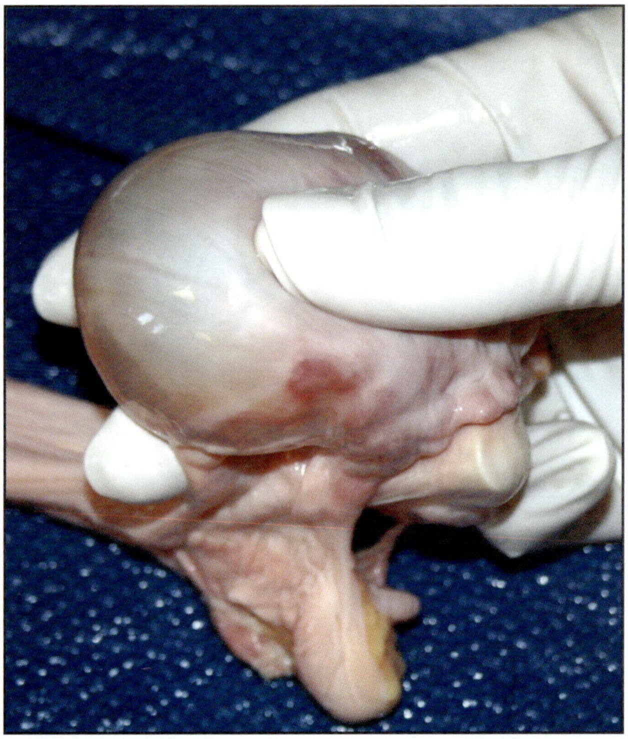

Figure 13-4 Large pre-ovulatory equine follicle.

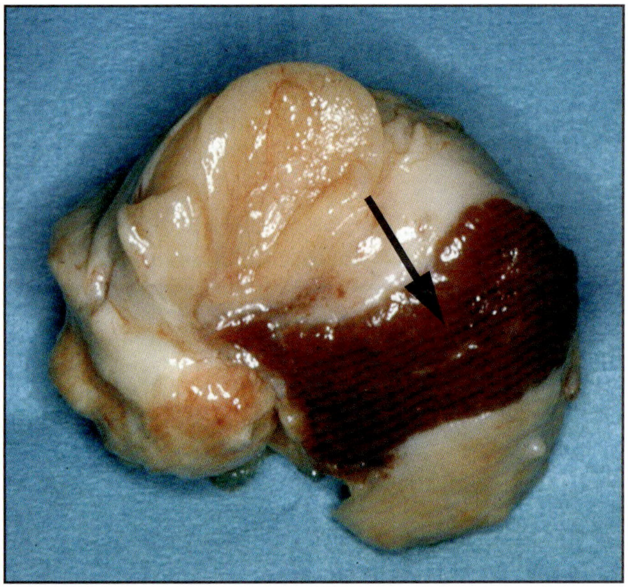

Figure 13-5 Mature equine corpus luteum (arrow).

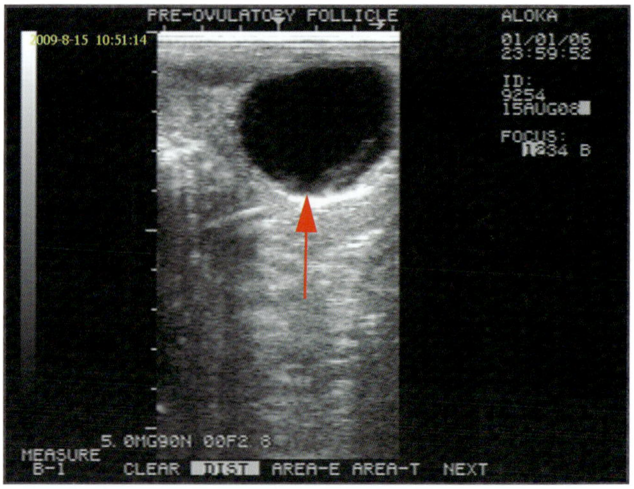

Figure 13-6 Ultrasonographic image of a large preovulatory follicle (arrow).

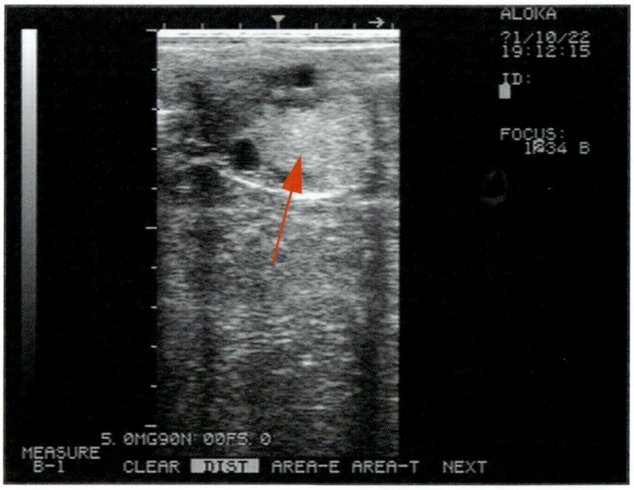

Figure 13-7 Ultrasonographic image of a corpus luteum (arrow).

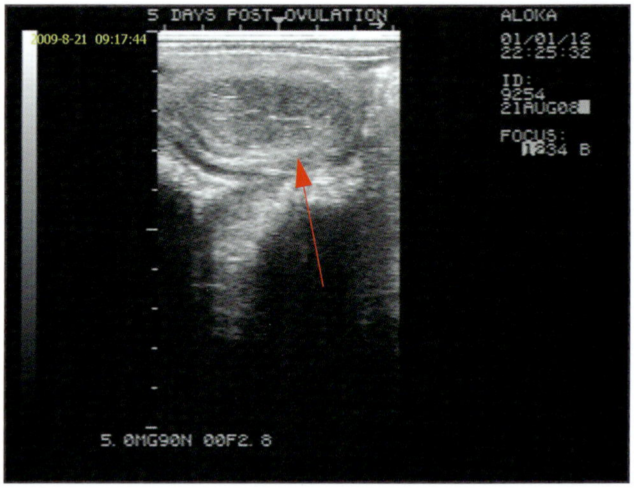

Figure 13-8 Ultrasonographic image of a uterus with no edema (arrow).

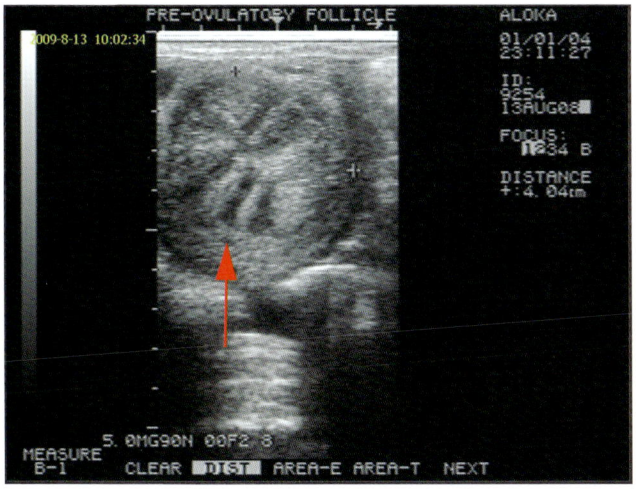

***Figure 13-9** Ultrasonographic image of an edematous uterus (arrow). Note the radiating pattern emanating from the center of the uterus.*

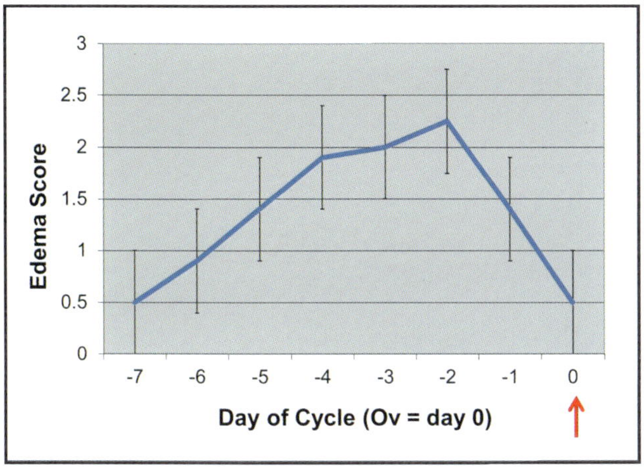

***Figure 13-10** Uterine edema pattern of a mare during estrus. Edema usually peaks 1-2 days prior to ovulation. The day of ovulation is indicated by the arrow.*

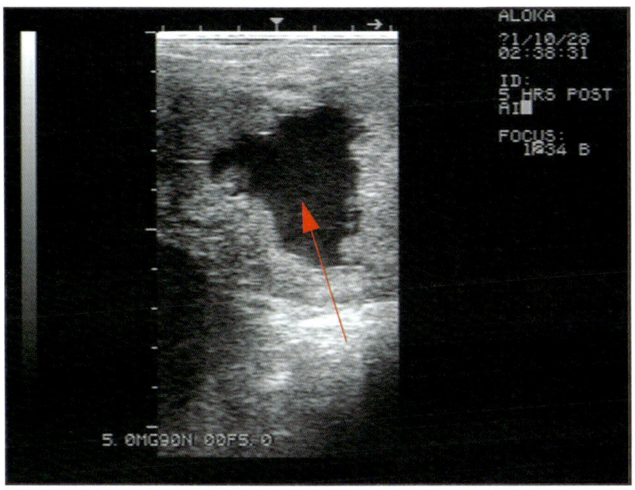

***Figure 13-11** Ultrasound image of echogenic fluid (arrow) within the uterine lumen of a mare with endometritis.*

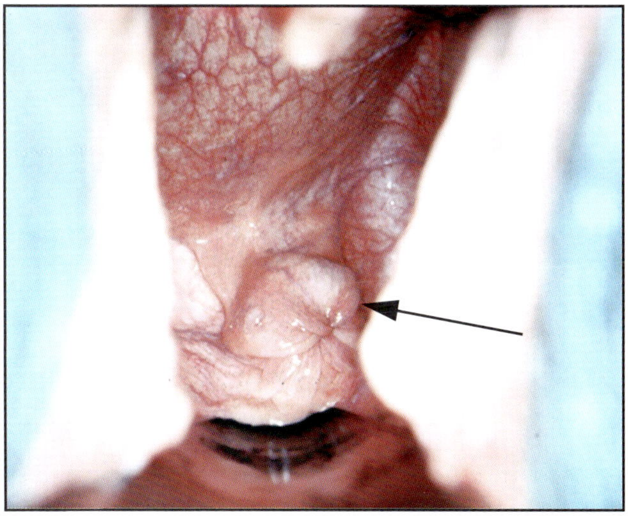

***Figure 13-12** Photograph of a relaxed cervix of a mare in estrus. (arrow).*

13.7 Vaginal Speculum Examination

A vaginal examination is performed using a Sterile Disposable Vaginal Speculum and Speculum Light to evaluate the vaginal vault and the external os of the cervix, determine the stage of the estrous cycle, and to detect pathologic conditions such as urine pooling, cervical discharge and trauma. The procedure is easy and inexpensive to perform.

The appearance of the external cervical os varies with season, stage of the estrous cycle, pregnancy status and presence of infection. When a mare is in winter anestrus, the cervix appears pale, dry and may be slightly open. During estrus, the cervix relaxes onto the floor of the anterior vagina, becomes edematous, pink and is moistened with clear mucous (Figure 13-12). In diestrus, the cervix is high on the anterior wall of the vagina, pale, dry and may be covered with a viscous, sticky mucous (Figure 13-13). The cervix of a pregnant mare is tightly closed and may have a thick mucous cap. In the presence of infection, the cervix becomes hyperemic, or reddened, and may have a purulent discharge.

Urine pooling is recognized by an accumulation of cloudy yellow fluid in the anterior vagina (Figure 13-14). Pooling of urine is most common in older mares with poor perineal conformation.

A persistent hymen may be present in a maiden mare, and is located at the junction of vestibule and vagina just cranially to the opening of the urethra (Figure 13-15). Vaginal varicose veins may be visi-

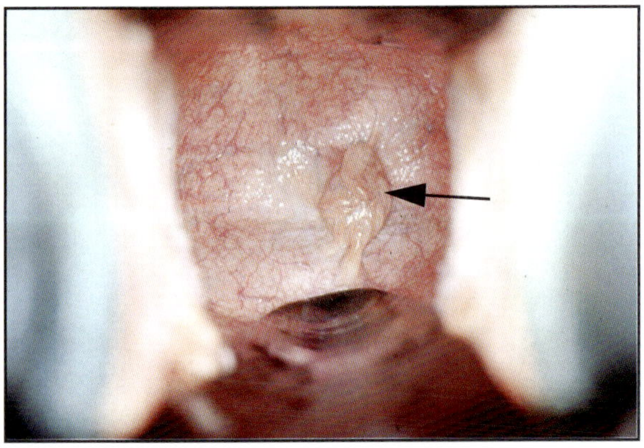

Figure 13-13 Photograph of a tight cervix of a mare in diestrus (arrow).

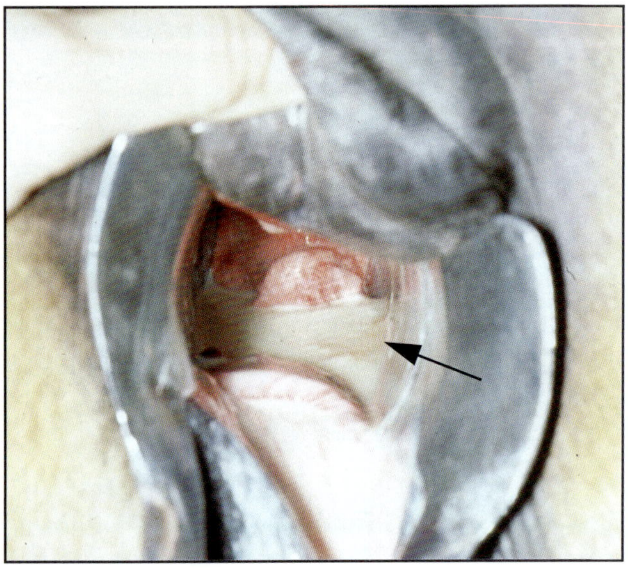

Figure 13-14 Urine pooling in the cranial vagina (arrow).

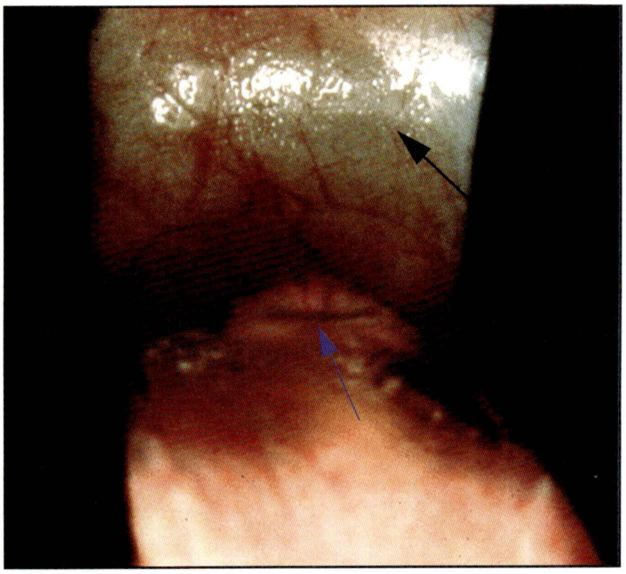

Figure 13-15 Persistent hymen in a mare (arrow). Note the opening of the urethra (blue arrow).

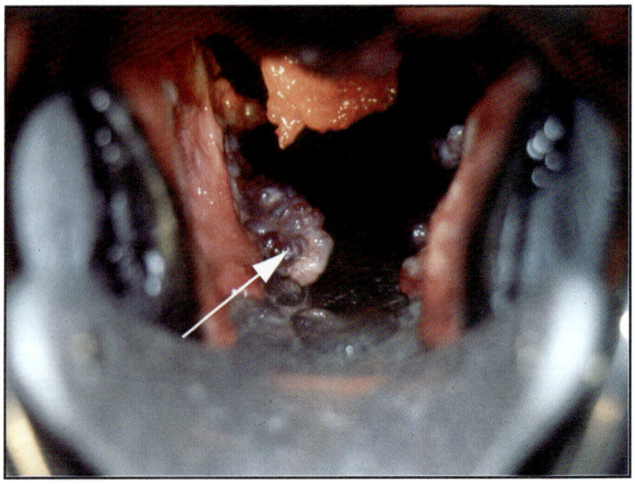

Figure 13-16 Vaginal varicose veins in a mare (arrow).

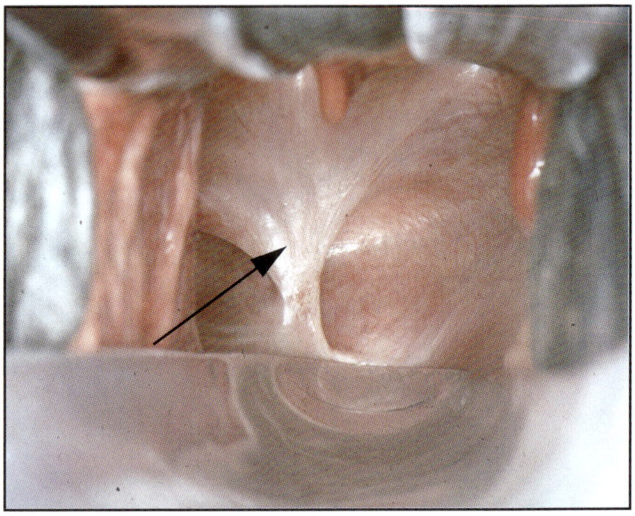

Figure 13-17 Cervical adhesions in a mare (arrow).

ble on speculum examination and are located near the junction of vestibule and vagina (Figure 13-16).

13.8 Digital Examination of the Cervix

After the speculum examination is completed, the cervix may be examined manually for patency and the presence of abnormalities. The examiner should wear a Sterile Obstetrical Sleeve and apply a small amount of Surgilube® Lubricating Jelly to the back of the sleeve in the finger and hand area. The hand is cupped and gently rotated while being inserted into the vulva, vestibule, and eventually the vagina. An index finger is inserted into the external cervical os, and the cervix is examined manually between the thumb and index finger for tone, patency and the presence of adhesions, lacerations or other abnormalities (Figure 13-17). During estrus, it may be possible to insert two to three fingers into the cervix, while it may prove difficult to insert a single

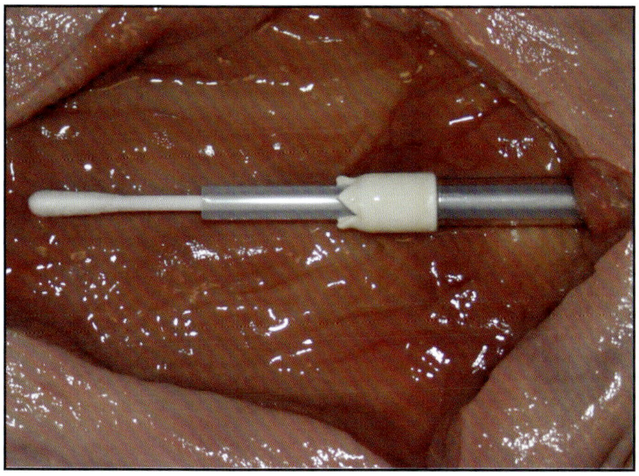

Figure 13-18 Uterine culture swab.

finger into the cervical os during diestrus due to the increased tone stimulated by high progesterone levels.

13.9 Uterine Culture

A uterine culture can help determine if a mare is free of infection, identify a potential pathogen, and determine the optimal antibiotic to use to eliminate the infection. Culture of the uterine lumen is usually done in conjunction with cytology for the diagnosis of uterine infection. Uterine infection, or endometritis, can be suspected in a mare that exhibits an abnormally short estrous cycle, has a vaginal or cervical discharge, an inflamed cervix on speculum examination, cloudy fluid in the uterus detected on ultrasound, and possibly failure to become pregnant when bred to a fertile stallion. Endometritis is a significant cause of reproductive failure in broodmares.

Collection of a culture from the uterus is relatively simple. The tail should be wrapped or held out of the way. The perineal area is thoroughly cleaned with soap and water, rinsed with clean water and then dried with paper towels. A sterile obstetrical sleeve, to which a small amount of Surgilube® Lubricating Jelly has been applied, is worn by the examiner. A sterile, disposable Culture Swab is guided into the vagina and then passed through the cervix into the uterus. The inner swab is advanced beyond the protective sheath until it contacts the endometrium and then is gently rotated, collecting a sample of fluid and cells from the uterine lumen and endometrial wall (Figure 13-18). The inner swab is then withdrawn into the outer sheath, and the entire culture instrument is withdrawn. Once outside the mare, the swab tip may be transferred into a special culture transport system, labeled and submitted to a microbiological laboratory for culture. The swab should be refrigerated if any significant time period is to elapse prior to submission of the culture.

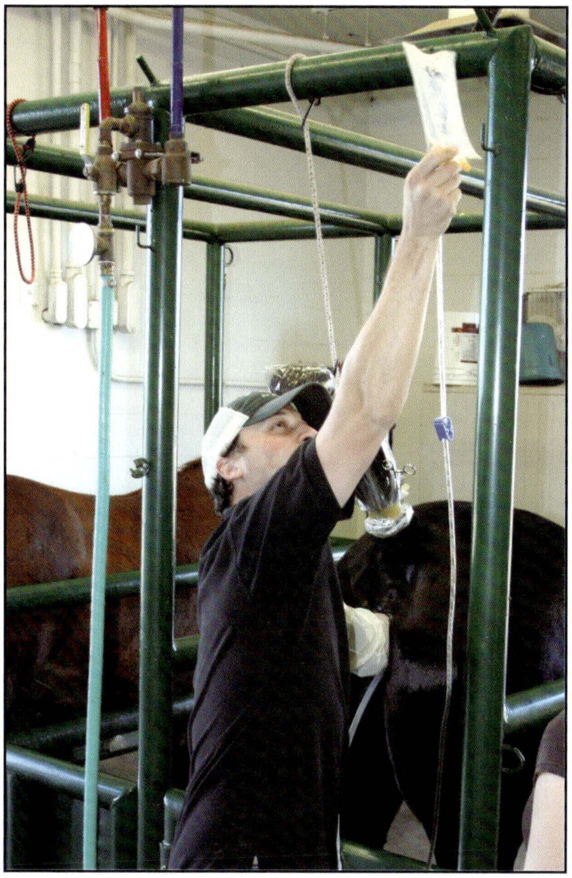

Figure 13-19 Infusion of 150 mls of sterile saline into the uterus during a low-volume lavage procedure.

An alternative technique for sample collection is to perform a low-volume uterine lavage. A sterile 28 to 34 gauge catheter is placed into the uterus and the cuff inflated. Approximately 150 to 500 mls of sterile saline are infused into the uterus via the catheter (Figure 13-19). The technician may choose to massage the fluid throughout the uterus per rectum to 'sample' the entire uterine lumen and to administer a dose of oxytocin to help facilitate fluid recovery. After 3 minutes, the fluid is allowed to exit the uterus and is recovered into the original fluid bag (Figure 13-20).The recovered fluid is subsequently distributed into 2 or more 50 ml Centrifuge Tubes with Cap. The tubes are centrifuged at 400 x *g* for 10 minutes. The supernatant is aspirated off and sterile swabs are used to collect the pellet. One swab/pellet is submitted for microbial culture and

Figure 13-20 Recovery of uterine fluid effluent into the original bag during a low-volume lavage procedure.

the second swab/pellet is utilized for cytologic evaluation.

The bacteria most commonly recovered from the uterus of mares are shown in Table 13-2. Yeast organisms are occasionally recovered from the uterus of older mares with a history of chronic reproductive problems.

Table 13-2 Prevalence of bacteria recovered from the uterus of mares.

Organism	Prevalence
Streptococcus equi subsp. *zooepidemicus*	40 to 50%
Escherichia coli	20 to 40%
Pseudomonas aeruginosa	< 5%
Klebsiella pneumoniae	< 5%
Miscellaneous organisms	10 to 20%

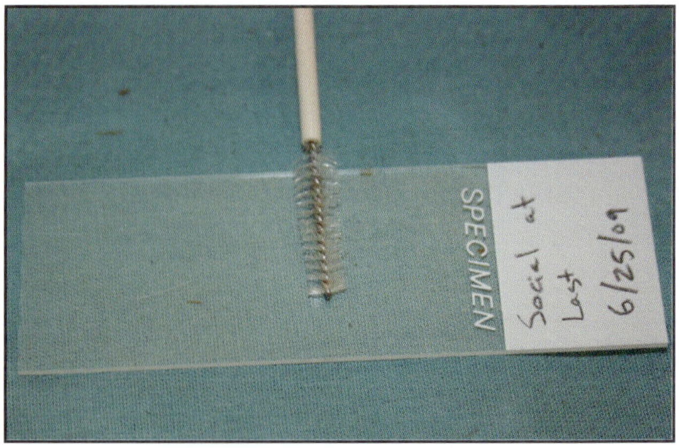

Figure 13-21 Rolling a cytology brush onto a glass slide in preparation for cytologic evaluation.

13.10 11.10 Endometrial Cytology

Cytologic evaluation of the uterus involves the collection and interpretation of cells lining the uterus (endometrium) and within the uterine lumen. Advantages of endometrial cytology for diagnosis of endometritis include the ease of sample collection and rapid availability of results. Endometrial cytology is one of the least expensive and most useful techniques routinely used to detect the presence of endometritis. A guarded Culture Swab or cytology brush is used to collect a swab of the uterine lumen and endometrium as previously described. The swab tip is then rolled along a Glass Slide (Figure 13-21), depositing cells and fluid collected from the endometrial surface. The slide is air-dried, fixed in alcohol and stained (i.e., Diff-Quick stain). Examination of the stained cytological specimen is done under a microscope.

The low-volume uterine lavage technique described in the previous section may also be used to collect material for cytological examination.

The quality of the cytology sample is first evaluated by observing the number of endometrial cells present. Then, the presence and relative number of inflammatory cells (white blood cells, especially neutrophils) (Figure 13-22 and Figure 13-23), bacteria, yeast and other debris is recorded (Figure 13-24). Presence of a significant number of white blood cells (i.e., more than 1 to 2 neutrophils per high power field) is an indication that significant inflammation is present. Absence of inflammatory cells usually indicates the absence of active inflammation (Table 13-3). However, some bacterial organisms (i.e. *E. coli*) may be present in the uterus

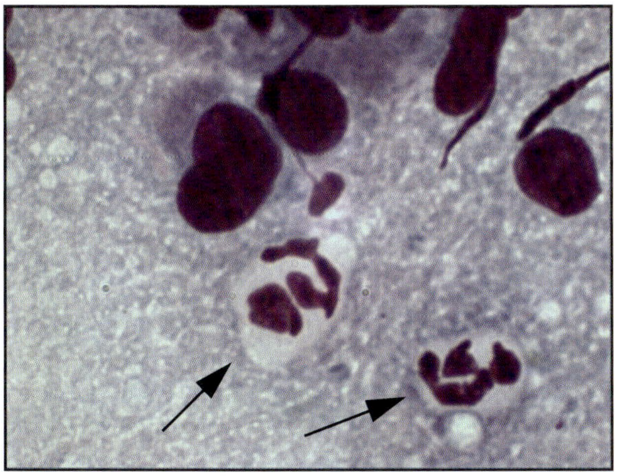

Figure 13-22 Inflammatory cells (arrows) observed during endometrial cytology from a mare with endometritis.

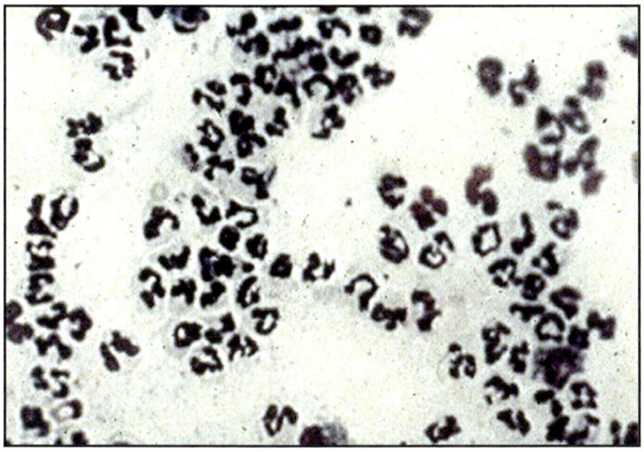

Figure 13-23 Inflammatory cells from the equine uterus.

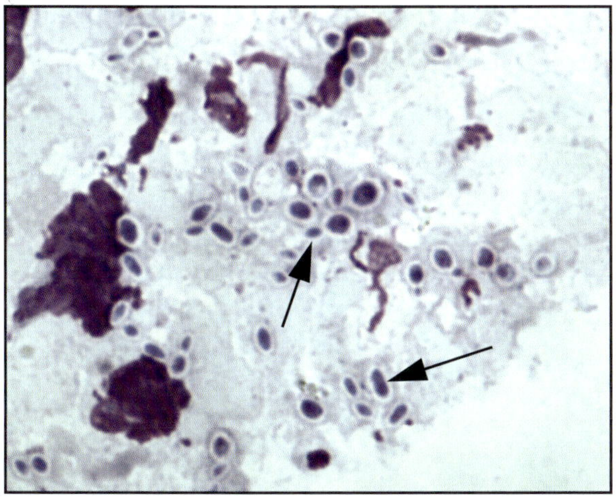

Figure 13-24 Yeast organisms (arrows) detected on endometrial cytology from a mare.

and not elicit a significant inflammatory response. In contrast, other bacterial organisms (i.e. *Streptococcus equi* subsp. *zooepidemicus*) are usually associated with a significant inflammatory response.

Table 13-3 Interpretation of endometrial cytology based on white blood cell (WBC) numbers.

# WBC/hpf	Interpretation
0	No inflammation
1 to 2	Mild inflammation
3 to 5	Moderate inflammation
> 5	Severe inflammation

13.11 Endometrial Biopsy

The endometrial biopsy technique involves collection of a small sample of the uterine lining (endometrium) for histologic evaluation(Figure 13-25). It is primarily used as an aid in the diagnosis of uterine disease and as a prognostic indicator of the ability of a mare to carry a foal to term.

Endometrial biopsy samples are examined for the presence of inflammatory (Figure 13-26) and

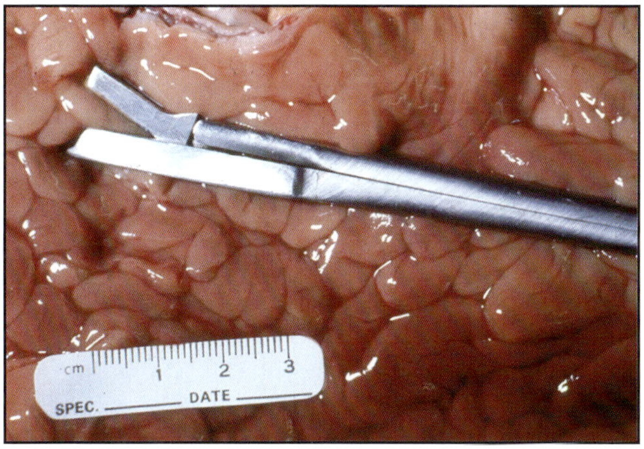

Figure 13-25 Uterine biopsy instrument for collection of endometrial biopsy samples.

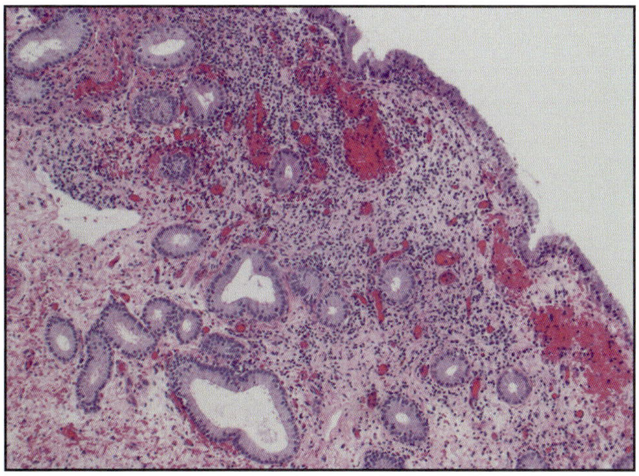

Figure 13-26 Inflammatory cells (lymphocytes) in the endometrial tissue.

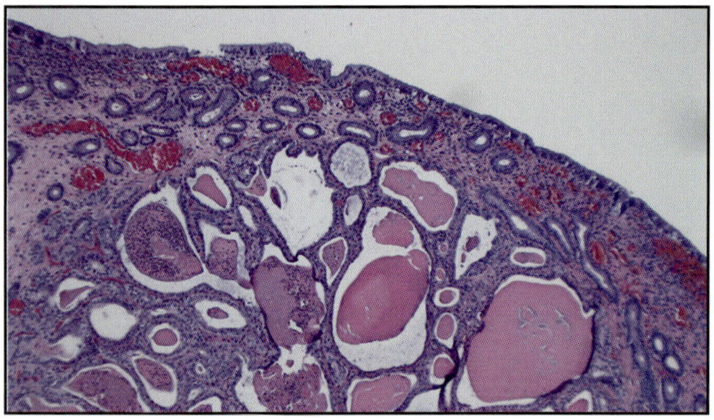

Figure 13-27 A 'nest' of dilated endometrial glands

degenerative changes (Figure 13-27). Inflammation represents a potentially treatable pathologic condition. In contrast to inflammation, fibrosis is a permanent, untreatable pathologic condition.

The endometrium is classified on a I-III grading scale based on biopsy characteristics. Grade I endometrium is essentially normal, with minimal inflammation or fibrosis. Grade III endometrium includes severe inflammatory and/or fibrotic changes. Grade II is a broad category encompassing all pathologic levels between Grades I and III.

It is possible for an improvement in endometrial grade if the inflammation present is reduced or eliminated with proper treatment.

The endometrial biopsy is often used to determine the prognosis for a mare to carry a foal to term. Expected foaling rates for each endometrial biopsy category are given in the following table (Table 13-4).

Table 13-4 Expected foaling rates of mares according to endometrial biopsy grade.

Grade	Degree of endometrial change	Expected foaling rate (%)
I	Absent	80 to 90
IIA	Mild	50 to 80
IIB	Moderate	10 to 50
III	Severe	<10

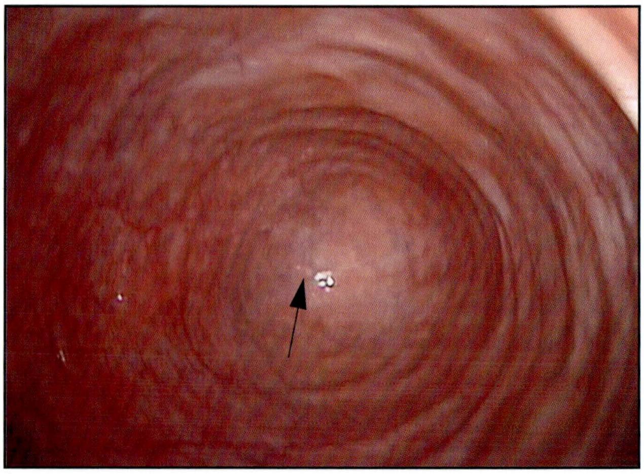

Figure 13-28 Hysteroscopic view of the inside of a uterine horn in a mare. The oviductal junction can be noted as a small papilla protruding into the uterus (arrow).

It must be emphasized that many additional factors, such as stallion and broodmare management, also play critical roles in conception and maintenance of pregnancy.

13.12 Hysteroscopy

The technique of direct visualization of the interior of the uterus, most commonly performed using an endoscope, is termed hysteroscopy (Figure 13-28). The endoscope may be used to detect intrauterine adhesions, cysts, and foreign bodies, as well as inflammation, fibrosis and other abnormalities.

13.13 Endocrinology

Analysis of reproductive hormones in the non-pregnant mare is most commonly performed to evaluate corpus luteum function and to diagnose ovarian abnormalities. Progesterone concentrations of < 1 ng/ml indicate an absence of luteal tissue, while concentrations > 1 ng/ml indicate the presence of an active corpus luteum. Testosterone and inhibin are occasionally measured to determine if an ovarian granulosa cell tumor (GCT) is present. Approximately 45 to 50 % of mares with ovarian granulosa cell tumors have elevated concentrations of testosterone. Mares with a GCT and elevated testosterone levels usually exhibit aggressive or stallion-like behavior. Inhibin is elevated in approximately 85 to 90% of mares with granulosa cell tumors (Figure 13-29). Anti-Müllerian hormone (AMH) concentrations are also elevated in a majority (95%) of mares with granulosa cell tumors.

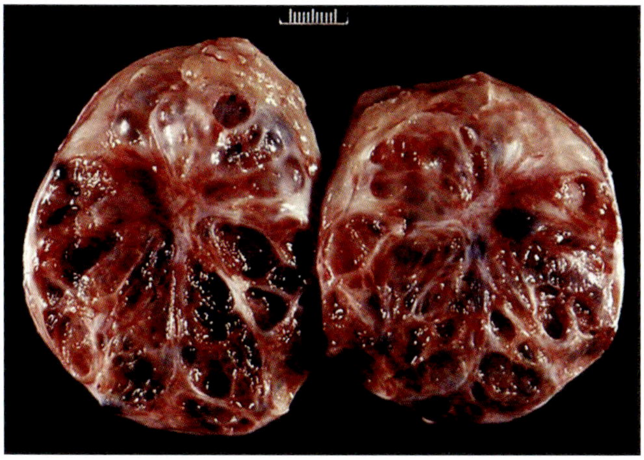

Figure 13-29 Granulosa cell tumor after surgical removal.

13.14 Chromosomal Abnormalities

Analysis of the chromosome number and structure, termed karyotyping, may be an important diagnostic test in the evaluation of primary infertility in the mare. The normal chromosome number of the horse is 64, consisting of 62 autosomes and 2 sex chromosomes. The karyotype of the normal mare and stallion are 64, XX and 64, XY, respectively (Figure 13-30 and Figure 13-31).

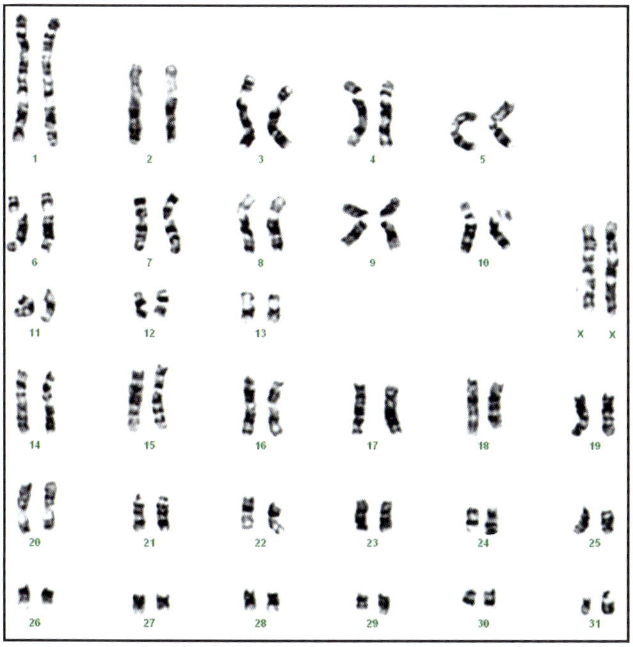

Figure 13-30 Karyotype of a normal 64, XX mare (courtesy of UC-Davis).

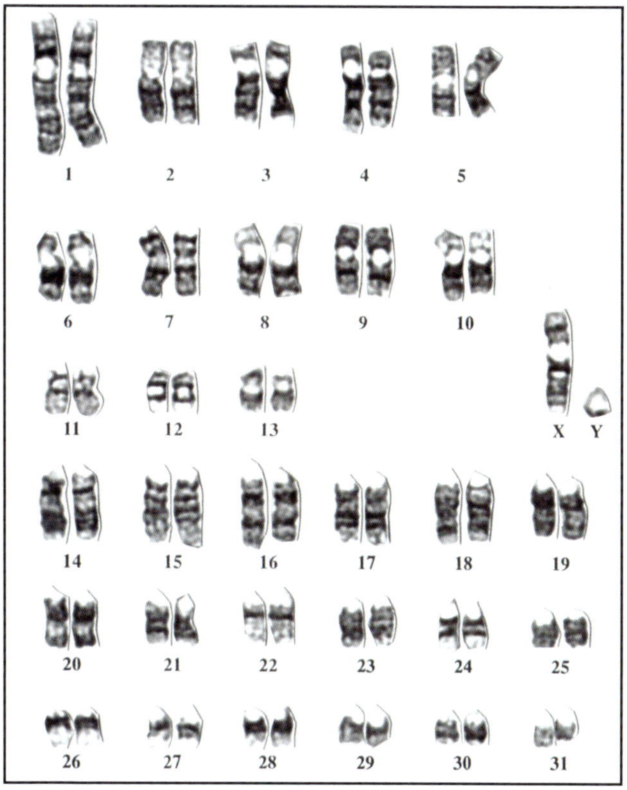

Figure 13-31 Karyotype of a normal 64, XY stallion or gelding (courtesy of UC-Davis).

The most commonly reported chromosomal abnormality of the horse is XO gonadal dysgenesis, a condition in which one of the sex chromosomes has been deleted, resulting in a 63, X karyotype. The equine condition is analogous to Turner's syndrome in humans. Horses with XO gonadal dysgenesis develop as phenotypic females due to the absence of a Y sex chromosome. Affected mares are often small in size for their age and breed, have small, inactive ovaries and are infertile. Several other chromosomal abnormalities have been reported in the horse, but are rarely encountered.

Chromosome analysis (karyotyping) is performed on blood or tissue samples by specialized diagnostic laboratories.

Chapter 14 Artificial Photoperiod and Hormone Therapy

14.1 Artificial Photoperiod to Modulate the Transition Period

The most common management strategy for advancement of the first ovulation of the year is by use of a stimulatory artificial photoperiod. Mares should be put under lights beginning in late November or early December to stimulate follicular development and ovulation by early February. In general, approximately 60 to 70 days of an artificial photo-period are required to induce ovulation. The most common techniques are to provide 16 hours of light and allow 8 hours of darkness (i.e. lights on at dusk and lights off at 11:00 pm) or to provide approximately 3 additional hours of artificial light beginning at dusk (Figure 14-1).

Incorporation of timing devices (Figure 14-2) to

Figure 14-2 Timer to control lights in a horse barn.

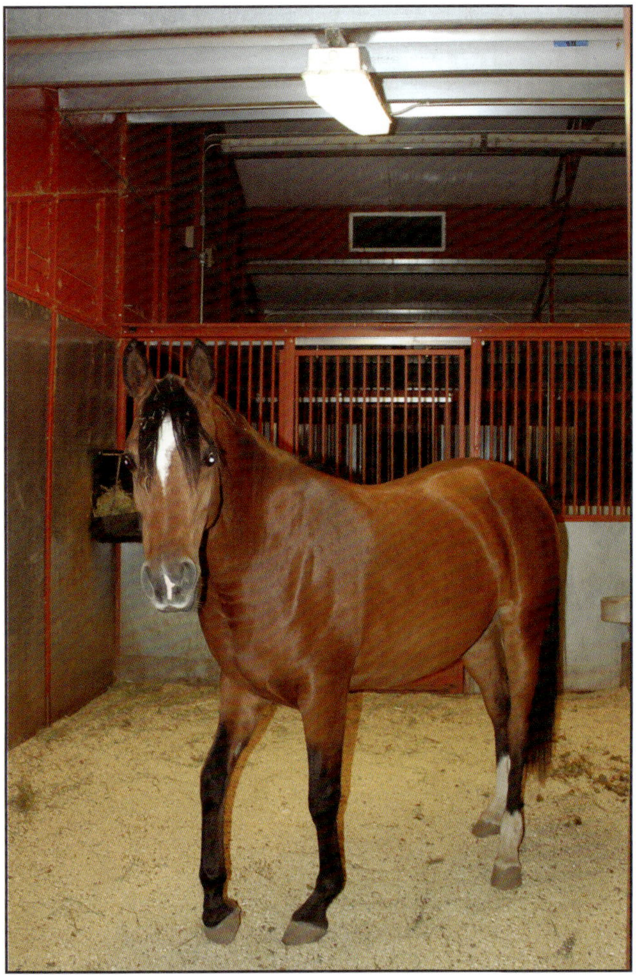

Figure 14-1 Fluorescent lights providing artificial photo-period.

control the lighting system is recommended. The type of light (i.e. fluorescent or incandescent) is not as important as the intensity and duration of the light. Follicular development will usually be stimulated if mares are housed under 10 or more ft. candles of artificial light. One 200-watt incandescent light bulb in a 12 ft by 12 ft stall is usually sufficient to provide 10 to 12 ft candles of light. Accurate photometers may be obtained or borrowed from local electrical contractors to test farm light programs.

Light of a specific wavelength (468 nm; blue light) and intensity (a minimum of 10 lux) can be directed into either one or both eyes and alter the pattern of melatonin secretion. A head mask (Equilume®) Light Mask) has been designed which contains an array of 5 LEDs covered with diffusing material so that it emits a low-level blue glow on a single eye (Figure 14-3). The mask may be programmed to begin emitting light at 4:00 pm and shut off at 11:00 pm. Initiation of low-level blue light exposure to mares on December 1 results in stimulation of ovarian follicular development and advancement of the breeding season that is equally effective in stimulating reproductive activity as traditional barn lights (i.e. stable lighting).

Potential advantages of the blue light mask to horse

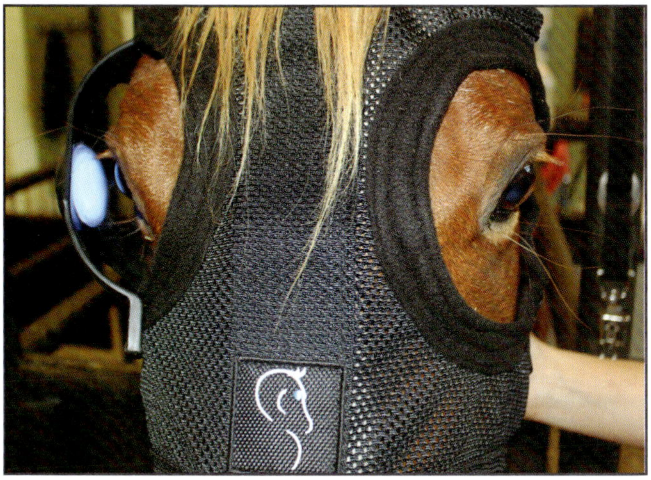

Figure 14-3 Equilume® blue light mask on a mare.

owners are that 1) their mare(s) can be maintained outdoors, which will reduce the time and cost of cleaning stalls and purchasing bedding and 2) the need to install stable light and timer systems for small breeders would be eliminated.

14.2 Hormone Therapy

A wide variety of hormone therapies are used in clinical practice in the reproductive management of mares.

Stimulation of Follicular Development

Hormone therapy has been utilized to advance the first ovulation of the year in seasonally anestrous mares, stimulate follicular development in postpartum acyclic mares and promote development of multiple follicles in cycling mares. The most successful strategies have incorporated natural or recombinant equine follicle stimulating hormone (FSH) or low-doses of a gonadotropin releasing hormone (GnRH) agonist.

Administration of purified equine FSH (eFSH) or recombinant equine FSH (reFSH) has been reported to be successful in stimulation of follicular development in seasonally anestrus mares. Unfortunately, there are no equine FSH products commercially available currently.

An alternative is twice daily low-dose (10 to 125 μg) administration of a GnRH agonist such as deslorelin, histrelin or buserelin. Mares in spring transition (i.e. with follicles ≥ 25 mm in diameter) are more likely to respond than mares in deep winter anestrus (i.e. follicles < 20 mm in diameter). Mares in deep winter anestrus that do respond to low-dose GnRH agonist therapy are more likely to revert back to anestrus after treatment is discontinued than mares initially treated during spring transition. In general, follicular development is evident within 3 to 5 days after the onset of therapy. It is recommended that human chorionic gonadotropin be administered to induce ovulation of a follicle stimulated by low-dose GnRH therapy.

Administration of progesterone or progestins during deep seasonal anestrus will not stimulate follicular development. However, progesterone treatment near the end of spring transition can be used to synchronize or 'program' the day of the first ovulation of the year. Common protocols include administration of altrenogest (i.e. Regu-Mate®) once daily for 14 days or administration of a combination of progesterone and estradiol once daily for 10 days, with administration of a dose of prostaglandins on the last day of therapy.

Induction of Ovulation

Induction of ovulation is advantageous if a mare is in a timed breeding, shipped semen, frozen semen or embryo transfer program. In addition, in mares with a history of accumulating fluid in the uterus following mating or insemination, it may be beneficial to induce ovulation and limit the number of times the mare has to be bred.

Human chorionic gonadotropin (hCG) was first used for induction of ovulation of mares in 1939. The biological action of hCG is due to its inherent luteinizing hormone (LH) like activity. hCG is generally administered when a mare is in estrus with a follicle ≥ 35 mm in diameter and endometrial edema is present. Ovulation is induced in 85 to 90 % of mares within 48 hours, with an average of 36 hours after hCG administration. hCG is most effective in inducing ovulation in young to middle age mares receiving the hormone for the first 2 or 3 times within a single breeding season. Efficacy at inducing a timed ovulation may be somewhat reduced if hCG is given to a mare repeatedly during the same breeding season.

Potent agonists of gonadotropin releasing hormone (GnRH) such as deslorelin (SucroMate™ and Ovuplant™), buserelin and histrelin have also been used to induce ovulation in cycling mares (Table 14-1). Administration of a GnRH agonist will stimulate LH release from the anterior pituitary which will subsequently stimulate follicle maturation, ovulation and formation of the corpus luteum. GnRH agonist administration will induce ovulation in 90 to 95 % of mares within 48 hours, with an average of approximately 40 hours.

Table 14-1 Hormone therapy to induce ovulation in cycling mares

Hormone	Dosage, Route, Frequency
Buserelin	1 to 1.5 mg, IM, once
Deslorelin	1.8 mg, IM, once
Histrelin	0.5 to 1.0 mg, IM, once
Human Chorionic Gonadotropin (hCG)	1,500 to 2,500 units, IV or IM, once

A convenient strategy to induce a timed ovulation in a mare being inseminated with frozen semen is to administer a GnRH agonist at 8:00 pm and anticipate ovulation at approximately 12:00 (noon), 40 hours later (Figure 14-4).

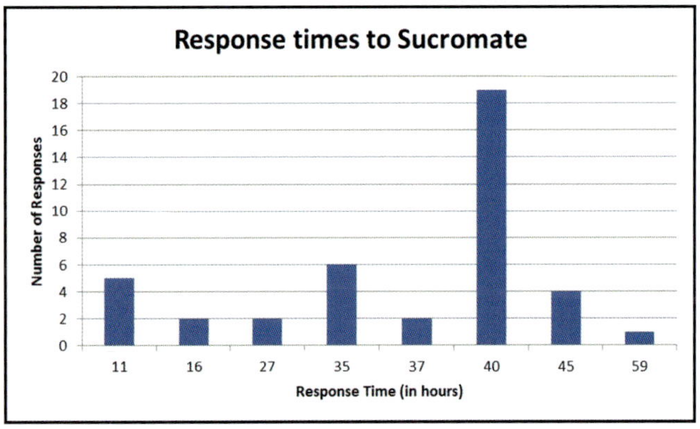

Figure 14-4 Interval from deslorelin (SucroMate™) administration at 8:00 pm to subsequent ovulation in mares being inseminated with frozen semen post-ovulation.

Pregnancy Support

Progesterone production by the corpus luteum is required for maintenance of pregnancy during the first 2 to 3 months of gestation. Progesterone levels less than 4.0 ng/ml are associated with an increased risk of pregnancy loss. Administration of exogenous progesterone for 'pregnancy support' and the risk of pregnancy loss due to 'progesterone deficiency' are controversial topics.

Progesterone/progestin supplementation for mares at risk is usually initiated either 1 to 2 days after ovulation is detected, after ultrasonographic detection of a pregnancy with concurrent presence of uterine edema and/or a small or absent corpus luteum, or measurement of low plasma progesterone levels. Therapy is often continued until day 120 of pregnancy, at which time production of progesterone by the placenta is adequate to maintain pregnancy. Options for progesterone/progestin support are presented in Table 14-2.

Table 14-2 Hormone therapy for maintenance of pregnancy.

Hormone	Dosage, Route, Frequency
Altrenogest	0.044 mg/kg, orally, q 24h
Altrenogest (high risk pregnancy)	0.088 mg/kg, orally, q 24h or 0.044 mg/kg, orally, q 12h
Progesterone	200 mg, IM, q 24h
Progesterone - Long Acting	1,500 mg, IM, q 7 days

Supplemental progesterone administration may be used to support problem pregnancies or pregnancies at risk due to placentitis, endotoxemia, colic or other medical problems. In these instances, altrenogest is commonly given at twice the 'normal' dose during the time the mare is at high risk or altrenogest therapy may be continued for the duration of the pregnancy. Additional treatments may include flunixin meglumine, antibiotics or other drugs depending on the specific medical condition.

Luteolysis and Short-Cycling

Luteolysis or destruction of the corpus luteum is the basis of therapeutic applications such as short-cycling, estrous synchronization, treatment of a persistent corpus luteum and termination of pregnancy. The equine corpus luteum takes approximately 5 days to become fully developed or mature and be responsive to prostaglandins. Administration of prostaglandins early in the post-ovulation period will adversely affect development of the corpus luteum. Repeated administration in the post-ovulatory period will result in failure of the corpus luteum to form (anti-luteogenic effect). Estrous synchronization may be achieved by administration of two doses of prostaglandins 14 days apart.

Prostaglandin products used in the horse include cloprostenol sodium (Estrumate®) and dinoprost tromethamine (Lutalyse®) administered as an intramuscular injection. Side effects of prostaglandin treatment include mild to moderate sweating, abdominal discomfort and transient diarrhea.

It is recommended that mares be examined by ultrasound prior to administration of prostaglandins to confirm that it is the correct mare, a corpus luteum is present, she is not pregnant and determine the diameter of the largest ovarian follicle. Overall, the average interval to ovulation following prostaglandin administration is 8.4 ± 2.5 days, and is inversely proportional to the diameter of the largest follicle at time of treatment (Table 3). Knowledge of the diameter of the largest follicle at the time of prostaglandin administration is very helpful in prediction of the duration to subsequent ovulation and potential avoidance of weekend semen shipments or times when a stallion is not available.

Table 14-3 Interval from prostaglandin administration in diestrus to subsequent ovulation in mares with a dominant follicle less than 35 mm in diameter.

Follicle Size (mm)	Cycles	Interval to Ovulation (days)
<10	6	11.8 ± 1.1^{a}
10 to 14	74	10.2 ± 0.2^{b}
15 to 19	83	9.1 ± 0.2^{c}
20 to 24	118	9.1 ± 0.2^{c}
25 to 29	122	9.1 ± 0.2^{c}
30 to 34	37	7.8 ± 0.5^{d}

Large diestrous follicles (≥35 mm) exhibit one of three outcomes following PGF treatment: ovulation within 48 hours in the absence of uterine edema (15 % of cases), ovulation after 48 hours accompanied by uterine edema (75 % of cases), or regression without ovulation followed by emergence of a new follicular wave (10 % of cases).

Pregnancy Termination

Elective termination of a pregnancy or a potential pregnancy may be indicated following an unplanned mating of a mare, breeding a mare with the wrong stallion or other clinical situations. Administration of a single dose of prostaglandins is usually sufficient for complete luteolysis and termination of pregnancy from day 5 post-ovulation until formation of the secondary corpora lutea. Multiple doses of prostaglandins may be required for complete luteolysis and termination of a pregnancy after day 35. Treated mares should be re-evaluated 5 to 10 days later to confirm that the pregnancy is no longer present.

Stimulation of Uterine Contractions

Stimulation of uterine contractions (i.e. an ecbolic effect) is used clinically for evacuation of uterine fluid, induction of labor and management of retained placentas. The two most common hormones with ecbolic effects used in equine practice are oxytocin and prostaglandins.

Oxytocin administration results in uterine muscular contractions for 30 to 45 minutes. Oxytocin may be administered 1 to 4 or more times per day in an attempt to evacuate fluid from the uterus of older mares or mares with persistent mating induced endometritis. In contrast, prostaglandin administration stimulates uterine contractions for 2 to 4 hours and may be more effective at evacuation of uterine fluid than oxytocin in some mares. A combination of oxytocin and prostaglandins may be administered to evacuate uterine fluid in some problem mares.

Administration of prostaglandins to mares either the day ovulation is detected or for 1 to 2 days after ovulation adversely affects the development of the corpus luteum and is associated with a reduction in pregnancy rate. In contrast, prostaglandin treatment prior to ovulation does not affect CL function. Oxytocin does not have any adverse effects on corpus luteum development when administered either prior to or after ovulation. Consequently, prostaglandins or oxytocin may be used to evacuate uterine fluid prior to ovulation, but oxytocin is a more appropriate choice for treatment after ovulation is detected.

Suppression of Estrus

Expression of behavioral estrus can have a profound negative effect on training and performance in some mares. Consequently, hormone therapy for suppression of estrus is common in the equine industry. Progesterone is the hormone that naturally suppresses expression of behavioral estrus. Administration of the synthetic progestin altrenogest once daily is generally effective at suppression of estrus in a majority of mares. Altrenogest treatment should be initiated at least 2 to 3 days prior to a performance event to allow sufficient time for behavioral modification. It is not recommended to use intramuscular progesterone/progestin products for suppression of estrus in performance mares due to the potential for inflammation at the injection site.

Administration of 60 units of oxytocin intramuscularly once or twice daily from day 7 to 14 of the estrous cycle has been reported to result in prolongation of the corpus luteum (pseudopregnancy) in approximately 60 to 70 % of mares treated and may be useful as a means of estrous suppression.

Cattle implants containing progesterone and estradiol have been administered to horses in an attempt to suppress heat. However, the implants do not suppress estrus due to the low amount of progesterone in the implants and the designed slow release rate (150 days). Consequently, the use of cattle implants for suppression of estrus in performance mares is not supported or recommended.

Other synthetic progestins, such as medroxyprogesterone acetate, hydroxyprogesterone caproate, norgestomet and megesterol acetate have also been administered to mares in an attempt to block estrus or maintain pregnancy. Unfortunately, none of the synthetic progestins other than altrenogest are effective in suppression of estrus or maintenance of pregnancy in mares since they do not bind adequately to the equine progesterone receptor. Consequently, although these products may appear to be convenient, they should not be used in horses due to lack of efficacy.

Administration of a vaccine against GnRH has also been used for suppression of estrus as well as contraception in mares, but is currently not commercially available in the United States.

Sterilized glass marbles have been inserted into the uterus of mares for the purpose of estrous suppression. Presence of a marble within the uterine lumen may induce formation of a persistent corpus luteum and elevated progesterone levels for 2 to 3 months. However, efficacy at inducing a persistent corpus luteum is low and anecdotal reports have indicated that complications may occur in some mares, such as uterine infections, fracture of the marble and difficulty in removal of the marble.

Stimulation of Behavioral Estrus

Estradiol-17β may be administered to an ovariectomized, seasonally anestrous or acyclic mare to stimulate behavioral estrus and allow the mare to be used as a tease mare or jump mare for semen collection. Estradiol administration will also result in a profound increase in uterine edema and promote cervical relaxation. Estradiol will not stimulate behavioral estrus when administered to a cycling mare in diestrus when progesterone levels are elevated. Conjugated estrogens (i.e. estradiol cypionate or estradiol valerate) will have a longer half-life and similar biological effects as the natural hormone estradiol-17β.

Induction of Labor

Oxytocin is the most common hormone used in equine practice to induce labor. Routine induction of labor is not recommended and should only be performed if the in utero fetus is sufficiently mature to survive after induced delivery. The following guidelines may be used to determine if the mare qualifies for induction:

- Gestation length of at least 330 days
- Mammary gland development and engorgement of the teats with colostrum
- Elevation in milk calcium

An effective protocol for induction of labor involves administration of a low dose of oxytocin, followed by a second dose 15 minutes later. The mare will usually rupture her chorioallantoic membrane approximately 10 minutes after the second dose of oxytocin and deliver the fetus within the subsequent 5 to 15 minutes.

Induction of Lactation

Failure of udder development and lactation may occur in pregnant mares grazing on pastures with tall fescue grass infested with an endophytic fungus. Agalactia may also occur in situations other than fescue toxicosis, such as a young mare giving birth to her first foal. Absence or inadequate lactation may result in failure of passive transfer of antibodies to the newborn foal and inadequate nutrition for a growing foal.

Lactation can be stimulated in mares by administration of a dopamine antagonist, such as domperidone or sulpiride. Pretreatment with estradiol enhances the effect of dopamine antagonist therapy on stimulation of prolactin secretion. Dopamine antagonists have also been used to induce lactation in nurse mares to be used for adoption of orphaned foals. The optimal choice for a nurse mare would be a mare that has foaled previously, lactated appropriately and exhibited good maternal behavior.

A protocol for induction of lactation in a nurse mare is as follows:

- Select a calm, gentle mare that has given birth and lactated previously.
- Administer estradiol intramuscularly once per day for 2 to 3 days. Potentially continue estradiol therapy every other day during the first few days of dopamine antagonist treatment.
- Begin daily administration of domperidone (1.1 mg/kg, orally, once daily).
- Start hand milking several times daily as the mammary gland increases in size and secretions start to be produced.
- Introduce the foal after the mare has started to produce milk.

Retained Placenta

Retention of the fetal membranes is one of the most common postpartum problems in the mare. An equine placenta is considered to be pathologically retained at 3 hours postpartum. Retention may include the entire chorioallantoic membrane or just the tip of the non-pregnant horn. The incidence of retained placentas increases in mares with dystocia, prolonged gestation, hydrops, cesarean surgeries or induced labor. Complications associated with retained fetal membranes include metritis, laminitis, septicemia and death.

Therapy for retained placenta in the horse include administration of oxytocin or prostaglandins, infusion of water in the allantoic cavity ('Burns Technique' or water technique) or infusion of water into an umbilical blood vessel ('Dutch Technique'). Additional treatments may include uterine lavage, intrauterine antibiotics, parenteral antibiotics, nonsteroidal anti-inflammatory drugs, and tetanus toxoid.

Chapter 15. Breeding Management of the Mare

Mares may be bred by natural cover or artificial insemination, depending on breed registry regulations, preference of the stallion owner and/or mare owner, location and availability of the stallion and mare, cost, safety concerns, experience of personnel, and other factors.

15.1 Natural Cover

Natural cover (also referred to as live cover or natural service) is the only breeding technique allowed in Thoroughbred mares if the foal is to be registered with the Jockey Club. Mares of other breeds may be bred by either natural service or artificial insemination techniques.

15.2 Pasture Breeding

In a pasture breeding program, a stallion is typically turned out with a band of up to 20 to 25 mares for approximately 60 to 90 days or more beginning in April or May (Figure 15-1).

The advantages of pasture breeding are decreased horse handling, decreased expenses for personnel, and decreased breeding expenses.

Disadvantages include potential for injury to the stallion or the mares, inability to detect reproductive problems with either the stallion or the mares while they are turned out together, spread of disease through the herd, and lack of an accurate conception date for calculation of a foaling date. It is often not possible to confirm that a given mare was even covered by the stallion.

***Figure 15-1** Stallion mating a mare in a pasture breeding program.*

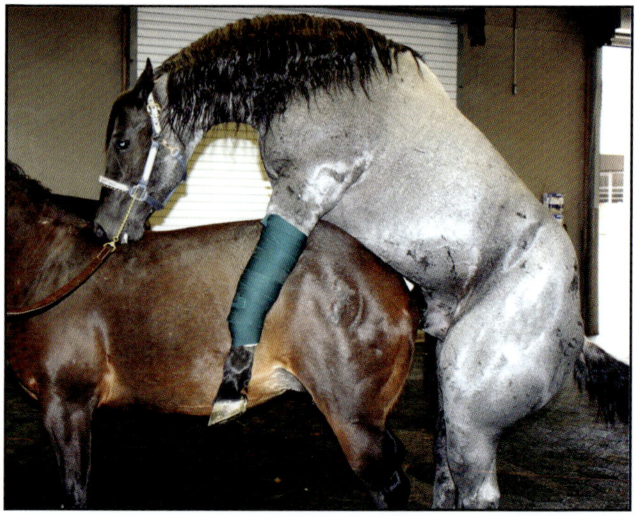

***Figure 15-2** Natural service where both stallion and mare are handled.*

15.3 Hand Mating

Hand mating implies that both the stallion and mare will be handled and restrained in a controlled breeding environment (Figure 15-2).

Advantages of hand breeding over pasture breeding are:

- Breeding can be scheduled and confirmed
- The mare can be examined before and after breeding to confirm ovulation and evaluate the reproductive tract
- Theoretically, hand breeding offers less risk to the stallion than pasture breeding
- A dismount sample can be collected from the stallion after mating to confirm ejaculation occurred and confirm the presence of live motile spermatozoa

Disadvantages of hand breeding are:

- Time required for satisfactory examination and teasing of mares
- Number of personnel involved in the breeding process
- Risk of injury to personnel in the breeding shed

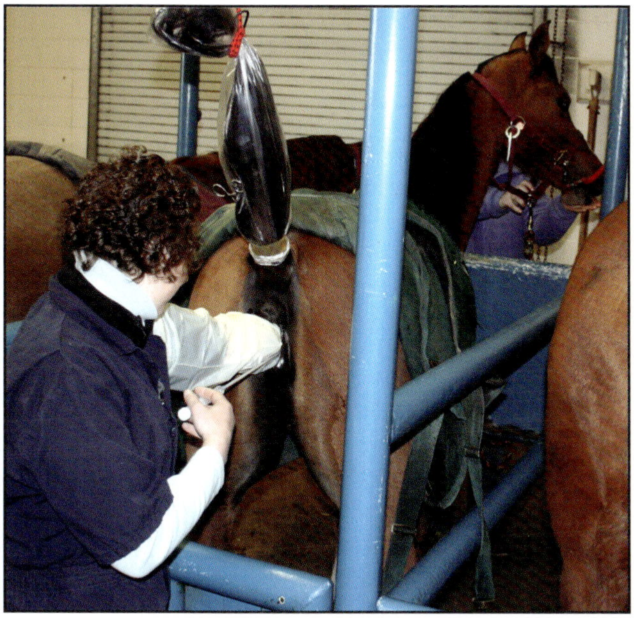

Figure 15-3 Artificial insemination of a mare.

15.4 Artificial Insemination

Artificial insemination (AI) of mares involves collection of semen from a stallion and deposition of that semen into the uterus of a mare in heat (Figure 15-3).

The ability to cool and freeze equine semen makes it feasible to ship semen from one location to another, giving mare and stallion owners more flexibility in their breeding program. A majority of breed associations have accepted the use of artificial insemination, cooled-transported semen and frozen semen. Consequently, mare owners have the opportunity to breed to stallions across the country or around the world.

15.5 Fresh Semen

When fresh semen is deposited into the reproductive tract of the mare, the sperm cells will usually remain viable for at least 48 hours. Therefore, a generally recommended breeding strategy consists of depositing fresh semen into the reproductive tract at least once every 48 hours while the mare is in heat, with at least one dose of semen being deposited within 48 hours prior to ovulation. Each insemination dose should contain at least 500 million progressively motile sperm, and should be diluted at least 1:1 with a satisfactory semen extender like E-Z Mixin® - CST (i.e. a skim milk-glucose type extender) containing an appropriate antibiotic. It is not recommended to use "raw" or un-extended semen for artificial insemination (AI).

15.6 Cooled Semen

Stallion semen may be cooled and transported from the site of collection to the location of the mare or semen may be cooled to use the next day on the breeding farm.

Spermatozoa that have been cooled for 24 hours will generally remain viable for an additional 24 to 48 hours after deposition into the reproductive tract of the mare. It is therefore recommended that the mare be inseminated with cooled semen within 24 to 48 hours prior to the anticipated ovulation. In most instances, it is anticipated that only one shipment of semen will be sent for a given mare in a single estrous cycle. In order to coordinate the timing of semen shipment, insemination and ovulation, the mare must be monitored closely by transrectal palpation and ultrasonography.

Semen can be shipped by counter-to-counter airline service and arrive later in the same day as collected or can be shipped by overnight courier service and arrive the next day.

Mares in a shipped semen program are almost always administered hCG or deslorelin to induce ovulation soon after insemination and to eliminate the need for a second semen shipment. The ovulation inducing agent may be administered at the time the semen is ordered, when the shipment of semen has been confirmed, or when the semen arrives.

The shipping container should be kept closed until the mare is ready for insemination. At that time, a dose of cooled semen is removed from the container, gently mixed, and inseminated into the mare without pre-warming. A small aliquot should be saved, warmed to 37° C for 10 minutes in an incubator and evaluated under a microscope for motility characteristics. It is expected that there will be some loss of motility during the cooling and transportation process. Each insemination dose of cooled semen should contain at least one billion progressively motile sperm at the time that it is packaged. A cooled semen sample would be considered good if progressive motility was at least 50 to 60 % after 24 hours of cooling.

The stallion manager may package and ship one or two doses of cooled semen for a given mare. A mare owner may request two doses, but the final decision is made by the stallion manager and is often dependent on the number of motile sperm collected from the stallion, the number of mares to be bred on the farm, and the number of cooled-transported doses requested for that day. If a single dose is sent, it is generally inseminated immediately upon arrival. If two doses are sent, the mare manager has several options for insemination. One option is to inseminate one dose of semen immediately upon arrival, keep the second dose cooled, and inseminate the second dose the next day. This tactic works well if the mare has a normal reproductive tract and if the semen retains adequate motility after 48 hours of cooling. If the second dose is to be kept cooled, it is recommended that a new frozen can or pack be placed into the passive cooling transport system or that the semen be placed in a small container in a refrigerator at 5 to 8° C.

A second option is to put both doses into the mare when the semen shipment first arrives. This may be beneficial in cases in which the uterus of the mare reacts to the presence of spermatozoa with a severe prolonged inflammatory response or if the motility of the stallion is known to be poor after 48 hours of cooled storage. The decision regarding how to use two doses of semen should be based on cooling characteristics of the semen and uterine health of the mare to be bred. A comparison of options for breeding management of mares if two doses of semen are presented in Table 15-1.

Table 15-1 Options for insemination of mares if two cooled doses of semen are available.

Mare Information	Stallion Information	Optimal Insemination Option
Young Maiden Mare	Semen with adequate longevity	AI with one dose at arrival of semen; AI with second dose the following day. Her uterus may not be able to hold the volume of two doses if inseminated at the same time and a substantial portion of the semen will be passed soon after insemination
Middle-aged broodmare	Semen with adequate longevity	Both options are available. One can inseminate with doses at the same time. Her uterus should be large enough to accommodate the volume of the combined doses; Alternatively, the second dose can be inseminated the next day
Older mare with a history of persistent mating-induced endometritis	Semen with adequate longevity	AI only once during a given estrous cycle; May choose to inseminate with only one dose (and discard the second dose) or use both doses at the same time; Start uterine therapy 4-6 hours after insemination. Do not AI a second time due to uterine hypersensitivity
Any type of mare	Semen with poor longevity	AI once with one or both doses of semen; Pointless to cool the second dose if low motility is predicted after an additional 24 hours of cooling; Spermatozoa may be better off in the reproductive tract of the mare

15.7 Frozen Semen

There are a number of strategies for successful use of frozen semen. The optimal strategy for a given mare may depend on the number of straws or doses available and the post-thaw motility. It is generally accepted that frozen-thawed spermatozoa will remain viable for only 12 hours in the reproductive tract of a mare and that the equine oocyte can remain capable of fertilization for only 6 to 12 hours after ovulation. Consequently, the timing of insemination and ovulation must be very tight when using frozen semen. If only a single dose of frozen semen is available, it may be optimal to inseminate immediately after ovulation is detected.

If the amount of frozen semen available is not limited, a common breeding strategy is to deposit one dose of frozen semen in the uterus within 12 hours prior to the expected ovulation and deposit a second dose within 6 to 8 hours after ovulation has been detected.

Alternatively, if only dose of frozen semen is available, a common strategy is to induce a timed ovulation by administration of a GnRH agonist (i.e. Deslorelin) at 8:00 pm when the mare is in heat and has a dominant follicle of the appropriate diameter (Figure 15-4); ovulation would be anticipated 40 hours later (or at approximately 12:00 noon). The mare is monitored by ultrasound every 6 hours and inseminated immediately once ovulation has been detected. A second option is to split the single dose and inseminate the mare with one-half of the dose prior to the anticipated ovulation and inseminate the other one-half dose after ovulation has been confirmed.

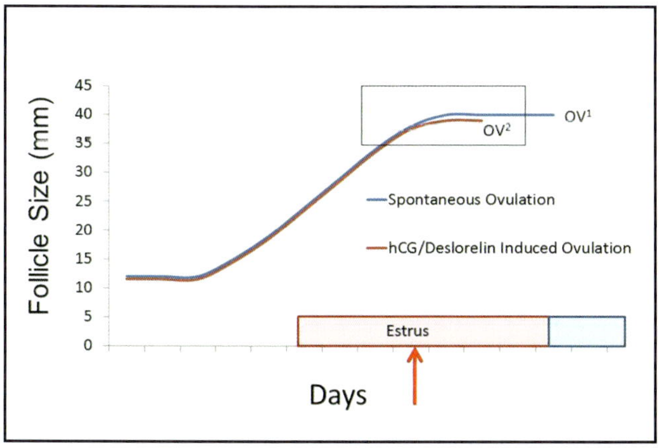

Figure 15-4 Window of opportunity for taking control of the pre-ovulatory follicle and inducing a timed ovulation when breeding mares with frozen semen. The arrow designates the time of administration of hCG or deslorelin, OV^1 - expected time of natural or spontaneous ovulation, OV^2 - expected time of ovulation after induction with either hCG or deslorelin. Note that the time of the induced ovulation occurs one or two days prior to the natural or spontaneous ovulation.

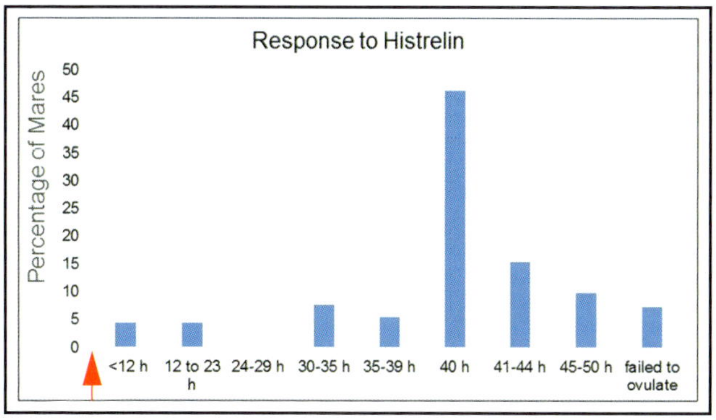

Figure 15-5 Graph of intervals to ovulation after administration of the GnRH agonist histrelin (arrow) to induce a timed ovulation. Note that the most frequent interval to ovulation is at 40 hours.

Unfortunately, not all mares administered deslorelin ovulate at exactly 40 hours. Ultrasound examinations must be performed periodically after deslorelin administration as some mares ovulate earlier than predicted and others ovulate later (Figure 15-5). In addition, some mares do not ovulate at all after deslorelin or hCG administration.

15.8 Summary

The length of time that sperm cells remain viable within the reproductive tract of the mare varies tremendously between fresh, cooled and frozen equine semen and varies with each stallion. Fresh semen will generally remain viable for at least 48 hours, cooled semen for 24 to 48 hours, and frozen semen only about 12 hours. Therefore, the goal of breeding management of the mare is to deposit semen into the reproductive tract at a time that will maximize the probability that viable sperm cells are present at ovulation. Breeding management techniques that are utilized include: 1) estrous detection, 2) transrectal palpation and/or ultrasonography, and 3) hormonal therapy. Although the use of cooled or frozen semen provides numerous advantages, owners and breeders must realize that the time and expense required for optimal breeding management may be much greater with cooled or frozen semen compared to that required for fresh semen or natural service.

Chapter 16. Reproductive Problems in the Mare

Reproductive problems are encountered in mares frequently over the course of a breeding season. A problem mare may be defined as:

- A mare that is not pregnant after being bred to a fertile stallion over 3 estrous cycles
- A mare that cannot successfully carry a foal to term
- A mare with known reproductive pathology
- A mare with behavioral issues related to reproduction.

A list of the common and less common reproductive problems in broodmares are presented in the table below.

Common Reproductive Problems	Less Common Reproductive Problems
Behavior	**Behavior**
Adverse behavior when in estrus	Persistent estrus
Silent heat	Stallion-like behavior
Ovary	**Ovary**
Hemorrhagic follicles	Ovarian tumors
Ovulation failure	Failure of follicular development
Persistent corpus luteum	
Premature luteolysis (endometritis)	
Oviduct	**Oviduct**
Parovarian cysts	Oviductal blockage
	Salpingitis
Uterus	**Uterus**
Persistent mating-induced endometritis (PMIE)	Fungal endometritis
Bacterial endometritis	Pyometra
Uterine cysts	Persistent endometrial cups
Endometrosis	Tumor (i.e. leiomyoma)
	Foreign body
Cervix	**Cervix**
Failure of cervical relaxation	Cervical adhesions
	Cervical lacerations
	Tumor (i.e. leiomyoma)
Vagina/Vestibule	**Vagina/Vestibule**
Urovagina	Lacerations
Vericose veins	Adhesions
Imperforate hymen	Vaginitis
Perineum	**Perineum**
Poor conformation	Squamous cell carcinoma
Inadequate vulva tone	Coital exanthema (EHV-3)
Perineal lacerations	
Melanoma (grey mares)	
Miscellaneous	**Miscellaneous**
Cushing's disease (PPID)	Chromosomal abnormalities
	Mastitis
	Inappropriate lactation

16.1 Anovulatory Follicles

Ovulation failure is a normal physiologic event for the mare during the spring and fall transition periods. The development of anovulatory follicles may occasionally occur during the physiologic breeding season. The cause(s) of ovulation failure are unknown.

There are two subtypes of anovulatory follicles. Approximately 85 % of anovulatory follicles are associated with hemorrhage and eventual luteinization (Figure 16-1). Hemorrhagic anovulatory follicles (HAF) occur when significant bleeding occurs into the lumen of the dominant follicle during estrus. Initially the blood does not clot due to anticoagulant factors present in equine follicular fluid. Eventually the blood clots and the fibrin scaffold-

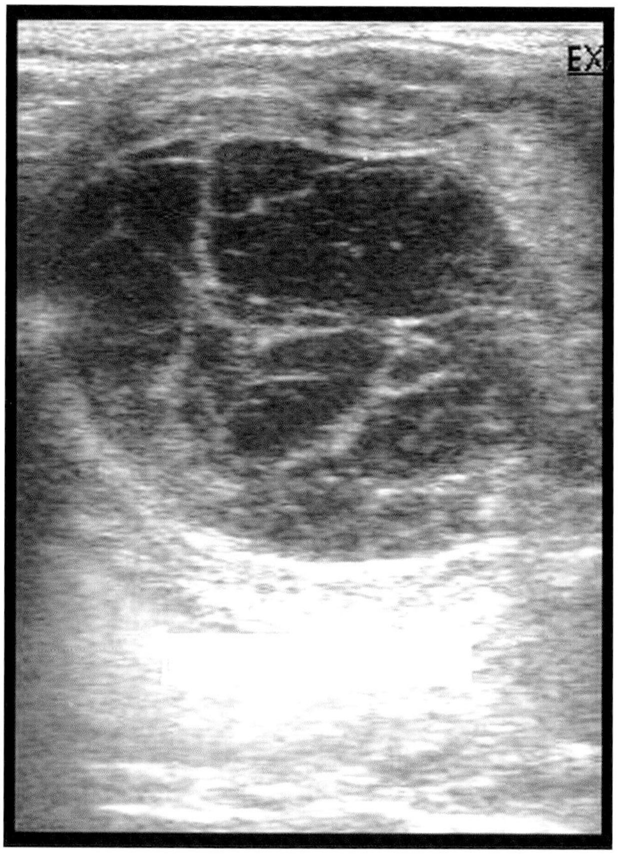

Figure 16-1 Hemorrhagic anovulatory follicle.

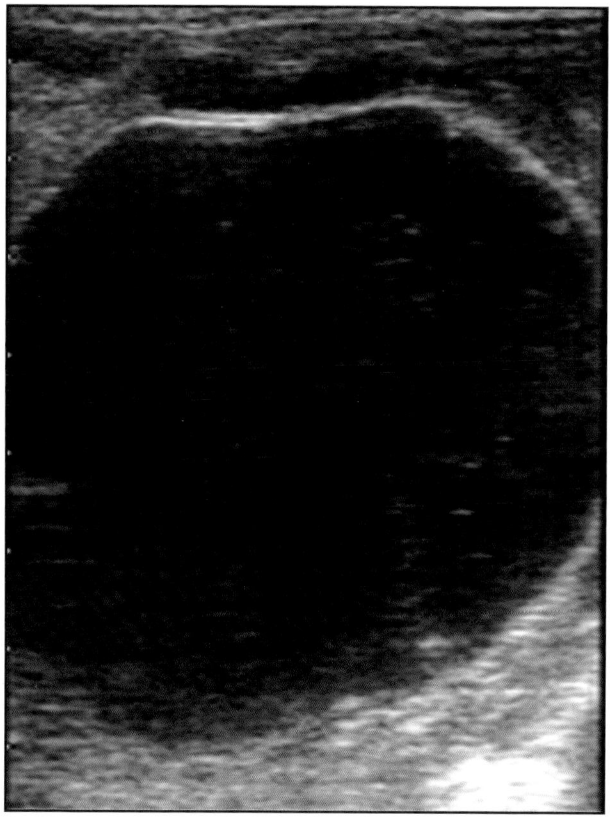

Figure 16-2 Persistent anovulatory follicle.

ing within the blood clot allows granulosa and theca cells to invade and luteinize. The now luteinized anovulatory follicle produces a large amount of progesterone. Approximately 15 % of anovulatory follicles remain as non-viable persistent anovulatory follicle (PAF) (Figure 16-2). As the follicle becomes non-viable, estrogen levels decrease, uterine edema goes away and the mare goes out of heat. A PAF does not luteinize and therefore does not produce progesterone.

In addition to the two primary subtypes of anovulatory follicles, a low percentage of mares may exhibit partial collapse of a follicle. Pregnancy rates associated with a partially collapsed follicle are low, possibly due to failure of the oocyte to be discharged from the follicle or possibly a deficiency in follicular or oocyte quality.

Luteinized HAFs and PAFs will both eventually regress spontaneously. A luteinized HAF can be eliminated with a single dose of prostaglandins administered 9 to 10 days after the initial recognition of echogenic particles within the follicular lumen. A PAF will not respond to prostaglandin administration as there is no luteinized tissue present.

16.2 Persistent Corpus Luteum

The corpus luteum that forms after ovulation is usually functional for 14 to 15 days in the nonpregnant mare. Corpora lutea that fail to regress at the normal time postovulation are considered to be pathologically persistent. The most common causes of a persistent corpus luteum are:

- Ovulation late in diestrus, resulting in a corpus luteum that is immature (<5 days old) at the time of prostaglandin release
- Embryonic loss after the time of maternal recognition of pregnancy
- Chronic uterine infections, resulting in destruction of the endometrium and therefore diminished prostaglandin release
- Inadequate prostaglandin release at days 13 to 15.

If untreated, the corpus luteum may persist for 2 to 3 months. This syndrome may be suspected clinically in mares that are not expressing normal estrous behavior during the physiologic breeding season, and it must be differentiated from the syndrome of mares with silent heat. In addition, mares that have been bred and do not return to heat and are later diagnosed as not pregnant may also have a persistent corpus luteum.

A persistent corpus luteum will be eliminated by the administration of a single intramuscular dose of prostaglandins.

16.3 Shortened Luteal Phase (Premature Luteolysis)

Diestrus in the normal mare lasts approximately 14 to 15 days. Premature destruction of the corpus luteum (luteolysis) may be associated with an early onset of estrus and a decrease in the interovulatory interval. The most common cause of premature luteolysis in the mare is endometritis. Inflammation of the endometrium can result in sufficient synthesis and release of prostaglandins to cause luteal regression. A mare that exhibits a shortened diestrus should be examined for endometritis. A culture, biopsy and cytologic examination of the uterus may be indicated.

16.4 Luteal Insufficiency

Primary luteal insufficiency implies a deficiency in progesterone production. Luteal insufficiency has been suggested to be a cause of subfertility in mares, although data is limited. Maintenance of pregnancy in some habitually aborting mares following administration of exogenous progestogens offers circumstantial evidence that progesterone insufficiency may be responsible for some cases of pregnancy loss. A blood progesterone concentration of $\geq$ 4.0 ng/ml is required to maintain pregnancy in the mare.

The most common treatment for luteal insufficiency in pregnant mares is daily administration of the synthetic progestogen altrenogest (Regu-Mate®) orally once daily. Options for duration of altrenogest supplementation include:

- Treatment until well after maternal recognition of pregnancy (i.e. after day 16) and measurement of endogenous progesterone $\geq$ 4.0 ng/ml
- Treatment until day 60 of pregnancy or greater (a time when secondary corpora lutea should be present and active in most mares) and measurement of endogenous progesterone level of > 4.0 ng/ml
- Treatment until day 120 of pregnancy
- Treatment until the end of pregnancy. This is the least common option and rarely indicated.

16.5 Ovarian Tumors

The most common ovarian tumor in the mare is the granulosa cell tumor (GCT). Granulosa cell tumors are almost always unilateral, slow growing, and benign. An examination of the affected ovary using transrectal ultrasonography typically reveals a multicystic or honeycombed structure (Figure 16-3 and Figure 16-4), but the tumor may also present as a solid mass or a single large cystic structure. The contralateral ovary is usually small and inactive, although mares with a GCT on one ovary and a

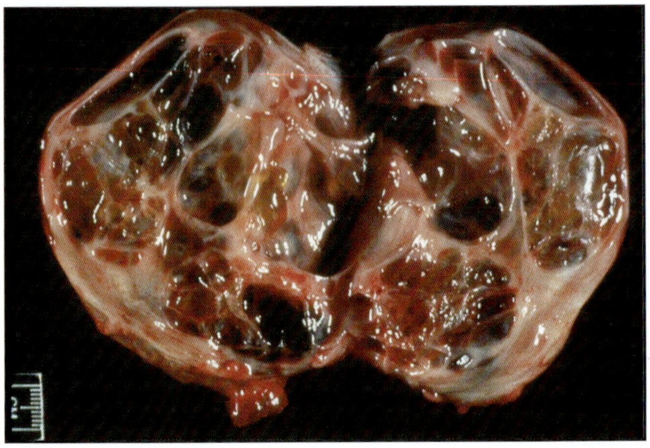

Figure 16-3 Photograph of a granulosa cell tumor surgically removed from a mare.

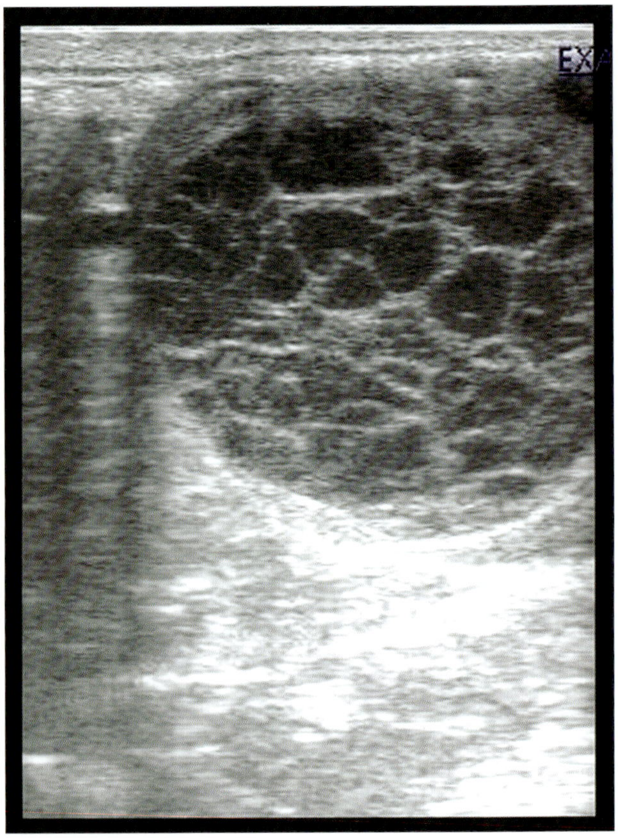

Figure 16-4 Ultrasound image of the ovary of a mare with a granulosa cell tumor.

functional contralateral ovary have been reported. Behavioral abnormalities such as prolonged anestrus, aggressive or stallion-like behavior, and persistent estrus may be expressed in affected mares.

Granulosa cell tumors are hormonally active, and clinical diagnostic assays for the detection of a GCT include the measurement of anti-Müllerian hormone (AMH), inhibin, testosterone, and progesterone (Table 16-1). AMH is elevated in approximately 95 % of mares with GCT, while inhibin is elevated in approximately 85 to 90% of affected mares. Testosterone may be elevated if theca cells are involved in the tumor (i.e., a granulosa-theca cell tumor, or GTCT). Testosterone is elevated in approximately 45 to 50 % of affected mares and is usually associated with aggressive stallion-like behavior. Progesterone concentrations in mares with a GCT are almost always below 1 ng/ml, since normal follicular development, ovulation, and corpus luteum formation do not occur and the tumor does not produce progesterone.

Table 16-1 Hormone concentrations in the normal nonpregnant mare and mares with a granulosa cell tumor.

Hormone	Normal Range	Levels in GCT mares
AMH	< 4.0 ng/ml	> 4.0 ng/ml
Inhibin	0.1 to 0.7 ng/ml	> 0.7 ng/ml
Testosterone	20 to 45 pg/ml	> 45 pg/ml (if GTCT)
Progesterone - Estrus	< 1.0 ng/ml	< 1.0 ng/ml
Progesterone - Diestrus	> 1.0 ng/ml	

Treatment of an ovarian granulosa cell tumor is surgical removal. Ovulation from the remaining ovary will occur approximately 6 to 8 months after tumor removal.

Other ovarian tumors include the cystadenoma (a tumor of the surface epithelium of the ovary) and the teratoma or dysgerminoma (germ cell tumors). These tumors are not considered to be hormonally active and do not cause regression of the contralateral ovary.

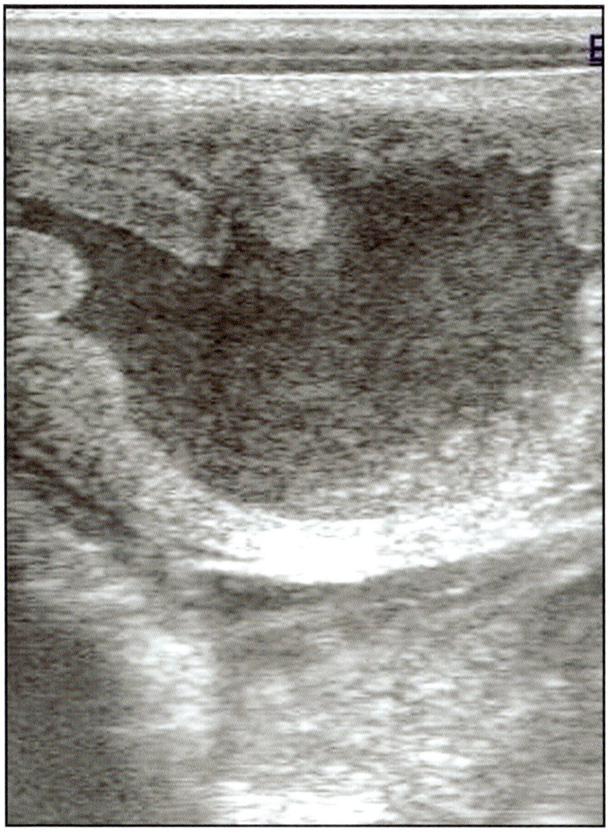

Figure 16-5 Ultrasound image of the uterus of a mare with mating-induced endometritis showing a large volume of echogenic inflammatory fluid.

16.6 Mating-Induced Endometritis

A transient inflammatory response in the endometrium is an inevitable consequence of mating by either natural service or by artificial insemination. The cause of mating-induced endometritis is due to an antigenic response to the presence of spermatozoa.

Diagnosis is made on the basis of the presence of echogenic fluid in the uterine lumen on ultrasound examination 12 to 24 hours after insemination of the mare (Figure 16-5), as most normal mares will have cleared the inflammatory fluid associated with the insemination of spermatozoa by that time period. Insemination with frozen-thawed spermatozoa into the equine uterus may lead to an enhanced inflammatory response, due to the absence of seminal plasma in frozen semen.

Management of persistent mating-induced endometritis is aimed at limiting the severity and duration of the inflammatory response and clearing the uterus of fluid, inflammatory by-products and bacteria.

Options include:

- Limiting the number of matings or inseminations; ideally the mare is bred once
- Uterine lavage 4 to 24 hours after breeding
- Administration of oxytocin 4 to 8 hours after mating to stimulate uterine contractions and provide physical clearance of fluid and inflammatory by-products

16.7 Bacterial Endometritis

Bacterial endometritis is a significant cause of decreased reproductive performance in mares due to failure of conception or early embryonic loss. A majority of young mares rapidly eliminate bacterial contamination of the uterus following mating, parturition, intrauterine manipulations or other events and are considered to be 'resistant' to infection. In contrast, some older mares may be unable to spontaneously eliminate pathogenic organisms from their uterus and are considered to be 'susceptible' to infection.

Factors predisposing mares to uterine infections include contamination at breeding, pooling of urine in the anterior vagina and uterus, trauma from parturition or breeding, and failure of natural uterine defense mechanisms. Poor perineal conformation, decreased muscular tone of the vulva and cranial displacement of the anal sphincter may lead to aspiration of air and fecal material into the reproductive tract.

Detection of a bacterial endometritis is based primarily on uterine culture and cytology (Figure 16-6 and Figure 16-7). Affected mares may have a history of short-cycling, repeated uterine infections and/or failure to conceive after having been bred to a fertile stallion. A uterine culture may detect the presence of a specific organism and antibiotic susceptibility tests can subsequently be determined. Cytologic examination of an endometrial swab may reveal an increase in white blood cells (neutrophils) and may reveal the presence of bacterial organisms.

Other diagnostic tests include:

- Polymerase chain reaction (PCR) analysis to detect DNA of microbial organisms
- Endometrial biopsy to detect inflammatory cells in the uterine lining

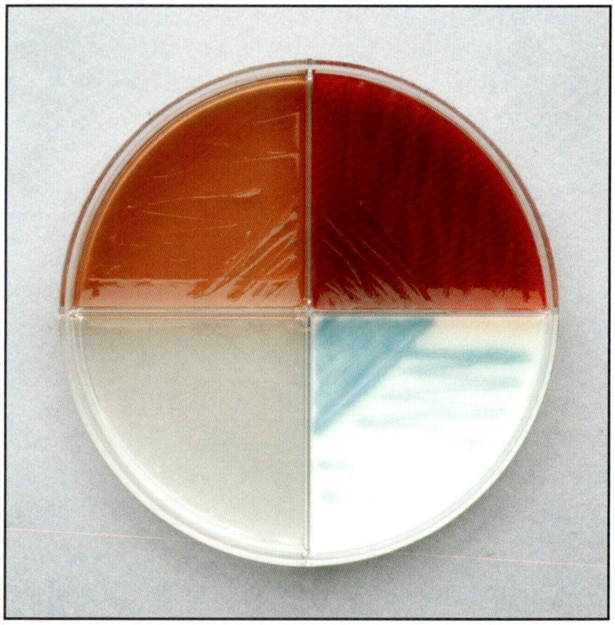

Figure 16-6 Uterine culture of a mare with bacterial endometritis due to Streptococcus equi subspecies zooepidemicus.

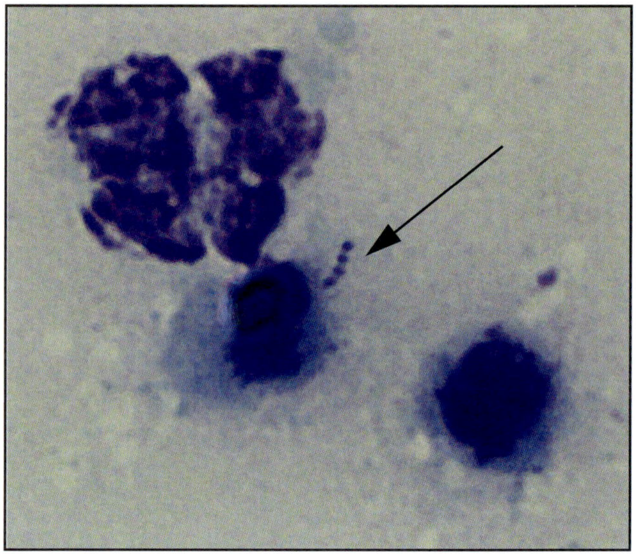

Figure 16-7 Uterine cytology of a mare with bacterial endometritis showing inflammatory cells and chains (arrow) of bacterial organisms (Streptococcus equi subspecies zooepidemicus).

- Ultrasonography to detect the presence of intrauterine fluid
- Low-volume uterine lavage to provide samples for culture, cytology or PCR

The most common bacterial organisms cultured from mares with chronic endometritis are *Streptococcus equi* subspecies *zooepidemicus*, *Escherichia coli*, *Pseudomonas aeruginosa*, *Klebsiella pneumoniae* and possibly *Staphylococcus aureus*. S. *zooepidemicus* is the most common organism associated with equine endometritis. *E. coli* infections are often associated with anatomic defects that predispose a mare to pneumovagina and fecal contamination.

The general principles of a treatment regimen are to remove the source of infection, aid in physical clearance of the uterus, eliminate pathogenic organisms by local infusion with antimicrobial agents and reduce future contamination by enhanced reproductive management. Treatments include:

- Correction of any predisposing factor for infection. A Caslick procedure should be performed if either the perineal conformation or the muscular tone of the vulva is inadequate.
- Uterine lavage to remove residual fluid, inflammatory by-products and bacteria.
- Intrauterine antibiotics. An empirical choice of antibiotics may be made initially, but continued treatment should be based on culture and antimicrobial susceptibility tests.
- Systemic antibiotic administration may be used alone or in conjunction with intrauterine administration of antibiotics for the treatment of bacterial endometritis.

16.8 Fungal Endometritis

Fungal infections of the uterus most commonly occur in older mares with reduced uterine defense mechanisms and occasionally in mares receiving prolonged antibiotic therapy. Fungal endometritis may be difficult to eliminate and may result in significant damage to the endometrium. Clinical signs vary in intensity from none to severe purulent endometritis with chronic infertility.

Diagnosis is typically based on uterine culture and cytologic examination (Figure 16-8 and Figure 16-9). Additional diagnostic tests may include low volume lavage for culture and cytology samples, and PCR to detect fungal DNA. The most common organisms cultured are *Candida albicans* and *Aspergillus fumigatus*.

It is not uncommon for mares with fungal endometritis to have a concurrent bacterial infection.

Therapy is directed at correcting predisposing factors and conformation defects, physical removal of uterine debris by lavage and elimination of infection by intraluminal infusion of antifungal drugs. Therapy for fungal endometritis includes:

- Correction of predisposing factors, such as poor perineal conformation, pneumovagina and urine pooling.
- Uterine lavage to remove inflammatory debris and microbial organisms.
- Intrauterine administration of an antifungal medication.
- Systemic administration of an antifungal medication.

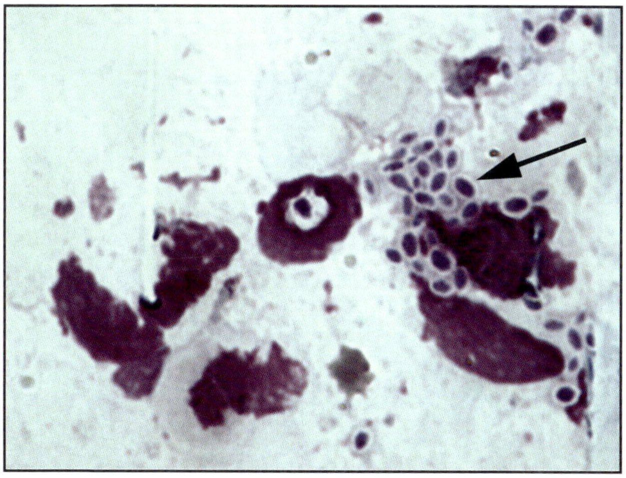

***Figure 16-8** Uterine cytology sample from a mare with fungal endometritis caused by the yeast Candida albicans (arrow).*

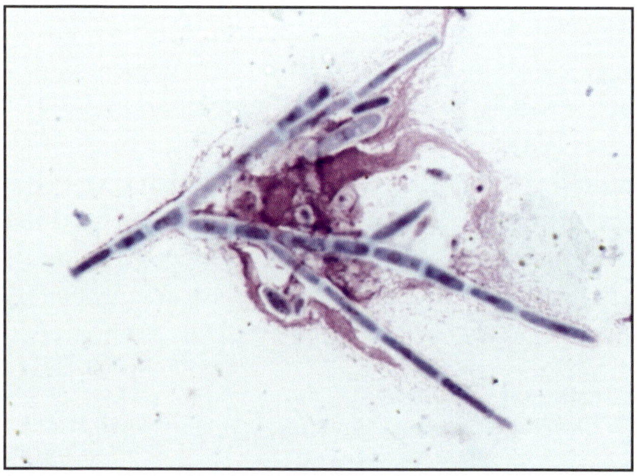

***Figure 16-9** Uterine cytology sample from a mare with fungal endometritis caused by the hyphate fungus Aspergillus fumigatus.*

Chapter 17. Artificial Insemination

Table 17-0 List and Part Number of ARS products used in this chapter.

Item	Part Number	Use/Comments
Cloth Adhesive Tape, 2”	537-675/6	Used to secure tail wraps on mares prior to AI
Sterile Obstetrical Sleeves	SLG-107/25	Used to provide sterility during the insemination process
Surgilube® Lubricating Jelly	SSL-101	Used to lubricate vulva of mare before insemination
Disposable Insemination Pipette, Sterile	544S Series	Used to deposit semen into uterus of mare during artificial insemination
All Plastic Syringe, Sterile	544S Series	Used to push semen through insemination tube
Sterile Disposable Vaginal Speculum	EDVS-102/10	Used in artificial insemination if it is not possible to use a hand for the process
Speculum Light	537-664	Used to light the vaginal speculum during the insemination process
25.5" Flexible Insemination Pipette	537-805	Used for low-dose or deep-horn artificial insemination

Artificial insemination (AI) refers to the deposition of spermatozoa into the reproductive tract of the mare utilizing a pipette or other instrument rather than by natural service. Most major equine breed organizations, other than the Thoroughbred, currently allow the use of artificial insemination.

A 'normal' stallion can theoretically impregnate hundreds of mares in a season in a successfully managed AI program. The limiting factors are: a) daily sperm production and output; b) percentage of progressively motile, morphologically normal spermatozoa in the ejaculate; c) inherent fertility of the stallion and mares; and d) reproductive management of the stallion and mares. Artificial insemination is a technique that may enhance reproductive efficiency and allow for greater progress in genetic advancement on a breeding farm as compared to natural service.

17.1 Advantages of Artificial Insemination

Semen collection and artificial insemination offer several advantages over natural service. First, semen can be evaluated after each collection and data should be recorded. Minor changes in semen quality should be noticed immediately. If a significant and consistent change in semen quality is observed, steps can be initiated to correct the problem or mares can be switched to another stallion. Secondly, it is possible to breed more mares by artificial insemination in a breeding season than a stallion can breed by natural cover.

Artificial insemination certainly allows more mares to be bred to a given stallion on any one breeding day than natural service. As a result, AI can limit or prevent overuse of a stallion and still enable most mares to be bred with an adequate number of spermatozoa on the optimal day of the estrous cycle. It may also allow for the effective use of older valuable stallions with poor semen characteristics.

It is generally accepted that insemination results in less contamination of the reproductive tract of the mare than natural service. This may be a significant advantage in older mares that are prone to uterine infections. There may not be as great an advantage in younger mares. In addition, if the stallion sheds pathogenic bacteria in his semen, mixing the semen with an extender containing an appropriate antibiotic may reduce or eliminate the number of organisms that are deposited in the mare.

Collection of semen from a stallion trained to mount a phantom and insemination into a mare held in examination stocks reduces the possibility of injury to personnel, the mare or the stallion during a live cover. Insemination also alleviates many potential problems associated with attempting to cover a mare that is not in good heat, mating horses of different sizes, or mating a mare with physical disabilities or in less than ideal body condition.

Finally, artificial insemination with cooled-transported semen or frozen semen gives mare owners access to a wider genetic pool than with natural cover. Access to equine genetics becomes global when artificial insemination is incorporated into a breeding management program. Considerable expense is also saved by not having to ship mares great distances and board them at the stallion station.

17.2 Facilities for Artificial Insemination

Physical facilities for housing, examination and insemination of mares should be safe, clean and efficient to manage. Accommodations should be made for the care and management of mares with foals at side and horses with special medical requirements. If mares are to be maintained for long periods of time, a herd health program that incorporates nutrition, vaccination, deworming, dental care, foot care and exercise should be developed.

The facility for insemination should be designed so that it is safe for both mares and personnel, out of the weather, able to be cleaned and disinfected, and allow for easy movement and restraint of mares and foals. A set of examination stocks are used for insemination on many breeding farms. A photograph of the examination stocks at Colorado State University is presented in Figure 17-1.

An adequate supply of warm water to wash the mare before insemination and suitable drain(s) to remove water are considered standard requirements for an insemination facility. A hose may be attached to a hot-cold water-mixing faucet with an in-line thermometer (Figure 17-2). Thus, water at the appropriate temperature for washing and rinsing mares is readily available.

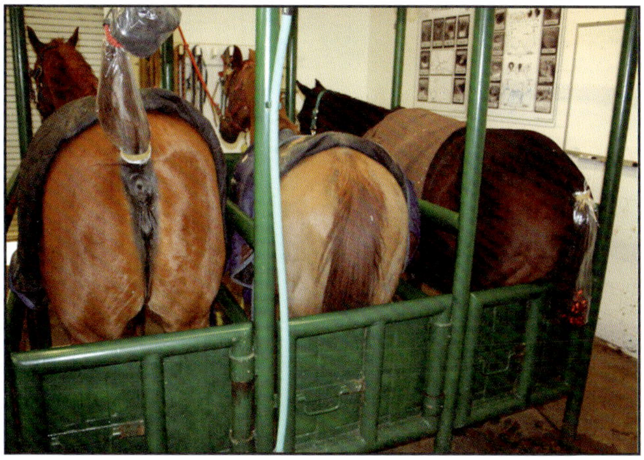

Figure 17-1 Mares in examination stocks at Colorado State University.

Figure 17-2 Close-up view of the hot-cold water-mixing faucet.

17.3 Materials and Equipment for Artificial Insemination

Materials are needed to clean the mare and for handling and deposition of semen. A tail wrap, non-residual soap (i.e. Ivory®), fresh clean warm water, and towels (paper or cloth) are needed to prepare the mare. Materials required for insemination of the mare include a Sterile Obstetrical Sleeve, Surgilube® Lubricating Jelly, a Disposable Insemination Pipette, and an All Plastic Syringe. The sleeve, pipette and syringe should all be sterile and individually wrapped. All plastic syringes are routinely used because rubber-tipped syringes have been previously reported to adversely affect sperm motility and viability. Insemination may also be performed using a vaginal speculum, light source, insemination pipette, and syringe.

17.4 Preparing a Mare for Insemination

The mare should be placed in examination stocks, if possible. The tail of the mare should be wrapped in a plastic bag or other suitable device (a palpation sleeve works well) and secured to the base of the tail with 2" Cloth Adhesive Tape or a short piece of rubber tubing and a small clamp. The tail can also be wrapped in gauze or a Velcro® sheath can be used to keep the tail hairs out of the way. The tail can be held out of the way using a stretchable rubber cord or an assistant can manually hold the tail.

Adequate and effective washing of the perineum is a critical aspect of the overall artificial insemination process. Failure to remove debris and bacteria may lead to a uterine infection if this material is transported into the uterus during the insemination process. Failure to completely rinse away soap or failure to dry the water from the perineum can adversely affect sperm motility if the semen comes into contact with either soap or water.

A liberal amount of warm water is applied to the perineal area to remove gross debris. A small amount of non-residual soap (i.e. Ivory®) is applied to either the gloved hand or the perineal area. The perineal area is gently, but thoroughly scrubbed (Figure 17-3). Cleaning should begin in the central region around the vulvar lips and then move to the anus and beneath the tail head, followed by the side regions adjacent to the vulva. After the entire area has been scrubbed, the region is subsequently rinsed with warm water. The procedure is repeated two more times, or more if necessary. The area is dried with clean disposable paper towels after the final rinse. The drying procedure is initiated directly on the vulvar lips, then moved to the anus, and then to each side. Be sure to carefully dry the area at the base of the tail, so if water is trapped in that area it does not run down onto the clean, dry perineum. It may be important to gently part the vulvar lips and pass a damp paper towel or small portion of moist roll cotton downward just within the vulva to remove any last particles of debris, soap or water.

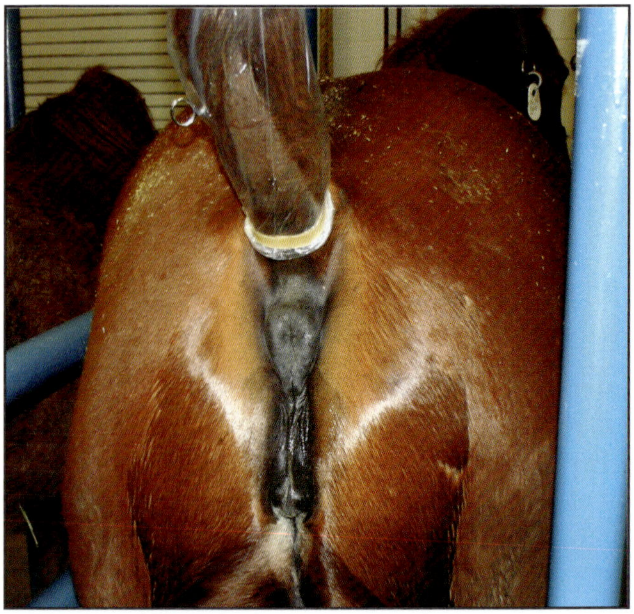

Figure 17-3 Washing a mare prior to insemination. Note that the tail is held out of the way by being wrapped and held up with a stretch cord.

17.5 Insemination Technique

The basic steps of artificial insemination involve drawing up the semen into a syringe connected to an insemination pipette and deposition of that semen into the uterus of the mare.

First, connect a sterile All Plastic Syringe of an appropriate size to a sterile Disposable Insemination Pipette. Initially, the majority of the pipette may be left within its protective plastic sheath to keep it sterile. The size of syringe chosen depends on the volume of the semen to be inseminated. Typically a 10ml, 20ml, 25ml, or 50ml volume syringe will be used.

Semen will typically be placed in a graduated cylinder, bag or centrifuge tube after collection. The insemination pipette should be removed from its protective plastic sheath. Dip the tip of the pipette into the container of semen. Slowly and gently withdraw one entire insemination dose up into the syringe by pulling back on the plunger of the syringe. The proper volume may be measured by noting the volume on the graduated cylinder before drawing up the dose, and then drawing until the graduated cylinder reads a volume equal to the initial graduated cylinder volume minus the volume of the insemination dose. To read the graduated cylinder properly it should be set on a level surface and the volume read with the eyes level with the bottom of the meniscus. The air initially present in the insemination pipette will form an air pocket in the syringe after it is filled. The air pocket will be used to expel all of the semen out through the insemination pipette into the mare's uterus.

Carefully remove a Sterile Obstetrical Sleeve from its package by grasping it at its shoulder end. Pull the sleeve up the entire length of the arm to be used for insemination. Place the tip of the Disposable Insemination Pipette into the palm of the gloved hand. Apply a small amount of Surgilube® Lubricating Jelly onto the knuckles of the gloved hand and then gently wipe the knuckles against the vulvar lips to lubricate them. Extend the fingers of the gloved hand. Initially introduce the hand through the vulva at an upward angle and then advance the hand horizontally once it has passed through the vestibule. Note: keep the fingers off the floor of the vestibule to avoid entering the urethral opening as the hand is advanced through the vestibule.

Carry the tip of the Disposable Insemination Pipette to the cranial end of the vagina. The tip of the pipette should be in the palm of the gloved hand with the tip of the pipette covered by the base of the thumb. Once the hand is fully advanced into the vagina, locate the external cervical os (opening into the vagina) protruding into the vaginal cavity. The cervix of a mare in estrus should be soft and relaxed, and may be resting on the floor of the vagina. Introduce the index finger of the gloved hand into the cervical canal, and gently advance the tip of the insemination pipette along the index finger, through the cervix and into the uterine body (Figure 17-4 and Figure 17-5).

The cervical canal is approximately 7.5 to 10 cm (3 to 4") in length, and the uterine body is 20 to 25 cm (8 to 10") in length. Ideally, the tip of the Disposable Insemination Pipette should be advanced 1 to 2" into the uterine body. No attempt should be made to advance the tip of the pipette into either uterine horn in a routine insemination. The goal is to deposit the semen into the uterine body (Figure 17-6).

After positioning the tip of the insemination pipette in the uterine body, withdraw the index finger from the cervical canal, and with the other fingers hold the cervix closed around the pipette. Raise the syringe containing the semen to approximately a

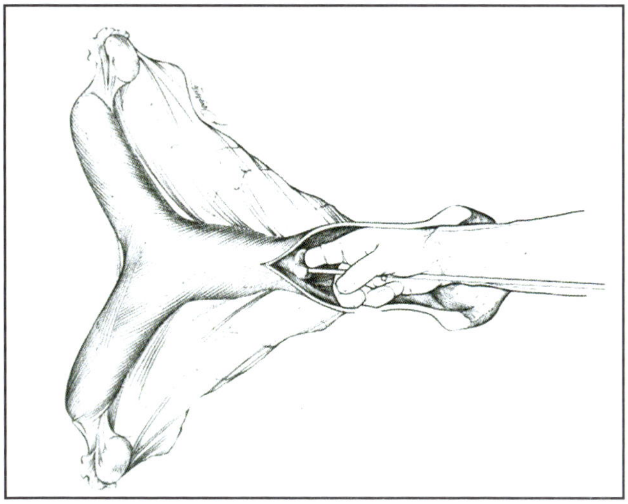

Figure 17-4 Drawing of the technique used to introduce the pipette into the cervix.

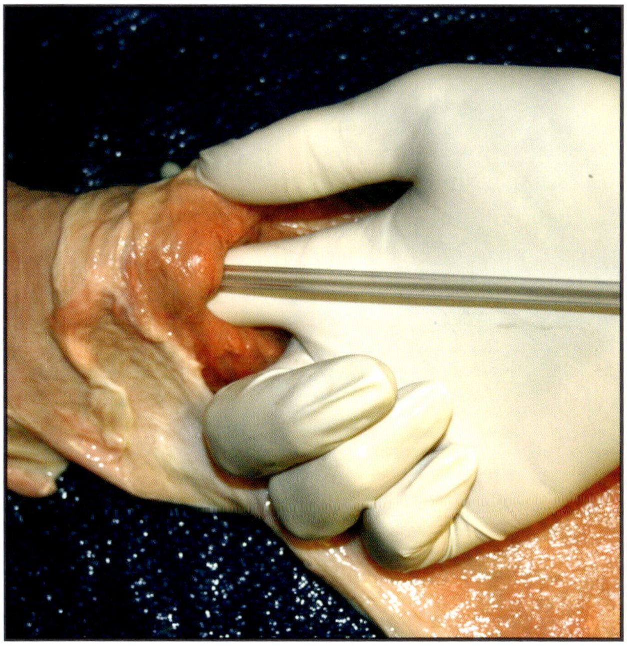

Figure 17-5 Introduction of an artificial insemination pipette along the index finger and through the cervical canal into the uterus.

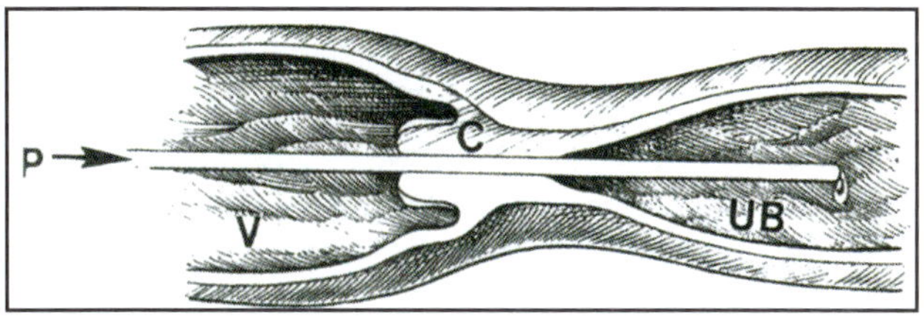

Figure 17-6 Schematic diagram showing the tip of an insemination pipette properly placed into the uterine body ready for deposition of semen. v = vagina, c = cervix, p = insemination pipette and ub = uterine body.

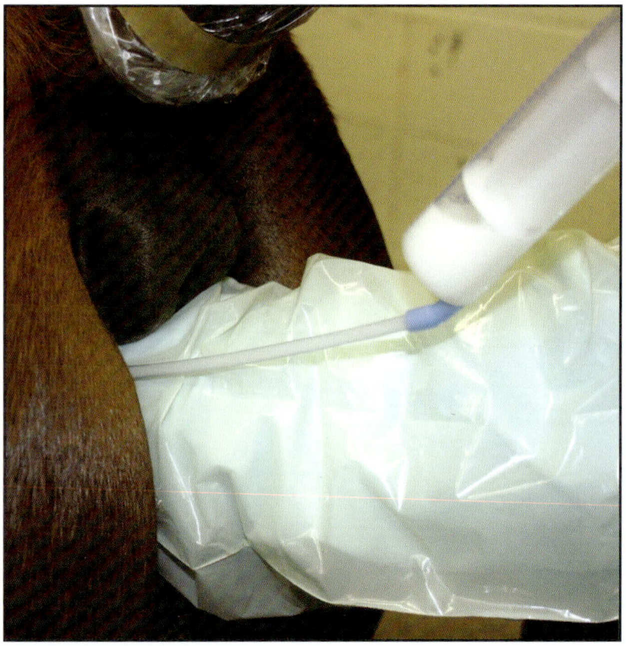

Figure 17-7 Expelling the semen through an insemination pipette by depressing the plunger of the semen syringe. Note that the syringe is lifted to a 45 angle to ensure that the air pocket enters the insemination pipette last and expels all the semen.

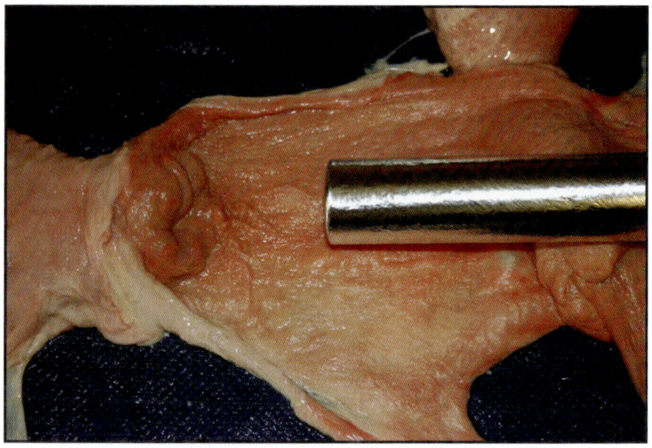

Figure 17-8 Positioning of a vaginal speculum to visualize the cervix for insemination.

45° angle, and slowly expel the semen by depressing the plunger (Figure 17-7). Raising the syringe at an angle will ensure that the air pocket enters the insemination pipette last and will fully expel all of the semen from the pipette. If the syringe has a tip that is off-center, it is important to position the syringe tip at the bottom, so that all semen will be expelled.

If resistance is felt when depressing the plunger, retract the insemination pipette slightly to pull it away from the uterine wall, which will usually allow the semen to flow freely. If resistance is not relieved, and too much force is exerted on the plunger, the syringe may detach from the insemination pipette, resulting in loss of semen outside the mare. Once semen has been deposited into the uterus, the insemination pipette is removed by pulling the gloved-hand backward and downward. Retracting the arm in this manner will minimize the amount of air introduced into the vagina as the gloved-hand is removed. Examine the insemination pipette immediately after it has been removed to verify that all semen was placed into the mare. Semen may be left in the insemination pipette as a result of: a) not using a sufficiently large air pocket, b) not positioning the syringe correctly, or c) depressing the plunger too rapidly (which forces air bubbles past the more viscous semen). If there is still a significant amount of semen left in the insemination pipette, disconnect the syringe from the pipette, draw more air into the syringe, re-attach it, and repeat the semen-deposition process.

17.6 Insemination through a Vaginal Speculum

If the mare has had an episioplasty or Caslick procedure (i.e. 'sutured'), or if for some reason it is not possible to insert the hand into the vagina, a vaginal speculum and a speculum light can be used for the insemination process. Using this technique, the Caslick would not have to be opened for insemination and subsequently re-sutured. Some mares may have to be lightly sedated for this procedure.

The mare is prepared as for standard insemination. A Sterile Disposable Speculum is lubricated and slowly inserted into the vulva at an upward angle. The cervix is visually located (Figure 17-8 and Figure 17-9), and the Disposable Insemination Pipette is introduced through the speculum into the cervical os and advanced through the cervical canal into the uterine body. Once the insemination tube is positioned appropriately, the semen is expelled by depressing the plunger slowly. The only difficult part is the initial positioning of the tip of the pipette into the external os. Once the tip is correctly placed, the tube can usually be easily advanced into the uterus.

Figure 17-9 Insemination of a mare through a vaginal speculum.

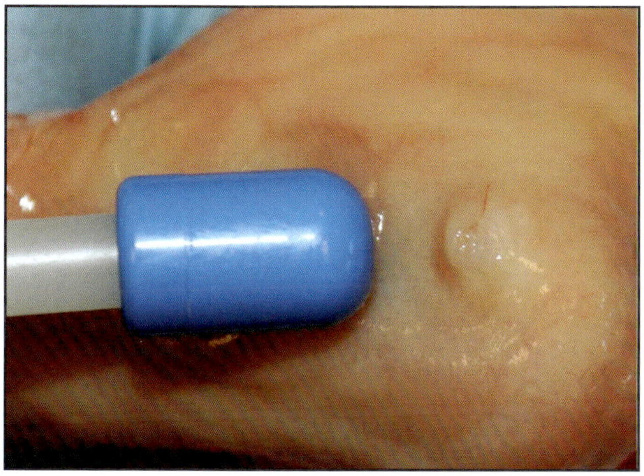

Figure 17-10 Positioning of the AI pipette adjacent to the utero-tubular junction (arrow) for deep-horn insemination of mares.

17.7 Deep-Horn Insemination

In some instances, it may be desirable to inseminate mares with either a reduced number of sperm or a decreased volume. This may be the case when a limited number of frozen semen straws are available, if breeding with epididymal spermatozoa or sex-sorted spermatozoa, or when a low number of sperm are collected in an ejaculate.

Studies have indicated that acceptable pregnancy rates can be achieved using what has been termed 'low-dose insemination techniques'. The number of spermatozoa deposited using low-dose protocols range from less than 5 million to 50 million or more spermatozoa in volumes ranging from less than a tenth of a milliliter up to one or two milliliters.

The most common low-dose technique used on breeding farms and veterinary clinics is a manual deep-horn procedure that does not utilize sophisticated or expensive equipment. In fact, the only equipment required for the procedure is a 25.5" Flexible Insemination Pipette. First, the preovulatory follicle is identified as being on either the left or right ovary. Next, a small volume of extended semen is drawn up into the tip of the pipette and the pipette is passed through the cervix into the uterine body using a traditional initial approach. Then, the arm of the person performing the procedure is introduced into the rectum and the location of the pipette tip is determined. The uterus is subsequently gently manipulated and the pipette is slowly passed up the uterine horn adjacent to the ovary containing the preovulatory follicle. The pipette is advanced until the tip is located at the end of the uterine horn near the utero-tubular junction or entrance to the oviduct (Figure 14-9). The semen is then deposited and the pipette withdrawn from the mare. This low-dose insemination technique is usually performed by a veterinarian.

In most instances the mare will be administered an ovulation inducing agent such as human chorionic gonadotropin (hCG) or deslorelin prior to or at the time of deep-horn insemination.

The second technique for low-dose insemination is hysteroscopy. With this procedure, the mare is sedated and a videoendoscope is passed through the cervix and the uterus is inflated with air. The scope is passed up the horn adjacent to the ovary containing the preovulatory follicle. A catheter containing a small volume of semen is passed down through a

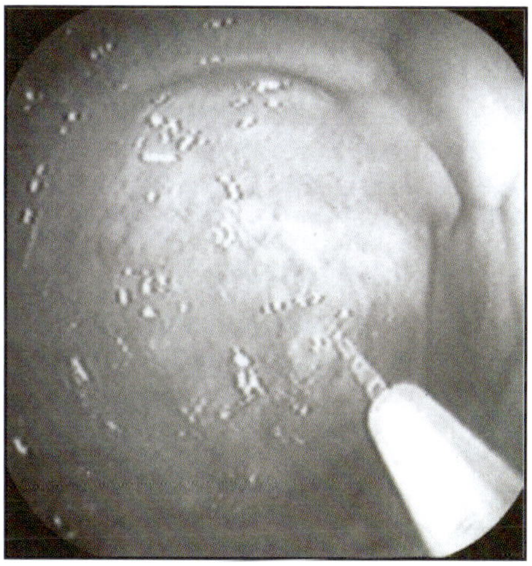

Figure 17-11 Deposition of semen onto the utero-tubular junction using hysteroscopy.

tube within the scope and out the end of the scope. The utero-tubular (oviductal) junction is visualized and the catheter tip is moved so that the small volume of fluid containing the spermatozoa is deposited directly onto the oviductal opening (Figure 14-10). The primary advantage of the hysteroscopy technique is direct visualization and precise deposition of semen onto the oviductal junction. Disadvantages include the initial cost of the videoendoscope, time required to set-up, perform and clean-up after the procedure, and the requirement for multiple trained personnel.

Controlled research studies have reported that there is no significant difference in pregnancy rates between the manual deep-horn technique and the hysteroscopic procedures. Both methods can yield acceptable pregnancy rates using low numbers of spermatozoa if the stallion has good inherent fertility.

There is no advantage in pregnancy rates between deep horn insemination and standard uterine body insemination when using frozen semen from fertile stallions. However, pregnancy rates can be enhanced using deep horn insemination with frozen semen from subfertile stallions or using a low number of frozen-thawed spermatozoa (i.e. a partial dose).

17.8 Pregnancy Rate after Artificial Insemination

Pregnancy rates are almost universally highest using properly extended fresh semen for artificial insemination. In general terms pregnancy rates are 5 to 10 percent lower using cooled-stored semen and often another 5 to 10 percent lower when using frozen semen (Table 14-1). There are always exceptions to these general concepts, with many fertile stallions having equal pregnancy rates with fresh and cooled semen. There are also individual stallions with very high pregnancy rates using frozen semen. However, there are also stallions with good fertility when breeding mares by live cover or inseminated using fresh semen, but poor pregnancy rates using cooled or frozen semen.

Table 17-1 Average pregnancy rates for mares bred with fresh, cooled, or frozen semen.

Semen Type	Expected Pregnancy Rates (% per cycle)
Fresh Semen	50 to 60
Cooled Semen	45 to 55
Frozen Semen	30 to 45

Additional Comments

- A complete array of all the equipment and supplies necessary for artificial insemination is available from ARS, either individually or as convenient kits
- Artificial Insemination Kits include a sterile obstetrical sleeve, insemination pipette and an all-plastic syringe
- The only additional item needed is sterile obstetrical lubricant, which can also be obtained from ARS (Item Number SSL-101/12)

Chapter 18. Physiology and Endocrinology of Pregnancy

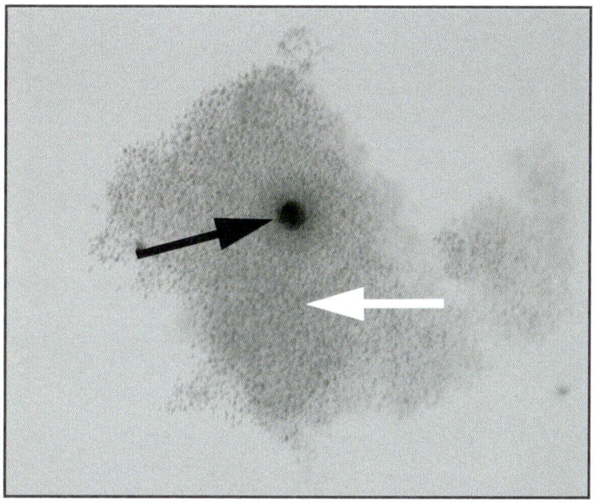

Figure 18-1 Photograph of an unfertilized oocyte (black arrow) surrounded by a thick layer of cumulus cells (white arrow).

18.1 Fertilization and Early Embryonic Development

The oocyte (egg) is surrounded by a layer of specialized cells called cumulus cells at the time of ovulation (Figure 18-1). The cumulus-oocyte complex forms a large, sticky gelatinous matrix that exits the follicle and is picked up by the infundibulum of the oviduct. The oocyte is rapidly transported down the infundibulum to the junction of the ampulla and isthmus regions of the oviduct. If the mare has been bred, several hundred to a few thousand spermatozoa may be present in each oviduct and about a dozen sperm may reach the vicinity of the oocyte.

Sperm undergo a series of changes in the mare reproductive tract, a process called capacitation, in order to have the ability to fertilize an egg. Capacitated sperm bind to specific proteins in the outer coat (zona pellucida) of the egg. Binding to the egg triggers the acrosome reaction, in which enzymes present in a specialized compartment located within the head of the sperm are released. The enzymes enable the sperm to penetrate through the zona pellucida. The plasma membranes of the sperm and egg subsequently fuse and the sperm is eventually engulfed into the egg.

The process of sperm capacitation includes:

- Changes in sperm surface membrane properties, such as removal or alteration of glycoproteins coating the surface of the sperm
- Alteration of the lipid structure of the sperm plasma membrane (i.e. loss of cholesterol), which results in decreased membrane stability and enhanced fluidity
- A change in motility from regular undulating low-amplitude 'wave-like' flagellar beats that result in a linear, forward progression of movement to a state of hyperactivity characterized by rapid, strong 'whip-like' beats that result in forceful vigorous, often non-progressive movement. Hyperactivation is dependent on an elevation of intracellular calcium
- Preparation of sperm to undergo the acrosome reaction

The egg subsequently undergoes a series of changes called the 'cortical reaction' to prevent additional sperm from penetrating through the zona pellucida. Fertilization of an oocyte with multiple sperm, or polyspermy, would result in failure of normal embryonic development. Fusion of the pronuclei of the sperm and egg, which contain chromosomes or DNA from the stallion and mare, respectively, results in formation of the genetic blueprint for the new embryo, now called a zygote.

An oocyte that has been successfully fertilized by a spermatozoon will begin the first cell division within 24 hr. The first cell division is called 'cleavage' and the two individual cells that result are termed blastomeres. Subsequent embryonic cell divisions occur at approximately 12 to 24 hour intervals. Early embryos are commonly referred to by the number of cells present, such as one-cell, two-cell, etc., up to the 16-cell stage. Tight junctions form between individual blastomeres at the 8- to 16-cell stage, causing the cluster of blastomeres to compact as the cells are drawn tightly together. The early embryo is still surrounded by the same zona pellucida that covered the oocyte.

Individual blastomeres are difficult to identify

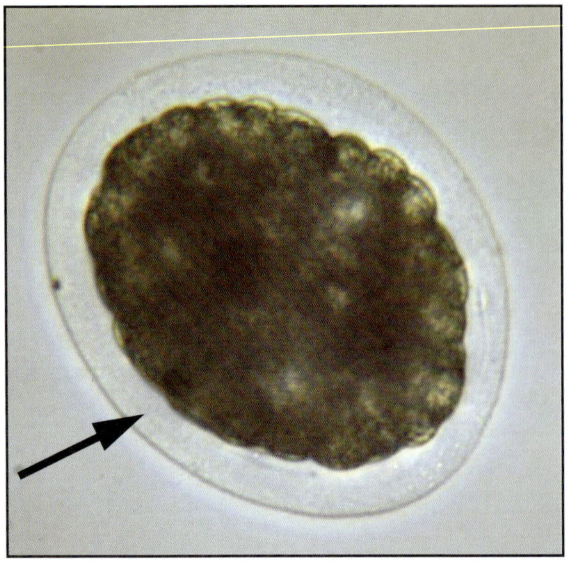

Figure 18-2 Photograph of a morula stage embryo. Note the thick zona pellucida surrounding the embryo (arrow)

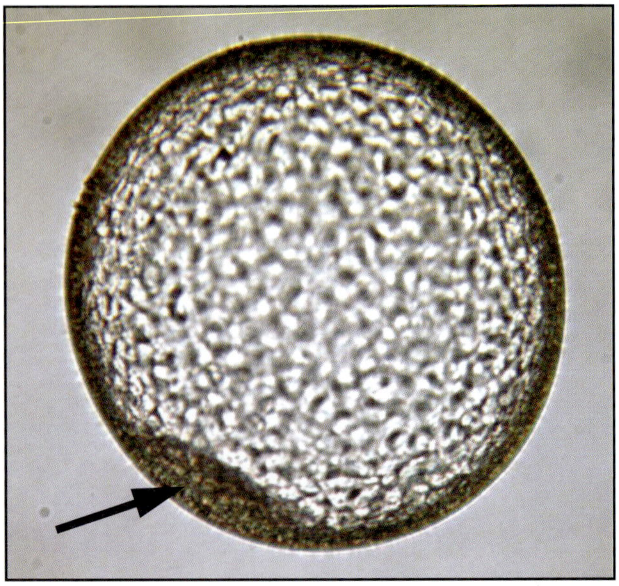

Figure 18-3 Blastocyst stage equine embryo. Note the inner cell mass (arrow).

when the embryo is between the 16- and 32-cell stage of development. Continued cell division and tight junction formation leads to the formation of a morula stage embryo which is comprised of $\geq$ 32 blastomeres (Figure 18-2)

18.2 Oviductal Transport of the Embryo

The mare is unique among domestic animals in that only live, healthy embryos are transported through the entire length of the oviduct and enter the uterus. Equine embryos produce a hormone called prostaglandin E_2 (PGE_2) which relaxes the circular smooth muscle of the isthmus region of the oviduct and allows the embryo to move distally toward the uterus. Unfertilized eggs do not produce PGE_2 and consequently are retained in the oviduct and eventually degenerate. Occasionally an unfertilized oocyte (UFO) will be recovered from the uterus during an embryo flush if it 'followed' a live embryo that secreted PGE_2 through the oviduct.

18.3 Entry of the Embryo into the Uterus

Equine embryos enter the uterus through a narrow passage called the utero-tubular junction (UTJ) approximately 5.5 to 6 days after ovulation. At this time most equine embryos are in either the morula or early blastocyst stage of development. Blastomeres of the morula stage embryo produce fluid which eventually forms a central cavity or blastocoele between cells of the embryo. The embryo is referred to as a blastocyst when the blastocoele cavity is fully-formed (Figure 18-3). A single layer of trophoblast cells initially lines the blastocoele and these cells will eventually form the placenta. A cluster of cells referred to as the inner cell mass form at one location along the inner surface of the trophoblast layer and project into the blastocoele cavity. The inner cell mass will eventually give rise to the embryo proper and fetus.

An acellular glycoprotein coat called the 'capsule' begins to form between the layer of trophoblast cells and the zona pellucida by day 6 to 7 after ovulation (Figure 18-4). The embryo subsequently begins a process of rapid expansion. The zona pellucida thins and is eventually shed, leaving the expanded-blastocyst stage embryo surrounded only by the capsule. The function or role of the capsule has been suggested to be protection from physical damage during migration through the uterus during the period of maternal recognition of pregnancy.

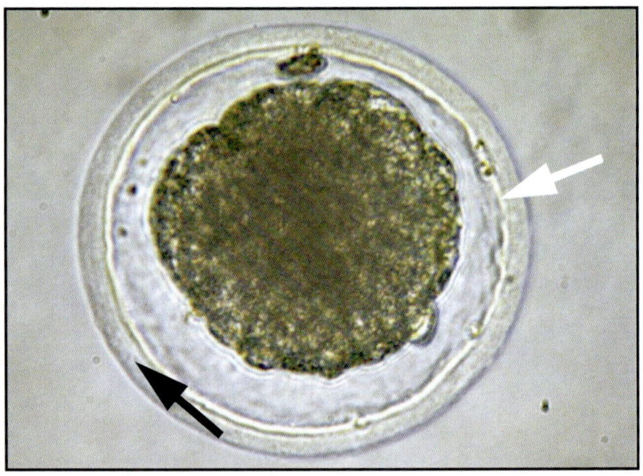

Figure 18-4 Compact morula stage embryo with a zona pellucida (black arrow) and a capsule (white arrow).

18.4 Nutritional Support of the Early Embryo

Progesterone produced by the corpus luteum stimulates the endometrial glands of the uterus to produce a protein-rich substance that has been referred to as histotrophe or 'uterine milk'. Histotrophe is the only source of nutrition for the pre-implantation embryo.

18.5 Embryonic Migration and Fixation

The equine embryo is unique amongst large domestic animals in that it migrates through the uterine lumen from the time it first enters the uterus until day 16 to 17 when mobility ceases and the embryo becomes fixed at the base of one uterine horn. Embryo migration is caused by myometrial contractions. Cessation of movement or 'fixation' is caused by a combination of increasing embryonic size and increasing uterine tone. Migration of the embryo is a critical component of maternal recognition of pregnancy and may also be important for efficient use of uterine nutrients.

18.6 Maternal Recognition of Pregnancy

In the pregnant mare, secretion of $PGF_{2\alpha}$ must be prevented in order to protect the corpus luteum from luteolysis and provide continued progesterone support for maintenance of pregnancy. The developing embryo is responsible for producing a signal that is detected by the uterus in a process known as 'maternal recognition of pregnancy'. Failure of the embryo to produce a sufficient signal or failure of the uterus to recognize the signal will result in the release of prostaglandins from the endometrium. Prostaglandins will travel systemically through the blood stream and cause regression of the ovarian corpus luteum. The subsequent decrease in progesterone will result in loss of the pregnancy.

Key factors in maternal recognition of pregnancy in mares are migration of the embryo throughout the uterus and production of the signal. It is critical that the embryo traverse the entire uterus several times per day during the period of maternal recognition, essentially informing the entire endometrium of its presence in order to prevent $PGF_{2\alpha}$ release. The window for maternal recognition of pregnancy in the mare is 12 to 14 days after ovulation. Unfortunately, the signal factor which has been identified in cattle, sheep, pigs and other species has yet to be identified in the horse.

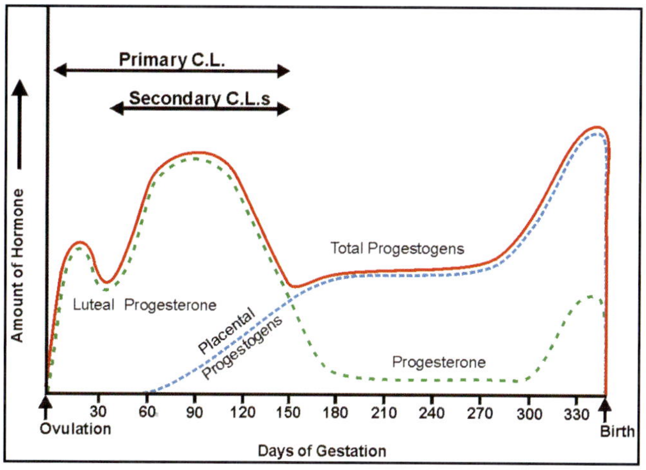

Figure 18-5 Progesterone concentrations in pregnant mares (Neely et al., Equine Reproduction; Veterinary Learning Systems Co., Inc., 1983, pp. 58-70).

18.7 Progesterone Support of Early Pregnancy

Progesterone is the most important hormone for maintenance of pregnancy (Figure 18-5). The pregnant mare is unique in that there are several sources of progesterone during pregnancy. The primary corpus luteum that formed within the ovary at the time of ovulation is the initial source of progesterone. Blood progesterone concentrations begin to increase above baseline (i.e. to > 1.0 ng/ml) the day after ovulation. Progesterone increases to peak levels at day 5 to 7 and then proceeds to decline gradually over the next 5 to 6 weeks in the pregnant mare. Concentrations of progesterone then increase dramatically after day 45 in response to the presence of equine chorionic gonadotropin (eCG) produced by the endometrial cups. Secretion of eCG stimulates follicular development and subsequent luteinization and/or ovulation, resulting in formation of multiple secondary corpora lutea. Production of progesterone from the ovaries increases and as a consequence blood progesterone levels increase and reach peak levels at 2 to 3 months of gestation. Ovarian contribution to circulating progesterone levels gradually decline and are minimal by the fourth to fifth month of gestation. Pregnancy is subsequently maintained by placental progestin production during the last two trimesters.

Supplementation of mares in early pregnancy with exogenous progesterone or a synthetic progestin has become commonplace. However, there is limited scientific evidence of luteal insufficiency as a common cause of early pregnancy loss. In addition, there is limited evidence that routine administration of progesterone to normal mares will either increase pregnancy rate or decrease the incidence of pregnancy loss. Progesterone supplementation does appear to be important in the maintenance of pregnancy in some individual mares. A blood sample may be collected from a pregnant mare for determination of endogenous progesterone levels. A progesterone concentration of ≥ 4.0 ng/ml is considered to be adequate for maintenance of pregnancy in most mares. Mares in the first trimester with progesterone levels < 4.0 ng/ml may be at some risk of pregnancy loss. It is important to consider stage of pregnancy when evaluating progesterone levels and attempting to determine clinical need for supplementation. Progesterone levels are commonly less than 4.0 ng/ml in normal pregnant mares beyond day 150 of pregnancy and supplementation is not usually warranted.

Clinical indications or observations that may support the use of progesterone supplementation include:

- A small corpus luteum noted during pregnancy examination 12 to 16 days after ovulation.
- Poor tone to the uterus and/or cervix during pregnancy examination.
- Presence of endometrial edema in an early pregnant mare.
- Blood progesterone level < 4.0 ng/ml during the first 2 months of pregnancy.
- Repeated history of early pregnancy loss (many factors may contribute to this problem).
- Failure to become pregnant after multiple estrous cycles (many factors may contribute to this problem).

Progesterone supplementation may begin 1 to 2 days after ovulation in mares with a known history of previous pregnancy loss or previous need for supplementation. In many other mares, supplementation begins when a potential problem is detected during a pregnancy examination (i.e. 12 to 16 days after ovulation).

Supplementation should continue until either a) a blood sample is collected and it is determined that an endogenous progesterone level of ≥ 4.0 ng/ml is present, or b) until 120 days of pregnancy, at which time the placenta should be producing sufficient progesterone and related progestin compounds to maintain pregnancy.

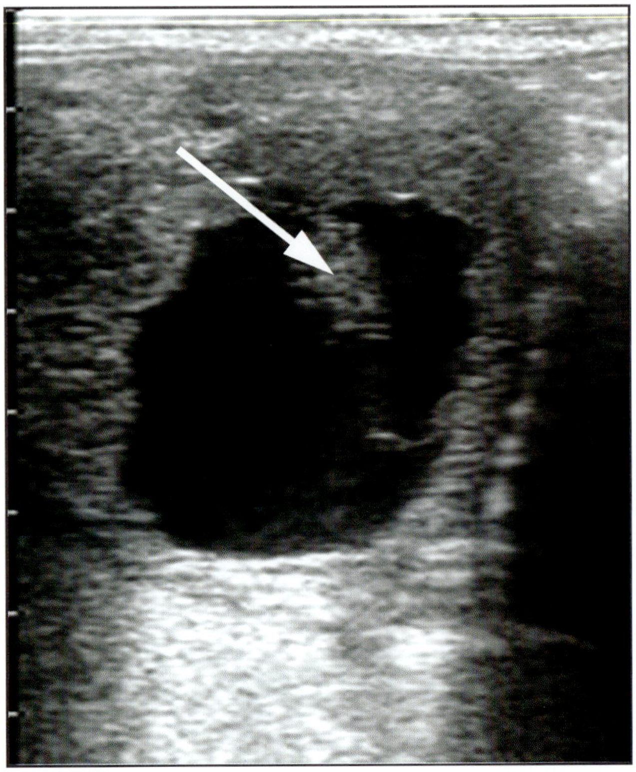

Figure 18-6 Ultrasound image of a normal 25 day pregnancy, with an embryo proper (arrow) within the fluid-filled embryonic vesicle.

18.8 Embryonic Heartbeat Detection

The inner cell mass of the blastocyst develops into a more extensive, but still microscopic embryonic disc by day 10 to 14. Ultrasonographically, the first visualization of the embryo proper can usually be made by day 24 to 25 after ovulation (Figure 18-6). A small flicker of an embryonic heart beat within the embryo proper can be detected by day 25 in most mares. Failure of an embryo proper to appear by day 27 to 28 is often the first indication that an 'empty trophoblastic vesicle' (ETV) has formed (Figure 18-7). An ETV will not continue as a normal developing pregnancy and is often reabsorbed by day 30. Affected mares usually have a persistent corpus luteum and may not return to estrus without prostaglandin treatment.

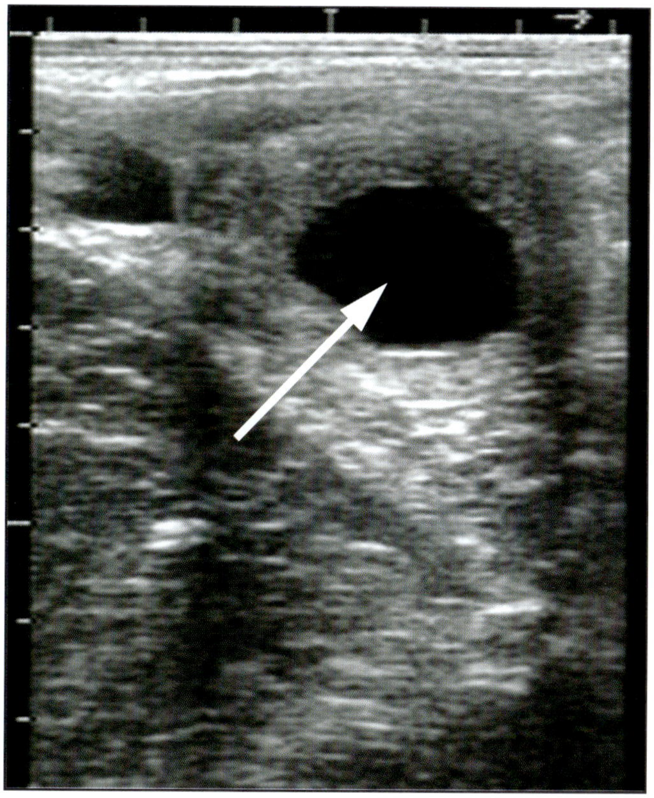

Figure 18-7 Ultrasound image of an empty trophoblastic vesicle in a mare at day 29 post-ovulation (white arrow). Note the absence of the embryo proper within the embryonic vesicle

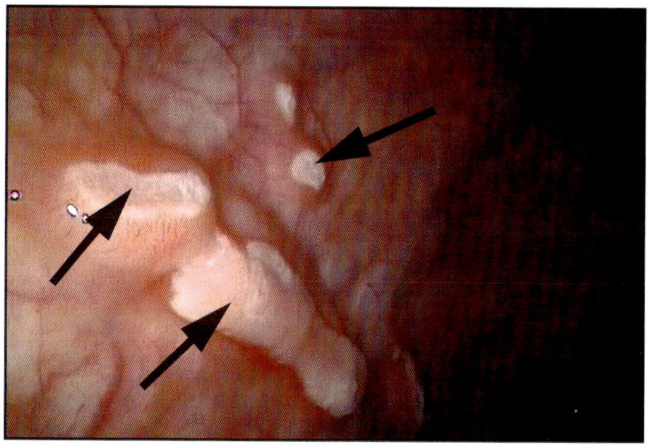

Figure 18-8 Videoendoscopic image of endometrial cups (arrows) within the uterus of a mare.

18.9 Endometrial Cups and Equine Chorionic Gonadotropin

Trophoblast cells from an area of the developing placenta called the chorionic girdle begin to invade the uterine epithelium at approximately 35 days of pregnancy. The cells form a series of discrete aggregates known as endometrial cups (Figure 18-8). Endometrial cups are unique to the horse and produce large quantities of a hormone called equine chorionic gonadotropin (eCG; formerly called pregnant mare serum gonadotropin, PMSG) (Figure 18-9). Endometrial cups continue to produce eCG until an immune response from the mare causes regression and elimination. Production of eCG from the endometrial cups plays an essential role in formation of secondary corpora lutea in the pregnant mare. Regression of secondary corpora lutea coincides with the disappearance of endometrial cups and a decrease in equine chorionic gonadotropin. Endometrial cups regress and eCG is absent in peripheral blood of most mares by 120 to 150 days of pregnancy.

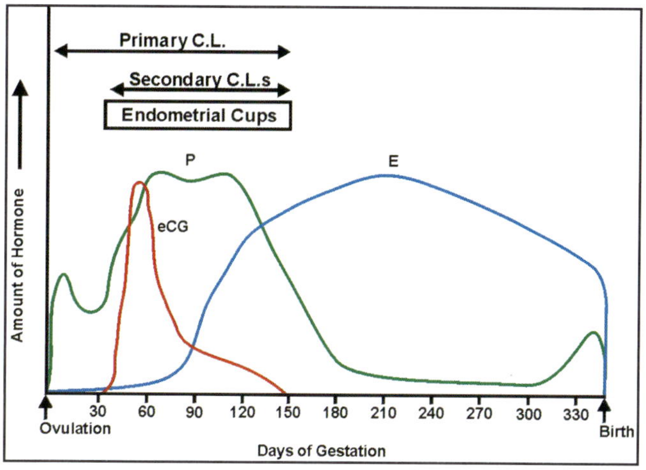

Figure 18-9 Reproductive physiology of the pregnant mare (from Allen et al., J Endocrinol 2002;172:237–246). P=progesterone, E=Estrogens, eCG=equine chorionic gonadotropin.

18.10 Secondary Corpora Lutea

The horse is the only large animal species to form secondary or accessory corpora lutea. Production of eCG from endometrial cups induces formation of secondary corpora lutea (Figure 18-10). Luteal structures may form following either ovulation of follicles or luteinization of follicles without ovulation. Mares may have multiple secondary corpora lutea on each ovary during the 2nd and 3rd month of gestation and as a consequence, the ovaries of a pregnant mare may become very large. Secondary corpora lutea typically regress between 140 and 160 days of pregnancy. It has been proposed that formation of secondary corpora lutea is a mechanism by which mares produce large amounts of progesterone throughout the first 4 months of pregnancy.

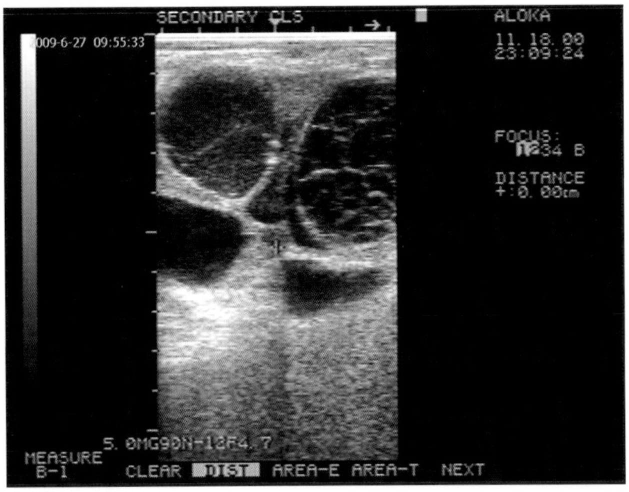

***Figure 18-10** Ultrasound image of an ovary with multiple secondary corpora lutea in a pregnant mare.*

18.11 Placental Progestin Production

The placenta is a significant source of progesterone and other progestins during the second and third trimesters of pregnancy. Production of progestins such as dihydroprogesterone (DHP), by the placenta, begins at approximately 70 to 80 days of gestation. Sufficient progestins are produced by the placenta by 90 days of pregnancy to maintain pregnancy in the absence of an ovarian contribution. Placental support of pregnancy continues from day 90 to term in the mare.

Several types of progestins are secreted by the fetal-placental unit during the last trimester of pregnancy. The clinical relevance is that multiple progestins other than progesterone are produced by the placenta and help support the ongoing pregnancy. Progesterone assays measure only 'natural progesterone' and not the various other progestins. Consequently, measurement of progesterone levels in a mare that is 6 or 7 months pregnant is likely to yield values between 2.5 and 4 ng/ml. This would be considered low for a mare in early pregnancy, but would be considered normal for a mare in later pregnancy, with the realization that other progestins produced by the placenta are helping to support the pregnancy and are not detected in a standard progesterone assay.

18.12 Estrogens of Pregnancy

Another unique feature of the horse is production of high concentrations of estrogenic compounds during pregnancy. An initial rise in estrogens occurs at approximately day 45 of pregnancy. This early rise of estrogens is from the ovarian corpus luteum in response to production of eCG from the endometrial cups. A second larger increase in estrogens begins at approximately 90 days of pregnancy and represents production from the fetal-placental unit (Figure 18-9).

The main estrogens produced by the pregnant mare are estrone, equilen and equilenin. Equilen and equilenin are estrogenic compounds found only in the pregnant mare. Equilen is slightly less biologically active than estrone, but is more biologically active than equilenin. Androgens produced by the fetal gonads are converted by the fetal placental into estrone, equilen and equilenin. Estrogen concentrations remain at basal levels until 90 days of gestation, then increase steadily from 90 to 210 days and then gradually decline until parturition. Measurement of estrone sulfate and/or total estrogens has been used as a marker for pregnancy and as an index of placental function and fetal viability.

18.13 Androgens of Pregnancy

A significant amount of androgens (i.e. testosterone and related hormones) are produced by the gonad of the equine fetus during mid-gestation. These steroid hormones produced by the fetus easily cross the placenta and enter the blood of the mare. As a consequence, testosterone levels in the blood of a pregnant mare increase from a baseline of < 50 pg/ml to levels of 200 pg/ml or more. Concentration of testosterone peaks at approximately 200 to 210 days of gestation and then decline to basal levels at the end of pregnancy.

The rise in testosterone occurs in conjunction with a phenomenon unique to the equine fetus, that of a marked hypertrophy of the fetal gonad in mid gestation (Figure 18-11). Testes of male fetuses and ovaries of female fetuses both undergo a transient yet dramatic increase in size. Gonadal hypertrophy peaks at approximately seven months of gestation and the testes or ovaries regress in size to quite small structures by the time the foal is born. Testosterone is produced in increasing quantities as the fetal gonad enlarges and decreases as the gonad regresses. There is no difference in testosterone levels in pregnant mares that are carrying male or female fetuses. Pregnant mares may exhibit aggressive or stallion-like behavior as they are exposed to increasing levels of testosterone from approximately 4 to 7 months of pregnancy. These some-

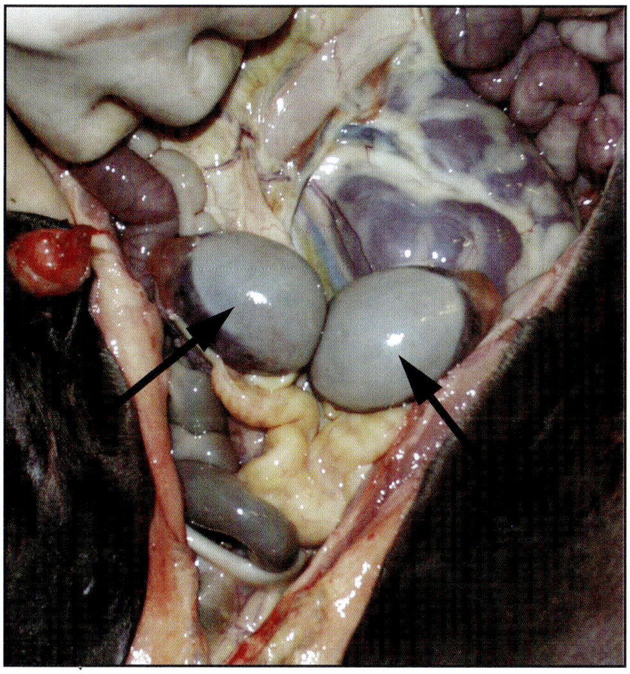

Figure 18-11 Testes of a male equine fetus at 7 months of gestation (arrows).

times adverse, obnoxious or dangerous behavioral characteristics tend to subside as testosterone levels decline in the last trimester. The biological reason for the temporary enlargement of the equine fetal gonad is unknown.

18.14 Relaxin During Pregnancy

Relaxin is a protein hormone produced in small quantities by several tissues in the body and in large quantities by the equine placenta. Concentrations of relaxin in the blood of the pregnant mare increase in the last half of gestation. One physiologic function ascribed to relaxin is softening of structures in the perineal area prior to the time of birth to allow for passage of the fetus. In theory, monitoring levels of relaxin could also be used as a marker for evaluation of placental health. However, there is currently no commercially available assay for routine measurement of relaxin levels in the mare.

Chapter 19 Pregnancy Examination

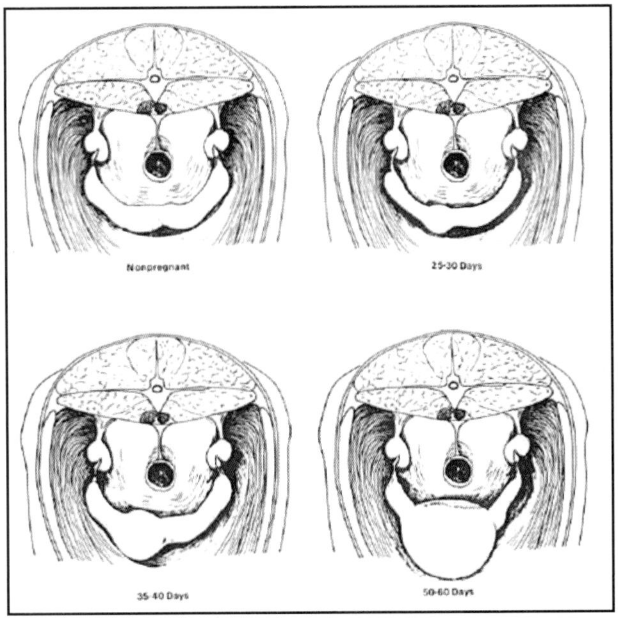

Figure 19-1 Evaluation of the pregnancy status of a mare based on manual palpation per rectum (from Neely et al., 1983).

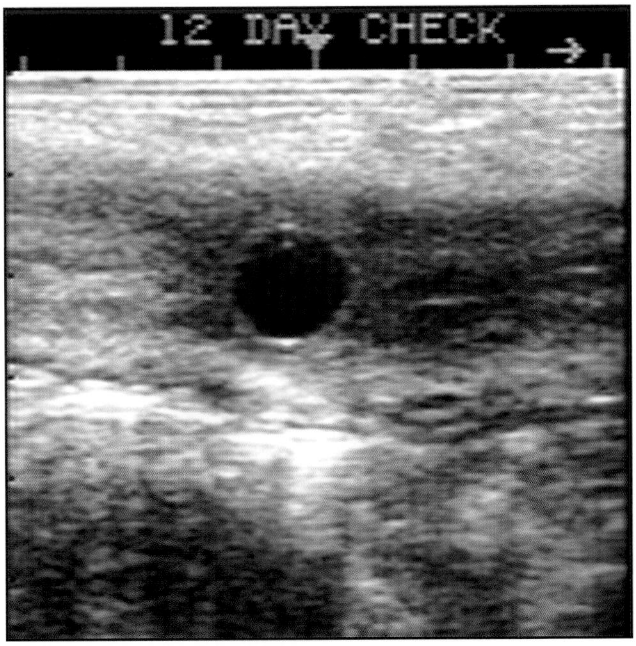

Figure 19-2 Ultrasound of a 12 day pregnancy.

Economic pressures of the equine breeding industry result in a demand for accurate early pregnancy diagnosis. This chapter will briefly review the techniques used and misused for pregnancy diagnosis in mares.

19.1 Behavior

Some horse owners presume that a mare that fails to come back into heat within 3 weeks after breeding is pregnant. That is not necessarily true. A substantial number of bred mares that fail to return to heat are not in fact pregnant. Reasons for a nonpregnant mare not coming back into heat include persistence of the corpus luteum (pseudopregnancy), seasonal effects on ovarian function, and some ovarian disorders.

19.2 Palpation of the Reproductive Tract

Palpation of the reproductive tract per rectum was the most common technique utilized for pregnancy determination prior to the advent of ultrasonography. A diagnosis of pregnancy by palpation is based on detection of a bulge in the uterus, typically at the base of one of the uterine horns (Figure 19-1), and the presence of good uterine and cervical tone. In maiden or barren mares, an initial diagnosis of pregnancy can be made by approximately 25 days after ovulation. In contrast, a positive diagnosis of pregnancy cannot be accurately made in many foaling mares until much later because of the increased size of the postpartum uterus. In addition, manual palpation is not a good technique to detect and manage early twins, detect a small amount of uterine edema, free fluid or evaluate the corpus luteum. As a consequence, ultrasonography has become the gold standard technique for detection of early pregnancy and monitoring ovarian and uterine function.

19.3 Ultrasound Examination

The most reliable technique for early pregnancy evaluation is ultrasonography (Figures 18-2 to Figure 19-5). Pregnancy diagnosis by ultrasound may initially be performed 12 to 16 days after ovulation. An ultrasound examination performed on or before day 16 is also beneficial for the identification and management of twins, scheduling of rebreeding in open mares, and early detection of problems associated with pregnancy. A follow-up examination with ultrasonography is generally recommended between 25 and 35 days of pregnancy to confirm that the pregnancy is still viable. The embryo proper, with a tiny heart beating regularly, can be seen within the fluid-filled embryonic vesicle on or after day 25. Mares determined to be open on the follow-up examination prior to day 35 can usually

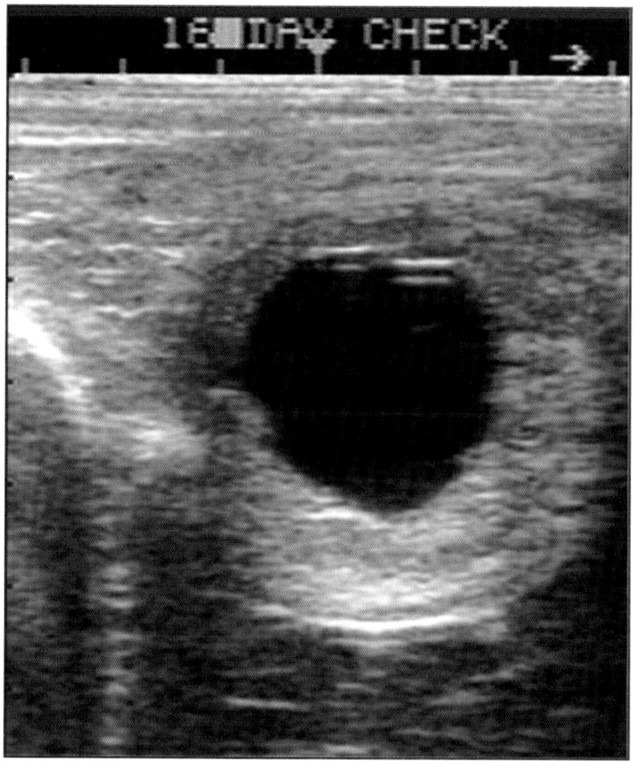

Figure 19-3 Ultrasound of a 16 day pregnancy.

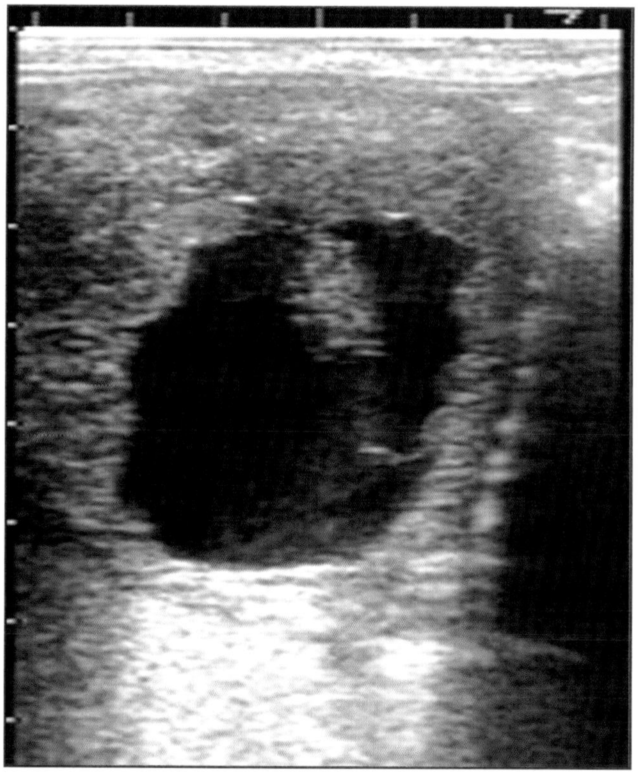

Figure 19-4 Ultrasound of a 25 day pregnancy.

be rebred that season. Administration of prostaglandins may be required to bring these mares back into heat as many will have a persistent corpus luteum. Unfortunately, most mares that lose pregnancies after day 35 will not cycle again that season

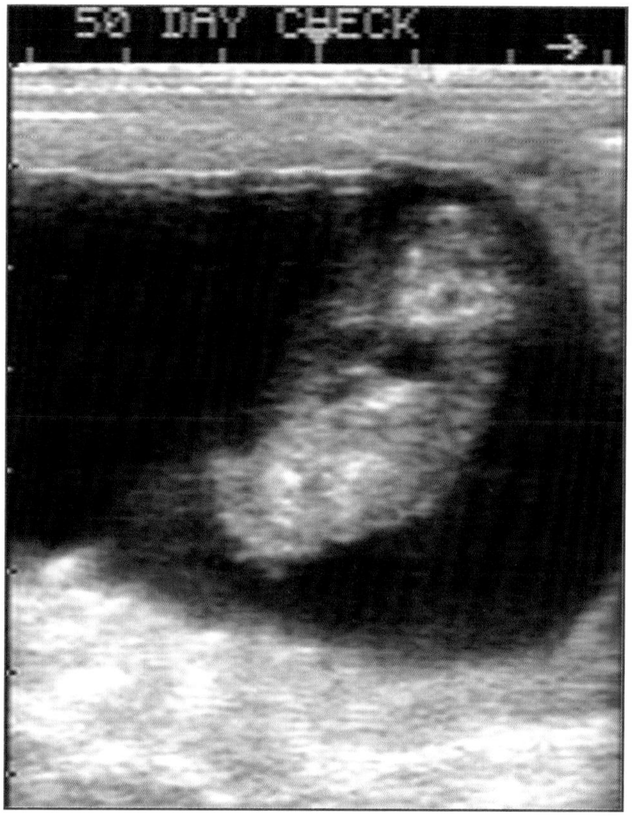

Figure 19-5 Ultrasound of a 50 day pregnancy.

or are very difficult to get in foal due to the presence of endometrial cups and production of equine chorionic gonadotropin.

19.4 Hormonal Tests for Pregnancy

Measurement of progesterone, equine chorionic gonadotropin (eCG) and estrogen in the blood of mares has been used separately or in combination as potential indicators of pregnancy (Table 19-1).

Measurement of progesterone in the blood of mares is of limited value for pregnancy diagnosis since normal (non-pregnant) diestrous mares, pseudopregnant mares and some non-pregnant mares with ovarian abnormalities may all have elevated levels of progesterone. In contrast, a very low progesterone level (less than 1 ng/ml) indicates that the mare is very unlikely to be pregnant or remain pregnant. Progesterone measurement is valuable in determining if a pregnant mare is producing sufficient progesterone to maintain her pregnancy. Normal progesterone levels vary with the stage of pregnancy so interpretation of progesterone results and management decisions must be made appropriately.

Table 19-1 Hormonal tests for pregnancy diagnosis in the mare.

Hormone	Source	Time Course	Comments
Progesterone (P4) and other progestogens	Corpus luteum and/or placenta	Initial elevation after primary ovulation; additional rise after formation of secondary corpora lutea begins on day 45 to 60	Not a direct indicator of pregnancy; levels > 1.0 ng/ml are associated with presence of luteal tissue in a non-pregnant or early pregnant mare; placenta begins to produce progestins by day 70 that may be detected in a progesterone assay; levels < 1.0 ng/ml are generally incompatible with pregnancy in the absence of additional progestin support
Equine Chorionic Gonadotropin (eCG) or Pregnant Mare Serum Gonadotropin (PMSG)	Endometrial cups	Cup formation begins at approximately day 35 of pregnancy; eCG may be detected in blood by day 35 to 42; maximum concentrations are reached by day 55 to 70; cups regress by day 120 to 150; eCG production and duration of secretion is highly variable between mares	Direct indicator of pregnancy; detection of eCG indicates presence of endometrial cups; false negatives may occur if testing before cup formation or after cup regression in a pregnant mare; false positive may occur following pregnancy loss after cup formation; some pregnant mares may not form endometrial cups
Estrogen (Estrone sulfate or Total Estrogens)	Ovary (CL) and fetal-placental unit	Initial rise at day 35 to 45 of ovarian CL origin; substantial increase at day 90 of placental origin	Direct indicator of pregnancy after day 90; also useful in monitoring health status of fetal-placental unit. Will decrease within 2 to 3 days after fetal demise
Relaxin	Placenta	Increased blood levels by day 80; levels remain elevated until foaling	Direct indicator of pregnancy in the mare; may be useful as a marker for placental health. Commercial testing not available
Testosterone	Fetal gonads	Increased blood levels in mare from first month of pregnancy; levels peak at 6 to 7 months and then decline	Not used as an indicator of pregnancy in the mare; levels increase in mares carrying either a male or female fetus

Detection of elevated levels of equine chorionic gonadotropin (eCG) in the blood of mares may be used as a method of pregnancy detection. This hormone is produced from groups of specialized placental cells called endometrial cups and eCG is only present in blood of pregnant mares from approximately 35 to 150 days of gestation. Two major problems exist with using eCG levels for pregnancy diagnosis. First, a false negative diagnosis (i.e. no eCG detected in a mare that is truly pregnant) can be made if a blood sample is collected prior to day 35 before endometrial cups form or after day 150 of pregnancy after regression of the cups. Second, a false positive pregnancy diagnosis (i.e. elevated eCG detected in a mare that is truly not pregnant) can be made if a blood sample is collected from a mare that lost her pregnancy after endometrial cup formation. Therefore, detection of elevated eCG in the blood of a mare will only confirm that endometrial cups are present and do not indicate true pregnancy status or fetal health.

Estrogens have also been used to determine the pregnancy status of mares. The estrogenic hormone estrone sulfate may be used to diagnose pregnancy after approximately 90 days of gestation. Small amounts of estrogens are initially produced by the ovary of the pregnant mare in response to rising levels of eCG. Larger amounts of estrogen are produced by the fetal-placental unit after day 90 of gestation. Measurement of estrogens after the third month of gestation is useful to both diagnose pregnancy and monitor fetal viability as fetal death leads to a rapid decline in estrogen levels.

In summary, ultrasonography is the most useful tool for early pregnancy diagnosis, identification of twins, and detection of uterine or ovarian problems. However, if endocrine tests are required for pregnancy diagnosis (i.e. in miniature mares or mares that cannot be examined by transrectal palpation and ultrasonography), especially if the breeding date is unknown, it is recommended that a combination of progesterone, eCG and estrogen assays be used. Pregnancy tests based on hormone levels in blood or urine are generally used if palpation and ultrasonography per rectum is not possible, unavailable, or if there are specific questions regarding the status of a pregnancy. Examples include determining if progesterone levels are adequate to maintain pregnancy and determining if endometrial cups have formed in a mare that may be losing her pregnancy.

19.5 Evaluation of Progesterone Concentrations

Measurement of plasma progesterone concentrations is valuable in the management of broodmares. Progesterone evaluation is helpful in identification of the presence of an active corpus luteum, monitoring of corpus luteum function across time, identification of certain forms of ovarian pathology (i.e. luteinized anovulatory follicle) and monitoring progesterone levels in pregnant mares.

Specific indications for progesterone analysis in pregnant mares include:

- Detection of a small corpus luteum during an early pregnancy examination in the presence of an embryonic vesicle; a small corpus luteum may suggest that progesterone levels are low
- Detection of endometrial edema during an early pregnancy examination in the presence of an embryonic vesicle; the presence of edema suggests that progesterone levels are low
- Monitoring progesterone levels in a problem mare or a mare with repeated pregnancy loss
- Monitoring progesterone level in a pregnant mare being supplemented with altrenogest to determine if progestin therapy can be discontinued; altrenogest is not detected in a traditional progesterone assay; consequently, a progesterone concentration $\geq$ 4.0 ng/ml is theoretically sufficient to maintain pregnancy without additional supplementation

19.6 Schedule of Dates for Ultrasound Examinations of a Pregnant Mare

A schedule of potential ultrasound examination dates is presented in Table 19-2. Frequency and schedule of initial and subsequent examinations are often dictated by factors such as availability of the mare or clinician, potential for twins, results of previous pregnancy examinations, a history of pregnancy loss in a particular mare, and economics.

Table 19-2 Schedule of potential ultrasonographic examinations in the early pregnant mare. Many modifications of this schedule are used in clinical practice.

Gestation Day Post-Ovulation	Examination Procedure
12 to 16	Initial pregnancy examination; identification and management of twins; evaluation of the corpus luteum, follicle status and presence of endometrial edema
25	Examination for an embryo proper; detection of a heart beat; re-confirm absence of twins
~ 35	Confirmation of pregnancy status at the stage of endometrial cup formation
~45	Confirmation of pregnancy status; may be required for insurance coverage of the pregnancy and/or payment of stallion service fees
~60	Evaluation of pregnancy status and supplementary CL development
65 to 90	Fetal sex determination
~ 150	Confirmation of pregnancy and administration of first equine herpesvirus (EHV-1) or rhinopneumonitis vaccine

Chapter 20 Management of Twins and Embryonic Loss

Figure 20-1 Healthy twin foals.

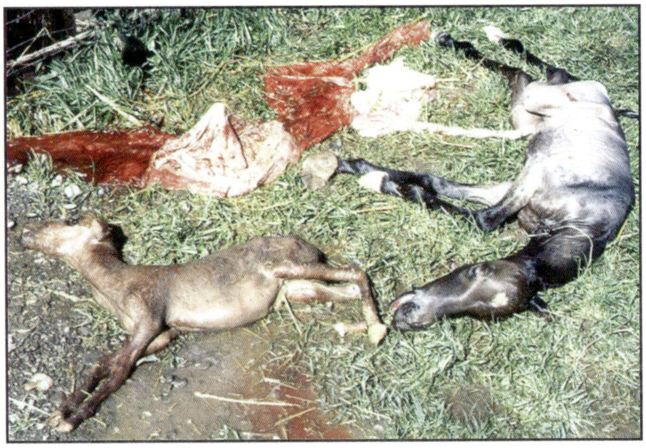

Figure 20-2 Aborted twin fetuses.

20.1 Twins

Twin pregnancies in the horse can occasionally proceed to term and produce healthy foals (Figure 20-1). However, historically twins have been a significant cause of reduced reproductive efficiency in the mare and usually result in abortion, stillbirth or early foal death (Figure 20-2). Routine early pregnancy diagnosis with ultrasound is the key for diagnosis and management of twins.

Identical twins result from the splitting of an embryo that formed after fertilization of one egg ovulated from a single follicle. In the horse, a majority of twins are a result of fertilization of two eggs ovulated from separate follicles and consequently are genetically non-identical (Figure 20-3).

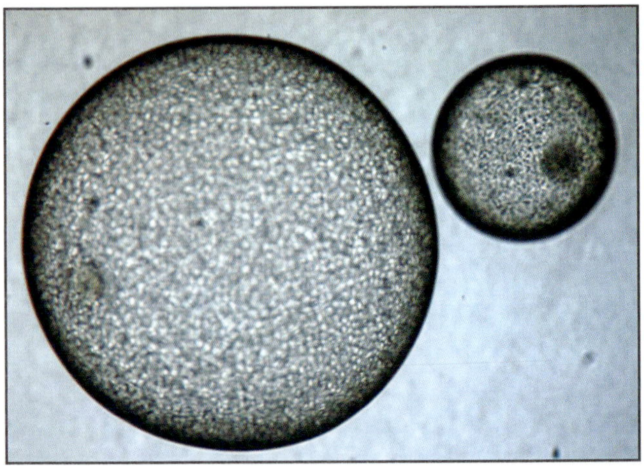

Figure 20-3 Photo of twin (day 8 and day 7 post-ovulation) blastocyst stage embryos.

Sperm from a fertile stallion can survive in the reproductive tract of a mare for several days. Twins may therefore develop from ovulations that occur on the same day or several days apart.

Early detection of twins is critical for proper broodmare management. The possibility of a twin pregnancy can be anticipated with the ovulation of two or more dominant follicles. An early diagnosis of twins may be made by transrectal ultrasonography as early as day 11 or 12 after ovulation. However, in most instances twin pregnancies are diagnosed on day 14 or 15 after ovulation (Figure 20-4).

Equine embryos migrates throughout the uterus until day 16 or 17 when they fix in one location. It is highly advantageous to identify twins during the mobility phase, so that one embryo can be eliminated when it is in a separate location within the uterus from the other embryo. If twins are located adjacent to each other in the same uterine horn (unilateral twins), it is more difficult to eliminate one without also damaging the other embryo. Rarely, two embryos may occupy a single embryonic vesicle (Figure 20-5).

Early management of twins is accomplished by disrupting one embryonic vesicle manually during palpation or ultrasonography per rectum (Figure 20-6). The remaining embryo has a high probability of being carried successfully to term.

Natural reabsorption or elimination of one embryo may occur if both embryos are adjacent to one

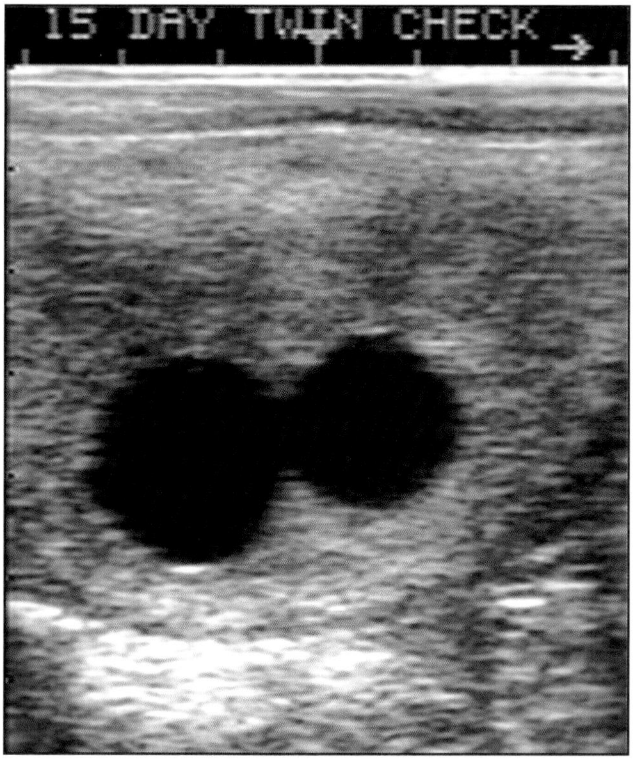

Figure 20-4 Ultrasound image of two embryonic vesicles adjacent to each other in one uterine horn.

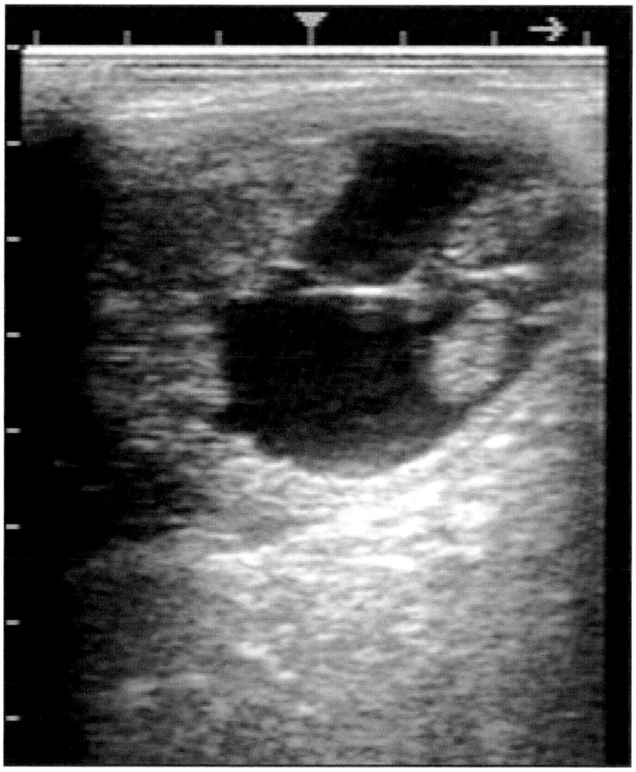

Figure 20-5 Ultrasound image of two embryos, each with a heartbeat, within one embryonic vesicle.

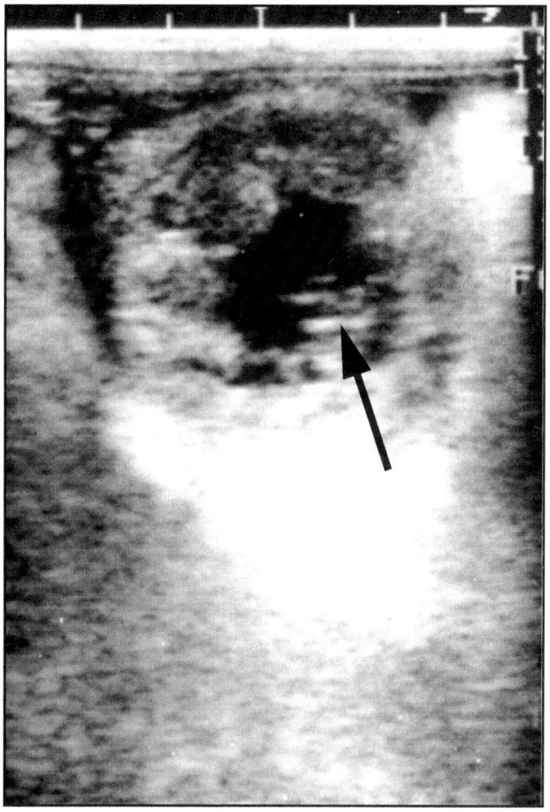

Figure 20-6 Disrupted embryonic membranes (arrow) after manual reduction of one embryo.

another in one uterine horn. It is less likely to occur if the embryos are located in opposite uterine horns.

Management of twins by manual reduction is most successful between 14 and 16 days postovulation. Twin management is easier, safer and more effective if performed early in pregnancy prior to the day embryos stop migrating. Delayed detection leads to increased risk, increased expense and increased chance of failure.

20.2 Embryonic Loss

Embryonic loss during the period from fertilization to the establishment of the endometrial cups ranges from approximately 20 % in young fertile mares to more than 70 % in aged subfertile mares. Pregnancy loss prior to the time of maternal recognition of pregnancy (day 12 to 14 postovulation) does not usually result in any aberrations of the estrous cycle (i.e. the mare returns to heat on schedule).

Pregnancy loss after the period of maternal recognition of pregnancy (i.e. after approximately day 14 post-ovulation) will often result in persistence of the corpus luteum or pseudopregnancy and a delayed return to estrus.

Causes of early embryonic loss may be associated with the mare, the embryo, or external factors. In many instances the cause of embryonic loss is not known.

Progesterone concentrations are often measured in mares with a history of infertility or early embryonic loss. A progesterone concentration of ≥ 4.0 ng/ml is considered to be adequate for maintenance of pregnancy. Mares with progesterone concentrations of < 2.5 ng/ml are considered to be at risk of pregnancy loss, while mares with progesterone levels between 2.5 and 4.0 are considered to be at a slight risk of pregnancy loss. Pregnant mares with low progesterone levels are often supplemented with exogenous progesterone or a synthetic progestins such as altrenogest.

Additional Comments

- Obstetrical lubricant for transrectal palpation and ultrasonography is available from Animal Reproduction Systems
- Pre-made Priority Care General Lube can be obtained in individual one-gallon jugs or by the case (four 1 gallon jugs per case)
- Alternatively, powdered obstetrical lubricant (ARS E-Z Lube Mix) can be acquired from ARS, which is mixed with water to produce a lubricant ideal for palpation and ultrasonography.
- Please check the ARS website for additional information www.arssales.com

Chapter 21. Management of the Late-Term Pregnant Mare

Table 21-0 List and Part Number of ARS products used in this chapter.

Item	Part Number	Use/Comments
Cohesive Bandage	WCB-101	Wrap the tail of the mare prior to foaling
2% Chlorhexidine Scrub	CS2-101	Wash the perineum and udder of mare prior to foaling

Pregnant mares due to foal in January, February or March may be housed under lights during the last 2 to 3 months of pregnancy. Exposure to an artificial photoperiod may shorten the gestation length by 7 to 10 days as compared to mares housed under ambient light conditions. More importantly, pregnant mares due to foal early in the season that are housed under a stimulatory photoperiod are at lower risk of postpartum anestrus than if housed under ambient light conditions.

Pregnant mares should be moved to the foaling facility at least 2 to 4 weeks prior to the anticipated foaling date. This will allow for acclimatization to the new environment and allow for development of immunity to local pathogenic organisms. Antibodies that are produced during this time will be sequestered into colostrum of the mare and passed to the foal at nursing.

21.1 Vaccination and Deworming of Pregnant Mares

Pregnant mares should be vaccinated against equine herpesvirus Type 1 (EHV-1), or rhinopneumonitis, at 5, 7 and 9 months of gestation to prevent or reduce the incidence of viral abortion. Late term pregnant mares should be vaccinated against tetanus, eastern and western equine encephalomyelitis (EEE and WEE), influenza, rhinopneumonitis, rabies and West Nile virus 4 to 6 weeks prior to foaling to allow for the production of maternal antibodies which will be sequestered by the mammary gland and passed to the foal in colostrum. Additional vaccines may be administered to late-term pregnant mares depending on geographic location, potential for exposure, and medical risk.

It is common practice to deworm mares immediately after foaling with ivermectin. The goal is to reduce the transmission of larvae of the intestinal threadworm (*Strongyloides westeri*) from the mare to foal. Larvae of this parasite can be transferred through milk to a newborn foal as it nurses. Parasitic infestation with *Strongloides westeri* is one of the many causes of diarrhea in young foals.

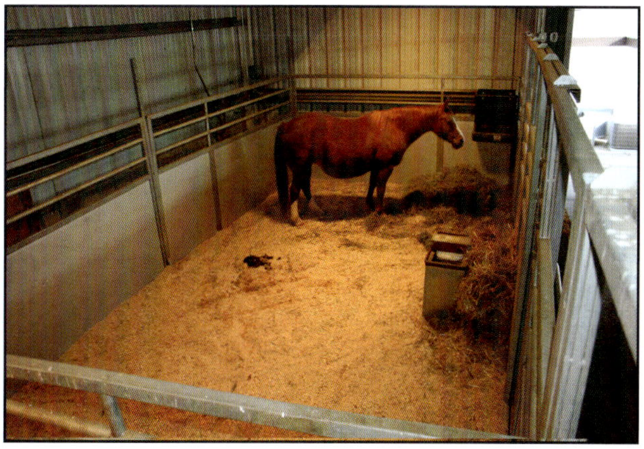

Figure 21-1 Foaling stall (12 ft by 24 ft) constructed by removing a partition between two smaller stalls.

21.2 The Foaling Site

The foaling site should be clean, dry, and visible (i.e. able to be monitored). A grass pasture or large foaling stall are common locations. The minimum size of a foaling stall should be 14 ft. by 14 ft. If a barn has stalls that are 12 ft. by 12 ft., it may be possible to remove panels between stalls to obtain a 12 ft. by 24 ft. foaling stall (Figure 21-1). Opinions vary as to the optimal bedding for a foaling stall, but fresh clean straw is the choice for a majority of facilities. It is important that the foaling stall be stripped completely, disinfected, and allowed to dry before being re-bedded for the next pregnant mare. Inadequate hygiene may result in the build-up of potentially pathogenic organisms and place subsequent foals born in the stall at risk of infectious diseases. Mares should be moved to the foaling stall or moved outside to pasture as parturition approaches.

21.3 Caslick Management

Pregnant mares should be examined for the presence of a Caslick vulvoplasty (Figure 21-2). If present, the Caslick should be opened fully (Figure 21-3) 1 to 2 weeks before the expected due date or sooner if it appears that the mare will foal early. Failure to fully open a Caslick can result in severe

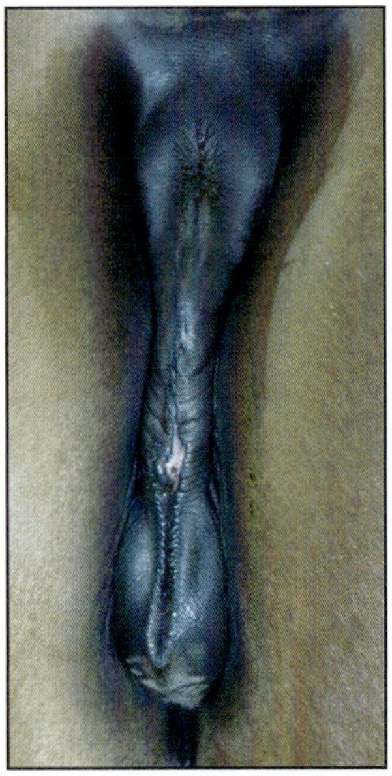

Figure 21-2 Mare with an intact Caslick, which surgically closed the top portion of the vulva to prevent ascending bacterial infection.

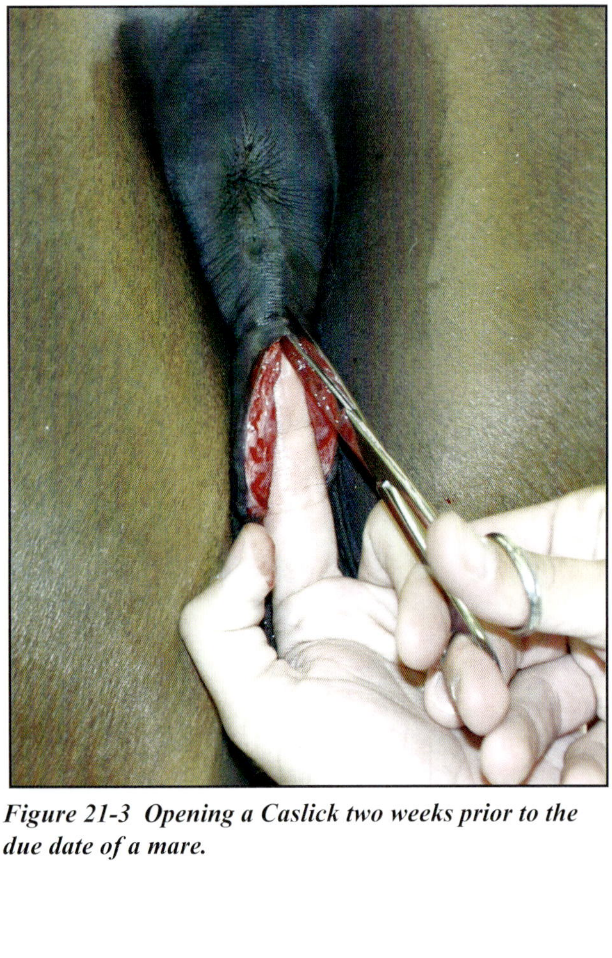

Figure 21-3 Opening a Caslick two weeks prior to the due date of a mare.

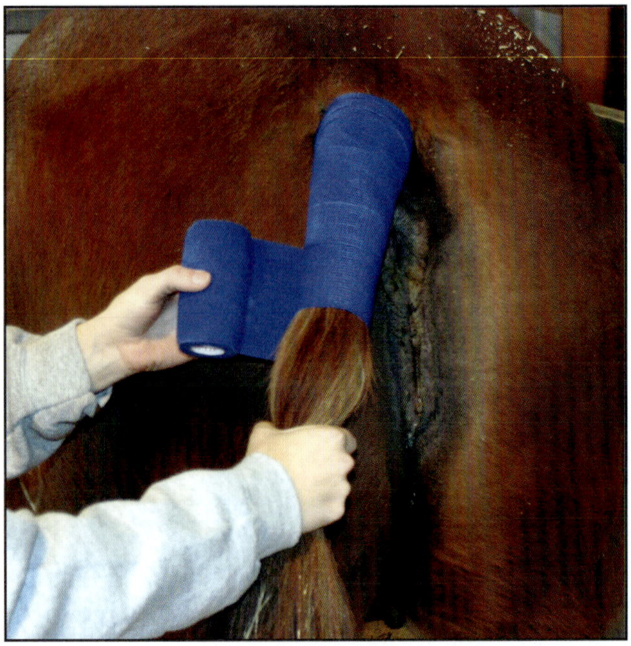

Figure 21-4 Wrapping the tail with an elastic wrap prior to foaling.

injury to the perineum during foaling.

21.4 Preparation of the Mare for Foaling

The tail of the mare should be wrapped with Cohesive Bandage or similar material prior to foaling (Figure 21-4 to Figure 21-6). The tail can get in the way if an obstetrical examination or delivery assistance is needed during foaling. In addition, wrapping will prevent the tail from gross contamination when the mare breaks her water, during the foaling

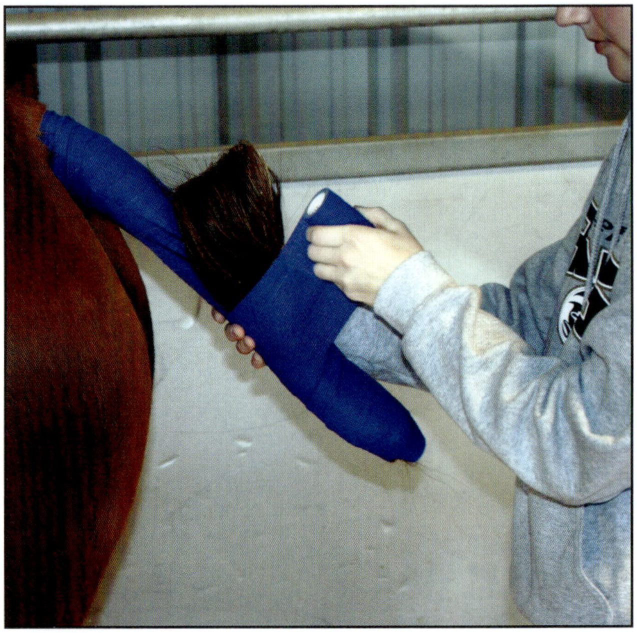

Figure 21-5 Wrapping the tail with an elastic wrap prior to foaling.

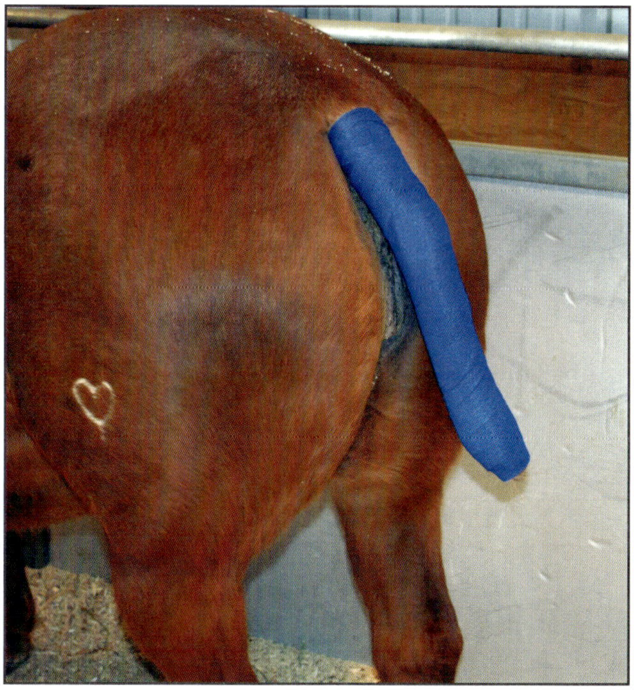

Figure 21-6 Tail wrapped and ready for foaling.

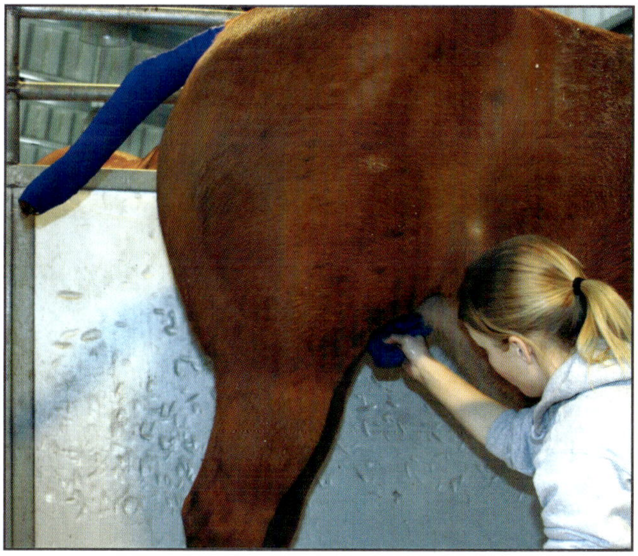

Figure 21-7 Washing the udder of a pregnant mare prior to foaling.

process, and while the placenta is present (i.e. before it passes).

The udder and perineum of the mare should be cleaned with 2% Chlorhexidine Scrub prior to foaling or immediately after foaling to decrease the incidence of bacteria-related diarrhea in newborn foals (Figure 21-7).

21.5 Screening for Neonatal Isoerythrolysis (NI)

The probability of a foal developing neonatal isoerythrolysis (NI), also known as 'Jaundice Foal Syndrome', can be determined by screening the blood of the pregnant mare for antibodies against equine red blood cell antigens 2 to 4 weeks prior to foaling. The blood type of the foal cannot be routinely determined prior to birth. If the mare does have antibodies in her blood directed against antigens present on the red blood cells of the foal, the foal will be at significant medical risk if it is allowed to nurse colostrum. Colostrum of an NI positive mare may have high levels of the offending antibodies and these antibodies can destroy red blood cells of the foal after colostrum is ingested and the antibodies absorbed.

If it is known that the mare does have anti-red blood cell antibodies in her blood prior to foaling, one can prevent the possibility of neonatal isoerythrolysis by intervention and management. Antibody screening is available at several diagnostic laboratories in the United States.

The at-risk foal should not be allowed to nurse colostrum from the mare. The foal should be supplied alternative colostrum, possibly from supplies previously tested and frozen. Colostrum from the mare containing anti-red blood cell antibodies should be collected every 1 to 2 hours for the first 24 hours after foaling and discarded. The foal should be fed an alternative milk source after receiving colostrum. The foal may be kept with the mare, but should wear a muzzle to prevent nursing. The muzzle can be removed and the foal allowed to nurse from the mare beginning approximately 24 hours after birth.

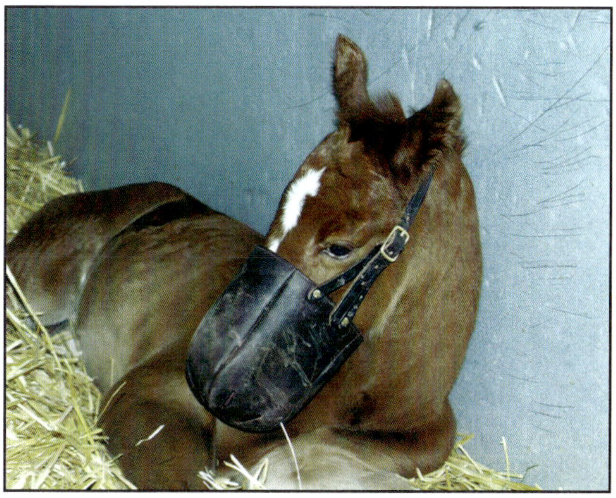

Figure 21-8 Newborn foal wearing a muzzle to prevent nursing from a mare with anti-red blood cell antibodies in her colostrum. The muzzle was removed at 24 hours of age.

Chapter 22 Prediction of Foaling

Table 22-0 List and Part Number of ARS products used in this chapter.

Item	Part Number	Use/Comments
Predict-A-Foal™	PAF-101	Milk calcium test designed to predict foaling
FoalWatch™	FW-K1700	Milk calcium test designed to predict foaling
pH Test Strips	PHS-101	pH test strips to predict foaling

The last few days prior to foaling can be especially tedious for the owner, farm manager or foaling staff. Late-term pregnant mares should be monitored closely to optimize services of farm or veterinary personnel, maximize use of foaling space, and to assist with the safe delivery of the foal if needed.

22.1 Physical Parameters

Clinical signs of impending foaling begin subtly a month or so prior to the expected due date (Table 22-1). Changes become more dramatic and occur more rapidly as the day of foaling approaches.

Table 22-1 Clinical signs of foaling.

Sign	Time Frame Relative to Foaling
Mammary gland development	Begins 2 to 6 weeks prior to foaling
Perineal relaxation	1 to 3 weeks prior to foaling
Engorgement of teat ends with colostrum	7 to 10 days prior to foaling
Waxing of teat ends	48 to 72 hours prior to foaling
Elongation and swelling of the vulva	0 to 24 hours prior to foaling
Dripping of milk from udder	12 to 24 hours prior to foaling

The first noticeable change is in the mammary gland, which begins to enlarge 2 to 6 weeks prior to term (Figure 22-1). Some mares may develop a large amount of edema around the udder before the gland itself becomes enlarged. Mammary gland development will be much more pronounced in

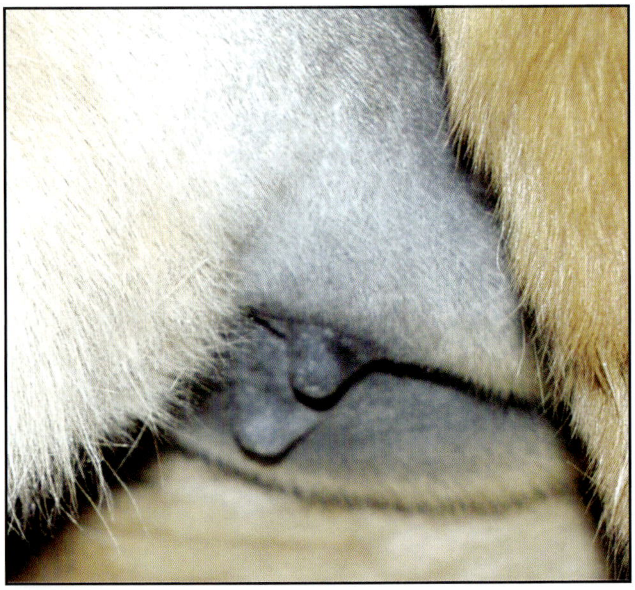

Figure 22-1 Early development of the mammary gland. The gland has started to enlarge ventrally and the teat ends are still flat.

mares that have previously had foals than in maiden mares. The teats or nipples will remain relatively flat until the last few days prior to foaling, at which time they will engorge with colostrum (Figure 22-2). The secretion by the mammary gland changes from a clear straw-colored fluid to a more turbid milk-like fluid as the due date draws near.

The mammary secretion becomes thick and honey-like as colostrum develops within the last day or two prior to foaling.

A thick, waxy exudate of dried colostrum often accumulates at the ends of the teats 24 to 48 hours prior to foaling (Figure 22-3). 'Waxing' of the teat ends is a classic sign that foaling is imminent. The extent of waxing can range from tiny droplets to elongated candle wax-like formations that project a half-inch or more from the teat ends. However, not

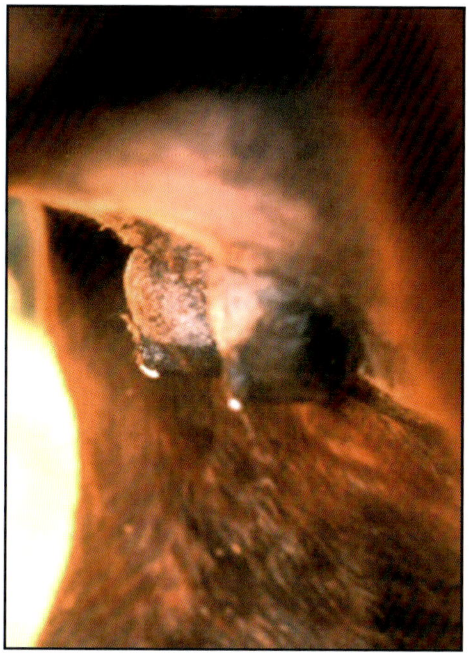

Figure 22-2 Fully engorged teats in a prepartum mare.

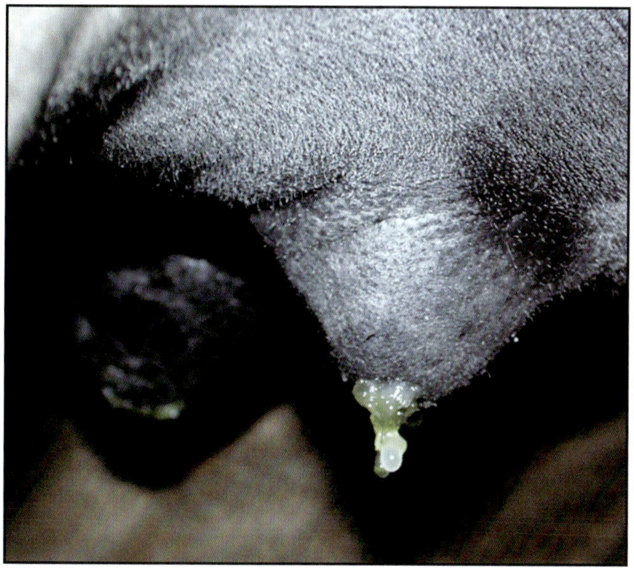

Figure 22-3 Waxing of teat ends in a prepartum mare.

all mares wax up and the duration from onset of waxing to foaling can be quite variable. In addition, some mares will transiently develop wax at the teat ends 1 to 2 weeks prior to foaling.

Waxing - Interpretation Relative to Foaling

- Approximately 70 % of mares wax up prior to foaling
- Approximately 70 % of mares that wax give birth within the next 24 to 48 hours

In the last 2 to 3 weeks of pregnancy the abdominal

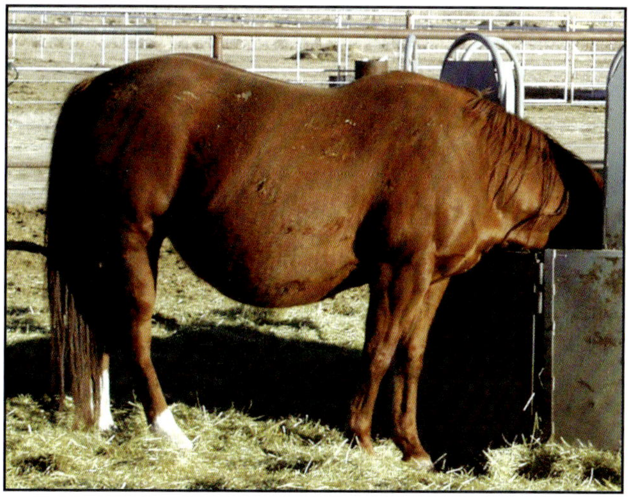

Figure 22-4 Late-term pregnant mare with a prominent 'dropped' abdomen.

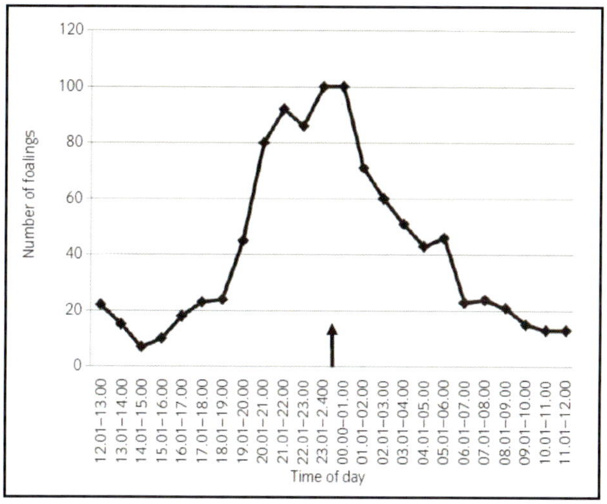

Figure 22-5 Number of mares foaling during a 24 hour period. The arrow designates midnight.

muscles relax causing a pronounced 'dropping' of the abdomen, which is especially noticeable in older mares (Figure 22-4). During the last week prior to foaling, the ligaments, muscles and other structures surrounding the mare's pelvis and perineum soften in preparation for birth. The vulva becomes relaxed, elongated and edematous in the hours immediately prior to foaling. The behavior of the mare often changes during the last few days or hours preceding foaling. Mares near term may tend to isolate themselves, go off feed and pass small amounts of manure or urine frequently.

A majority of mares foal out at night, although a low percentage of mares will give birth during daylight hours (Figure 22-5).

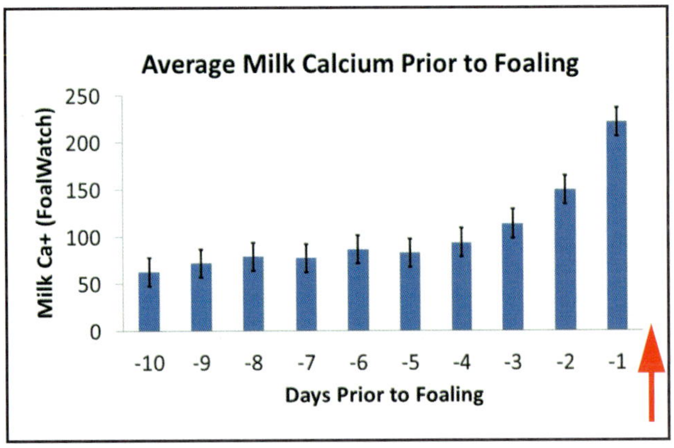

Figure 22-6 Graph of average milk calcium levels prior to foaling (arrow) in mares.

22.2 Monitoring Milk Calcium Levels

Prediction of foaling based on changes in calcium concentrations in mammary secretions has been used successfully for many years. Calcium concentration in milk increases sharply as the mare approaches the time of foaling (Figure 22-6). It is recommended that testing be initiated several days prior to the expected due date and performed once daily in the evening. Testing in mares with an unknown breeding date should begin when significant udder development is noted and a small amount of secretion can be obtained.

One commercial test, Predict-a-Foal^{TM} uses a test strip that measures both calcium and magnesium. The strip is dipped into a specific dilution of milk and distilled water and observed for color change in any of the 5 test squares (Figure 22-7). The chance of a mare giving birth within the next 12 to 24 hours increases as the number of squares that change color increases. The Predict-a-Foal^{TM} test is easy to use, easy to interpret, and repeatable.

A second test, FoalWatch^{TM}, titrates the concentration of calcium carbonate in a milk sample. A milk sample is obtained and a specific volume (1.5 mls) is mixed with a specific volume of distilled water (9 mls). An indicator dye is added and small amounts of the test sample are aspirated into a calibrated titration chamber until the color in the chamber turns from orange-pink to blue (Figure 22-8, 21-9 and 21-10). Level of calcium carbonate is determined using a scale provided on the glass chamber.

Calcium levels above 200 ppm indicate that the mare has a high probability of foaling within the next 48 to 72 hours, whereas mares with a milk calcium level of less than 50 ppm are unlikely to foal in the next 24 hours.

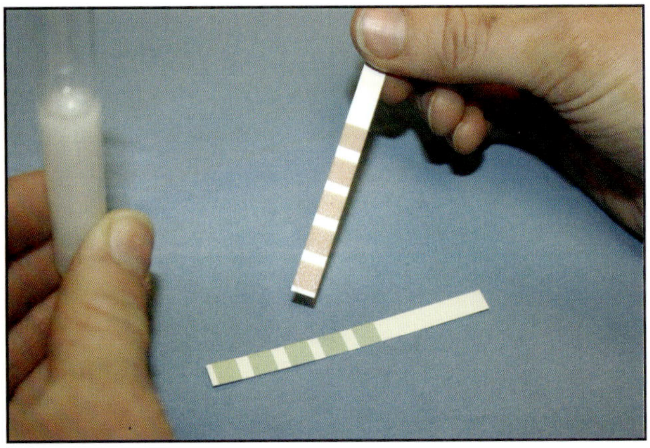

Figure 22-7 Predict-A-Foal^{TM} indicator strips. The number of boxes (originally green) that turn pink indicates the relative concentration of calcium in the milk sample.

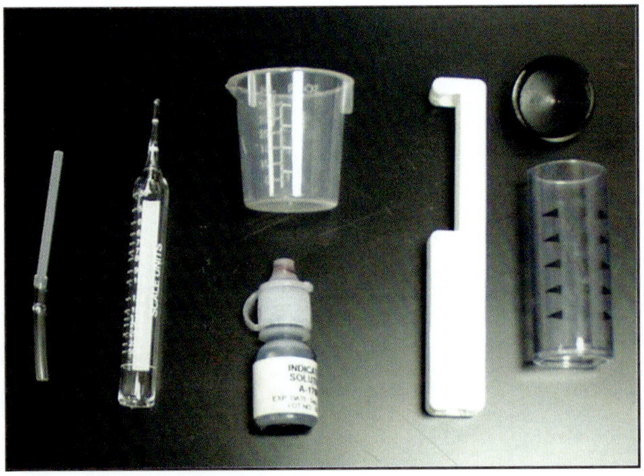

Figure 22-8 Components of the FoalWatch^{TM} test kit for measurement of milk calcium in order to predict foaling.

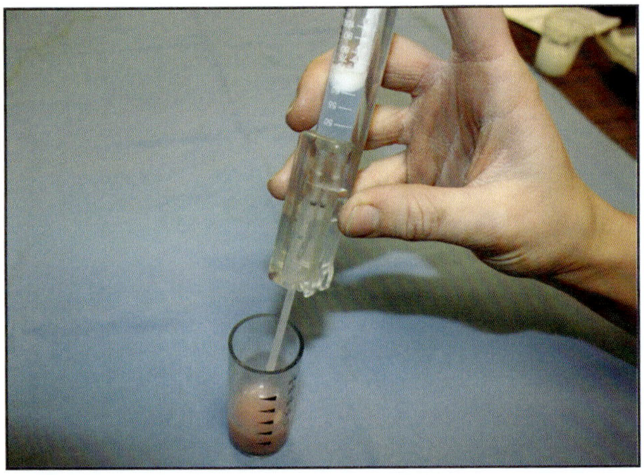

Figure 22-9 Titration of calcium concentration in a mare milk sample using the FoalWatch^{TM} test.

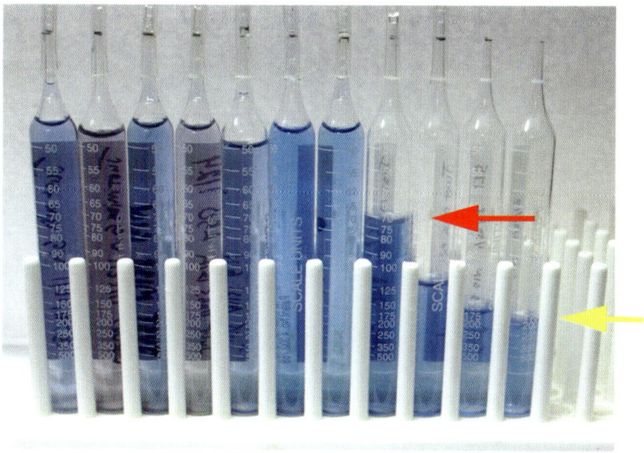

Figure 22-10 A series of FoalWatch™ milk calcium test results on a mare as she approached her due date. Calcium levels in the first 7 samples were undetectable (< 50 ppm). Milk calcium in the 8th sample was 70 ppm (red arrow) and increased to approximately 200 ppm on the final sample prior to foaling (yellow arrow).

Data from the clinical program at Colorado State University indicate that many mares give birth with milk calcium levels less than 200 ppm (Figure 22-11). In addition, any dramatic rise in milk calcium in a mare near her due date may be indicative of impending foaling.

Evaluation of calcium levels in mammary gland secretions is useful in prediction of when mares are likely to foal and are also useful in predicting that a given mare is unlikely to foal in the next few days. Calcium testing may not be necessary on farms if trained foal-watch personnel are available. However, the tests may be quite valuable on smaller operations with limited staff.

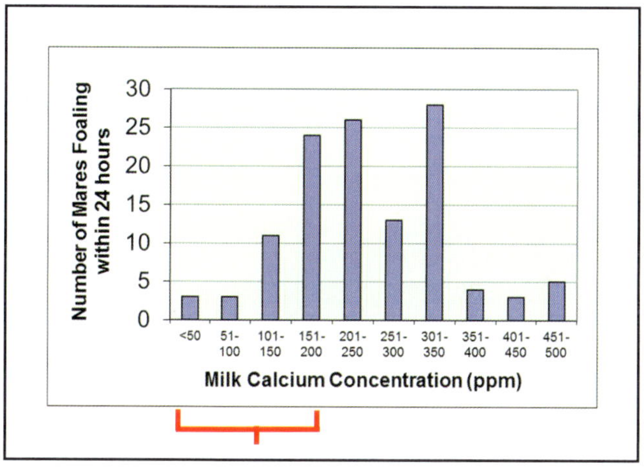

Figure 22-11 Graph of milk calcium levels in mares immediately prior to foaling. Note that a relatively large number of mares foaled with a milk calcium level less than 200 ppm (red bracket) and 3 mares foaled with a milk calcium level of less than 50 ppm.

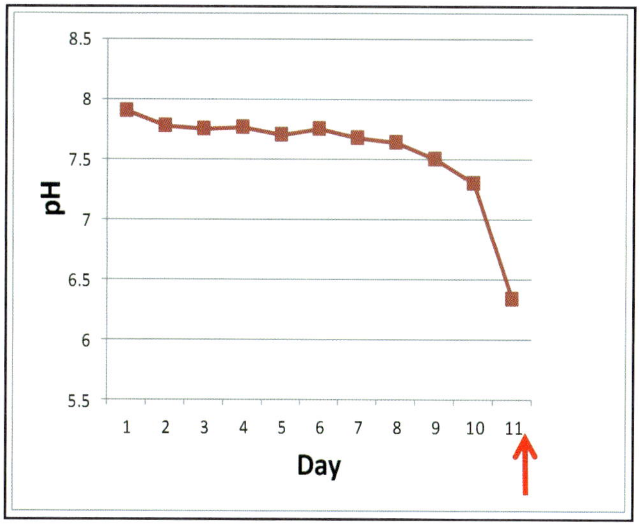

Figure 22-12 pH in mare milk relative to the day of foaling (arrow).

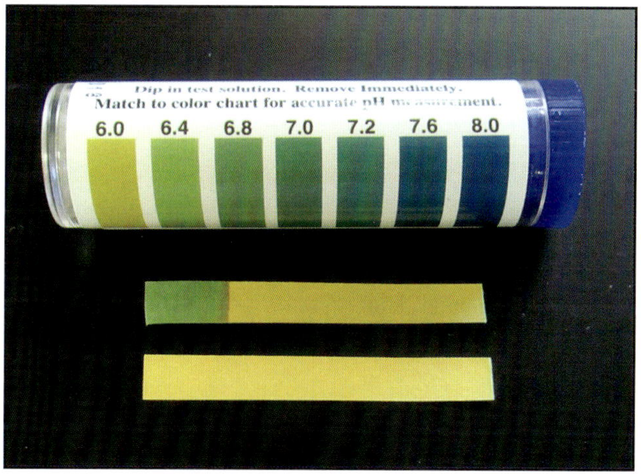

Figure 22-13 pH test strips and color chart ranging from 6.0 to 8.0.

22.3 pH in Milk as a Predictor of Foaling

The pH of a mare's milk often decreases markedly within the 24 hour period prior to foaling. The normal pH of mare's milk in the week prior to foaling is typically 7.0 to 7.4. A drop in pH to ≤ 6.4 is often associated with foaling within the subsequent 24 hours (Figure 22-12). The most accurate method to measure milk pH is a commercial pH meter, but cost of the device may preclude routine use on a breeding farm or ranch. An alternative is to use commercial pH test strips (Figure 22-13) calibrated in the range of 6.0 to 8.0.

22.4 Labor Alert Devices

Labor alert devices are intended to signal an owner or foaling attendant that the mare is in the process of giving birth. The design of the devices vary between units.

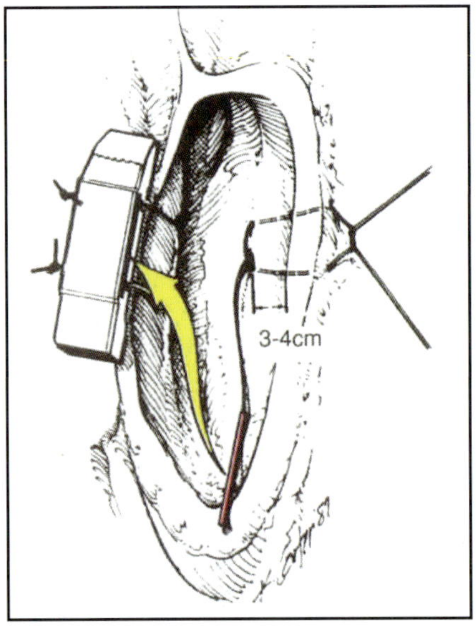

Figure 22-14 Diagram of Foalert transmitter (left) and magnet (right) sutured onto the vulva of a mare.

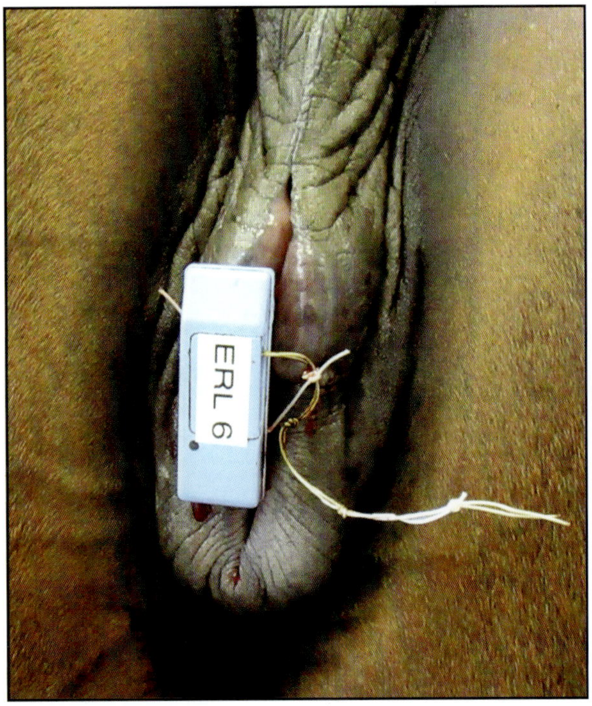

Figure 22-15 Foalert labor alert device placed on the vulva of a mare.

The Foalert system utilizes a transmitter sutured to the vulva of the mare (Figure 22-14 and Figure 22-15). Separation of the vulva lips at foaling pulls a magnet out of the transmitter, which activates the transmitter to send a signal to receiver which has an audible alarm. The receiver can also be attached to an auto-dialing device which can be programmed to activate a pager or send a message to one or more phones pre-programmed into the unit.

Labor alert devices are beneficial in that mares can

Figure 22-16 Web-based video camera above a foaling stall.

be monitored continuously without constant or periodic observations. Labor alert devices may be most effective in allowing farm personnel to go about their routine chores or business during the daytime when one does not necessarily expect a mare to foal.

22.5 Video Monitoring Systems

Video systems, either direct or web-based, are becoming common on broodmare farms to monitor late-term mares (Figure 22-16 and Figure 22-17). These systems allow for close supervision of mares without the necessity of the foaling attendant to wait by the stall or to make repeated visits to the stall every 15 to 30 minutes throughout the night. An added benefit is that video systems minimize disturbances to the nervous mare by decreasing stall visits. However, in the end someone still needs to monitor the mare and positioning of the mare relative to the camera may limit visibility.

Figure 22-17 View of a mare in a foaling stall with a color web-based video camera system.

Chapter 23. Normal and Abnormal Foaling

Table 23-0 List and Part Number of ARS products used in this chapter.

Item	Part Number	Use/Comments
CoTear™ Cohesive Bandage	WCB-101	Wrap the tail of the mare prior to foaling.
Chlorhexidine Scrub	CS2-101	Wash the perineum and udder of mare prior to foaling.
Umbilical Tape	UT-101-12/24	Used to tie off the umbilical stump immediately after foaling (if needed; used as an alternative to an umbilical clamp).
Umbilical Clamp	UC-101/10	Used to clamp off the umbilical stump immediately after foaling (if needed; used as an alternative to umbilical tape); usually removed or will fall off after 2-3 days.
Stainless Steel Mayo Scissors	CS-101	Multiple uses including opening a placenta in a 'red-bag' birth, cutting umbilical tape or tail wrap material, or occasionally cutting the umbilical cord.
Chlorhexidine Solution	CSD-101	Diluted 1:1 and used as a navel disinfectant.
Nylon Placenta Cord	CN-48/6	Used to tie the placenta above the hocks of the mare after foaling; prevents the mare from stepping on or tearing placenta.
60" Nylon Obstetrical Strap	NOS-101	Used under the direction of a veterinarian to assist in the foaling process if needed.
ARS E-Z Breather™ Foal Resuscitator	EB-101	Used to provide emergency resuscitation to newborn foal if necessary.
Sterile Obstetrical Sleeves	SLG Series	Should be worn if the position of the fetus inside the birth canal needs to be checked during labor.
Surgilube® Lubricating Jelly	SSL-101	Should be used with the sterile obstetrical sleeves when checking fetal orientation in birth canal.
ARS Foaling Kit	AFK-101 or AFK-201	Comprehensive kit of foaling equipment and supplies.

23.1 Signal for Birth

A key concept regarding the onset of foaling is that the fetus initiates or triggers the birth process. Parturition will generally occur when the fetus is physiologically ready to survive outside of the mare.

23.2 Preparation of the Mare for Birth

A series of brief tasks should be completed as the time of foaling approaches. The vulva of the mare should be checked for the presence of a Caslick surgery. If the surgery had been performed, it is recommended that the sutured vulva be opened 7 to 14 days prior to the calculated due date. The site should be opened earlier if the mare bags up significantly prior to her due date.

It is recommended that the tail of the mare be wrapped prior to foaling, primarily for cleanliness and to prevent tail hairs from getting in the way in the event that assistance is required during delivery (Figure 23-1). A variety of materials may be used to wrap the tail, including Cohesive Bandage, rolled gauze, polo wraps, neoprene wraps, etc.

The perineum and udder of the mare should be washed with 2% Chlorhexidine Scrub as the hour of foaling nears (Figure 23-2). Cleaning the perineum and udder of the mare prior to foaling or immediately after foaling may reduce the incidence of septicemia and diarrhea in newborn foals by decreasing the number of bacteria the foal is exposed to early in life, especially as the foal first

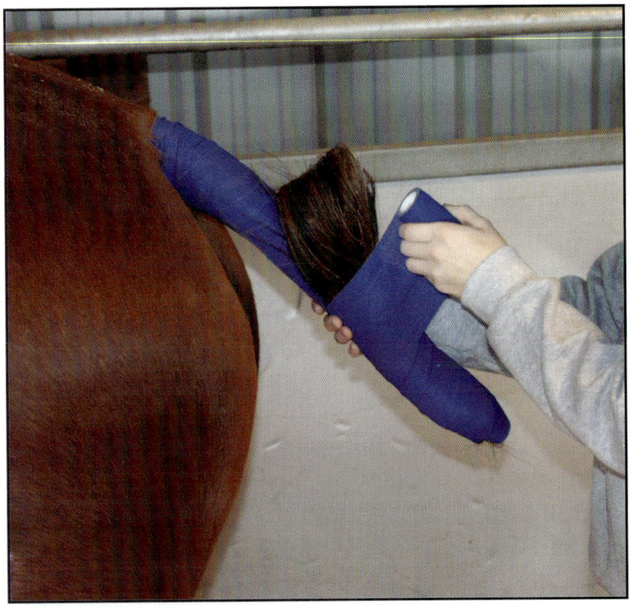

Figure 23-1 Wrapping the tail of a pregnant mare prior to foaling.

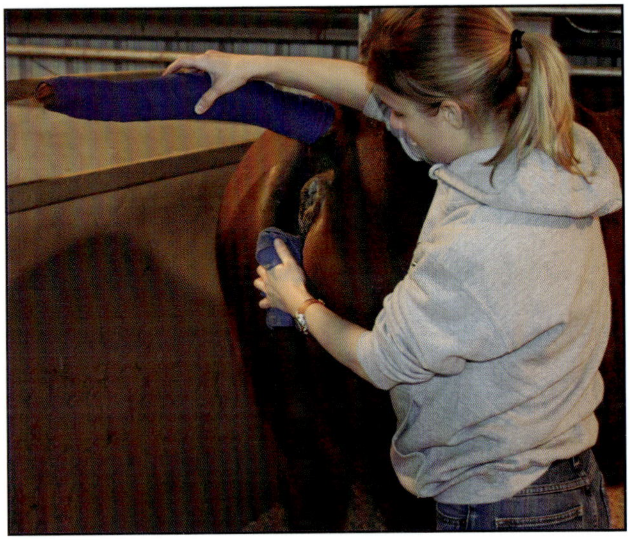

Figure 23-2 Washing the vulva of a prepartum mare.

begins to nurse.

23.3 Stages of Normal Labor

Labor is divided into 3 stages (Table 23-1). The fetus is typically positioned with its back toward the mare's abdomen and the head toward the mare's pelvis prior to foaling. During Stage 1 of labor, the head and forelimbs extend and rotate into a dorsal position for delivery. In Stage 2 of labor, the fetal head, forelimbs and shoulders enter the birth canal and the fetus is delivered. Fetal movements, uterine contractions and mare movements combine to reposition the fetus for delivery. Stage 3 consists of passage of the fetal membranes or placenta.

Table 23-1 Summary of the stages of labor in a mare.

Stage	Characteristics	Duration
I	Restlessness Signs of mild colic Tail switching Frequently lying down and rising Sweating	1 to 4 hours
II	Rupture of the outer water sac (chorioallantoic membrane) Active straining Strong, 'explosive' efforts Appearance of smokey-grey amnion at vulva Birth of foal	5 to 20 minutes
III	Passage of placenta	1 to 3 hours

Stage I. The first stage of labor begins with the onset of uterine contractions and ends with the rupture of the chorioallantoic membrane or outer placental membrane (i.e. the mare 'breaks her water'). The start of Stage I is difficult to determine since the initial mild uterine contractions may occur without overt clinical signs. The mare may be restless or nervous, lie down and stand up frequently, paw at the ground, nibble a little hay or grass, pass small amounts of urine or feces, look at her flanks and/or show signs of abdominal discomfort. She may exhibit patchy sweating behind the elbows, in the flanks and along the neck (Figure 23-3). Milk may begin to squirt from her teats as a result of oxytocin secretion.

The force of the uterine contractions eventually exerts enough pressure to push the placenta through

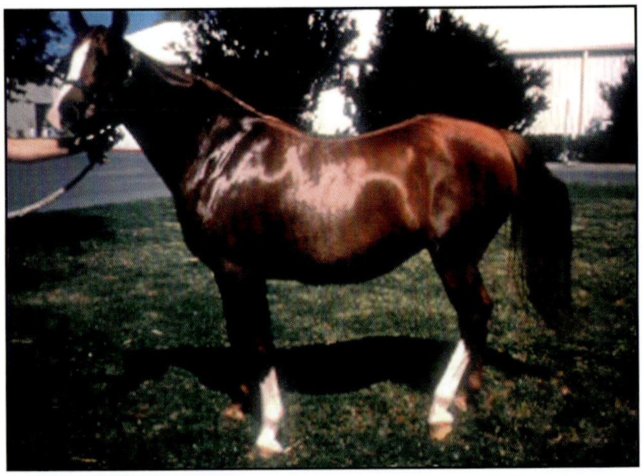

Figure 23-3 A mare in Stage I of labor with sweat along the neck and chest.

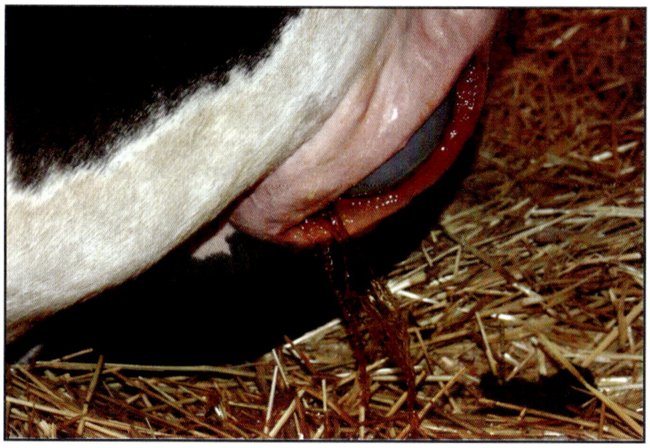

***Figure 23-4** Mare 'breaking her water' and releasing allantoic fluid at the start of Stage II of labor.*

the cervix where the chorioallantoic membrane ruptures at the 'cervical star', releasing allantoic fluid. This is visible as an outpouring of fluid from the vulva (i.e. the mare has 'broken her water') (Figure 23-4). The duration of Stage I is usually 1 to 4 hours. Stage I may be shorter and less obvious in mares that have had several foals (i.e. multiparous mares). If the chorioallantoic membrane fails to rupture, it may pass through the cervix and vagina and be visible outside of the vulva (see the section on Premature Separation of the Placenta or 'Red Bag').

Stage II. The second stage of labor begins with rupture of the chorioallantoic membrane and ends with delivery of the foal. Contraction of the uterus pushes the fetus into the birth canal. Cervical stimulation triggers a neuroendocrine reflex (Ferguson reflex) which results in release of oxytocin from the posterior pituitary of the mare. Oxytocin stimulates additional uterine contractions which begin to expel the fetus.

The first structure normally visible at the vulva is the amnion or inner placental membrane (Figure 23-5). The amnion is recognized as a translucent, light gray to white membrane and is filled with amnionic fluid. The amnion is usually visible within 1 to 5 minutes after rupture of the chorioallantois. As uterine contractions continue, the front feet and nose of the fetus protrude through the vulva (Figure 23-6). One forelimb usually precedes the other by 4 to 6 inches. This results in slight angling of the shoulders and thereby reduces the width of this area as it passes through the mare's pelvis. The nose of the fetus should appear by the

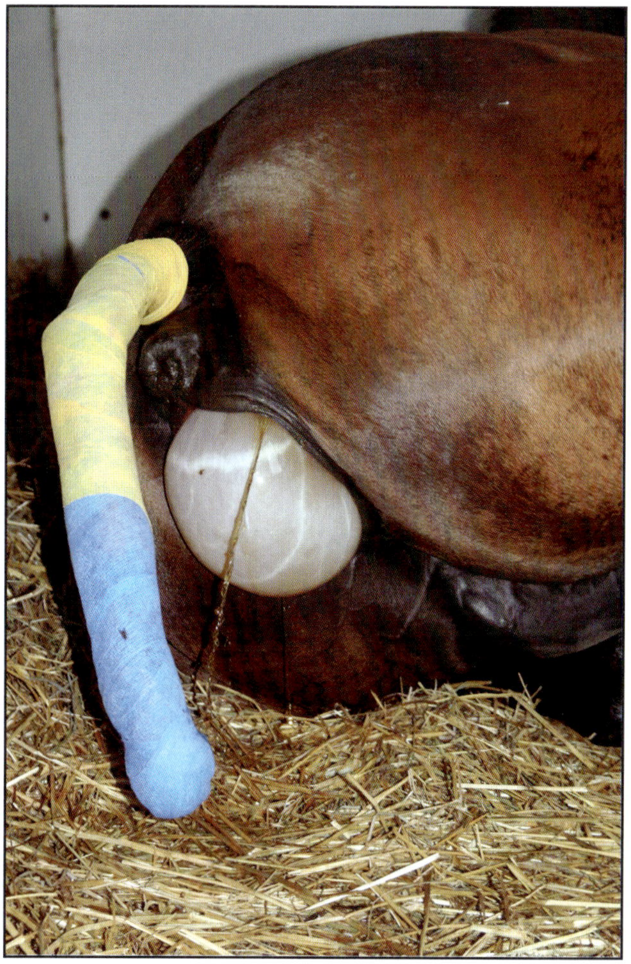

***Figure 23-5** Translucent white amnion protruding through the vulva of a mare in normal Stage II of labor.*

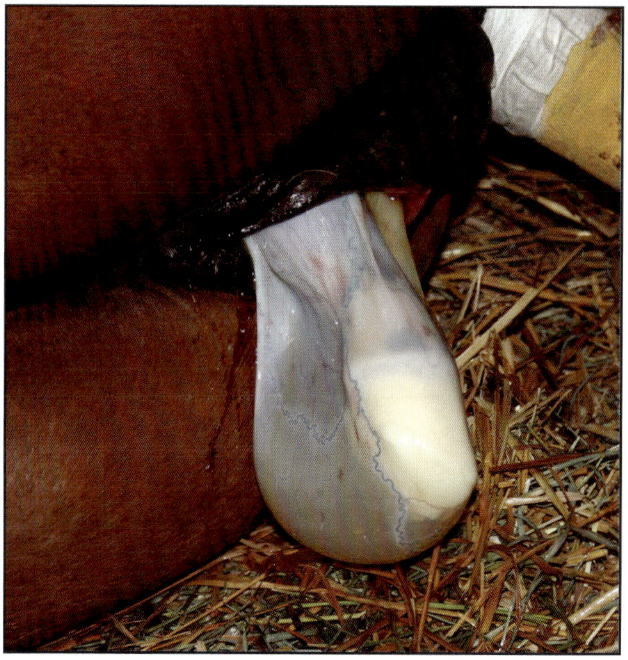

***Figure 23-6** Photograph of front legs of the fetus protruding through the vulva of a mare in Stage II of labor.*

Figure 23-7 Photograph of the amnion breaking off the nose of a newborn foal.

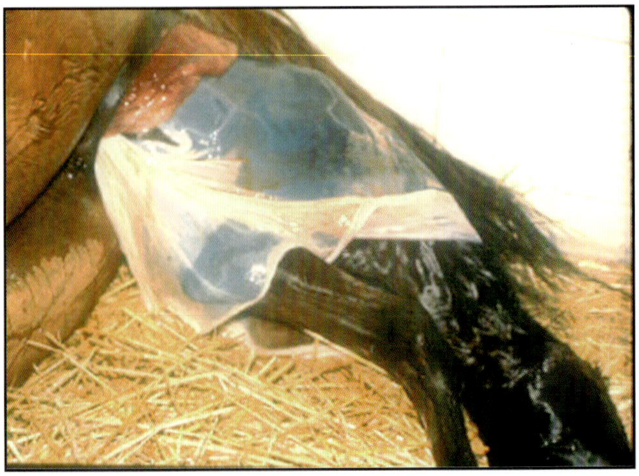

Figure 23-8 Photograph of the front half of the foal protruding through the vulva of a mare in Stage II of labor.

time the carpal (knee) joints are observed. If not, intervention may be indicated as the head may be in an abnormal position and a normal unassisted foaling may be difficult or impossible. The soles of the hooves are directed downward if the foal is in the normal delivery position.

Techniques to distinguish between front legs and back legs include:

- The first two large movable joints on the front leg (fetlock and carpus) flex in the same direction.
- The first two large movable joints on the back legs (fetlock and hock) flex in opposite directions.

Spontaneous rupture of the amnion often occurs after the fetus is at least midway through the birth canal (Figure 23-7 to Figure 23-9). There is no need to manually remove the amnion from the head of the foal until after the chest has passed through the birth canal. If the amnion remains intact after the foal has been delivered, it should be immediately removed from the head or the foal may die from suffocation. Gentle traction on the front legs may be applied in synchrony with the mare's contractions at this time if necessary.

The mare usually lies down for the final contractions that push the fetus completely out. Straining usually decreases markedly when the foal's hips clear the vagina. It is best if the mare is allowed to lie quietly with minimal disturbance for several minutes after foaling. This allows the foal to orient to its new environment and may potentially allow for transfer of blood from the placenta into the foals circulatory system prior to rupture of the umbilical cord.

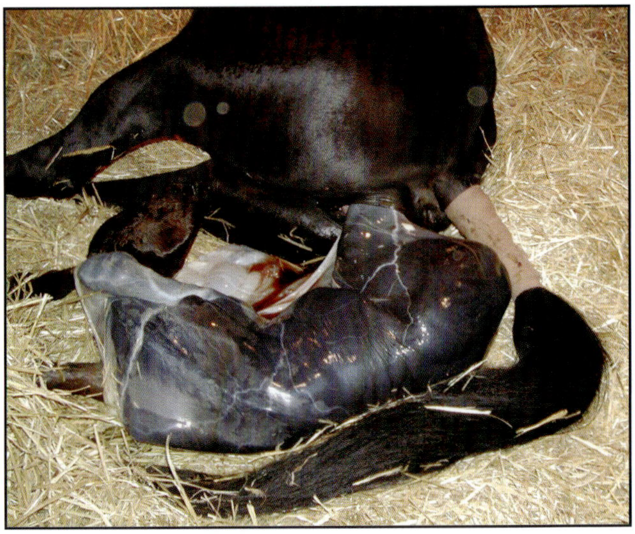

Figure 23-9 Photograph of the newborn foal and mare resting after delivery.

It is usually not necessary or recommended to cut or manually break the umbilical cord. The cord normally breaks when the mare stands or the foal attempts to rise (Figure 20-10). If necessary, manual breakage of the cord can be accomplished by grasping the cord with one hand on each side of the natural point of breakage, which is usually 1 to 2 inches from the foal's abdomen. Direct tension on the cord attachment to the abdominal wall should be avoided. This may result in rupture of the cord at

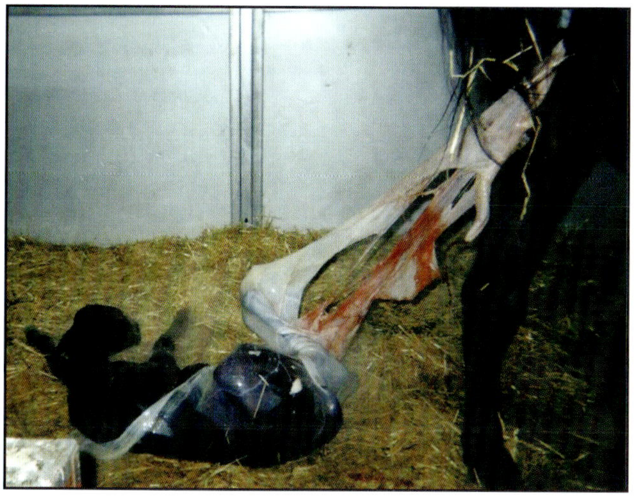

***Figure 23-10** Umbilical cord stretching and about to break as the mare stands after delivery.*

the level of the abdomen or even below skin level (i.e. without an umbilical stump) and will increase the likelihood of an infection in the umbilical cord (i.e. 'navel ill').

If it is necessary to cut the umbilical cord, it is recommended that the cord be tied with Umbilical Tape or an Umbilical Clamp be placed 1 to 2 inches from the abdominal wall. The cord can then be cut with Stainless Steel Mayo Scissors on the side of the tape or clamp away from the foal. Failure to tie or clamp the cord prior to cutting with a sharp knife or scissors may result in excessive hemorrhage. The umbilical stump should be disinfected with Navel Dip (i.e. 2% Chlorhexidine Solution diluted 1:1 with distilled water) immediately after the cord breaks.

Stage II of labor normally lasts 15 to 20 minutes from when the mare 'breaks her water' until the foal is delivered. Labor may be shorter in mares that have previously delivered a foal. The mare should be examined if the fetus has not been delivered within 15 to 20 minutes after the mare has broken her water, if labor has stopped completely, or if the normal progression of foaling has been interrupted. A delay in labor may result in compromise to the health of the fetus when oxygen delivery is decreased as the placenta begins to separate from the uterus of the mare. If a problem is suspected and if the foaling attendant is experienced, he or she should quickly but effectively clean the perineal area with 2% Chlorhexidine Scrub and then perform a vaginal examination. The position of the foal within the pelvic canal should be determined and a judgment made as to the ability of the mare to deliver the foal with minimal or no assistance. This can be accomplished using Sterile Obstetrical Sleeve and Surgilube® Lubricating Jelly under the direction of a veterinarian. If it is determined that the mare cannot deliver the foal without assistance, the foaling attendant should start to implement the dystocia/emergency foaling plan that should be in place prior to the foaling season on every farm. The plan may consist of calling for additional help from the farm or a neighboring farm, calling a local veterinarian to come to the farm, or transporting the mare to a veterinary clinic.

If the foaling attendant is not experienced, help should be summoned if the mare has not made significant progress or delivered a foal within 15 to 20 minutes from the time the water broke. Knowing when to call for help is one the most critical and time-sensitive decisions that can be made on a broodmare farm. In general, the only bad decision is not calling for help or taking action. Failure to take action may put the life of the foal at risk within a few valuable minutes. Any factor that slows the delivery process is detrimental, because the placenta may separate rapidly and the supply of oxygen to the fetus can be subsequently reduced. The incidence of fetal or neonatal death increases if an expedient delivery is not forthcoming.

Stage III. Expulsion of the placenta or fetal membranes is the final stage of parturition. After the foal is delivered, the amnion may be tied using the Nylon Placenta Cord so that it hangs just above the hocks (Figure 23-11). This prevents the mare from stepping on it and yet provides sufficient weight and traction on the umbilical cord to aid in the separation of the chorioallantois from the uterus. When separation is complete the entire placenta is expelled (Figure 23-12). The placenta is usually passed within 30 to 120 minutes after an uncomplicated foaling. An equine placenta is considered to be abnormally retained after 3 hours. Techniques for examination of the placenta after it has passed are discussed in the Postpartum Mare Section.

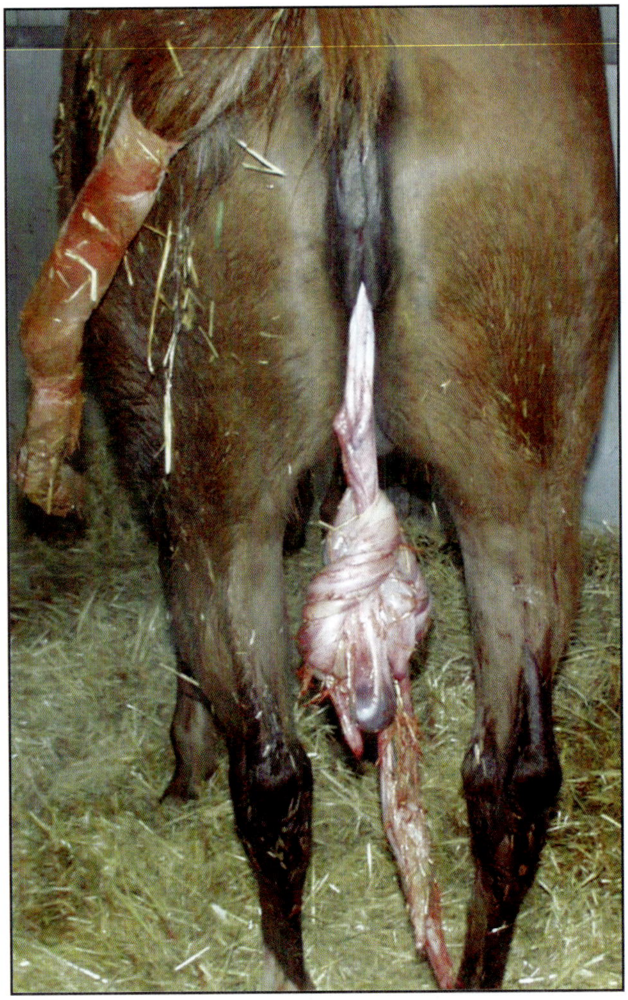

Figure 23-11 Photograph of the umbilical cord and amnion tied above hocks.

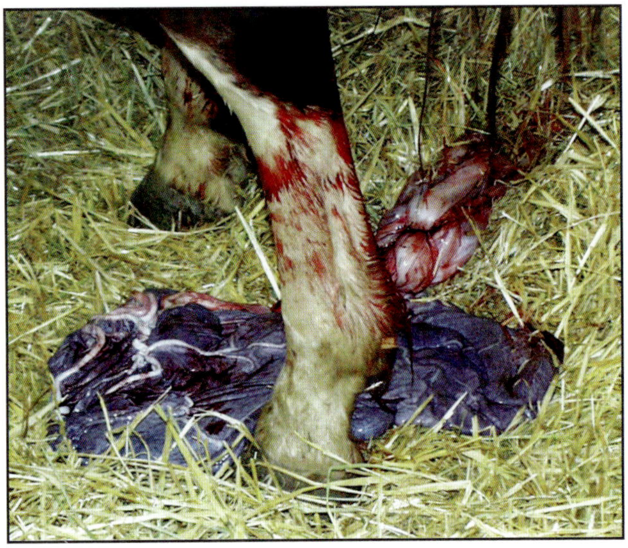

Figure 23-12 Photograph of the placenta after it has been passed onto the stall floor.

23.4 Dystocia

The term dystocia refers to an abnormal or difficult birth. Dystocia occurs in approximately 8 to 12% of all foalings and is more common in mares during their first foaling (i.e. maiden mares) than in mares that have previously given birth to one or more foals. As noted previously, active (Stage II) labor is usually completed within 15 to 20 minutes. An owner or foaling attendant should be concerned if a foal has not been born within 15 to 20 minutes after a mare 'breaks her water'.

The most common cause of dystocia in the mare is an abnormal alignment of the head or forelimbs of the foal in the birth canal (i.e. the pelvis of the mare). Failure of the foal to be properly oriented will almost always prevent normal passage through the birth canal.

Intervention is often required in a difficult birth to assist with delivery of the foal. The ultimate goals in assisting in a dystocia are to save the life of the foal, save the life of the mare and to preserve the future fertility of the mare. Time is critical during an equine dystocia. It has been estimated that for each 10 minute increase in duration of labor beyond 30 minutes, there is a 10 percent increased risk of failure of the foal to survive.

It is strongly recommended that an emergency plan be formulated prior to the foaling season to prepare for a difficult birth or a medical problem with a newborn foal. The plan should be the result of a conversation between the mare owner, farm manager, foaling attendant, and the farm veterinarian. All personnel involved with foaling should be trained and ready to assist. In addition, a foaling kit should be readily available near the foaling stall.

Management of a dystocia is dependent on training, experience, and availability of farm personnel as well as the proximity of veterinary services. It is recommended that a foaling attendant call for assistance ('on-farm' or veterinary as appropriate or as needed) in the following circumstances:

- If there has been no progress toward delivery after 15 to 20 minutes
- If progress abruptly stops
- If the mare becomes acutely painful or shocky
- If a moderate to severe dystocia is suspected

- If they are unsure of a potential problem
- If they do not have the knowledge, training, or ability to identify or correct the problem

Table 23-2 outlines the most common causes of dystocia in the mare categorized by management difficulty. Mild dystocias are commonly managed on the farm by foaling personnel. More complicated dystocias may require advanced training or experience and often require veterinary intervention. Veterinary advice or assistance should immediately be sought if the problem cannot be safely and quickly corrected by farm personnel.

Table 23-2 Causes of Dystocia.

Correction Difficulty	Foaling Complication or Issue
Mild	Elbow lock Upside-down foal Backwards foal Uterine inertia 'Red-bag' (premature placental separation)
Moderate	Front leg(s) flexed at the knee (carpus) Neck flexed ventrally; muzzle below pelvic brim 'Hip-lock'
Difficult	Front leg(s) flexed at shoulder Neck flexed to side; muzzle not reachable 'Breech' presentation Transverse presentation Twins (when both entering birth canal simultaneously)

Veterinary intervention may include sedation of the mare, an epidural anesthetic to decrease pain and straining and/or general anesthesia to facilitate safe evaluation of the mare and to reposition the fetus into the correct orientation to allow for a controlled vaginal delivery. In some instances a vaginal delivery is not possible and a Cesarean surgery may be required to resolve the dystocia.

If a foaling attendant has been trained and ready to assist with the delivery of a foal that is properly oriented in the birth canal (i.e. frontwards presentation, right side up, and both front feet and the head extended), the following guidelines would apply, as recommended by the Equine Reproduction Laboratory at Colorado State University:

1. Place a loop of the 60" Nylon Obstetrical Strap or obstetrical chain on each front leg above the fetlocks.

2. Pull when the mare has a uterine contraction; stop pulling when the mare relaxes in between contractions.

3. Do not exceed the force of two people when assisting.

4. Never use any mechanical devices to pull a foal

5. Pull in an outward (initially) and then slightly downward direction (Figure 23-13).

6. 'Walk' the shoulders of the foal through the birth canal one at a time.

If no significant progress is made toward resolution of the problem within 5 to 10 minutes of assisting, it is recommended that a call be placed for additional help. It is always better to call early if a problem exists than to wait too long and wish a decision had been made sooner.

Special immediate attention must be given to the foal following a dystocia. Resuscitation equipment like the E-Z Breather™ Foal Resuscitator should be available on farms that foal out a lot of mares and farm personnel should be trained in the proper care and use of the equipment.

The foal is at high risk of many neonatal diseases including neonatal maladjustment syndrome, failure of passive transfer, ruptured bladder and trauma, such as rib fractures. The mare should also be examined in due course following resolution of a

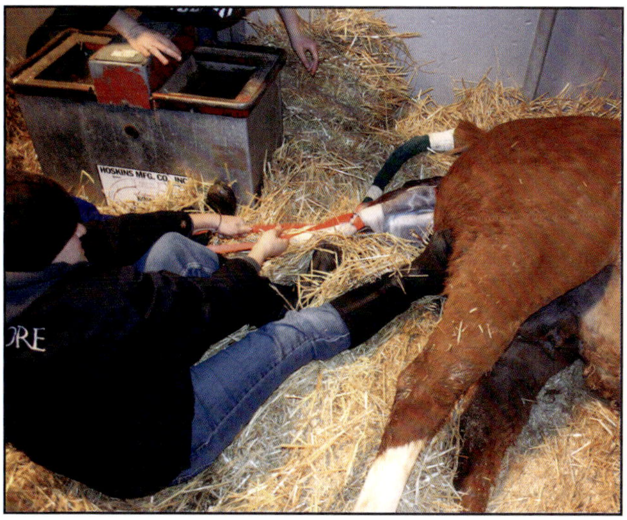

Figure 23-13 Assisting with the delivery of a foal using obstetrical straps.

dystocia. It is common for the placenta to be retained following a dystocia and preventative treatments are often instituted after a dystocia has been relieved. Finally, the reproductive tract of the mare (i.e. perineum, vagina, cervix and uterus) should be carefully examined by a veterinarian for trauma that may limit her future reproductive performance.

23.5 Premature Separation of the Placenta ('Red Bag')

The equine placenta consists of an outer membrane called the chorioallantois, that is attached to the uterus, an inner membrane called the amnion, which surrounds the foal and the umbilical cord. The chorioallantois is connected to the uterine wall by millions of microscopic 'Velcro-like' attachments called microcotyledons, except for the area of the placenta that is in direct contact with the cervix. Absence of uterine glands on the cervix leads to a failure of microcotyledon development on the adjacent part of the placenta. Consequently, whereas a majority of the outer chorionic surface of the placenta has a brick-red velvety appearance due to the presence of the microcotyledons, the region of placenta abutting the cervix lacks microcotyledons and has a smooth white appearance. This area is known as the 'cervical star'. Attachment of the placenta to the uterus via the microcotyledons is critical for the transfer of nutrients and oxygen from the mare across the placenta to the fetus during pregnancy.

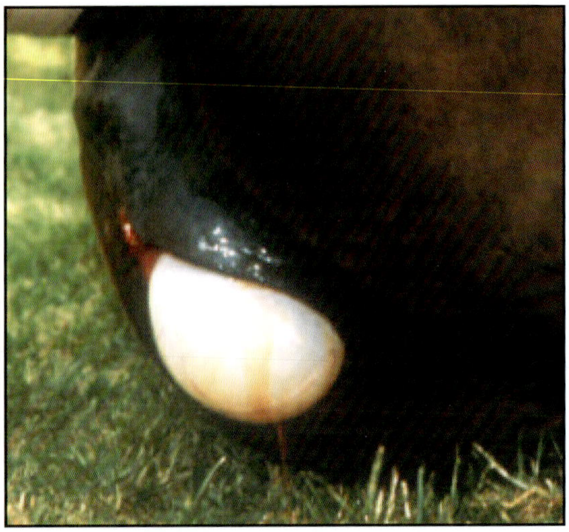

Figure 23-14 Amnion protruding through the vulva during a normal foaling.

Figure 23-15 Chorioallantoicmp membrane protruding through the vulva, indicative of premature separation of the placenta or 'red bag'.

With the onset of labor, the cervix starts to relax and the uterus begins to contract. Increased pressure from the uterus causes the chorioallantois to bulge into the open cervix. In the normal progression of foaling, the chorioallantois ruptures at the cervical star and results in the release of a large quantity of allantoic fluid (i.e. the "water breaks"). A thin, transparent, white membrane, the amnion, should begin protruding through the vulva within 1 to 5 minutes after the mare breaks her water (Figure 23-14). As the mare continues to push, front legs and then a nose should appear inside the amnionic sac. The foal is usually delivered within 15 to 20 minutes after the mare breaks her water.

Occasionally, a different series of events occurs during the labor process. Premature separation of the outer placental membrane away from the uterine wall may lead to protrusion of the intact fluid-filled chorioallantois through the vulva (Figure 23-15 and Figure 23-16). The dark red color of the outer surface of the chorioallantois gives rise to common term for premature separation of the placenta "redbag". Confirmation of the condition may be made by observing the cervical star on the chorionic surface.

Failure of the outer placental membrane to rupture during labor and the subsequent separation of the attachments between the uterus and placenta lead to a rapid decrease in oxygen transport to the fetus. As a consequence, the fetus may suffer from lack of oxygen (hypoxia) or may die of asphyxiation if the condition is prolonged or progresses.

Figure 23-16 Another example of 'red-bag'.

Owners or foaling personnel must quickly recognize the red bag condition and intervene immediately. The placental membrane should immediately be opened with a sharp instrument such as a knife or Stainless Steel Mayo Scissors that are kept in the foaling kit near the foaling stall. This will result in a release of allantoic fluid and a transient delay in uterine contractions. Veterinary assistance should be summoned and the foal delivered as soon as possible. Oxygen should be administered to the newborn foal if available. Foals may develop problems associated with hypoxia even though they may appear to be normal at birth.

The incidence of premature separation of the placenta has been reported to be 1 to 2% of all births and accounts for 5 to 10% of all cases of abortion, stillbirth and perinatal death. The most common causes of red bag are placental infections (placentitis), fescue toxicity and stress. Chronic placental separation from the uterus may occur over a period of several days or weeks during late gestation as a consequence of placentitis. The condition may be associated with a cervical discharge, mild blood loss out the vulva or a premature increase in mammary development. A diagnosis of placental separation may be possible by ultrasound examination of the late-term pregnant uterus.

Recognition of premature placental separation and appropriate intervention are the key factors for survival of the foal.

23.6 Foaling Kit

Mare owners are encouraged to keep basic critical supplies on hand during the foaling season. The items in the ARS Foaling Kit are considered to be the essential supplies needed for routine management of the late-term mare and newborn foal. Owners should contact their veterinarian about additional medical supplies or equipment that may be recommended. A list of supplies included in the kit is provided in Table 20-3. It is recommended that owners receive specific instructions or training from their veterinarian regarding appropriate use of obstetrical equipment, recognition of complications of the foaling process, and medical care of the newborn foal. In the event of a complication, the person attending the foaling is encouraged to immediately call the farm manager, owner or veterinarian for additional help or instructions.

Table 23-3 ARS Foaling Kit supplies.

Item	Use
General Use	
Fast Reading Digital Thermometer	Evaluation of body temperature of mare and/or newborn foal
Double Head Stethescope	Evaluation of heart rate and respiratory rate in mare and/or newborn foal
Stainless Steel Mayo Scissors	Multiple uses, including opening a placenta in a 'red-bag' birth, cutting umbilical tape, tail wrap material, or occasionally cutting the umbilical cord
ARS Penlight	Most mares foal out at night; a small flashlight may be very handy at that time
"*Techniques in Equine Reproduction*" book	Guide to foaling and mare and foal care
NI Test Submission Form	Fill out owner and mare information and send with blood sample from mare prior to foaling for evaluation of antibodies against other horse red blood cell antigens.

Item	Use
Pre-Foaling Supplies	
Blue ARS Terry Towel	Used to stimulate and dry foal immediately after birth
Predict-A-Foal™	As aid in the prediction of foaling date.
CoTear™ Cohesive Bandage	To get tail hairs out of the way prior to and during the foaling process.
Sterile Obstetrical Sleeves (2 small hand; 2 standard hand size)	Used if needed to check the position of the fetus during the foaling process.
Surgilube® Lubricating Jelly	Applied to sleeve prior to checking position of fetus (if needed)
Wrist Length Gloves (2 pairs of medium; 2 pairs of large)	General purpose, non-latex gloves used when washing mare prior to foaling, handling placenta, etc.
2% Chlorhexidine Scrub	Used to wash udder and perineum of mare prior to foaling.
Foal Supplies	
Umbilical tape (two 12" strips)	To tie off the umbilical cord immediately after foaling (if needed; used as an alternative to an umbilical clamp)
Umbilical clamps (2 each)	To clamp off the umbilical cord immediately after foaling (if needed; used as an alternative to umbilical tape); usually removed or will fall off after 2 to 3 days
Navel Dip (1% Chlorhexidine Solution)	Used to dip the stump of the umbilical cord (navel) immediately after foaling to help seal the vessels within the cord and disinfect the area to reduce the probability of a bacterial infection (navel ill)
Navel Dipping Tubes	Use to dip navel stump with disinfectant; pre-labeled to identify individual foals.
Fleet Enema	Administered to newborn foal at 1 to 2 hours of life to prevent or treat a meconium impaction
Equine Colostrum Refractometer*	Used to evaluate the quality of the colostrum of the mare after foaling
500 ml Colostrum Collection Cup	Convenient when collecting a large volume of colostrum from a mare immediately after foaling for freezing.
250 ml Sterile Plastic Colostrum Storage Bottles	Used for storage of colostrum in freezer. Convenient size and pre-labeled.
Cotton Gauze 4x4 Colostrum Filters	Used to strain colostrum to remove dirt and debris.
Folding Disposable Funnels	Use to aid in pouring colostrum into 250 ml Sterile Colostrum Storage Bottles for Freezing
Plastic Placenta Bag with drawstring	Used to weigh and dispose of placenta.
Nylon Placenta Cord	Used to tie placenta above hocks of the mare after foaling; prevents mare from stepping on and tearing placenta.
60cc Catheter-tip Dosing Syringe	Used to administer oral medications to foal under supervision or instruction of a veterinarian.
Nasal Aspirator	Used to clear foal's nasal passages if necessary.
60" Nylon Obstetrical Strap	Use under the direction of a veterinarian to assist in the foaling process if it has halted.
E-Z Breather™ Foal Resuscitator*	Use on newborn foals if emergency resuscitation is needed.

* Items included in Deluxe Foaling Kit.

Chapter 24 The Postpartum Mare

Figure 24-1 Photograph of a mare attempting to eat her placenta.

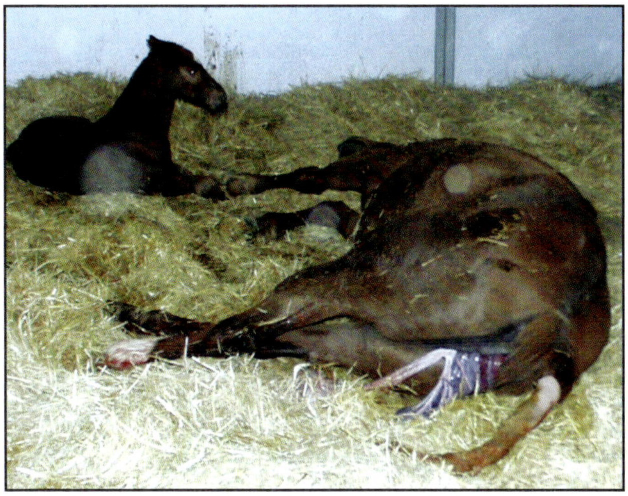

Figure 24-2 Mare exhibiting abdominal pain after giving birth.

24.1 Passage of the Placenta

Separation of the placenta from the uterus begins prior to foaling and complete expulsion usually occurs within 30 minutes to 2 hours after foaling. Rupture of the umbilical cord after delivery of the foal causes collapse of the fetal placental blood vessels and subsequent shrinkage of the microscopic placental attachment sites. Uterine contractions post foaling in combination with gentle continuous traction from the weight of the amnion pulling on the umbilical cord eventually results in release of the placenta from the uterus.

The placenta should be removed from the foaling stall as soon as it is passed. Occasionally a mare my attempt to eat the placenta and may end up with a choke or colic (Figure 24-1).

24.2 Postpartum Pain

Uterine contractions that continue in the immediate postpartum period may be associated with signs of mild to severe abdominal pain or colic (Figure 24-2). It may be beneficial to administer a dose of an analgesic medication such as flunixin meglumine (Banamine®) or phenylbutazone to a mare exhibiting abdominal pain in the postpartum period. Alleviation of pain may allow an affected mare to interact and bond with her foal more effectively. In addition, mares that continue to exhibit pain after foaling often do not allow their foal to nurse. Adequate pain management may therefore facilitate nursing and passive transfer of maternal antibodies in colostrum. A majority of mares do not appear to require analgesic treatment in the postpartum period.

The presence of severe abdominal pain after foaling or the reoccurrence of pain following initial relief of pain with analgesic therapy may be a sign of a more significant medical complication than just postpartum uterine contractions. Medical possibilities include displacement or torsion of a portion of the intestinal tract, intussusception of a uterine horn or impending uterine prolapse, internal hemorrhage of a large blood vessel (i.e. ruptured uterine artery) or other factors. A veterinary examination should be performed if a mare has significant pain following foaling or if pain returns after temporary relief following administration of an analgesic medication.

24.3 Reproduction in the Postpartum Mare

The first estrus or heat period that occurs after foaling is called the 'foal heat'. Mares usually first come into behavioral estrus by 6 to 8 days postpartum. The average interval from foaling to first ovulation is approximately 10 to 12 days, although mares can ovulate as early as 7 to 8 days or as late as 14 to 15 days postpartum and be considered clinically normal. Pregnancy rates are usually higher for mares that ovulate 10 or more days after foaling as compared to mares that ovulate prior to day 10 post foaling.

24.4 The Breeding Decision

Mare owners and breeding managers must decide whether or not to breed mares on the foal heat. Reviews of breeding records indicate that mares initially bred on their foal heat will maintain a foaling interval of approximately 12 months (i.e. have an opportunity to have a foal every year). Obviously, not every mare becomes pregnant after a foal heat breeding, but the average interval from foaling to pregnancy for mares initially bred on the foal heat is about 25 days. The potential interval between sequential births is approximately one year when this 25-day period is added to a 340 day gestation length.

In contrast, waiting until the second (30-day) heat to begin breeding will inevitably result in a longer foaling-to-conception interval. Owners that choose not to breed mares on the foal heat must accept the fact that eventually each mare will have to be left open for a season every 4 to 6 years when the potential foaling date becomes too late in the season. The economic implications of the lost foal crop and continued costs of board and care for barren mares during this 'lost year' are obvious.

24.5 Reproductive Evaluation of the Postpartum Mare

A majority of mares have significant inflammation present in their uterus during the first week postpartum and bacteria can be cultured from the uterus of many mares during their foal heat. Although many breeding programs specify that mares will not be bred unless a negative uterine culture is obtained (i.e. the mare is 'clean' or free of infection), research has indicated that the presence or absence of bacteria is not correlated to fertility in foal heat mares. This will not hold true for cycles after the foal heat, where presence of uterine bacteria is a significant cause of reduced fertility.

24.6 Reproductive Activity of the Postpartum Mare

A majority of mares have a foal heat cycle and ovulation and subsequently continue to cycle at approximately 21-day intervals (Table 21-1). However, some mares will have a foal heat cycle and ovulation followed by a variable period of anestrus until the mare resumes normal cyclic activity. A low percentage of mares will have minimal to no follicular development following foaling and will not cycle at all for 2 to 3 months. Failure to develop follicles and/or ovulate after foaling is due primarily to the effects of season (i.e. photoperiod). Consequently, mares that foal in January through March in the Northern Hemisphere are most likely to be affected. Failure of follicular growth in postpartum mares has occasionally been attributed to lactation and some mares return to estrus soon after the foal is weaned. Other factors that may play a role in mares that do not cycle after foaling include inadequate nutrition or poor body condition, medical or health issues, and adverse environmental conditions (i.e. extremes of hot or cold).

Table 24-1 Reproduction in the postpartum mare. Note that some mares that foal out in late winter or early spring (scenarios 2 and 3) may experience a period of postpartum anestrus and not resume normal estrus until April or May.

Scenario	Follicular Development	Foal Heat Ovulation	Continued Cyclicity	Comments
1	*Yes*	*Yes*	*Yes*	Most common
2	*Yes*	*Yes*	*No*	Less common; seasonally dependent
3	*Variable*	*No*	*No*	Uncommon; seasonally dependent

24.7 Management Options for Postpartum Mares

A number of strategies have been used in an attempt to enhance fertility of mares in the early postpartum period. Exposure of pregnant mares to an artificial photoperiod during the last trimester will shorten the length of gestation by 7 to 10 days and decrease the risk of a mare returning to a state of ovarian inactivity or anestrus following foaling. Administration of progesterone or Regu-Mate® to postpartum mares has been used in an attempt to delay the first ovulation and enhance pregnancy rates, but results have been inconsistent. It used to be common practice to lavage the uterus of mares 1 to 2 days after foaling. However, clinical trials concluded that routine uterine lavage did not increase pregnancy rates in normal post-foaling mares. Oxytocin or prostaglandins are sometimes used in post-foaling mares to promote uterine contractions and thereby eliminate fluid and debris and decrease the size of the uterus in an attempt to enhance foal heat conception rates.

In most situations, a foal heat breeding can be considered if the following criteria are met:

- No dystocia during the foaling
- No retained placenta
- No prolonged uterine discharge
- Ovulation occurs on or after day 10 postpartum

Mares that experienced foaling or postpartum complications (i.e. dystocia, retained placenta, prolonged discharge, etc.) may have a decreased foal heat pregnancy rate or an increased embryonic loss rate. Consequently, it may be advisable to breed such mares on the second postpartum estrus (30 day heat) or a later heat period.

A simple strategy to optimize post-partum conception rates in mares with an uncomplicated foaling is to have the mare examined by ultrasound on days 7 and 9 post-foaling (Table 24-2). Mares that ovulate on or before day 9 are not bred, but are administered prostaglandins 5 days after ovulation to bring them back into heat (i.e. short-cycled). Mares that still have a large follicle 9 days post-foaling are bred using standard techniques. The use of ovulation-inducing agents (i.e. hCG or GnRH) is discouraged until day 9 or 10, since ovulations early in the postpartum period may not be as fertile.

Table 24-2 A simple breeding management strategy for foal heat mares.

Day	Procedure
7	Reproductive Evaluation • If ultrasound exam is normal and the mare did not have a dystocia, retained placenta or prolonged vaginal discharge, plan on breeding on foal heat.
9	Ultrasound Examination • If mare has ovulated, wait 5 to 7 days and administer prostaglandins. • If mare has not ovulated, breed.
11	Ultrasound Examination • If mare has ovulated, schedule a pregnancy examination in 14 to 16 days. • If mare has not ovulated and a large (> 35 mm) follicle is present, administer an ovulation-inducing agent (i.e. hCG, deslorelin) and breed.
13	Ultrasound Examination • Confirm ovulation, schedule pregnancy examination.

Another strategy for breeding post partum mares is to let them go through their foal heat and short-cycle with a dose of prostaglandins 17 days post foaling.

24.8 Aggressive/Protective Behavior in Post-Partum Mares

Occasionally a normally placid mare may exhibit extreme aggression or foal-protective behavior toward other horses or toward humans after giving birth. The adverse behavior is usually manifested within a few hours after the foal is born and may last for several days or weeks. The mare may assume a threatening posture, pin her ears back, charge or aggressively attack and bite.

The behavioral change is often unpredictable, but a mare that shows aggressive-protective behavior after birth of one foal is likely to show similar adverse behavior after birth of subsequent foals.

Safety needs to be the first priority when faced with an aggressive-protective mare. It may not even be possible to enter the foaling stall to halter the mare or otherwise restrain the mare to perform a newborn foal exam, dip the umbilicus or collect a blood sample for an IgG test. Consequently it may not be possible or safe to attempt to sedate the mare. In some instances addition of a behavioral modulating compound (i.e. Zylkene® or Confidence Eq®) in sweet feed may help suppress aggressive behavior.

24.9 Foal Rejection

Rejection of a foal by its dam can take several forms. The mare may ignore the foal, avoid the foal or prevent the foal from nursing, or may become aggressive toward the foal. Mares in the latter category may assume a threatening posture, pin their ears back when the foal approaches, charge or chase the foal, squeal at the foal, or in more serious cases, may kick at or bite the foal. Mares have, on rare occasions, seriously injured or killed their foals in the first few days after giving birth.

Foal rejection may occur in any horse breed, but is most common in Arabians. Rejection is most likely to occur in mares giving birth to their first foal. Mares that have rejected a foal in the past have an increased chance of rejecting a subsequent foal. In addition, mares that are separated from their foal for a prolonged time interval in the early postpartum period have an increased risk of foal rejection.

Mares that ultimately reject their foals are not as likely to express normal maternal behaviors in the early post-partum period, such as licking their foals, nickering to their foals and standing guard over or next to their foals.

Failure to allow nursing will result in an inability of the foal to acquire maternal antibodies from colostrum necessary to protect against pathogenic disease organisms. In addition, affected foals will be deprived of important nutritional support in the neonatal period.

Mares exhibiting a tendency toward foal rejection should be monitored closely for the first 48 hours or more after foaling. The vast majority of rejection-type behavioral interactions occur within the first 12 hours after birth. Therefore, in at-risk mares it is best to avoid interrupting the bonding that naturally occurs between mare and foal early in life.

Management of foal rejection may initially include restraint of the mare by hand, judicious use of a twitch, hobbles or cross-ties, or by placing the mare behind a bar or within a nursing chute to allow the foal to have an unimpeded opportunity to suckle.

In mild cases, distraction of the mare with grain may be sufficient to allow the foal time to nurse without the mare becoming nervous and moving away. If the foal does not or cannot nurse, colostrum from the mare should be milked out and fed to the foal by bottle or by nasogastric tube.

In some instances, the mare may need to be muzzled to prevent biting of the foal. The mare may also need to be tranquilized periodically during the first few day post-partum with a medication such as acepromazine, xylazine, detomidine or alprazolam (Xanax®) to decrease aggression or anxiety.

Administration of the oral progestogen Regu-Mate® has also been used in cases of foal rejection in an attempt to suppress or modulate aggressive behavior. Treatment of the mare with an analgesic, such as flunixin meglumine (Banamine®), may be indicted if the mare appears to be rejecting nursing attempts by the foal due to post-foaling pain or mammary gland discomfort. Inflammation of the mammary gland, or mastitis, may contribute to refusal of a mare to allow nursing.

If other techniques are not successful, some breeders advocate turning a mare exhibiting mild foal rejection behavior out into a paddock with her foal along with another mare and foal in the hope that natural maternal protective instincts will enhance acceptance of her own foal.

It may take several days of patient, diligent work to assist a mare to accept her foal. However, if the process is unsuccessful the foal may be fostered onto a nurse mare. Hand-rearing a rejected foal as an orphan is a labor intensive alternative if a nurse mare is not available.

Rejection of a foal by its biological dam can be difficult to watch. Fortunately, many mares will overcome their initial avoidance or rejection behavior and eventually accept their foal.

Chapter 25. The Placenta

Table 25-0 List and Part Number of ARS products used in this chapter.

Item	Part Number	Use/Comments
Plastic Placenta Bag with Drawstring	Purchase at local grocery store (0.9 mil thickness or higher)	Use to weigh and dispose of placenta
Vinyl Wrist Length Exam Gloves	WLVG-108	Wear when handling and examining placenta
Retained Placenta Kit	RPK-101	Contains all equipment needed to perform the 'Dutch Technique'

25.1 Placental Evaluation

The placenta is the connection between the developing fetus and the uterus of the mare. A healthy functional placenta is critical for fetal nutrition and gas exchange. Examination of the placenta after foaling can offer valuable insight into the *in utero* health of the newborn foal. Consequently, it is recommended that owners, farm managers or foaling attendants remove the placenta from the stall as soon as it has passed (Figure 25-1) and perform an evaluation of each placenta. Examination of a normal placenta should only take a few minutes and should be accomplished as soon after foaling as possible. The information gained may be critical for early medical management of the foal and/or the mare.

Placentas are usually placed in a Plastic Placenta Bag with drawstring or bucket until they can be examined. Remove the placenta from the temporary storage container and rinse it free of gross debris with a hose and tap water. Vinyl Wrist Length Exam Gloves should be worn during handling and examination. If possible, the weight of the placenta should be determined (Figure 25-2). Tip: weigh the placenta in a plastic bucket and then subtract the weight of the bucket. An inexpensive bathroom scale is sufficient. Under normal circumstances, the weight of the placenta should be approximately 11% of the body weight of the foal. An increased weight may be the result of edema associated with factors such as fescue toxicosis or may be due to an infectious condition such as placentitis. Both conditions may be associated with a medically compromised foal.

The placenta consists of three primary components, the outer placental membrane or chorioallantois, the inner placental membrane or amnion, and the umbilical cord. In a normal foaling, the thicker

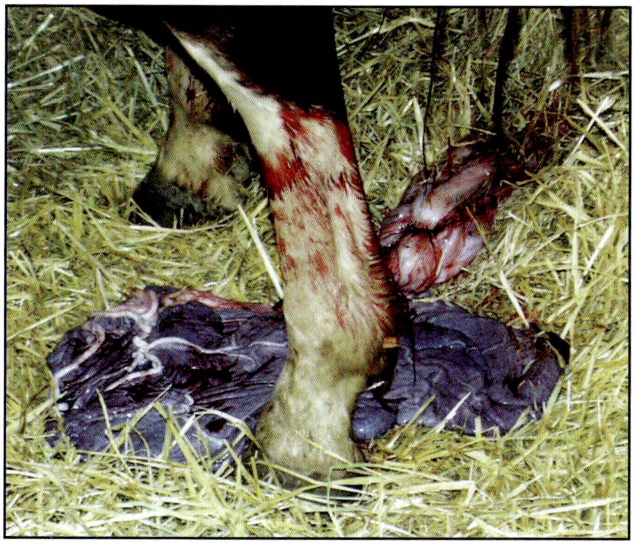

Figure 25-1 Photograph of a recently passed placenta.

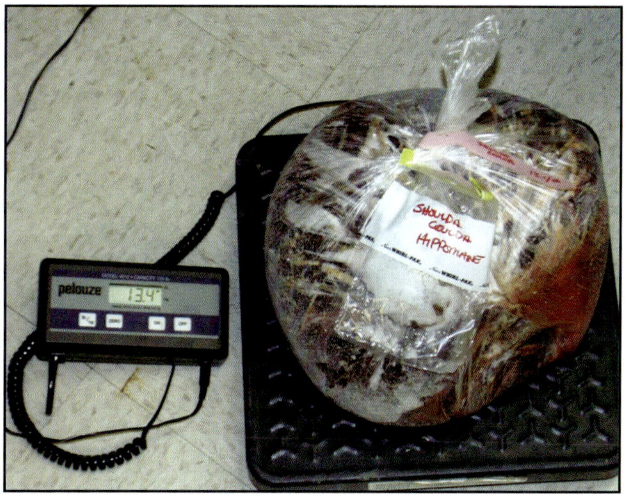

Figure 25-2 Weighing a placenta on the scale.

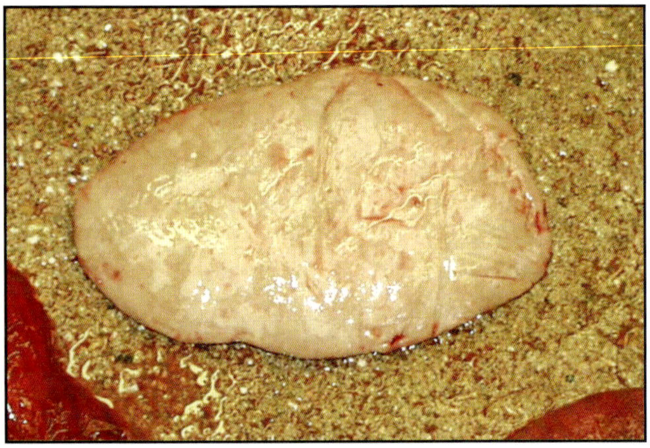

Figure 25-3 Photograph of a Hippomane.

outer placental membrane is almost always turned inside-out as the placenta is passed. A hippomane, also called an 'allantoic calculi', which is a soft, flat, oval mass tan to brown in color and about 4" to 6 " in diameter is commonly passed as the mare gives birth (Figure 25-3). Folklore suggests that the hippomane is either a twin that did not survive, was present in the mouth of the fetus, or was part of the liver of the fetus. These are all incorrect. A hippomane is simply a mass of lipids, placental cells and debris that aggregates in the allantoic cavity of the placenta. Hippomanes do not form in the amnionic cavity where the fetus is located.

For initial examination, the outer placental membrane (chorioallantois) should be turned right-side out, with the chorionic side outward, and then spread out on a clean flat surface (Figure 25-4). The chorionic (side toward the uterus) surface has a brick-red velvety appearance due to the presence of microcotyledons. Microcotyledons are the microscopic villi or finger-like projections that provide the 'Velcro®-like' attachment of the placenta to the uterine lining (see Physiology of Pregnancy Chapter). The allantoic (side toward the foal) surface is

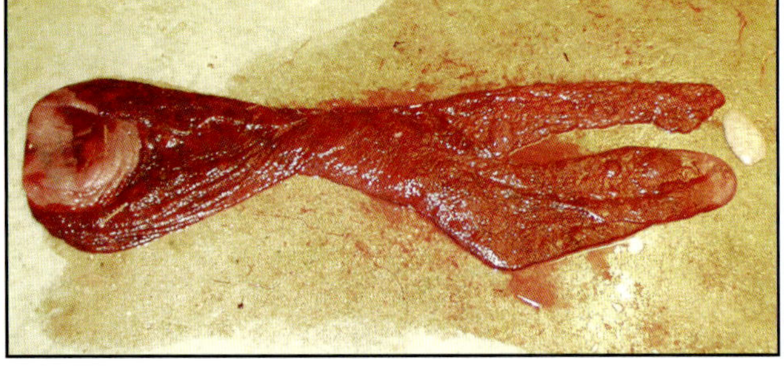

Figure 25-4 Photograph of a placenta with the chorionic surface visible.

Figure 25-5 Photograph of a placenta with the allantoic side visible.

smooth and light pink/purple in color and blood vessels are visible coursing along its surface (Figure 25-5).

The membranes may be laid out with the chorioallantois in an "F" or "Y" shape, with the two horns of the placenta forming the arms of the "F" or "Y" and the body of the placenta forming the base. The umbilical cord and amnion should protrude from the base or body of the placenta.

One of the first observations made is that the tips of the placental horns differ significantly in size and thickness (Figure 25-6). The larger placental horn housed the fetus and is referred to as the pregnant horn. The tip of the pregnant horn is always thicker than the tip of the smaller non-pregnant horn.

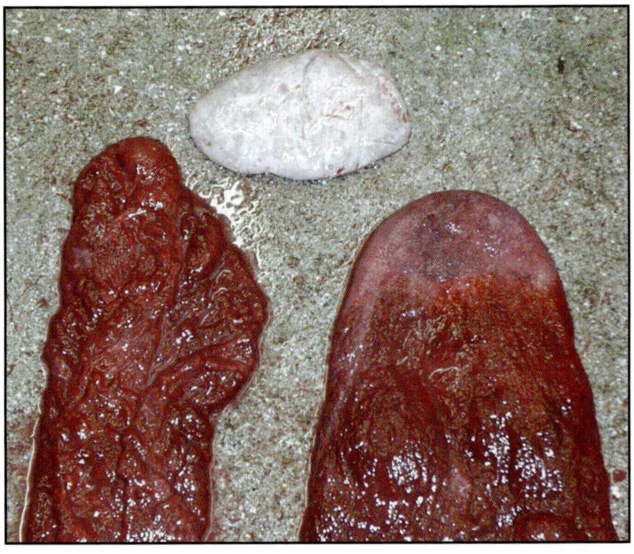

Figure 25-6 Close-up photograph showing the difference in thickness between the pregnant (right) and nonpregnant (left) horn tips. A hippomane is also present in the photograph.

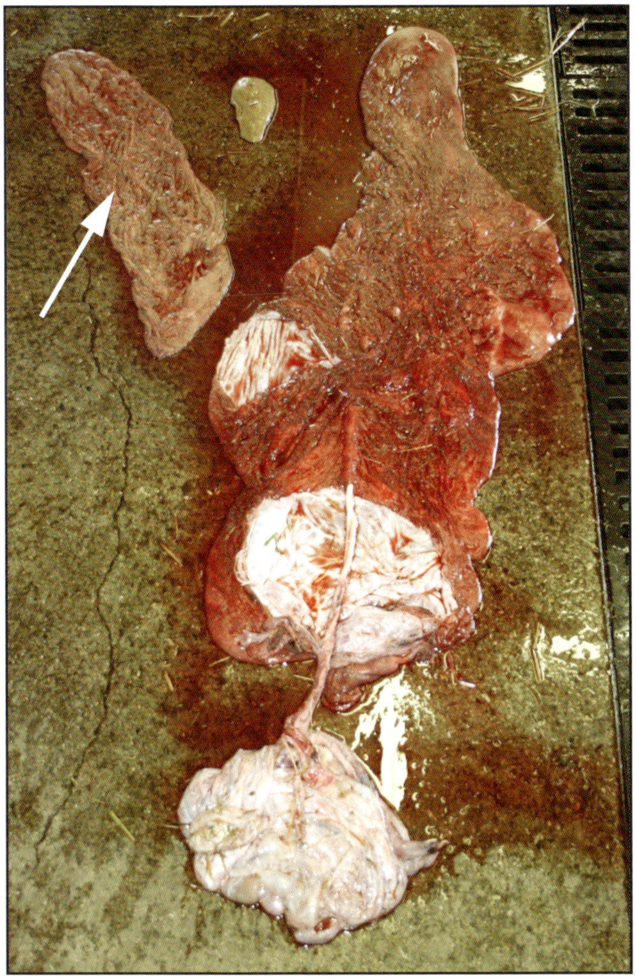

Figure 25-7 Placenta from a mare in which the entire non-pregnant horn (arrow) was retained for several hours in the uterus after a majority of the placenta had passed.

The chorioallantois should be examined to determine if it was passed intact or if a piece is missing and potentially still inside the mare. The portion of the placenta most likely retained is the tip of the non-pregnant horn (Figure 25-7). Retention of even a small piece of placenta in the uterus poses a very serious threat to the health of the mare. Refer to the section on 'Retained Placenta' for more information.

The area around the cervical star (Figure 25-8) should be examined for thickening, presence of inflammatory or infectious material, abnormal texture or color (Figure 25-9 and Figure 25-10). All of which may indicate the presence of placentitis. Since the placenta is of fetal origin, an infection of the chorionic surface adjacent to the cervical star may be associated with *in utero* fetal infection and a septic foal after delivery.

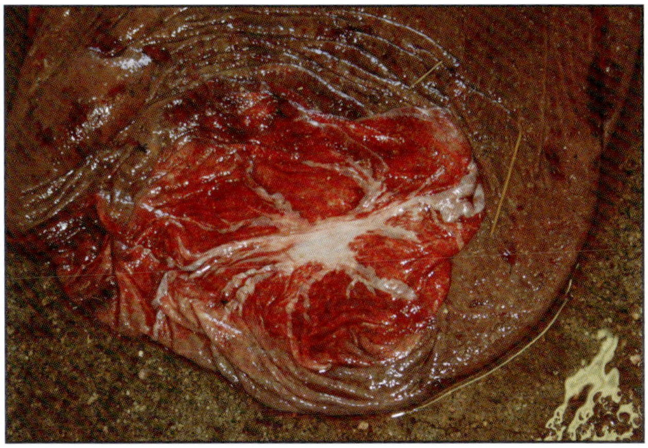

Figure 25-8 Cervical star region of the chorionic surface of an equine placenta.

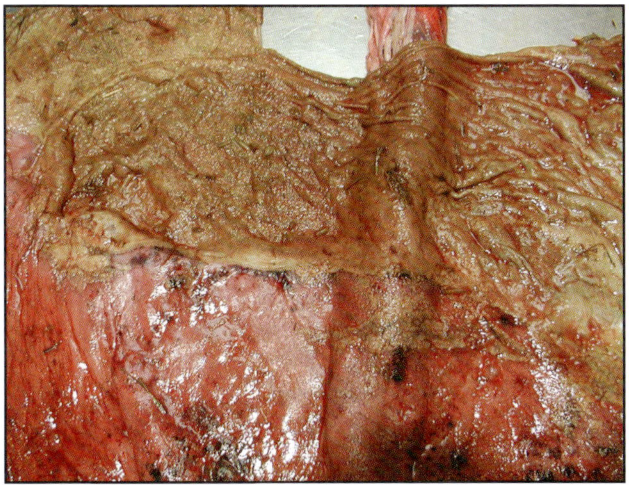

Figure 25-9 Discolored region around the cervical star suggestive of ascending placentitis.

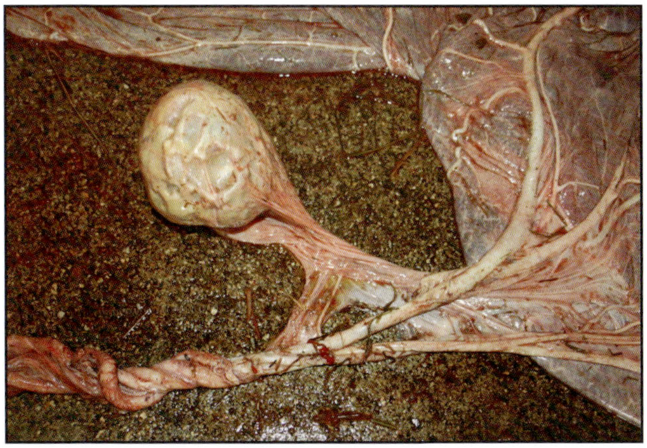

Figure 25-11 Yolk sac remnant attached by a stalk to the umbilical cord.

Occasionally, a single thick walled sac, possibly with an ossified rim or capsule, may be observed on a stalk emanating from the umbilical cord (Figure 25-11). The structure is a remnant of the embryonic

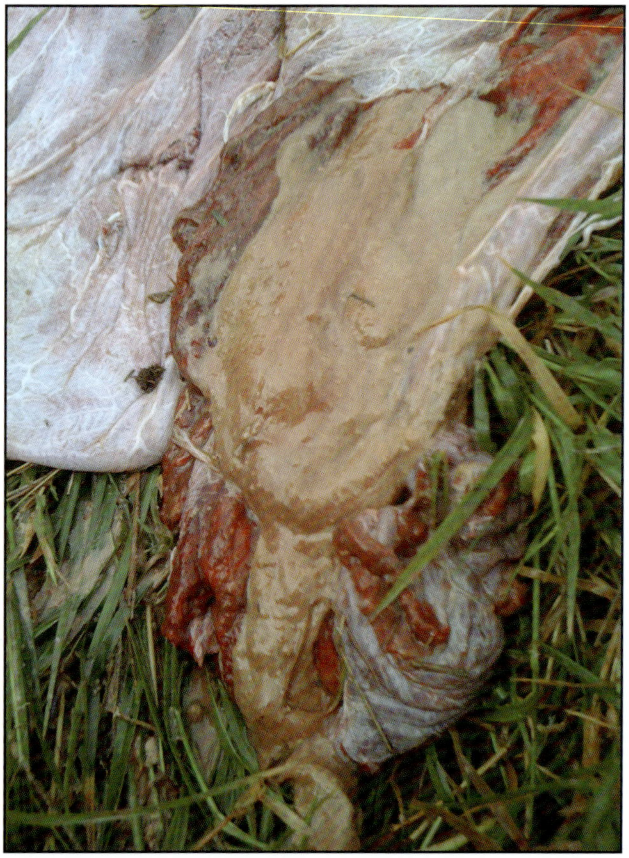

Figure 25-10 Infectious debris adherent to the cervical star area of the chorionic surface of an equine placenta indicating ascending placentitis.

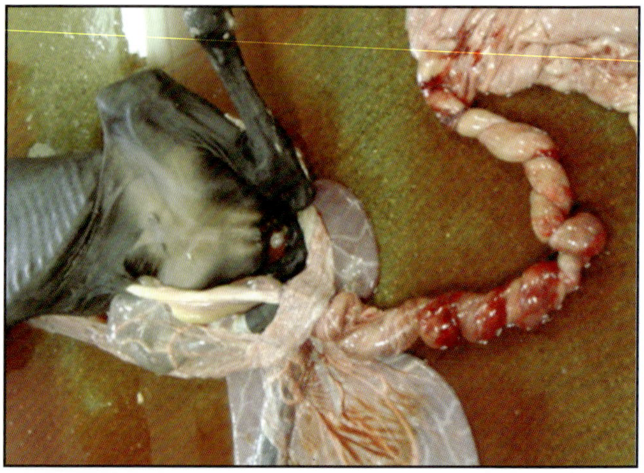

Figure 25-12 Twisted umbilical cord causing fetal death and abortion.

yolk sac. It is commonly mistaken for a non-surviving twin. The only pathology associated with a yolk sac remnant is if the structure wraps around and constricts the umbilical cord preventing normal blood flow to or from the fetus.

The most common abnormality of the umbilical cord is a twisted cord which may restrict blood flow to the fetus and may consequently result in fetal death and abortion (Figure 25-12). There is an association between an abnormally long umbilical cord and excessive twisting of the cord. Twisted umbilical cord is now a more common cause of non-infectious abortion than twins, since the advent and common use of ultrasonography in the early detection and management of twins.

An alternative technique for examination of the placenta is to inflate the chorioallantois with water. The placenta should be rinsed off and turned right side out as previously described. A garden hose is passed through the ruptured cervical star area and the chorioallantois is inflated with tap water as the cervical area of the placenta is clamped by hand around the hose to prevent leakage (Figure 25-13). This technique will allow one to rapidly determine if the placenta is intact and will provide an excellent view of the chorionic surface.

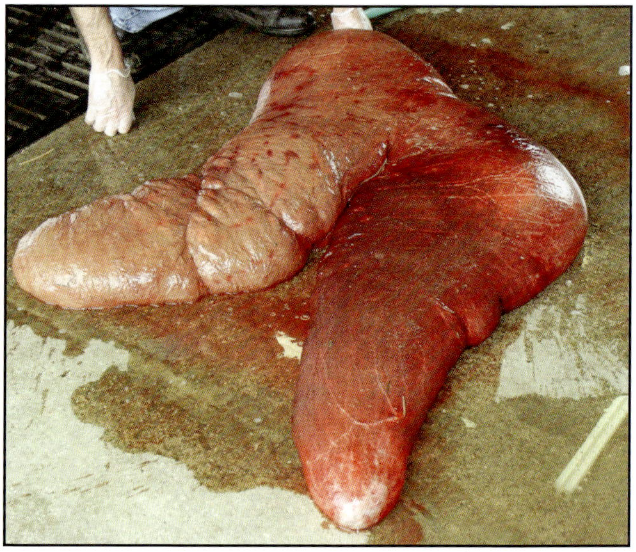

Figure 25-13 Photograph of a placenta inflated with water.

Evaluation of the placenta is a valuable procedure that can positively impact the health and welfare of both the newborn foal and the mare. It is recommended that a veterinarian be contacted for an initial lesson in field evaluation of the placenta and that he or she be notified if abnormalities are identified in subsequent placental examinations. It may be recommended to submit samples of abnormal placental tissue or the entire placenta to a qualified diagnostic laboratory for further evaluation.

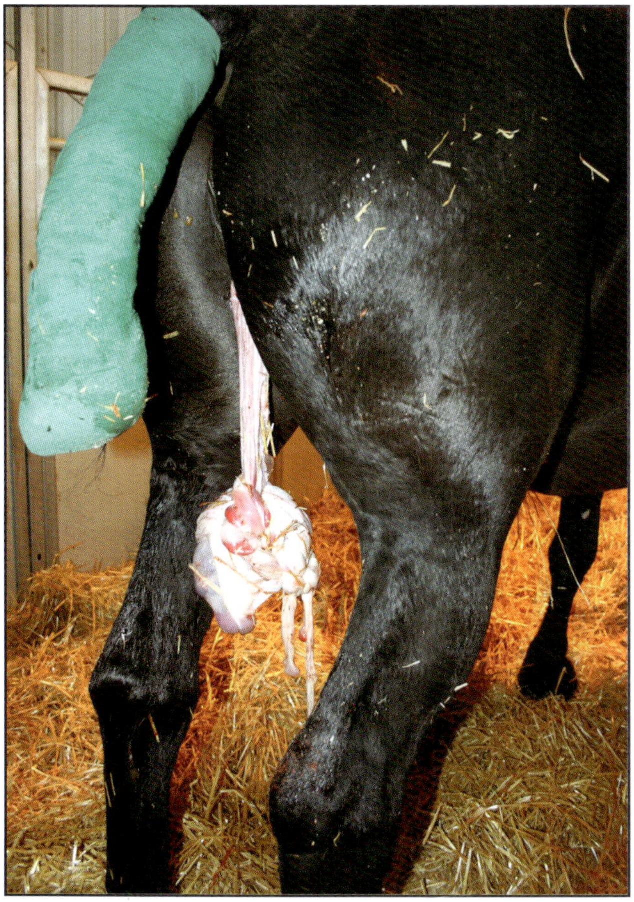

Figure 25-14 Retained placenta in a Friesian mare.

25.2 Retained Placenta

Retention of the placenta is one of the most common problems of the mare in the early postpartum period. A placenta is considered to be abnormally retained if it has not passed within 3 hours after foaling (Figure 25-14). The incidence increases following abortion, dystocia, obstetrical manipulations, Cesarean surgery, induction of labor, placental infections, fescue toxicity and other factors. The percentage of broodmares that retain their placenta ranges from 2 to 10%. Mares with a history of retained placenta have an increased risk of having another retained placenta in the future. Friesian mares have a breed predisposition for retention of the placenta. An association has been reported in Friesian mares between placental retention and low blood calcium levels.

Mares may retain the entire chorioallantois (outer placental membrane) or only a portion of one horn tip within the uterus following foaling. Detection of a retained placenta may not be obvious if only a portion of the placenta remains in the mare. A foaling attendant should examine the entire placenta once it has passed to determine if both horn tips are present. If the placenta is spread out in an 'F' or 'Y' pattern, the tip of one horn will be noticeably thicker than the tip of the other horn. The tip of the thin non-pregnant horn is the one more commonly still attached to the uterus and retained while the rest of the placenta has passed. It is important to emphasize that a mare may become just as ill if only a part of the placenta is retained as she will if the entire placenta is retained. Mares with a retained placenta may not exhibit clinical signs of illness in the first few hours after foaling. However, many mares become depressed, go off feed, and have an elevated body temperature if the placenta has been retained more than 12 to 24 hours. Rapid bacterial growth within the uterine lumen in the presence of placental membranes may lead to a toxic uterine infection and subsequently laminitis or founder. A retained placenta is therefore potentially life threatening to a mare.

Horse owners and breeding farm managers are encouraged to examine the placenta after each mare foals. Treatment for retained placenta should be instituted early, since significant complications can occur. It may be advantageous to administer oxytocin to mares with a history of retained placenta within 1 to 2 hours after foaling.

Mare owners should contact their veterinarian prior to the onset of the foaling season to discuss strategies for early intervention in the event that a retained placenta should occur. The future health of the mare may depend on it.

25.3 Management of Retained Placenta

Initially, the amnion should be tied in a knot above the hocks of the mare to prevent the mare from stepping on or kicking at the placenta. Tying up the amnion may also help prevent the amnion from being torn away from the remainder of the fetal membranes. If the amnion is not attached, there may be insufficient weight applied to the umbilical cord to stimulate release of the chorioallantois from the uterus.

Strategies for the management of a retained placenta vary with the duration of retention and health of the mare. Possible techniques include:

- Oxytocin administration
- 'Burns' technique
- 'Dutch' technique
- Manual technique (last resort)
- Administration of a calcium-magnesium-borogluconate solution

Oxytocin. Initial treatment often involves administration of one or two doses of oxytocin to promote uterine contractions and expulsion of the placenta. On an equine breeding operation it is common for farm personnel, under directions from a veterinarian, to administer an intramuscular dose of oxytocin to a mare that has not passed her placenta within 3 hours. A second dose is often administered 1 to 2 hours later if the placenta still has not passed. If the placenta has still not passed within 1 to 2 hours after the second dose, it is recommended that a veterinarian be consulted.

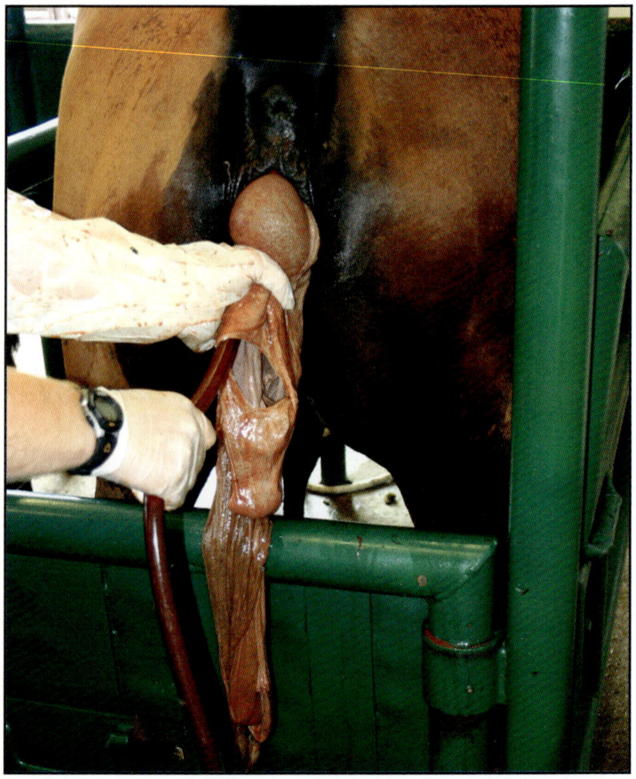

Figure 25-15 Passing a stomach tube along the umbilical cord into the allantoic cavity.

'Burns' Technique. A procedure called the 'water technique' or 'Burns technique' may be utilized if oxytocin therapy is not successful. A sterilized stomach tube is passed along the umbilical cord into the allantoic cavity of the retained chorioallantoic membrane (Figure 25-15). The chorioallantoic membrane is manually clamped around the stomach tube and a large volume (3 to 5 gallons) of warm water, to which a small volume of povidone-iodine solution has been added as a disinfectant, is pumped into the allantoic cavity. The water refills the allantoic cavity and is allowed to remain in the chamber for 3 to 5 minutes. The fluid is then allowed to egress from the allantoic cavity.

In a majority of cases, refilling the allantoic cavity and re-distending the chorioallantoic membrane results in a dissociation of the remaining microcotyledons of the chorionic membrane that are still attached to microcaruncles of the endometrium. Subsequently, the now freed chorioallantoic membrane is able to be passed in its entirety.

The water technique is only effective if the chorioallantoic membrane is intact. Water cannot fill and distend the allantoic cavity if the chorioallantoic membrane is torn. In the event that the Burns Technique does not result in separation/release of the chorioallantois from the uterus, the procedure still essentially acts as a placental lavage to remove some of the bacteria and associated toxins.

'Dutch' Technique (Umbilical Blood Vessel Infusion Technique). In this procedure, tap water is slowly infused into one of the umbilical blood vessels. Infusion of water results in distention of capillaries and formation of edema within the chorion which may result in release of microcotyledons from the maternal endometrium.

Equipment needed for the 'Dutch Technique' includes:

- Water source
- Garden hose
- Adapter for garden hose
- Stallion catheter or foal stomach tube or urinary catheter

An adapter and catheter are available in the ARS Retained Placenta Kit.

The 'Dutch technique' is performed as follows:

1. A small incision is made into one umbilical blood vessel (Figure 25-16)

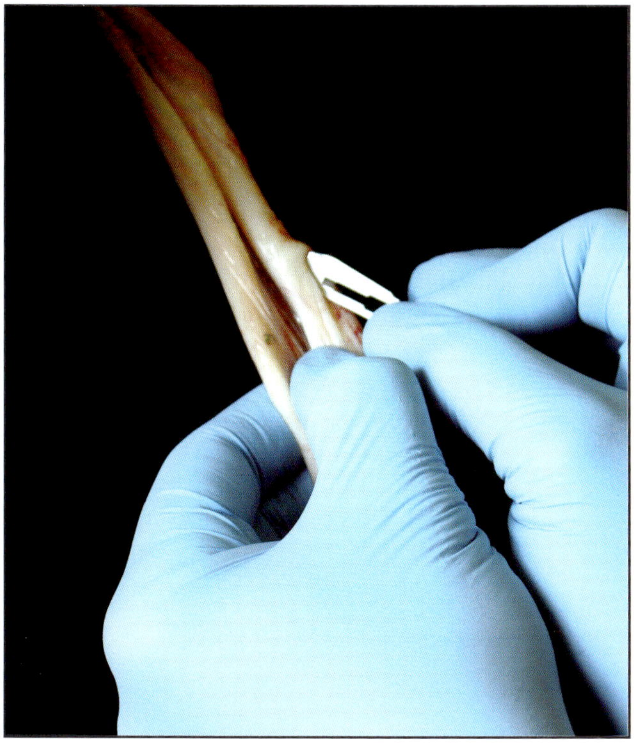

Figure 25-16 Making an incision into an umbilical artery or vein with a scalpel blade.

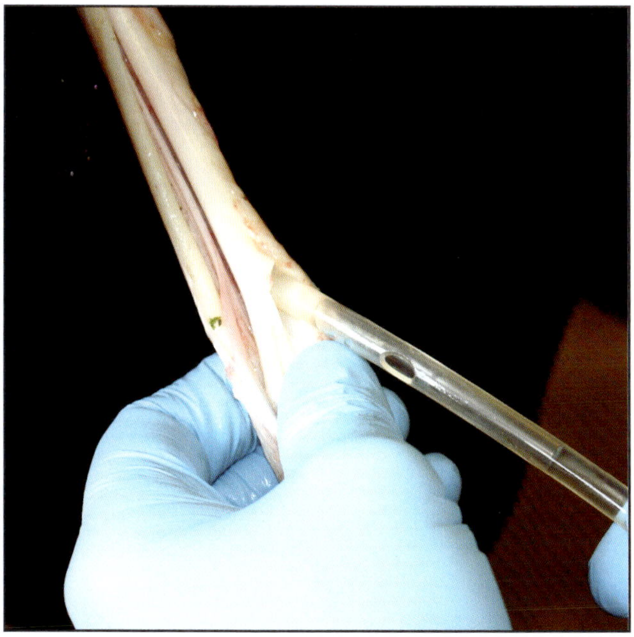

Figure 25-17 Insertion of a stallion catheter into the incised umbilical blood vessel.

2. A small catheter (i.e. a 6 mm stallion catheter or foal stomach tube) is passed proximately up the vessel (Figure 25-17)

3. An adapter, purchased at a hardware store, is fitted onto a standard garden hose and connected to the catheter (Figure 25-18)

4. Water is slowly infused into the blood vessel

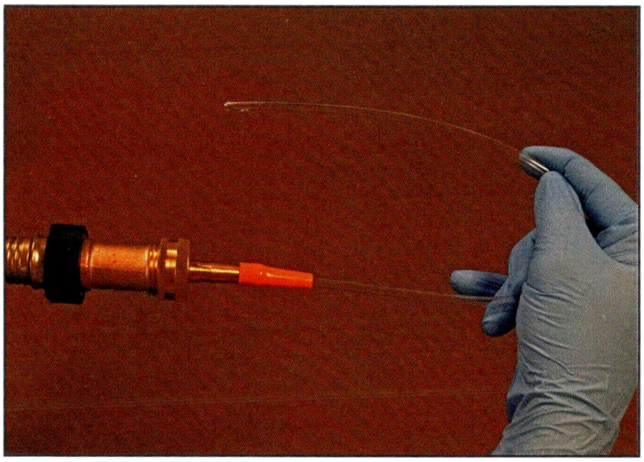

Figure 25-18 Adapter with valve connecting the garden hose to the catheter (ARS Retained Placenta Kit).

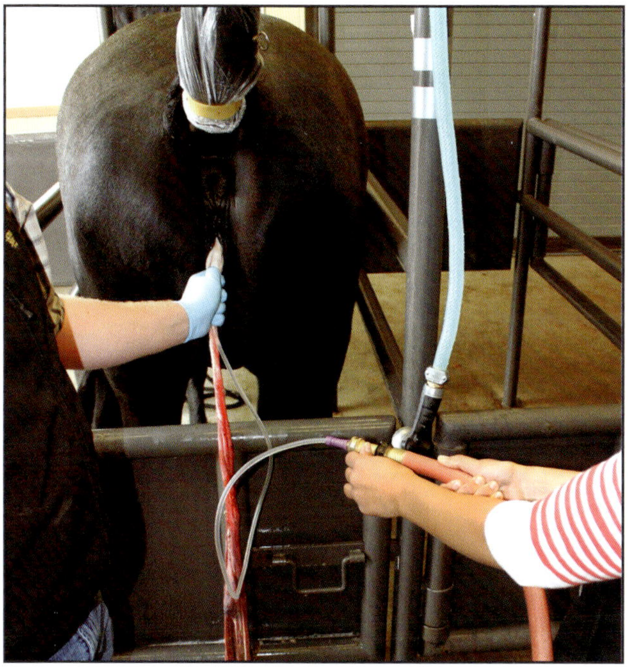

Figure 25-19 Infusion of water into an umbilical blood vessel in a mare with a retained placenta.

through the catheter for 3 to 5 minutes (Figure 25-19)

5. The water is held in the retained membrane for approximately 5 minutes

6. Gentle traction is placed on the placental tissue to encourage passage (Figure 25-20 and Figure 25-21).

The technique is successful in a majority of cases of retained placenta. If the 'Dutch Technique' is not initially successful, the procedure may be repeated utilizing a different umbilical blood vessel.

Manual Removal. Manual removal of retained placentas in mares is controversial. Manual

Figure 25-20 Retained chorioallantoic membrane starting to protrude through vulva.

Figure 25-21 Chorioallantoic membrane being completely passed after using the 'Dutch Technique'.

removal has been associated with severe hemorrhage, placental tearing, delayed uterine involution, endometrial damage, intussusception of a uterine horn and partial or complete uterine prolapse. It may be advantageous to initiate other options before attempting to manually remove a retained placenta. However, implementation of a careful technique to gently dissociate the chorioallantois from the endometrium has been used successfully in many clinical cases.

Additional Treatments for Retained Placenta

Calcium Gluconate. Administration of a calcium-magnesium-borogluconate solution along with oxytocin has been described for mares with refractory cases of retained placenta. Friesian mares that retain their placenta often have lower blood calcium levels than similar mares that do not retain their placenta. Consequently, intravenous administration of a calcium containing solution may be beneficial in treatment of retained placentas in Friesian mares and possibly mares of other breeds.

Other Treatments. If the entire chorioallantois or a portion of the chorioallantois (i.e. tip of the non-pregnant horn) remain retained for more than 6 to 12 hours after foaling, additional medical treatments and management practices may be indicated to prevent toxic metritis and laminitis.

Additional treatments may include:

- Systemic administration of broad-spectrum antibiotics
- Intrauterine infusion of antibiotics or antiseptics to prevent bacterial growth in the uterus postpartum
- Oxytocin administration
- Uterine lavage to promote uterine involution and remove bacteria, debris and inflammatory fluid from the uterine lumen
- Nonsteroidal anti-inflammatory drugs (i.e. flunixin meglumine) to prevent endotoxemia and laminitis
- Acepromazine and/or topical nitroglycerine (2 %) to promote peripheral vasodilation and prevent laminitis
- Frog support pads to help prevent laminitis
- Housing mare and foal in a deeply bedded stall to prevent laminitis.
- Other therapies may include administration of anti-endotoxin hyperimmune plasma and polymixin B to prevent endotoxemia, tetanus vaccination and possibly a Caslick vulvoplasty to limit aspiration of air into the uterus

Medical therapy in at-risk mares should be instituted early, since complications can be severe and life-threatening.

Chapter 26 Colostrum Evaluation and Management

Table 26-0 List and Part Number of ARS products used in this chapter.

Item	Part Number	Use/Comments
Equine Colostrum Refractometer	ECR-101	Used to evaluate colostrum quality of mare prior to nursing.
500 ml Plastic Measuring Cup	PMC-101-500	Used to collect a larger volume of colostrum from a mare immediately after foaling for freezing.
Udderly EZ Milker	UEZ Milker	Used to collect a large volume of colostrum or milk from a mare without hand milking.
Cotton Gauze 4x4's	CG-44/200	Used to filter gross debris and dirt from colostrum before storing.
250ml Plastic Colostrum Bottles	537-800/6	Used to store colostrum for later use with mare's name and colostrum information.

26.1 Colostrum

Colostrum is the thick, sticky yellow fluid produced by the mammary gland of the mare during the last few weeks of pregnancy. It is comprised of carbohydrates, fats, proteins and electrolytes. Colostrum is rich in antibodies or immunoglobulins that are critically important for immune protection of the newborn foal. The process by which foals acquire antibodies from the colostrum of their dam is called 'passive transfer of immunity'.

The multi-layered epitheliochorial placenta of the horse prevents *in utero* transfer of antibodies from the blood of the mare to the fetus. As a consequence, foals are born without any antibody protection. The newborn foal is thus entirely dependent on antibodies from colostrum for protection against infection during the early neonatal period.

Under normal circumstances, a foal will stand and nurse within 1 to 2 hours after it is born. Specialized cells (enterocytes) in the small intestinal mucosa absorb the colostral antibodies by a process called pinocytosis (engulfment of fluid droplets).

The capacity of the small intestine to absorb and transfer antibodies is greatest during the first 6 to 8 hours after birth. It declines substantially after 12 hours and within 24 hours after birth the specialized intestinal cells are replaced by cells incapable of transferring antibodies. Consequently, ingestion of colostrum by the foal after 24 hours of age will not result in an increase in blood antibody levels.

Foals need to ingest approximately two liters of good quality colostrum within the first few hours of life to acquire sufficient antibodies to protect against infectious diseases.

Mares only produce colostrum during the final one to two weeks at the end of gestation. Colostrum is rapidly depleted as the foal nurses throughout the first day of life. Within 24 hours after foaling, the mammary gland no longer contains colostrum and the milk produced thereafter does not contain high concentrations of antibodies.

26.2 Evaluation of Colostrum Quality

Evaluation of mare colostrum immediately after foaling and prior to nursing can be helpful in predicting if failure of passive transfer is likely to occur. This is especially true in situations in which colostrum has been lost due to premature leakage from the mammary gland, or if colostrum quality is poor. Evaluation is also valuable in determining the quality of colostrum to be harvested and stored frozen in a colostrum bank.

Quantitative measurement of IgG levels in colostrum can be obtained by a radial immunodiffusion (RID) assay. Unfortunately, the RID technique is not a test that can be performed easily on a farm and takes approximately 24 hours to obtain results. Qualitative assessment of colostrum can be performed using an Equine Colostrum Refractometer to evaluate optical density. Optical density is correlated with antibody (IgG) content of colostrum.

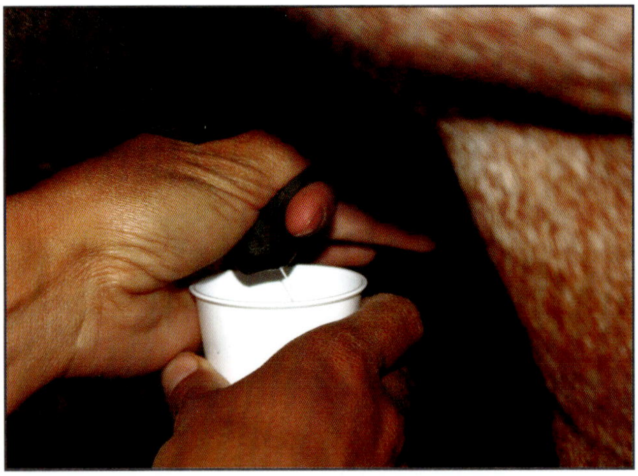

Figure 26-1 Collection of colostrum sample.

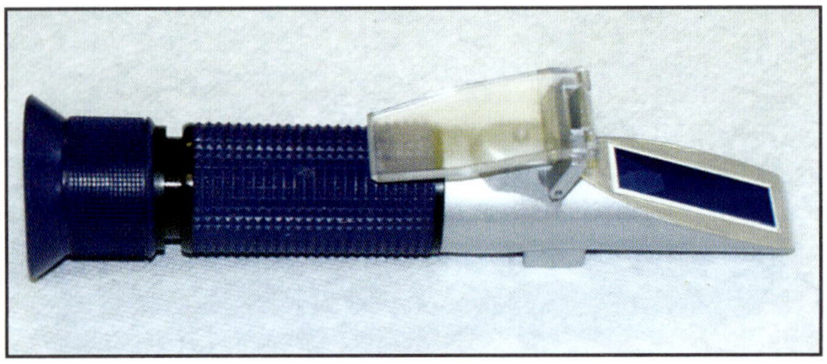

Figure 26-2 ARS Equine Colostrum Refractometer.

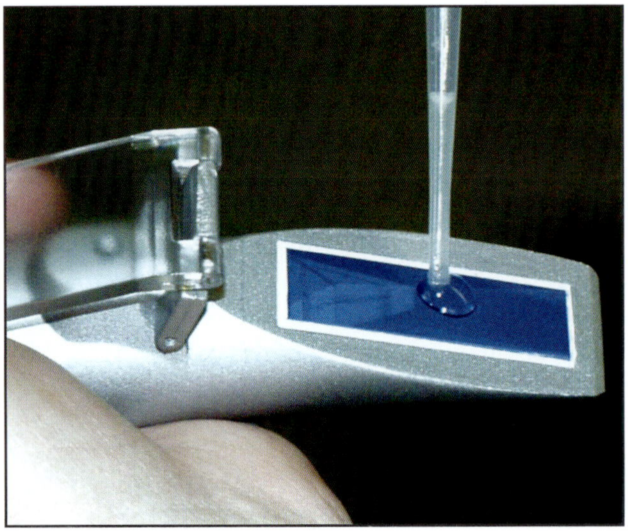

Figure 26-3 Placement of a drop of colostrum on the prism of the refractometer.

26.3 Equine Colostrum Refractometer

Refractometry measures the concentration of dissolved solids in a solution. To evaluate colostrum using an Equine Colostrum Refractometer, a small amount of colostrum is collected (Figure 26-1), and one to two drops are placed on the prism (Figure Figure 26-2 and Figure 26-3) and the daylight plate

Figure 26-4 Evaluation of the percent score and quality grade on the scale visible through the eyepiece (arrow).

is closed. Closure of the daylight plate spreads the colostrum evenly across the prism. The refractometer is held in the direction of a light source and the deviation or refraction of light is evaluated on a scale as a percentage score (Figure 26-4). The level or location of the color (blue) on the scale is determined. The scale contains graduations (%) and a quality assessment score for accurate interpretation.

Colostrum with a low amount of dissolved solids (i.e. low IgG level) will have a lower amount of light scatter and a lower percentage score. Colostrum with high amounts of dissolved solids (i.e. high IgG levels) will cause more light scatter and therefore have a higher percentage score. Refractometer evaluation of equine colostrum has been shown to be highly repeatable and highly correlated with IgG levels as measured by the radial immunodiffusion assay.

26.4 Interpretation and Colostrum Management

The relationship between Brix refractometry score (%), IgG content as determined by RID assay and overall colostrum quality assessment is presented in Table 26-1 below:

Table 26-1 Colostrum quality as assessed by IgG concentration and Brix refractometry score.

Colostrum Quality	IgG Conc. (mg/dl)	Brix (%)
Very Good	> 8,000	> 30
Good	5,000 - 8,000	20 - 30
Fair	2,800 - 5,000	15 - 20
Poor	< 2,800	<15

Successful passive transfer of antibodies from the mare to her foal depends on many factors, including quality and quantity of colostrum, timing of the ingestion of colostrum, health status of the foal, and absorption of antibodies by the small intestine. Assessment of colostrum quality evaluates only one component of the passive transfer process. However, if it can be determined that the quality of the colostrum produced by a mare is inadequate, the foal can be supplemented early in life with additional frozen-thawed colostrum of good quality or with an oral colostrum substitute containing equine antibodies.

26.5 Colostrum Bank

An owner or farm manager generally does not know in advance which foal will need supplemental colostrum. An on-site supply of frozen colostrum can be critical for the health of a valuable neonate.

The best colostrum donors are mares that have had one or more foals and are 4 to15 years of age. Vaccination 4 to 6 weeks prior to foaling will stimulate the immune system of the mare, increase antibody content of colostrum and consequently increase the quality of colostrum to be collected for storage. Colostrum volume and quality are not as good from young maiden mares or aged mares. Mares that have dripped milk for several hours prior to foaling (Figure 26-5) may not have a large volume of good quality colostrum remaining in their udder and may not make suitable donors for a colostrum bank.

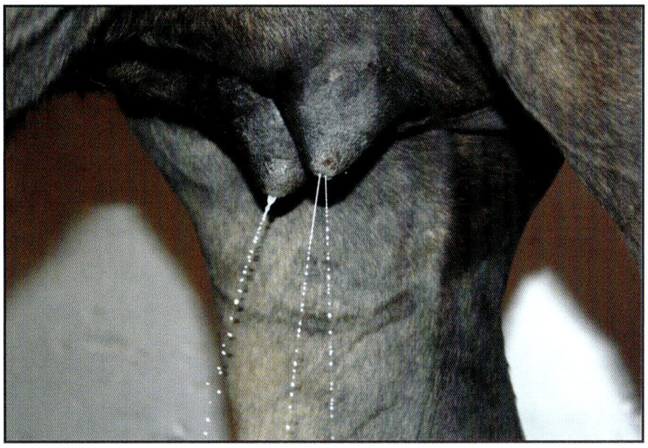

Figure 26-5 Mare dripping colostrum prior to foaling.

Colostrum should not be saved from a mare with a history of having a foal affected by neonatal isoerythrolysis (NI or Jaundice Foal Syndrome) or a foal that died from unknown causes within the first few days after birth.

Good quality colostrum is thick, yellow in color, and sticky in texture. Poor quality colostrum is often watery, white in color and non-viscous in texture. Good colostrum has a Brix score of ≥ 20%, with a higher Brix score indicating better quality colostrum.

Ideally, colostrum to be banked should also be tested for the presence of anti-RBC antibodies, to prevent the possibility of inducing neonatal isoerythrolysis in a foal receiving stored colostrum. Testing for NI antibodies can be performed at several veterinary diagnostic laboratories throughout the United States.

The technique for harvesting colostrum for banking is relatively simple. The udder of the mare should be washed with warm water and soap to remove debris and bacteria. It is recommended that colostrum be collected from one side of the mammary gland from a donor mare in the first hour after foaling before her foal has nursed. A total of 8 to 16 oz may be safely harvested from the mare without adversely affecting the ability of her newborn foal to acquire sufficient colostrum for adequate passive transfer of antibodies.

Options for collecting colostrum include hand milking (Figure 26-6), using an inverted syringe (Figure 26-7), or using a commercial milking device (Figure 26-8). Stripping or milking colostrum by hand directly into a 500ml Plastic Measuring Cup will make it easy to evaluate the volume that has been collected.

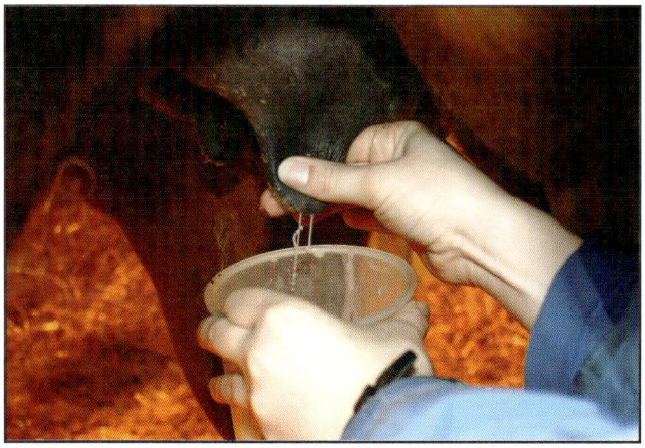

Figure 26-6 Hand milking colostrum from a mare.

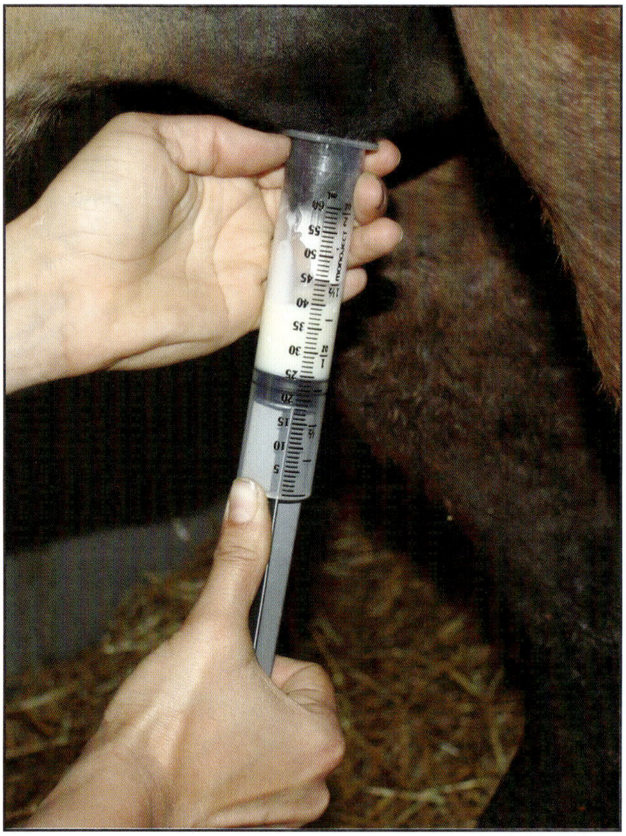

Figure 26-7 Using an inverted syringe to collect colostrum from a mare.

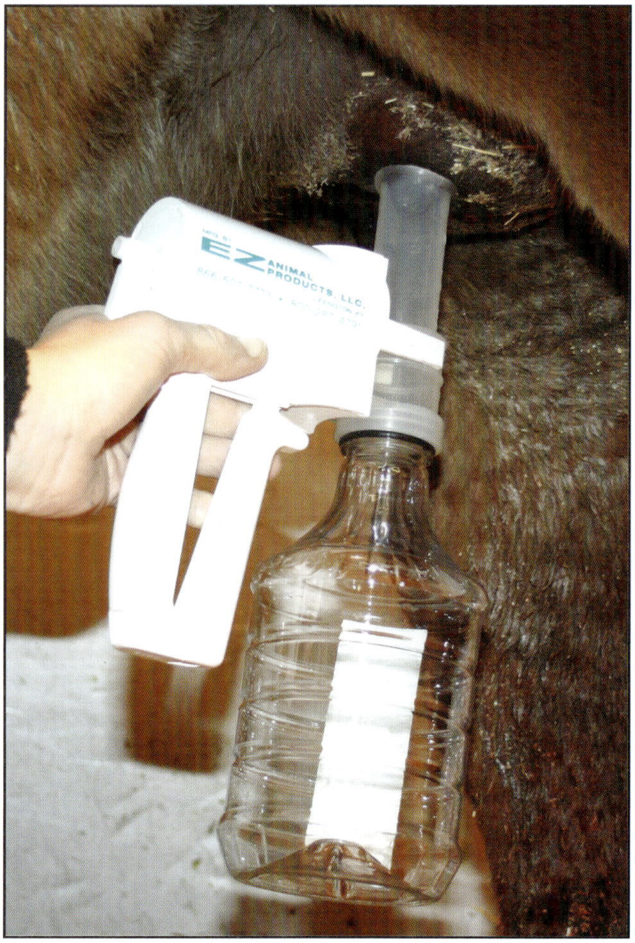

Figure 26-8 Use of the Udderly EZ Mare Milker to collect milk from a mare.

A commercial product called the Udderly EZ™ Milker is a hand-held trigger-operated pump that can safely and effectively harvest colostrum and milk from mares.

Figure 26-9 Straining colostrum through a gauze filter prior to freezing in a plastic bottle.

Harvested colostrum should be passed through a Cotton Gauze 4" X 4" filter into a storage container (Figure 26-9). Colostrum should be stored in a 250ml Plastic Colostrum Bottle labeled with the donor mare's name, collection date and colostrum quality. Glass bottles or plastic freezer bags are not recommended for storage of frozen colostrum. Frozen equine colostrum can be safely stored for 1 to 2 years in a standard -20° C freezer (Figure 26-10). Colostrum should be harvested each breeding season to replenish the colostrum bank with a fresh supply.

Frozen colostrum should be thawed in a water bath at room temperature (Figure 26-11). Thawing in hot water or in a microwave will destroy the antibodies and render the colostrum useless. It is recommended that colostrum be administered immediately after thawing.

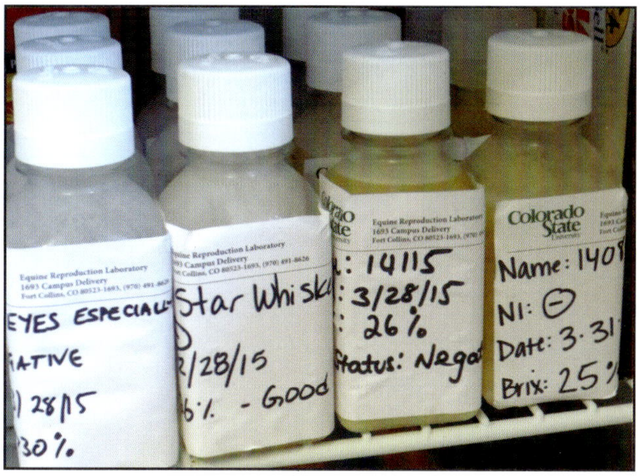

Figure 26-10 Bottles of frozen equine colostrum.

Figure 26-11 Thawing a unit of colostrum in a bucket of warm water.

Colostrum is considered to be 'liquid gold' by horse breeders and veterinarians alike. Make deposits in the colostrum bank early and often during the breeding season; dividends will be provided later in the year.

Chapter 27. Care of the Newborn Foal

Table 27-0 List and Part Number of ARS products used in this chapter.

Item	Part Number	Use/Comments
ARS Foaling Kit	AFK-101 or AFK-102	Comprehensive kit of foaling equipment supplies
Nasal Aspirator	NA-101	Use to clear mucus from nostrils of newborn foals (if necessary)
ARS E-Z Breather Foal Resuscitator	EB-101	Used to resuscitate newborn foal that is not breathing
ARS Terry Towel	TTB-101/6	Use to rub down foal after birth
Double Head Stethoscope	DHS-101	Use to listen to heart and lungs of foal
Umbilical Clamp	UC-101/10	Use to clamp off the umbilical cord after birth (an alternative to umbilical tape)
Umbilical Tape	UT-101	Use to tie off umbilical cord after birth (an alternative to umbilical clamp)
Stainless Steel Mayo Scissors	CS-101	Use to cut the umbilical cord after tying or clamping if necessary
Navel Dip (1% Chlorhexadine solution)	CSD-101	2% Chlorhexidine Solution diluted 1:1 with distilled water; use to disinfect the navel stump immediately after birth and 2 to 3 times a day for 2 to 3 days after birth
Navel Dipping Tube	537-806	Use to disinfect navel stump with Navel Dip
Cotton Gauze 4x4	CG-44/200	Use to strain colostrum to remove dirt and debris prior to storage
250 ml Plastic Colostrum Bottle	537-800/6	Use to store colostrum for later use
Fast Reading Digital Thermometer	THM-105	Use to monitor body temperature of newborn foal and/or mare
Equine Colostrum Refractometer	ECR-101	Use to evaluate colostrum quality
ARS Foal IgG Test	DENK-925 or DENK-1025	Use to measure antibody (IgG) level in foals
Fleet Enema	FE-101	Use to assist with passage of meconium
EZ-Pass™ Foal Enema Kit	EZPF-101	Treatment of refractory meconium impactions

All newborn are faced with a dramatic environmental change at the moment of birth. A foal must instantly adapt in order to survive. An owner or foaling attendant should be trained, ready, and able to assist if necessary. It is important to keep track of critical events, such as the time the mare broke her water, the time the foal was born, and time when the foal first stood, nursed and passed meconium. The mare and foal should be left alone as much as possible after foaling to allow time for social bonding to occur. The placenta should be saved and examined as this may provide valuable information as to the foal's in utero environment and potential exposure to pathogens (See “The Placenta” on page 181). The ARS Foaling Kit (See “ARS Foaling Kit supplies.” on page 175), emergency contact list, telephone, emergency intervention protocol, and possibly even transportation (i.e. truck and trailer) should be readily available to the foaling attendant.

27.1 A-B-C Guidelines for Foal Resuscitation

A specific series of events must occur during and immediately after birth to optimize foal survival.

Fortunately, these events occur spontaneously in the vast majority of foalings and no intervention is required. However, foaling attendants must understand these principles and should be prepared to intervene during a foaling and attend to the immediate needs of the newborn foal if necessary (Table 27-1).

Table 27-1 The A-B-C Guidelines for foal resuscitation are listed below.

Order	Event
A	Establishment of an airway
B	Establisment of breathing
C	Establishment of circulation

Intervention may be indicated in the absence of spontaneous breathing, if breathing is irregular or abnormal, in the absence of a heartbeat, or if the newborn foal is flaccid and non-responsive. Foals born as a result of induced labor or by Cesarean section may be at increased need for resuscitation or immediate care.

It would be ideal if all farm personnel received training in birth resuscitation of foals. Many resuscitation procedures are basic and require a minimal, but critical understanding of normal events, recognition of problems, knowledge of resuscitation equipment, and how to properly implement resuscitation techniques, if needed.

27.2 Establishment of an Airway

The foal must be able to breathe on its own once it exits the protected environment of the uterus and is detached from the umbilical cord. Occasionally a foal is born with the thin, white amnion still covering its nose, preventing normal respiration. An alert foaling attendant must quickly recognize this problem and immediately remove the amnion from the head and neck area (Figure 27-1).

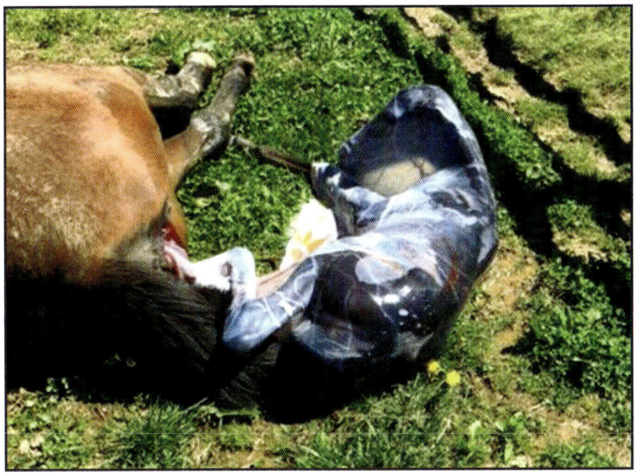

Figure 27-1 Newborn foal with amnion covering the head. The amnion was quickly removed allowing the foal to breathe.

There is usually limited fluid or mucus that occludes the upper airway passages of a foal. Most of the amnionic fluid is probably pushed out of the respiratory tract (i.e. lungs and upper airways) when the chest is compressed as it passed through the birth canal. One can 'strip' some fluid from the external nares area with simple digital compression with fingers followed by a forward movement. Rarely, an attendant may have to suction mucus from the nasal passages of a foal using a Nasal Aspirator. It is not recommended to hold a foal vertically from the hind legs to 'promote drainage of fluid from the lungs'. If any fluid exits after this ill-advised maneuver, it is probably the contents of the stomach. Holding a foal elevated in this manner may actually make it more difficult for the foal to breathe.

If there is visual evidence of yellow-brown meconium staining on the foal or the amnion, it is recommended that a veterinarian be consulted, as this may indicate that the foal may also have meconium in its airways and could have other issues related to pre and/or intrapartum stress.

27.3 Establishment of Breathing

A newborn foal should take its first breath within a few moments after the chest has passed through the birth canal. If the foal has not initiated breathing immediately after it was born, the attendant should immediately enter the foaling stall and briskly rub the foal down with the ARS Terry Towel. The goal is to stimulate the foal sufficiently to begin breathing. If the foal still has not taken a breath, stimulate the inside of its nostrils with a piece of straw or stick a finger in its ears. Flexion of the forelimbs has also been described as a technique to initiate respiration by stimulating stretch receptors.

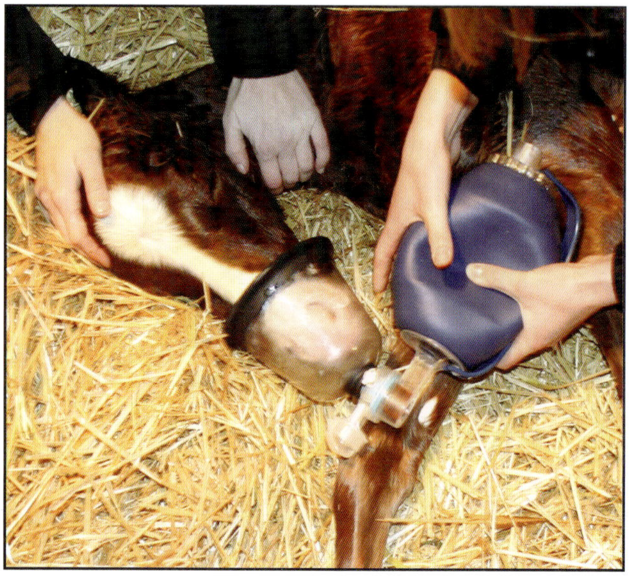

Figure 27-2 Placing an EZ Breather™ over the nose of a newborn foal.

If these techniques fail, one should quickly begin manual resuscitation efforts using a device designed for respiratory use (i.e. the E-Z Breather™ Foal Resuscitator system). The foal is placed on its right side, if possible. The cone of the EZ Breather™ system is placed over the nose of the foal (Figure 27-2). The rubber gasket provides a seal against the foal's face. Once firmly seated, the bag is compressed with both hands to deliver air into the lungs of the foal and then released. The attendant should deliver 10 to 20 'breaths' per minute. An assistant (if available) should gently put pressure on the esophagus (left side of neck) to prevent air from being forced into the gastrointestinal tract. A brief pause should occur every 30 seconds to check if the foal is breathing on its own. Once the foal is breathing, it should be placed in a sternal position to allow for expansion of both lung fields.

An oxygen tank (i.e. E-Tank) may be present on many larger broodmare farms so that a newborn foal can be supplemented with oxygen if needed.

Farm personnel should be trained prior to the onset of the foaling season in the use of oxygen supplementation if such a tank is to be made available.

The normal respiratory rate of a newborn foal may range from 70 to 80 breaths per minute and will gradually decrease to 30 to 40 breaths per minute over the first few hours. Respiratory rate may increase if the ambient environmental temperature is high. The breathing pattern should be regular and without excessive abdominal effort. A sleeping foal may exhibit an irregular breathing pattern with periods of apnea that alternate with fast, shallow breathing.

27.4 Heart Rate and Rhythm

A heart beat should be evident immediately after birth. The heart rate of a newborn foal is approximately 80 to 120 beats per minute. This will decrease over a few hours to 40 to 80 beats per minute. To check if the heart is beating in a newborn foal, place the Double Head Stethoscope on the lower left side of the chest (behind the elbow) and listen for a heart beat or place a hand on the lower left side of the chest and manually feel for a heart beat. If a heartbeat cannot be heard or felt in an obtunded foal, call for back-up assistance immediately. Cardiac compressions, performed by a trained attendant, or emergency medications, delivered under the advice or supervision of a veterinarian, may be indicated in the absence of a detectable heartbeat.

The oral mucous membranes (i.e. gums) of a newborn foal should be pink, moist and, when blanched with firm digital pressure, should become pink again within 1 to 2 seconds (i.e. capillary refill time).

27.5 Rupture of the Umbilical Cord and Umbilical Care

The umbilical cord normally breaks approximately 2 inches from the body wall of the foal when the mare stands or the foal struggles to rise (Figure 27-3 and Figure 27-4). There is no reason to break the cord prematurely as long as the mare and foal are lying quietly and there are no obvious complications. Although it is controversial whether or not any significant amount of placental blood is actually transferred into the foal following birth, it may be best to allow for that possibility. Consequently, early clamping, tying, or manual disruption of the cord is discouraged unless absolutely necessary.

If it does become necessary to break the cord, manual rupture can be performed by firmly grasping the cord on both sides of the normal breakpoint and tearing it. Do not attempt to break the cord away from the abdomen of the foal simply by pulling on it. Tearing is preferable to cutting since cutting does not allow the natural retraction and occlusion of the

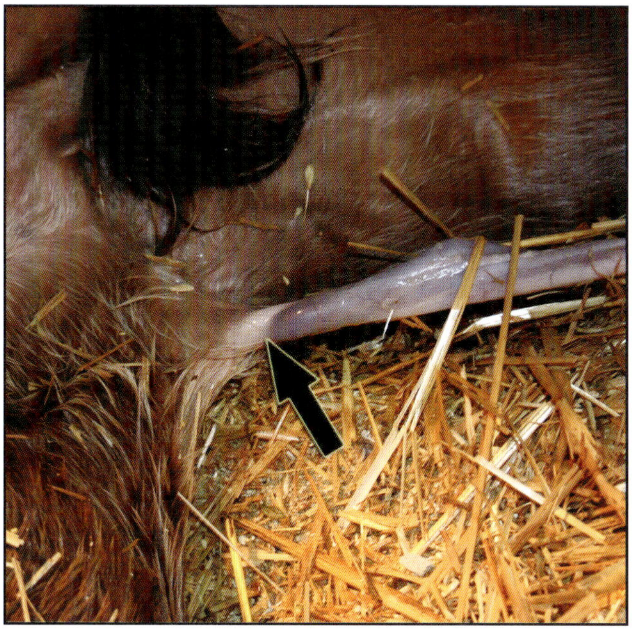

Figure 27-3 Umbilical cord still attached to a newborn foal. The area of normal disruption is indicated by the arrow.

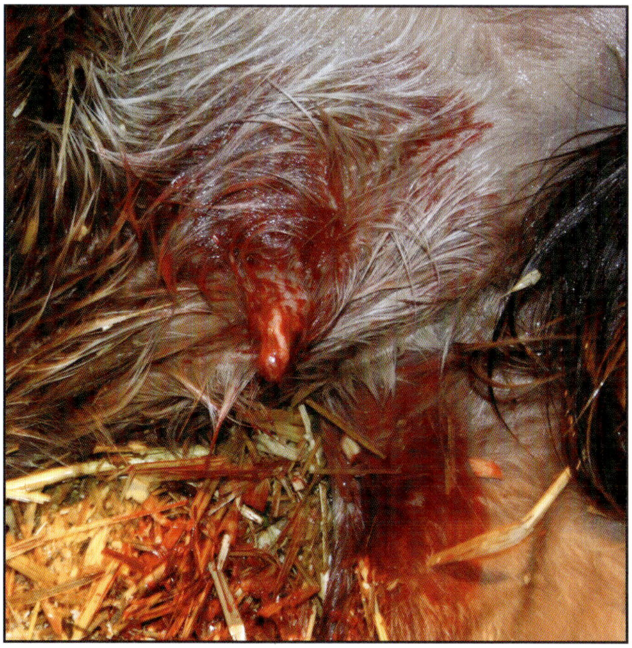

Figure 27-4 Umbilical stump after normal breakage of the cord.

umbilical vessels, and has been associated with a higher incidence of excessive bleeding, patent urachus and umbilical infections. Alternatively, an Umbilical Clamp (Figure 27-5 or Umbilical Tape can be applied to the cord approximately 2 inches from the body wall and a pair of Stainless Steel Mayo Scissors used to cut the cord distal to the clamp.

It is recommended that the umbilical stump be disinfected immediately with Navel Dip (1% Chlorhexidine solution) after the cord has ruptured (Figure 27-6). This will prevent bacteria from entering the open umbilical vessels and infecting the newborn foal. Choices for umbilical disinfectant treatment include chlorhexidine, povidoneiodine, and 2 % iodine. It is currently recommended to use a diluted chlorhexidine solution to safely and effectively disinfect the umbilical stump of new-born foals. The umbilical stump should be completely immersed in a Navel Dipping Tube of disinfectant for several seconds. Disinfectant treatment should be applied 2 to 3 times per day for 2 to 3 days.

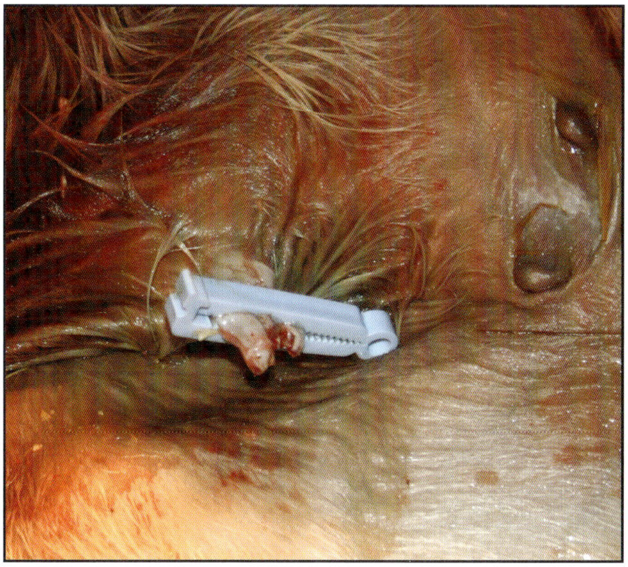

Figure 27-5 Umbilical clamp applied to the umbilical stump of a newborn foal.

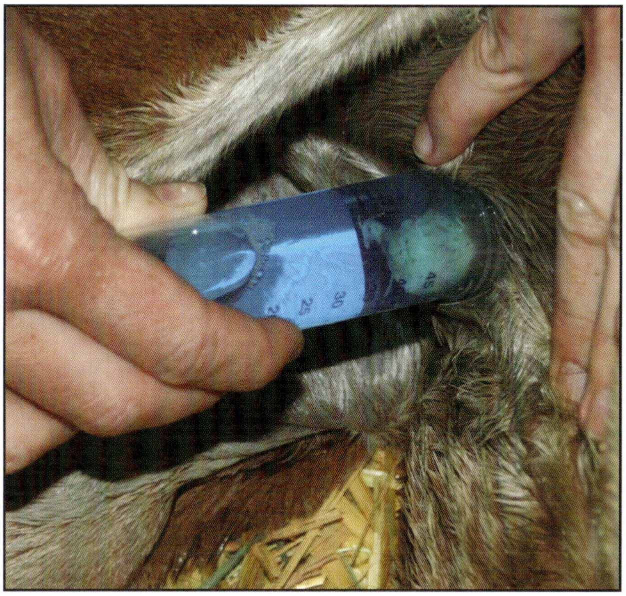

Figure 27-6 Dipping the navel of a foal with chlorhexidine solution.

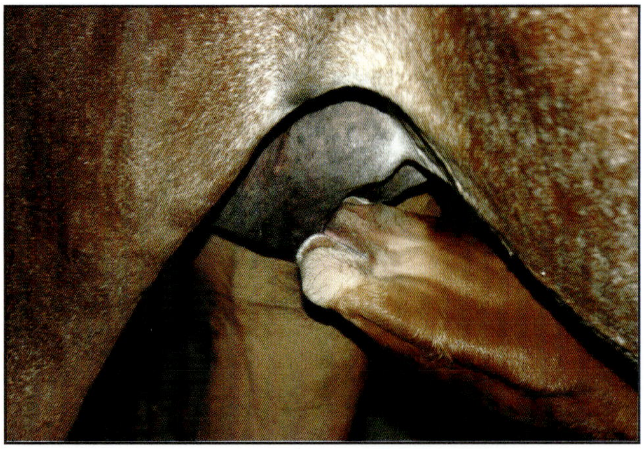

Figure 27-7 Newborn foal nursing from its dam.

27.6 Nursing and Ingestion of Colostrum

Nursing and ingestion of colostrum are critical to the well being of a newborn foal. The foaling attendant and/or farm personnel should observe the foal to determine if it has stood and nursed on its own or if assistance is required. Thankfully, the vast majority of foals will stand and nurse unassisted within the first 1 to 2 hours after being born (Figure 27-7). A few foals will stand unassisted, but may need some guidance to find the udder. Observing dried milk on the face and nose of the foal and a full, tight udder on the mare suggests that the foal is not nursing effectively or maybe not at all. In some circumstances a young, inexperienced mare may not let her foal nurse and intervention may be needed.

Newborn foals enter the world without antibody protection. Foals are entirely dependent on antibodies absorbed following ingestion of mare colostrum in the first few hours of life for protection against infectious diseases, a process called passive transfer of immunity. Exposure of foals to infectious disease organisms in the first few hours or days of life can have a devastating effect if the foal does not obtain immune protection from colostrum.

Mares produce colostrum only during the last 1 to 2 weeks of gestation as antibodies are actively transported from their blood and concentrated in the mammary gland. After suckling colostrum, specialized cells that line the small intestine of the newborn foal absorb antibodies and transfer them into the foal's blood. Absorption of antibodies by these specialized cells is greatest during the first 6 to 8 hours after birth and stops by 24 hours of age.

Failure of passive transfer (FPT) of antibodies occurs in 10 to 20% of newborn foals. The most common causes of FPT are poor quality colostrum and premature lactation. Mares that drip or run milk for several hours prior to giving birth are losing colostrum that is vital to the survival of their foal. In that situation, it is recommended that colostrum be stripped or milked out of the mare, tested for quality using an Equine Colostrum Refractometer and saved for the foal. The colostrum should be strained through a Cotton Gauze 4" X 4" into a 250ml Plastic Colostrum Bottle and either refrigerated or frozen if foaling does not appear to be imminent. Other causes of inadequate transfer of antibodies include failure of colostrum production (i.e. due to fescue toxicity), inability or lack of desire by the foal to nurse, prematurity, dysmaturity, foal rejection by the mare and failure to absorb antibodies that are ingested.

If colostrum of a post-partum mare is tested with the refractometer and determined to be of marginal or poor quality, it would be beneficial to supplement the foal with frozen-thawed colostrum from another mare or administer a colostrum substitute orally within the first few hours of life. Early intervention and oral supplementation can eliminate the need for intravenous plasma transfusion later.

27.7 Passage of Meconium and Meconium Impaction

Meconium is the first feces passed by a newborn foal and is comprised of digested amnionic fluid, gastrointestinal secretions, and cellular debris swallowed by the fetus while in utero. It is usually dark greenish brown or black in color, firm pellets to pasty in consistency, and is generally passed within the first 3 hours after birth. Failure to pass meconium results in significant abdominal pain in the neonate.

A foal is considered to have retained meconium or a meconium impaction if frequent unsuccessful attempts to pass meconium occur within the first 12 to 36 hours of life. It has been estimated that 1 to 2 % of all foals are affected by meconium impactions. Colt foals reportedly have a higher incidence of meconium impactions than filly foals.

Mild clinical signs are usually apparent within 6 to 24 hours after birth and include failure to completely pass meconium, a progressive increase in abdominal pain, and frequent posturing and straining to defecate (Figure 27-8). Affected foals may also be depressed and reluctant to nurse.

The standard initial treatment for foals with a meconium impaction is administration of an enema. A commercial sodium phosphate enema (Fleet® Enema) is safe, easy to administer and generally effective. Enemas should be warmed prior to use and may be kept in an incubator until needed or warmed to approximately 37° C in a water bath. The protective cap is removed from the enema bottle, the lubricated tip is gently inserted fully into the rectum, and the plastic bottle is gently squeezed to deliver the contents (Figure 27-9). In most instances, foals are administered the entire contents of the enema bottle (100 to 133 mls or approximately 3.5 to 4.5 oz). The rectal mucosa of the foal is very tender and friable. Proper restraint and careful passage of the applicator tip into the rectum are imperative to prevent trauma.

Breeding farms may choose to routinely give all newborn foals an enema within the first 1 to 2 hours after birth or may selectively administer enemas only to foals that do not pass meconium on their own. Either type of management strategy is acceptable. Foals that do not successfully pass meconium in the first few hours of life should be treated because of the potential for significant complications, including colic, failure to nurse adequately,

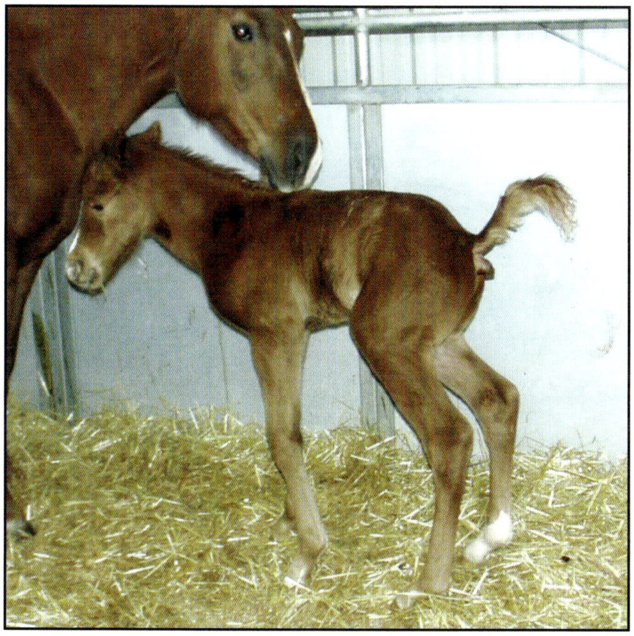

Figure 27-8 A foal with a meconium impaction straining to defecate.

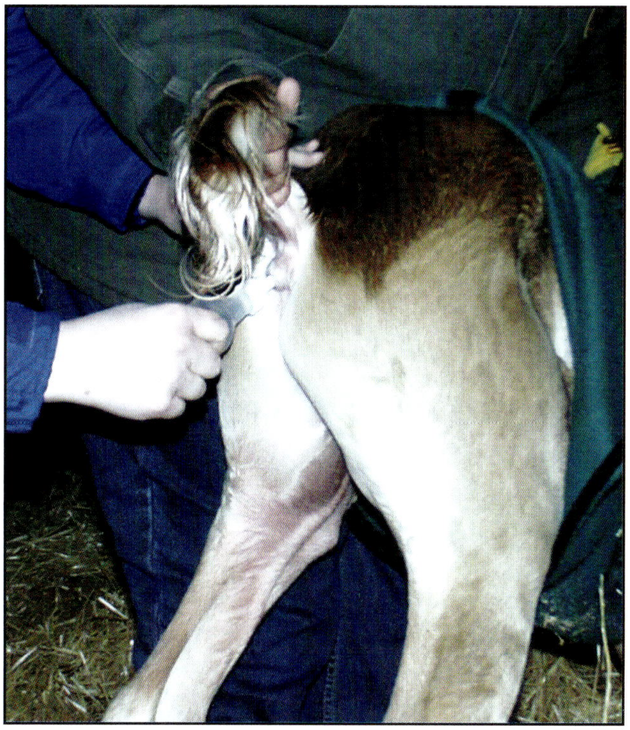

Figure 27-9 Administration of a sodium phosphate enema.

inflammation of the colon and rectum and potentially translocation of bacteria resulting in sepsis.

If administration of 1 to 2 sodium phosphate enemas does not resolve a meconium impaction, a veterinarian should be contacted. Administration of an acetylcysteine enema, using the E-Z Pass™ Foal Enema Kit, may be successful in the medical resolution of meconium impactions.

Contents of the EZ-Pass foil packet are added to 100 mls of tap water within the plastic administration bottle supplied in the enema kit. The acetylcysteine solution is slowly infused into the rectum through a soft, flexible Foley-type catheter (Figure 27-10). The catheter is clamped shut and the solution allowed to remain in the rectum for 15 to 30 minutes before the clamp is opened and the catheter removed. The foal should be then be monitored for complete passage of the retained meconium and observations continued for the next 24 to 36 hours. The presence of yellow 'milk stool' indicates that meconium has passed completely and that digested colostrum is now being voided. As with many medical conditions, early recognition and treatment is important in the successful management of meconium impactions.

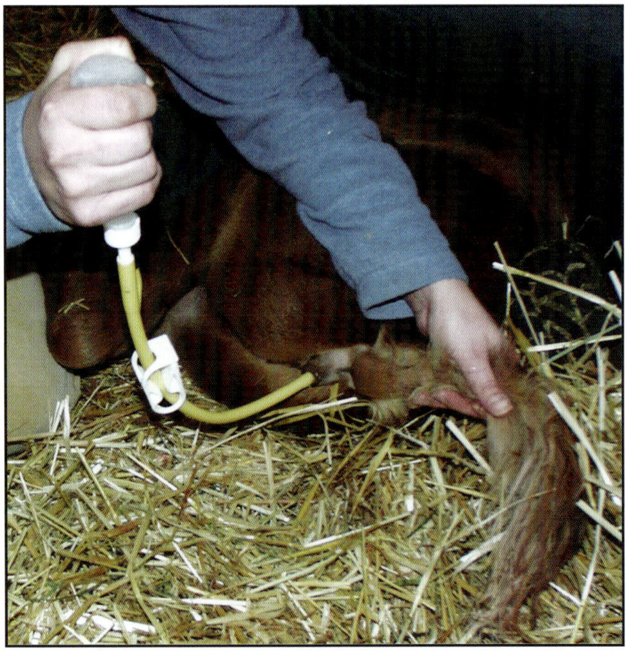

Figure 27-10 Acetylcysteine enema treatment.

27.8 1-2-3 Rule

As a general rule of thumb, critical events in the life of a newborn foal should occur by the time periods after foaling outlined in Table 27-2.

Table 27-2 The 1-2-3 rule of events in the life of a newborn foal.

Time from Foaling	Event
1 hour	Standing unassisted
2 hours	Nursing from mare
3 hours	Passing Meconium

27.9 Testing for Passive Transfer of Antibodies

Owners or farm managers should consult with their veterinarian regarding collection of blood sample(s) from the foal and testing for IgG antibodies. In some circumstances, farm personnel will collect an appropriate blood sample and measure IgG levels on the farm. Another option is for farm personnel to collect the blood sample(s) at the recommended time post foaling and take the sample(s) to a veterinary clinic for evaluation. A third option would be to have a veterinarian collect the blood sample during a newborn foal examination performed 12 to 24 hours after foaling. Timing of the sample collection, interpretation of results, and appropriate therapeutic options are all critically inter-related. Again, it is best to have a meeting between ownership, farm personnel, and the farm veterinarian before the onset of the breeding-foaling season to discuss sample collection and testing options.

Early testing for antibody levels in a neonatal foal can identify potential cases of FPT and allow for early intervention and medical management. It is recommended that a blood sample be collected from a newborn foal approximately 12 hours after birth to evaluate circulating IgG levels prior to 'closure' of the gastrointestinal tract to antibody absorption. If IgG levels are < 400 mg/dl at 12 hours, oral supplementation with frozen-thawed colostrum or a commercial colostrum substitute should be performed (Table 27-3). If IgG levels are 400 to 800 mg/dl, the need for intervention and therapy is dependent on potential pathogen exposure and/or the medical condition of the foal. Foals with partial failure of passive transfer are at risk of developing infections and may benefit from IgG supplementation. In contrast, foals with partial FPT born into a clean environment with low pathogen exposure potential and good preventive management practices may not need supplemental IgG. Antibody levels of > 800 mg/dl at 12 hours of age indicate that adequate passive transfer of immunoglobulins occurred and no additional testing or intervention is necessary under most management conditions.

Table 27-3 Antibody levels in foals with adequate passive transfer and failure of passive transfer of maternal immunity.

Foal Plasma IgG Concentration	Interpretation
> 800 mg/dl	Adequate passive transfer
400 to 800 mg/dl	Partial failure of passive transfer
< 400 mg/dl	Failure of passive transfer
< 200 mg/dl	Complete failure of passive transfer

Testing a foal at 24 hours of age or more will determine the final extent of passive antibody absorption. It is critical to understand that no significant amount of antibodies is absorbed if oral supplementation is provided after 24 hours of age. Foals greater than 24 hours of age identified with FPT require intravenous administration of plasma to successfully increase blood antibody levels. Although plasma transfusions are commonly per-

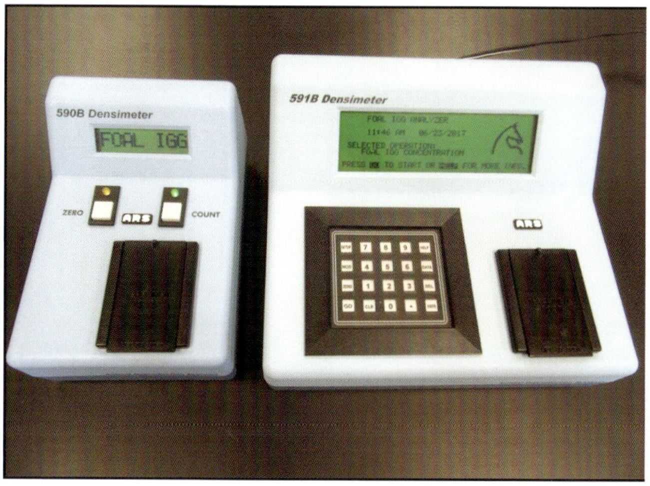

Figure 27-11 The 590B and 591B Densimeter can be calibrated to perform quantitative IgG analysis.

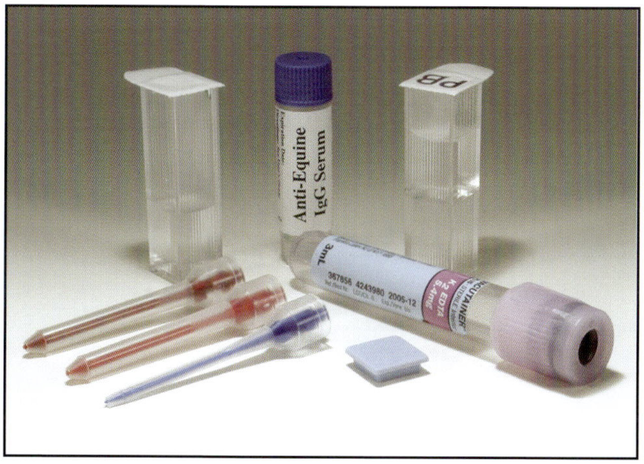

Figure 27-12 The IgG kit sold by ARS contains all the necessary reagents to quantitatively determine a foals' IgG level.

formed in foals for disease prevention and medical therapy, oral administration of colostrum early in the first day of life (i.e. at ≤ 12 hours of age) is unquestionably easier and safer to perform. A quantitative turbidimetric immunoassay screening test for evaluation of IgG levels in foals has been developed (See "Guide to the ARS Foal IgG Test" on page 203) (Figure 27-11 and Figure 27-12). The test is rapid, accurate and sensitive in detection of failure of passive transfer in foals. A small blood sample (1 to 2 mls is adequate) is collected into a vacutainer tube containing EDTA (i.e. a 'purple-top' tube) and either centrifuged at 300 x *g* for 5 minutes or placed upright on a flat surface and the blood cells allowed to settle to the bottom. Only a small quantity of plasma (25.7 µl) is used in the assay, which takes less than 10 minutes to complete. The test has been calibrated against the single radial immunodiffusion test, which is considered the gold standard for immunoglobulin testing, and results are presented in mg/dl.

Early testing of a newborn foal can detect potential cases of failure of passive transfer in time for oral supplementation with frozen colostrum to be effective. A timely diagnosis and early therapeutic intervention will often circumvent a life-threatening medical crisis in a young foal.

27.10 Follow-up Care and Other Observations

The newborn foal and dam should be observed carefully by farm personnel for the first 2 to 3 days after foaling to monitor activity level, health, social bonding, and nursing. Normal foals nurse frequently and generally keep the udder of the mare drained. Foaling attendants and farm personnel should be instructed to specifically observe the newborn foal for normal urination and defecation and to alert appropriate personnel if the foal appears to have problems voiding urine or is straining to defecate. The strength and activity level of the foal should progressively increase over time. Foals with medical conditions may become weak, depressed, and stop nursing over a very short time period. Early recognition of changes in the behavior or attitude of the foal may be critical.

Foals that were born following a difficult birth (dystocia) or in a red-bag delivery should be closely monitored for behavior over the first 48 to 72 hours, as hypoxemic events that occurred during foaling may not be immediately apparent. Foals may sustain fractured ribs during a dystocia, assisted foaling, or even an apparently uneventful foaling. Affected foals may exhibit localized swelling, pain, difficulty in breathing, or other problems.

The body temperature of the foal should be measured using the Fast Reading Digital Thermometer if the foal appears to be depressed, not nursing, reluctant to move, or less active than normal. The normal body temperature of a newborn foal ranges from approximately 37.2 to 38.7 °C (99.0 to 101.5 °F). A body temperature below or above this range is considered abnormal and appropriate personnel should be notified. Note that it is common for a newborn foal to shiver occasionally during the first 3 to 4 hours after birth to generate heat. In some instances, a young foal may need extra bedding (i.e.

deep straw), a blanket, or heat lamps to help it keep warm.

It is recommended that a routine newborn foal examination be performed by a veterinarian within 12 to 24 hours after birth to evaluate health status and determine if medical therapy is indicated. As noted previously, a veterinarian should be contacted immediately in the event of a difficult birth, retained placenta, or sick newborn.

The placenta can be evaluated at the time of the newborn foal examination if it has not been looked at previously by farm personnel or if abnormalities were observed. The placenta should be refrigerated if a significant time delay is anticipated between foaling and placental evaluation. A blood sample can also be collected from the foal for measurement of IgG levels, if the timing is appropriate.

27.11 Neonatal Maladjustment Syndrome (NMS)

Neurosteroids (i.e. pregnanes) function to keep an equine fetus quiescent in utero. Pressure applied to the chest of the foal during passage through the birth canal is hypothesized to be the physical trigger that switches the physiological state of consciousness from that of somnolence or sedation in a fetus to that of awake, alert and interactive in the neonate. In the normal foal, neurosteroid levels decline rapidly following birth.

However, in some foals, neurosteroid levels remain elevated for days and affected foals exhibit decreased awareness of their environment, decreased affinity for the mare, decreased interest or ability to nurse and are generally in an obtunded or stuporous mental state.

Application of continuous moderate pressure for 20 minutes to the chest of foals showing signs of NMS may stimulate a transition to consciousness (Madigan Chest Squeeze Technique).

- E-Z Squeeze™ Foal Rope is placed around the cranial chest, incorporating a front leg and secured snugly. Incorporation of a front leg prevents the rope from slipping caudally and also prevents occlusion of the airway
- The rope is arranged in a series of 2 half-hitches with loops around the chest and the half-hitches located along the back of the foal (Figure 27-13). It is important to keep the loops snug against the chest.

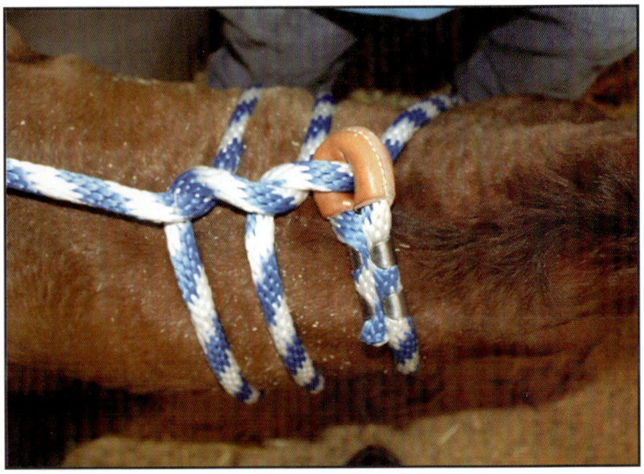

Figure 27-13 Dorsal view of a foal with the initial loop incorporating a front leg (arrow) and two additional half-hitches

- Application of moderate continuous pressure on the rope from behind the foal will provide uniform chest compression as the rope tightens through the half-hitches. It may be prudent to cover the head with a towel.
- The foal may struggle briefly with initial pressure and then will lay down(Figure 27-14). Apply continuous pressure for 20 minutes and then remove the rope and allow the foal to stand without assistance.

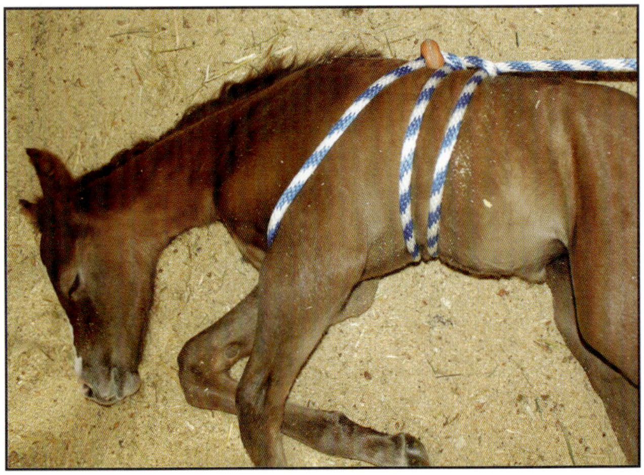

Figure 27-14 Foal recumbent after gentle application of the chest squeeze.

For more information on the Madigan Chest Squeeze, please visit the ARS website at

www.arssales.com

Chapter 28. Guide to the ARS Foal IgG Test

Table 28-0 List and Part Number of ARS products used in this chapter.

Item	Part Number	Use/Comments
ARS Foal IgG Test Supply Kit	IGG-101-KIT	Supply kit for measuring antibody (IgG) level in foals
590B Foal IgG Analyzer Kit	DENK-1025	590B Densimeter calibrated for Foal IgG (Complete Kit)
591B Foal IgG Analyzer Kit	DENK-925	591B Densimeter calibrated for Foal IgG (Complete Kit)
590 Series Foal IgG Upgrade	IGG-101-590-UG	Foal IgG upgrade for existing 590 Series Densimeter.
591 Series Foal IgG Upgrade	IGG-101-591-UG	Foal IgG upgrade for existing 590 Series Densimeter.
ARS 180 µl Positive Displacement Pipette	594KR-1800	Used to precisely measure volumes of foal plasma, buffer or anti-equine IgG serum during the Foal IgG test; pipette can be used to dispense 25.7 µl or 180 µl volume depending on the disposable tip used
Kimwipes®	537-669	General laboratory tissue; used to remove excess fluid from pipette tip prior to dispensing into a test cuvette

Items in the ARS Foal IgG Test Supply Kit

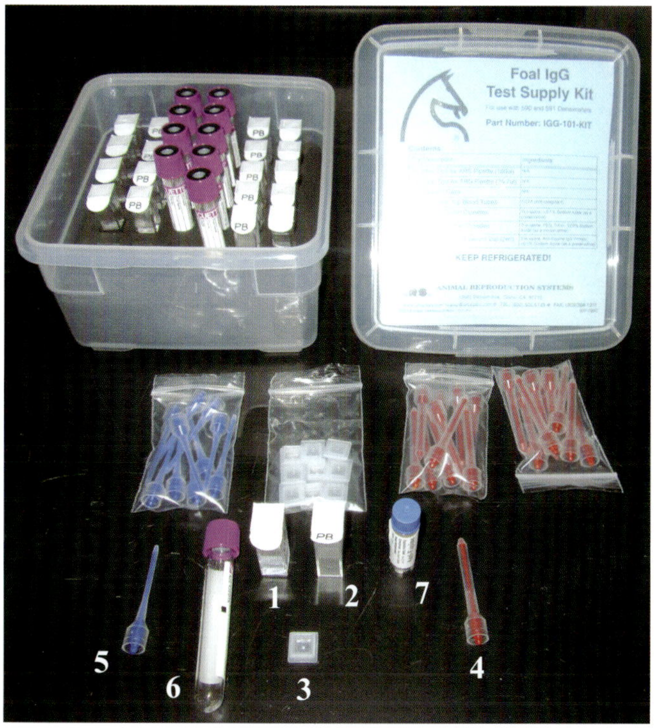

Figure 28-1 ARS IgG Test Supply Kit components.

1 - Dilution cuvettes (10)
2 - Measurement cuvettes (labeled 'PB') (10)
3 - Caps to seal cuvettes (20)
4 - Red 180 µl pipette tips (20)
5 - Blue 25.7 µl pipette tips (10)
6 - Lavender top EDTA Vacuette tubes (3 ml) (10)
7 - Vial (2 ml) anti-Equine IgG serum (1)

Additional items needed that are not provided in the kit (Figure 28-2)

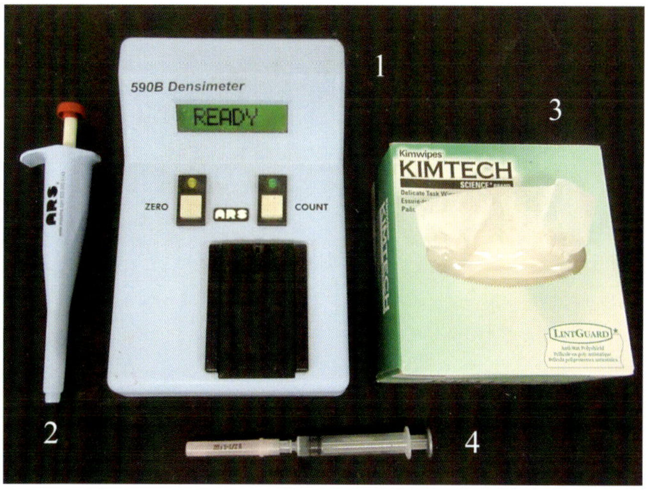

Figure 28-2 Additional equipment and supplies needed to perform the ARS Foal IgG Test.

1 - 590B Densimeter or
591B Densimeter (not shown)
2 - 180 µl Positive Displacement Pipette
3 - Kimwipes®
4 - Syringe and needle

The ARS IgG Test is an immunoturbidometric assay. The basis of the assay is immunocomplex formation between equine IgG antibodies that are present in the plasma of foals after ingestion of colostrum and an anti-equine IgG antibody. If limited to no passive transfer of antibodies has occurred, there will be minimal immunocomplexes formed and the test cuvette will remain clear or only slightly cloudy/turbid. In contrast, if a significant amount of maternal antibodies have been absorbed into the foal's blood, a large amount of immunocomplexes will form and the test cuvette will turn very cloud or turbid. The amount of anti-equine IgG and the volume of foal plasma added to the assay are constants, so the degree of turbidity is dependent on the IgG content of the foal plasma. The degree of turbidity is assessed by the percentage of light transmission, which is then converted into IgG concentration in mg/dl by a calibrated spectrophotometer (ARS Densimeter). The ARS Foal IgG assay has been validated against the single radial diffusion assay, which is the gold standard for IgG determination.

28.1 IgG Test Procedure

Step 1. Collect 1 to 2 mls of blood from the foal using a syringe (Figure 28-3) and immediately transfer the blood into a 3 ml purple/lavender top Vacuette tube containing the anticoagulant EDTA. Place the tube upright and allow the blood to stand for 15 to 20 minutes at room temperature and let the red blood cells separate from the plasma. Alternatively, the Vacuette tube may be centrifuged at 300 x *g* for 5 minutes to separate the cellular components from the plasma.

Remove test kit components from refrigerator and allow to equilibrate to room temperature for 10 to 15 minutes. Turn on the 590B Densimeter while holding down the ZERO button. Release the ZERO button once information is visible on the display. This will automatically select the IgG Test format.

Step 2. Carefully withdraw 25.7 µl (25.7 microliters) of plasma from the top of the Vacuette using a new disposable blue pipette tip attached to the Positive Displacement Pipette (Figure 28-4). Wipe off the exterior of the tip with a Kimwipe® or other tissue to remove any extra plasma on the surface.

Add the 25.7 µl of plasma to the 4.0 ml cuvette of dilution buffer (unmarked top). Partially peel back the cuvette cover to add the plasma. It is recommended that the tip of the pipette be submerged in the buffer while dispensing the plasma contents (Figure 28-5).

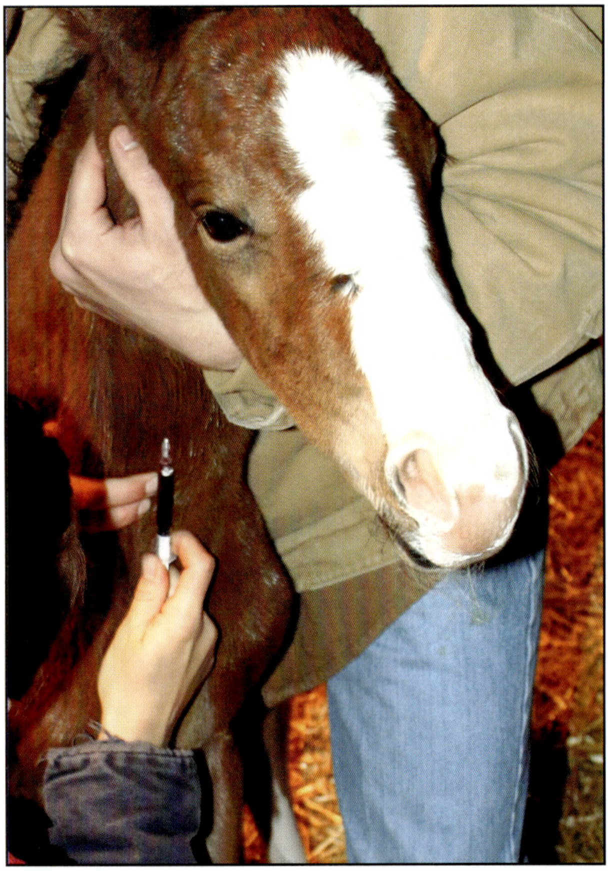

Figure 28-3 Collection of a blood sample from a foal at 12 hours of age.

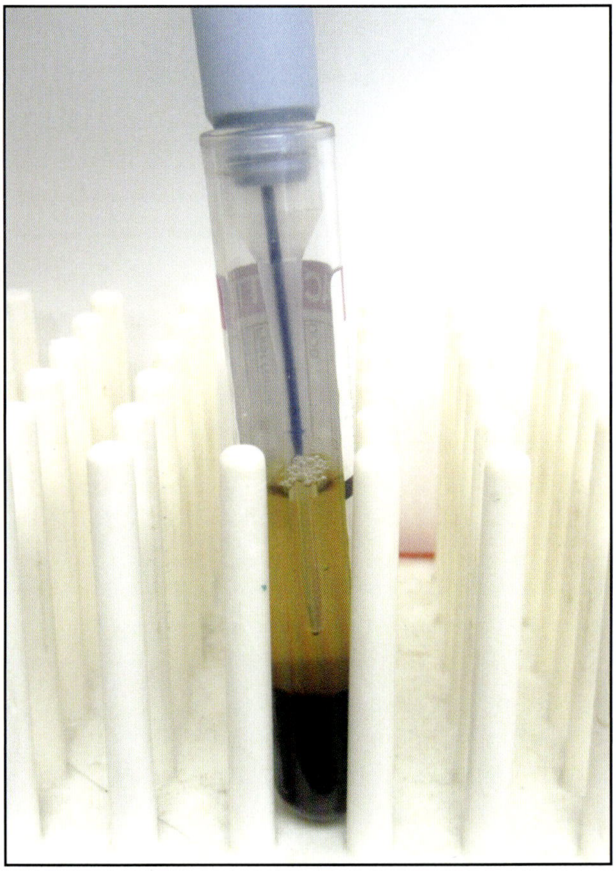

Figure 28-4 Collection of a 25.7 µl sample of foal plasma from a purple top EDTA Vacuette tube.

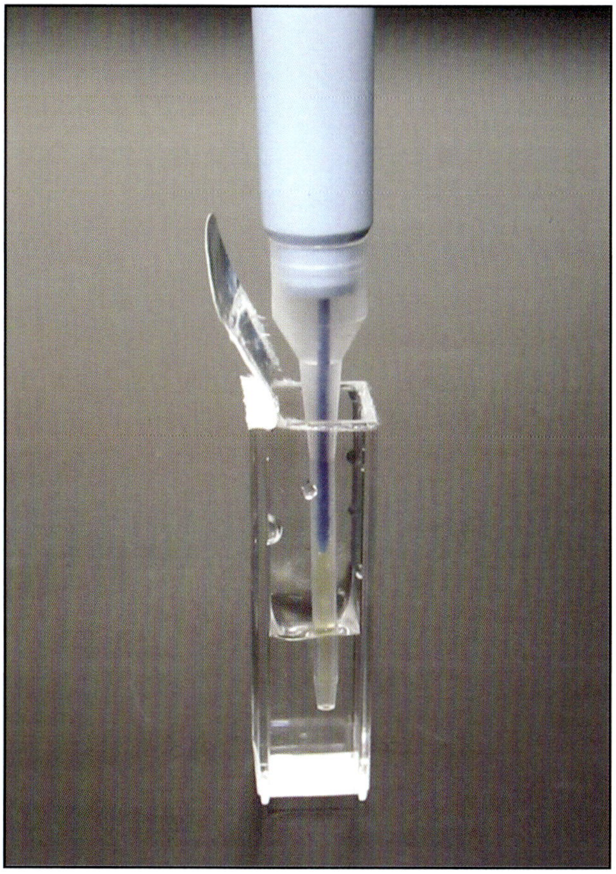

Figure 28-5 Dispensing the 25.7 µl volume of plasma into the 4.0 ml cuvette.

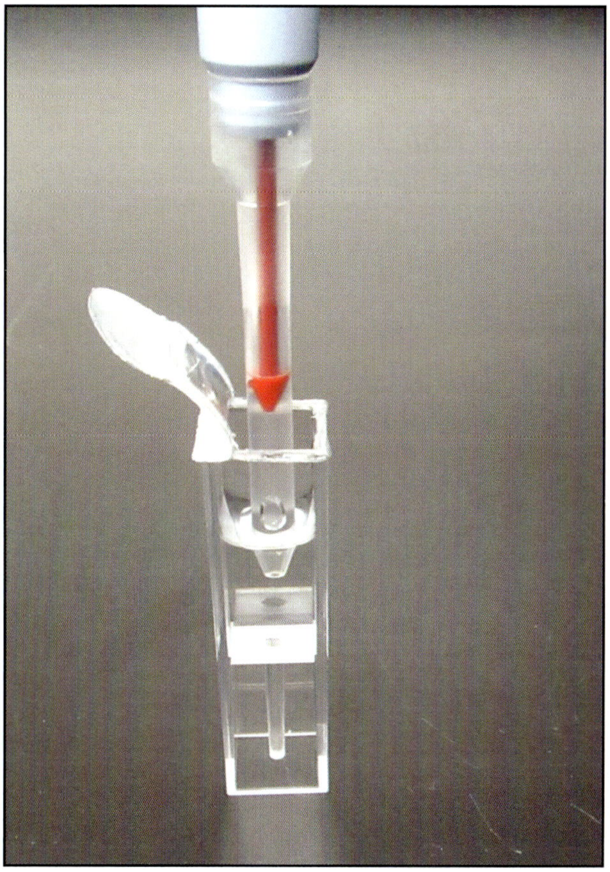

Figure 28-6 Depositing 180 µl of diluted plasma into the 2.0 ml cuvette (marked PB).

Re-cover the dilution buffer cuvette, or seal with a disposable cuvette cap, and gently invert 10 times to mix contents.

Step 3. Carefully withdraw 180 µl of the diluted plasma sample from the cuvette using a red 180 µl pipette tip attached to the Positive Displacement Pipette. Carefully wipe off exterior of pipette with a tissue to remove excess fluid. Add the aliquot of diluted plasma to the 2.0 ml cuvette of polymer buffer (marked PB) (Figure 28-6). Again, partially peel back the cover to add the sample. Re-cover the cuvette or seal with a disposable cuvette cap and gently invert 10 times to mix contents.

Step 4. Insert the 2.0 ml cuvette into the Densimeter, making sure a ribbed side is facing forward and also making sure not to touch the smooth sides (Figure 28-7). Press the ZERO button. Wait until the cuvette is ZEROed and the LED indicates to ADD ANTIBODY (Figure 28-8).

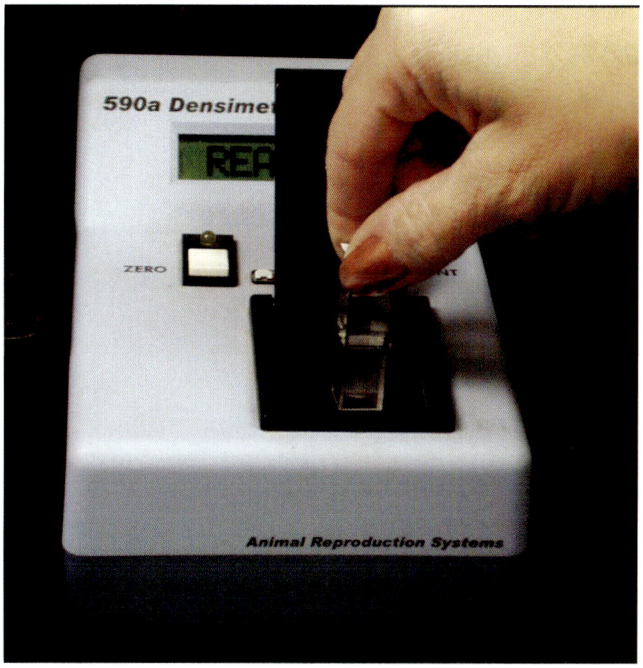

Figure 28-7 Placement of the 2.0 ml cuvette into the Densimeter.

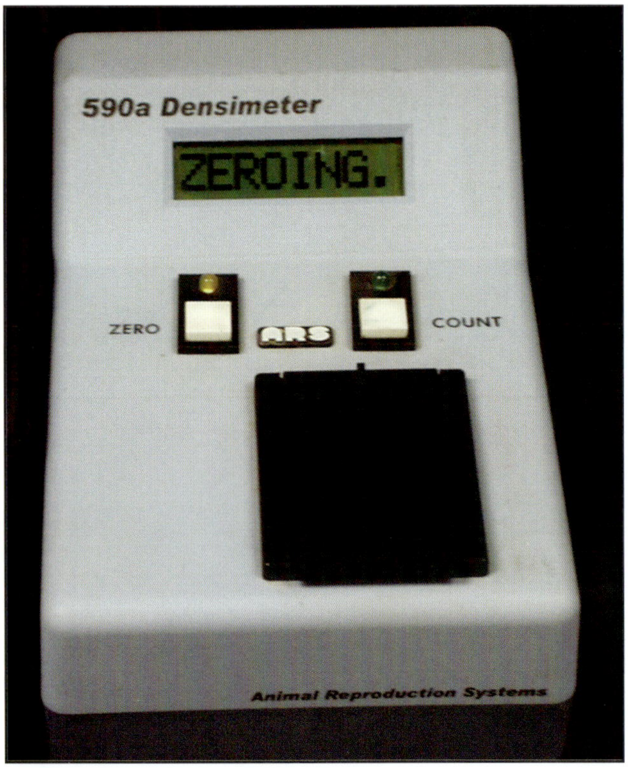

Figure 28-8 Zeroing the Densimeter.

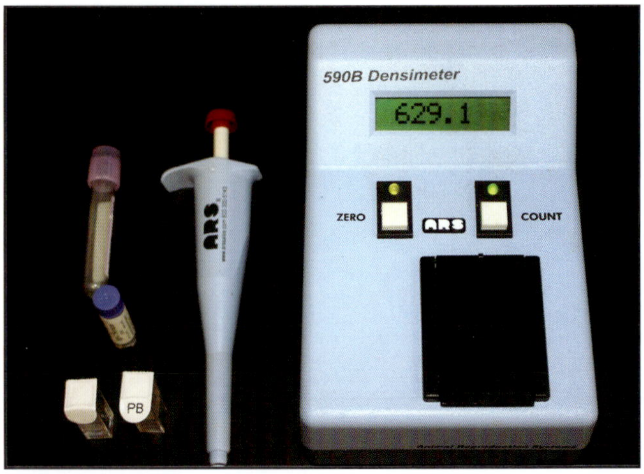

Figure 28-9 IgG concentration in a foal plasma sample at 12 hours of age. The IgG in this sample was 629.1 mg/dl and the foal was subsequently supplemented with frozen-thawed colostrum.

Step 5. Add 180 µl of anti-Equine IgG serum using a new red 180 µl pipette tip attached to the Positive Displacement Pipette. Remember to use a new tip each time to prevent contamination of the vial. Seal the cuvette and invert 10 times to mix contents.

Step 6. Replace the 2.0 ml cuvette into 590a Densimeter and press COUNT button. The Densimeter will count down for 5 minutes and will then automatically evaluate the IgG content. The Densimeter will report the IgG value in mg/dl Figure 28-9). Record the value immediately as the number will remain visible for only 5 minutes.

If you fail to record the IgG value before the 5 minute mark and the value is no longer visible, simply press the count button to display the last result.

Figure 28-10 Turbidity in the 2.0 ml cuvette (left) after addition of anti-equine IgG in a foal with high antibody transfer.

Additional Comments

- Immune complexes form almost immediately after addition of the anti-equine IgG to the cuvette containing the foal plasma. The degree of turbidity can be visually assessed before the cuvette is placed into the Densimeter (Figure 28-10).
- Foal plasma samples with an IgG content greater than 2,000 mg/dl will be read out on the LED as > 2,000 mg/dl (Figure 28-11).

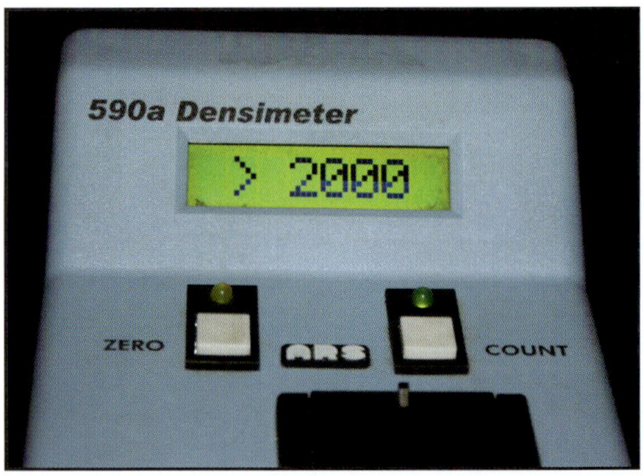

Figure 28-11 Foal IgG concentration of more than 2,000 mg/dl.

28.2 Interpretation of Results

IgG Level	Interpretation
> 800 mg/dl	Adequate passive transfer of colostral antibodies
400 to 800 mg/dl	Partial failure of passive transfer
< 400 mg/dl	Failure of passive transfer
< 200 mg/dl	Complete failure of passive transfer

28.3 Early Testing (approximately 12 hours of age)

Collection and evaluation of a blood sample collected approximately 12 hours after birth of the foal will allow for the early identification of passive antibody failure or the early identification of adequate antibody transfer.

If IgG level is < 200 mg/dl, indicating complete failure of passive transfer, the foal should be supplemented with a minimum of 1 liter of good quality frozen-thawed colostrum and may require intravenous plasma transfusion as well to raise serum IgG levels sufficiently to protect against potential infectious diseases.

If IgG levels are < 400 mg/dl at 12 hours, oral supplementation with frozen-thawed colostrum or a commercial colostrum substitute should be performed.

If IgG levels are 400 to 800 mg/dl, the need for intervention and therapy is dependent on potential pathogen exposure and/or concurrent medical conditions. Foals at risk of developing sepsis may be benefited from IgG supplementation. Foals born into a clean environment with low pathogen exposure potential and good preventive management practices may not need supplemental IgG.

If IgG levels are > 800 mg/dl, no additional testing or intervention is necessary under most management conditions.

It must be recognized that antibodies will continue to be absorbed during the interval between the initial test (12 hours) and the time when the gut closes to further antibody absorption (24 hours). Blood antibody levels should continue to increase if the mare still has colostrum in her mammary gland, the foal is still actively nursing, and if absorption is still occurring. Consequently, if plasma IgG levels are at the upper end of the 400 to 800 mg/dl range at 12 hours of age, it is quite likely that IgG levels will be > 800 mg/dl at 24 hours of age.

If IgG levels in the foal are low at 12 hours, it is strongly recommended that another blood sample be collected and evaluated between 24 and 48 hours of age, whether or not the foal was administered supplemental IgG. If levels are still not adequate in the second sample, intravenous plasma transfusion is recommended.

28.4 Later Testing (> 24 hours of age)

Collection and evaluation of a blood sample after 24 hours of age will determine the final extent of passive antibody absorption.

If IgG levels are < 400 mg/dl, intravenous administration of plasma is indicated (Figure 28-12). Oral supplementation is not effective after 24 hours of age in enhancing blood IgG levels of foals. It is strongly recommended that a second test be performed 24 to 48 hours after the plasma transfusion to evaluate blood IgG levels and response to treatment.

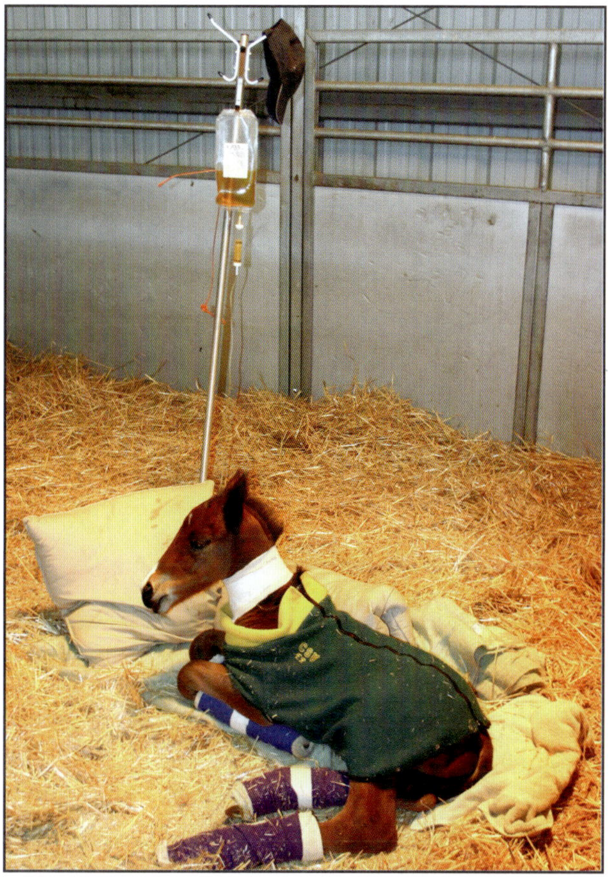

Figure 28-12 Intravenous plasma transfusion into a foal with low plasma IgG at 24 hours of age.

If IgG levels are 400 to 800 mg/dl, intravenous plasma transfusion is recommended if exposure to potential pathogens is high or if other medical conditions are present.

If IgG levels are > 800 mg/dl, no intervention or treatment is required and no further testing is necessary.

> **Comment:**
>
> The ARS IgG test can also be preformed on 591 series Densimeters. Figure 28-13 through Figure 28-23 show the step-by-step screen shots that prompt the user through the entire ARS IgG test.

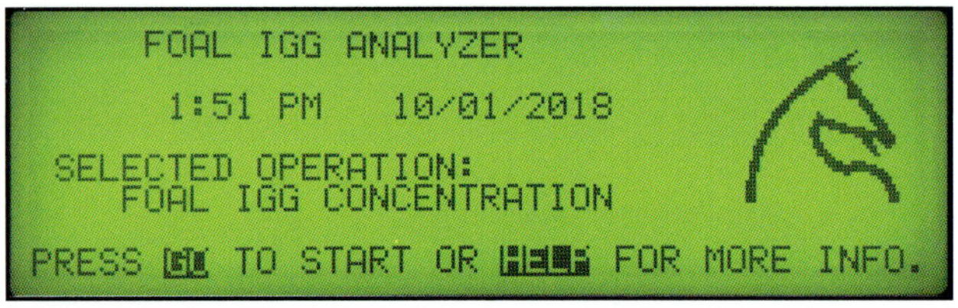

Figure 28-13 591B Foal IgG start screen.

Figure 28-14 591B warming supplies instruction.

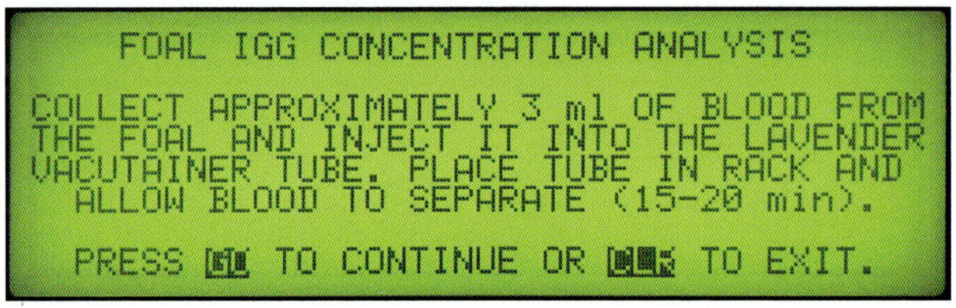

Figure 28-15 591B collect blood from foal instruction.

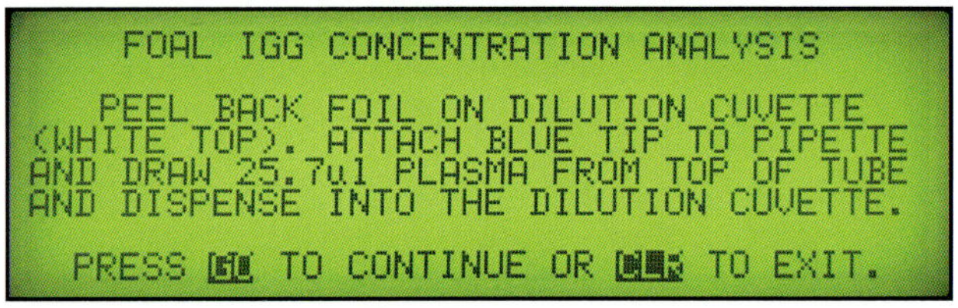

Figure 28-16 591B add plasma to dilution cuvette instruction..

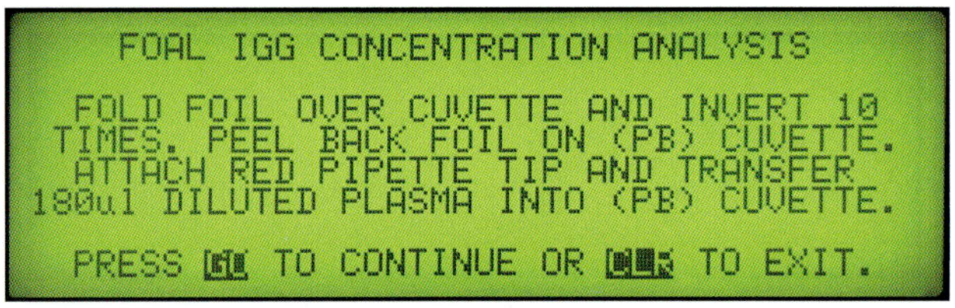

Figure 28-17 591B transfer diluted plasma instruction.

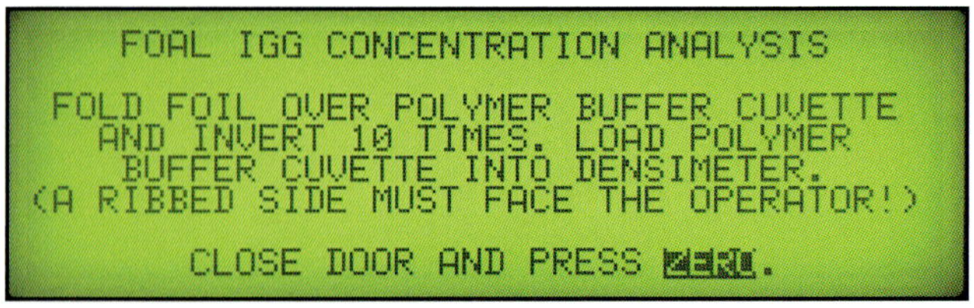

Figure 28-18 591B mix diluted plasma before zeroing instruction..

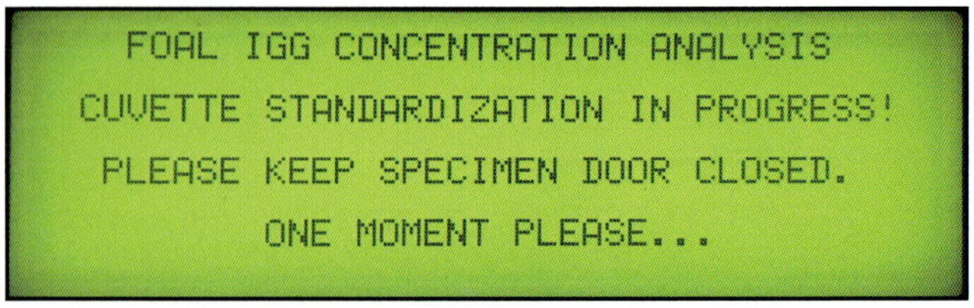

Figure 28-19 591B display during 'Zeroing' Densimeter.

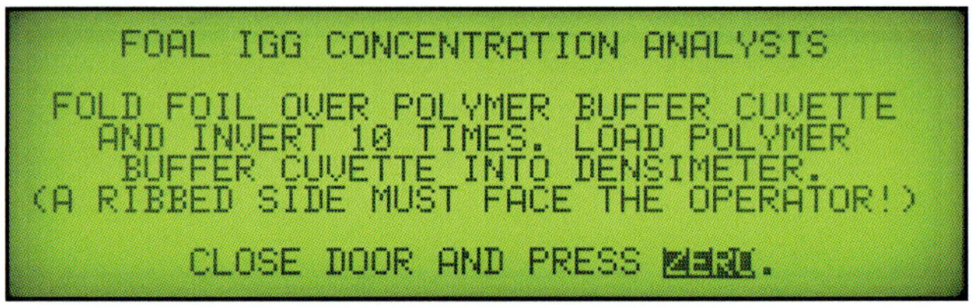

Figure 28-20 591B mix diluted plasma before zeroing instruction..

Figure 28-21 591B add anti-IgG serum to cuvette instruction..

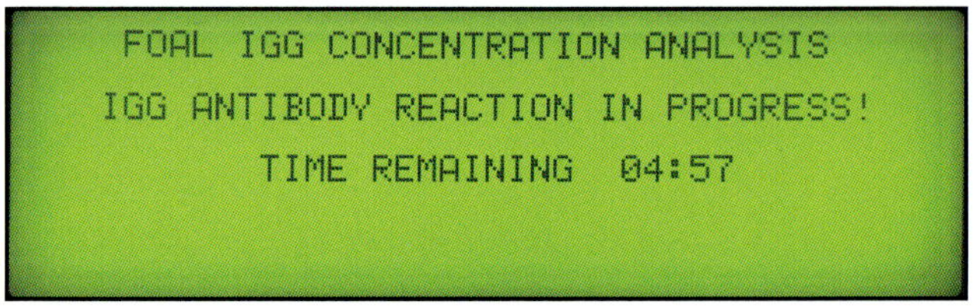

Figure 28-22 591B display during automatic countdown incubation timer.

Figure 28-23 591B final results screen showing IgG concentration of 342.1 mg/dl.

Chapter 29 Care of an Orphan Foal

Item	Part Number	Use/Comments
Equine Colostrum Refractometer	ECR-101	Used to evaluate colostrum quality of mare prior to nursing.

29.1 Initial Evaluation

The health status of the orphan foal should be determined. Evaluations may include a complete physical examination and diagnostic tests, as indicated, possibly including:

- Complete blood count (CBC), if indicated
- Serum chemistry panel, if indicated
- IgG test to evaluate passive transfer

Routine medical and nursing care should be provided as needed, including, but not limited to:

- Umbilicus should be disinfected in a newborn foal
- Tetanus antitoxin if vaccination status is unknown
- Antibiotics if foal is at risk of pathogen exposure
- Colostrum or plasma should be administered, depending on age of foal, if IgG is less than 400 to 800 mg/dl

29.2 Colostrum

The next priority for an orphaned newborn foal is an adequate quantity of good quality colostrum. A newborn foal should ultimately receive a total of 1 to 2 liters of good quality colostrum divided over several feedings in order to acquire sufficient antibodies for immune protection.

Colostrum quality can be estimated with an Equine Colostrum Refractometer or a colostrometer or directly assessed by measurement of IgG content in a single radial immunoassay (Table 1).

Administration of colostrum may be accomplished using a bottle and nipple or through passage of a nasogastric tube. If sufficient equine colostrum is not available, a commercial equine IgG antibody preparation (i.e. Seramune™) or hyperimmune equine plasma may be administered.

Table 29-1 Quality assessment of equine colostrum.

Colostrum Quality	IgG Conc. (mg/dl)	Brix (%)	Specific Gravity
Very Good	> 8,000	> 30	≥ 1.10
Good	5,000 - 8,000	20 - 30	1.08 - 1.09
Fair	2,800 - 5,000	15 - 20	1.06 - 1.07
Poor	< 2,800	<15	< 1.06

29.3 Nurse Mare

Once the foal has been provided colostrum, the optimal approach would be to foster the foal onto a nurse mare if one is available. Options for a nurse mare include a mare that lost her foal, a mare that has recently weaned her foal and is still lactating or induction of lactation in a non-pregnant mare. In addition, the prospective nurse mare should have a good temperament and be of a size appropriate for the breed of the foal.

Appropriate restraint of the prospective nurse mare may be important during the initial fostering or grafting procedure.

Techniques during initial grafting may include:

- Manual restraint and/or distraction of the mare with grain (Figure 29-1)

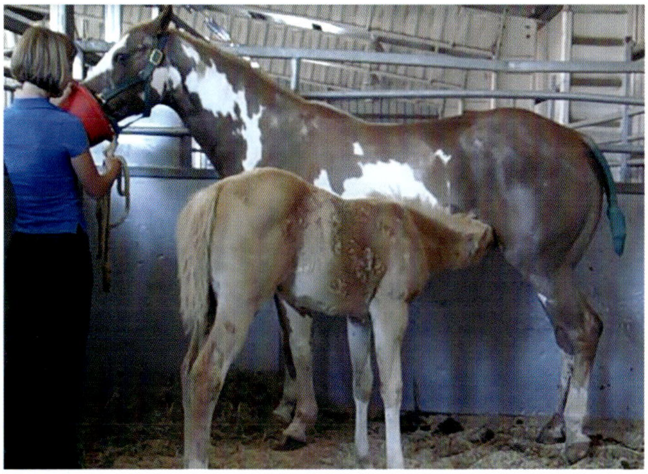

Figure 29-1 Feeding a prospective nurse mare grain while attempting to foster a foal onto her.

- Other options include sedation, blindfolding (Figure 29-2), hobbles, olfactory blockage with scents applied around nostrils of mare or a grafting spray applied onto the foal (i.e. MotherUp®)
- Prostaglandin therapy to stimulate maternal behavior
  - Administer 3 to 5 mls of cloprostenol (250 μg/ml) intramuscularly
  - Wait until the mare is actively sweating
  - Introduce foal to mare slowly
- It is helpful if the foal is hungry, active and willing to seek the udder during the initial introduction to the nurse mare
- Monitor reaction of the nurse mare during grafting process and stop the procedure if adverse events occur
- Continued assessment of the behavior of the mare and nursing of the foal over the subsequent 24 to 48 hours

Patient and experienced personnel and a gentle accepting nurse mare candidate are all tremendously valuable in the grafting process.

29.4 Milk Replacer

If a foal cannot be fostered onto a nurse mare, it can be hand-reared using a commercial milk replacer or a milk substitute. Commercial mare milk replacers provide a convenient means of supplying nutrients to the foal. Milk replacers are dehydrated, nutrient-rich, milk-like products and can be found at most feed stores. Only those designed for foals should be used; one should avoid using milk replacers from other species (e.g. calf, lamb, etc.). Good quality mare milk replacers come with a complete set of instructions on how to use the product. There are numerous mare's milk replacer powders commercially available.

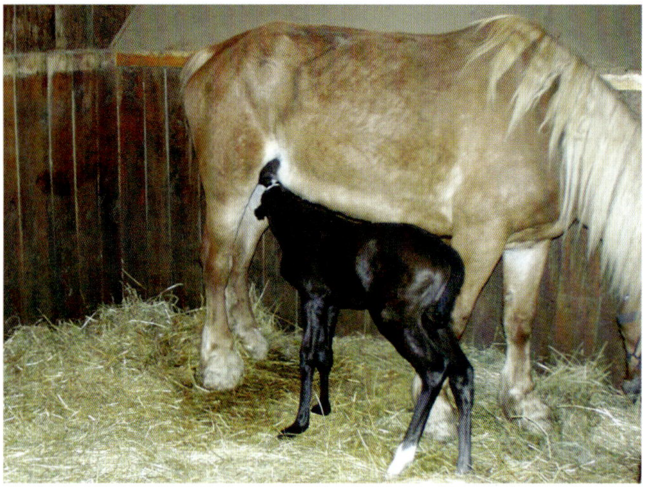

Figure 29-2 Orphaned 3-day-old Thoroughbred foal fostered onto a Belgian nurse mare. The mare was blindfolded and fed grain during the initial introduction.

Milk replacers should contain about 15 % fat, 22 % crude protein and have a fiber content of less than 0.5 percent. If a foal becomes constipated when fed a commercial milk replacer, it may be beneficial to provide a more dilute solution. If this is done, a greater volume of diluted milk replacer solution should be fed to provide the recommended total dry matter intake.

A commercial milk replacer can be fed to the foal using either a nipple bottle or a wide-mouthed bucket (Figure 29-3 and 26-4). A bucket may be

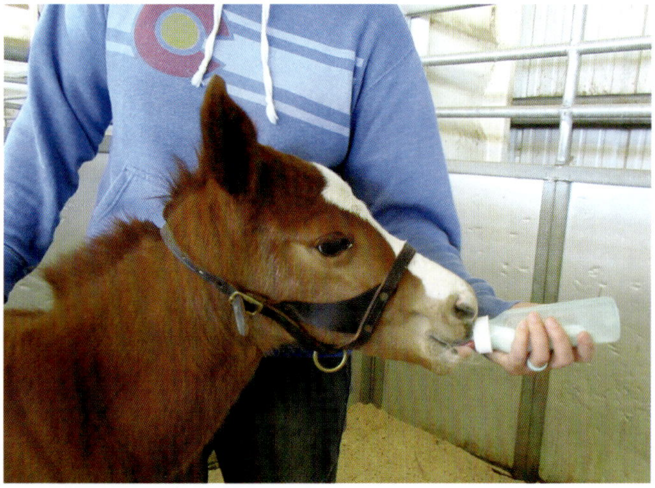

Figure 29-3 Feeding an orphan foal with a bottle.

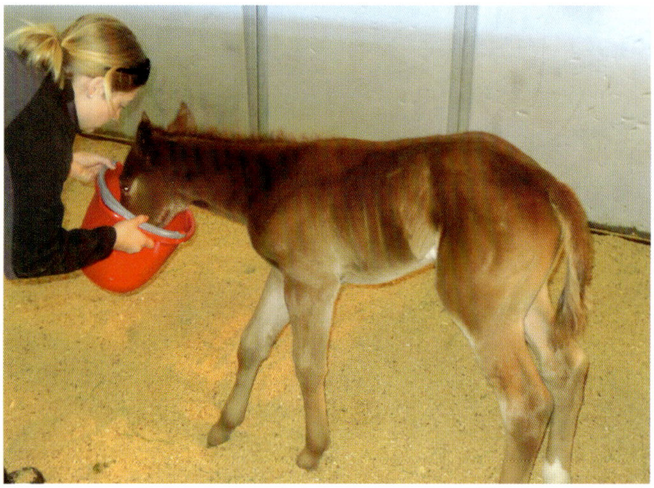

Figure 29-4 Teaching an orphan foal to drink out of a bucket.

preferred because it involves less labor (i.e. no around the clock feedings) and allows the foal constant access to the milk replacer which more closely simulates a nursing foal's pattern of feeding.

However, if a foal is not allowed frequent access or goes relatively long periods without the replacer (6 to 8 hours), it may gorge itself upon reintroduction and experience digestive disturbances. Constant access to the milk replacer prevents this problem.

Teaching the foal to drink from a bucket is relatively easy; however, the type of bucket used is important. It should be relatively wide-mouthed and shallow (approximately 12 inches in diameter and 8 inches in depth).

To teach a foal to drink out of a bucket, one should first place a finger in the foal's mouth to stimulate the suckling reflex and then gradually lower the hand into the bucket until the foal's mouth comes into contact with the milk replacer. Although this requires patience with some foals, most foals can learn to drink from a bucket within 1 to 3 lessons.

Milk replacer should always be kept fresh and clean. Once mixed, it should be fed within 12 hours to prevent spoilage. The foal will drink approximately 1.5 to 2 gallons in a 24 hour period. Some milk replacers contain acidifiers to preserve them for a longer period of time. However, the ideal regime is to supply the foal with an amount of reconstituted milk replacer that will be almost completely consumed between each of the feedings (minimum of two feedings per day).

Milk substitutes should be fed to a total volume of approximately 10 % of the foal's body weight at one day of age. The amount fed should be gradually increased to 25 % of body weight per day from day 10 until weaning.

Whole milk from a cow or goat has almost twice the fat content and only two-thirds the sugar content of mare's milk. An adequate foal milk replacer can be produced by adding one teaspoon of white corn syrup to 8 ounces of low-fat (2 %) cow's milk.

Alternatively, dextrose (not table sugar) can be added at a rate of 4 teaspoon per 24 ounces of low-fat cow's milk to approximate the content of mare's milk. Table sugar may cause diarrhea and thus should be avoided. Goat's milk has been used on many occasions to feed an orphan foal. Goat's milk

Figure 29-5 Orphan foal nursing from a dairy goat.

can cause firm stools and impactions when fed to foals. Consequently, administration of 0.5 to 1.0 ounces of mineral oil (orally once to twice daily) may be beneficial if constipation occurs. In some cases, a dairy goat has been used to provide milk for an orphan foal (Figure 29-5). A safe stable structure that the goat can climb on should be provided; the foal is able to nurse once the goat has climbed onto the structure.

Foals should be fed every one to two hours during the first few days after birth. The frequency of feeding can be decreased to every four to six hours after two weeks of age. Overall weight gains in foals reared on an artificial diet are similar to gains in foals allowed to nurse from their dams.

29.5 Induction of Lactation

Stimulation of milk production in a non-pregnant mare may be accomplished by a combination of exogenous hormone therapy and hand milking. A technique that has worked well in our clinical practice is as follows:

- Select a calm, gentle mare that has given birth and lactated previously.
- Administer estradiol once daily for 2 to 3 days
- Administer the dopamine antagonist domperidone (Equidone®) twice daily for 7 to 14 days
- Start hand milking 4 to 6 times daily on the 4th to 7th day of treatment, when the mammary gland has increased in size (Figure 29-6).
- Oxytocin may be administered during milking to promote milk let-down.

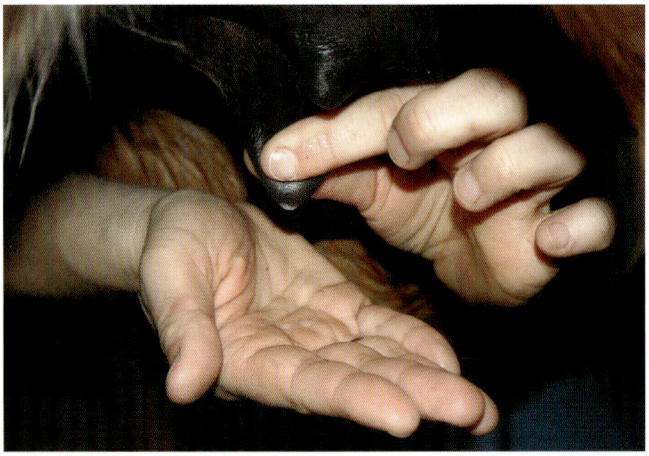

Figure 29-6 Expression of milk from a mare induced to lactate.

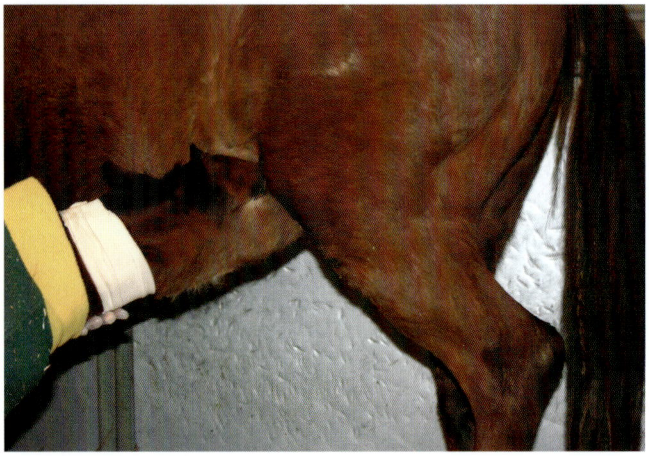

Figure 29-7 Orphan foal nursing from a mare induced to lactate.

- Introduce foal after 3 to 4 days of milking, when milk production has increased (Figure 26-7).

29.6 Additional Considerations

- Provide milk replacer pellets in a creep feeder for an older orphan
- Raise orphan foals in a group rather than alone
- Provide an adult equine 'chaperone' if a nurse mare is not available

Appendix 1 Calculation of Relative Gravitational Force for any Centrifuge

Selection of the speed for centrifugation is dependent on the following factors:

- Type of centrifuge (i.e. rotating radius)
- Whether or not a cushion is used
- Whether or not a colloid or density gradient is used

The relative centrifugal force (i.e. gravitational force; *g*-force or x *g*) of any centrifuge can be determined if revolutions per minute (rpm) and the rotating radius (r) of the arms of the centrifuge are known (Figure A-1).

Figure A-1 The rotating radius of a centrifuge is the distance measured from the center of the centrifuge to the end of the bucket when held horizontally.

A Nomograph chart (Figure A-2) can be used to determine the relative centrifugal force (gravitational force; *g*-force; x *g*) if the rotating radius of the centrifuge is known and the speed (revolutions per minute) of the centrifuge can be controlled. A line is drawn between the rotating radius (left side of chart) and the speed (rpm; right side of chart). The point at which the line intersects the relative centrifugal force scale determines the *g*-force (center of chart) for that specific centrifuge. Again, if the rotating radius is known and the rpm can be controlled, the *g*-force can be calculated.

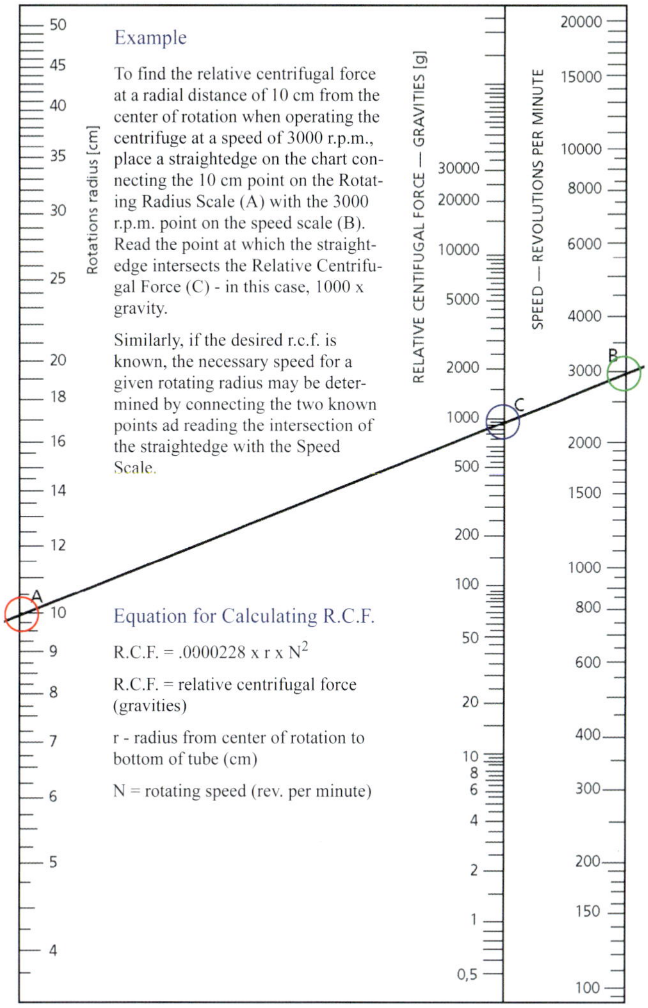

Figure A-2 Nomograph to determine relative centrifugal force (RCF). Using the chart, a g-force of 1,000 (blue circle) can be obtained from a centrifuge with a rotating radius of 10 cm (red circle) if the RPM is set at 3,000 (green circle).

Appendix 2 Test Freezing Stallion Semen

A split ejaculate test freeze should be performed the first time semen from an individual stallion is frozen. A test freeze is designed to compare post-thaw motility characteristics between several freezing extenders. The ultimate goal is to identify a cryopreservation protocol for an individual stallion that maximizes sperm survival after freezing and thawing. It is important that the test freeze compare multiple freezing extenders on the same ejaculate.

Example Test Freeze Protocol using E-Z Freezin® Equine Semen Extenders

1. Thaw one packet of each of the following ARS freezing extenders

E-Z Freezin® 'LE'

E-Z Freezin® 'MFR5'

E-Z Freezin® CryoMax™ LE

E-Z Freezin® CryoMax™ MFR5

2. Collect semen from the stallion for the test freeze
3. Evaluate semen for volume, concentration and motility (total and progressive)
4. Extend raw semen with E-Z Mixin® 'BF' (1:1 semen:extender)
5. Transfer extended semen into one or more 50 ml conical tubes
6. Optional: place 3.0 mls of cushion at bottom of conical tube, below extended semen
7. Centrifuge to concentrate spermatozoa (900 x *g* for 10 minutes without cushion or 1,000 x *g* for 25 minutes if a cushion is used)
8. Aspirate off seminal plasma supernatant and remove cushion below sperm pellet (if a cushion was used)
9. Combine pellets from all tubes into one 50 ml conical tube (if more than one tube was used for centrifugation)
10. Transfer an approximately equal volume of the combined pellets into each of 4 new 50 ml conical tubes
11. Re-suspend pellets in the conical tubes with 1.0 ml of each of the four freezing extenders to be evaluated
12. Perform a sperm count using a hemocytometer
13. Further dilute semen to a final concentration of 200 million sperm per ml using the appropriate freezing extenders to be evaluated
14. Package extended semen in labeled 0.5 ml straws
15. Load straws on a freezing rack and place in refrigerator for 30 minutes to cool to 5°C
16. Place freezing rack 3 cm over liquid nitrogen for 10 minutes
17. Plunge straws into liquid nitrogen
18. Thaw one or two straws frozen in each extender in a 37°C water bath for 30 seconds
19. Evaluate total and progressive sperm motility after warming to 37°C for 10 minutes
20. Select the extender with the best post-thaw sperm motility for use in the future

Appendix 3 Liquid Nitrogen (LN2) Safety

Properties of Liquid Nitrogen

The temperature of liquid nitrogen is -196° C (-320° F)

Liquid nitrogen expands tremendously upon vaporizing (x 700 fold)

One liter of liquid nitrogen expands to 24.6 cubic feet of nitrogen gas

Hazards of Liquid Nitrogen

Liquid nitrogen can cause severe frostbite

Expansion of liquid nitrogen upon vaporizing can cause an explosion if in a sealed container

Vaporized liquid nitrogen can displace oxygen in a non-ventilated area (room, vehicle, etc.) and subsequently lead to suffocation

Precautions when handling Liquid Nitrogen

Do not allow LN2 or objects frozen by LN2 to contact skin

Do not allow LN2 to become trapped in clothing near skin

Avoid spilling or splashing LN2 when transferring

Never allow any unprotected part of your body to touch objects cooled by liquid nitrogen

Use only approved unsealed containers designed for LN2

- Never use containers with tight seals
- Sealed containers may explode

Handle LN2 Dewars with care as they can be damaged easily

Maintain adequate ventilation when transporting LN2 containers

Never dip a hollow tube into LN2; liquid may squirt up the tube

Use solid metal or plastic dipsticks to check LN2 fluid levels (i.e. not a wooden 'yardstick')

Use and store in well ventilated areas

- LN2 can displace oxygen and cause asphyxiation

Wear protective clothing

- Safety goggles should always be worn when handling LN2
- Face shield
  - Recommended when pouring or filling
- Insulated cryo gloves
  - Should be loose fitting so that they can be immediately removed if LN2 splashes into them
- Lab coat with long sleeves
  - To minimize skin contact
- Long pants
- Proper footwear
  - No canvas shoes
  - No open-toed shoes

Disposal of Liquid Nitrogen

Never dispose of liquid nitrogen in confined areas or places where others may enter

Do not pour down a sink or drain

Dispose of excess LN2 in an outdoor area to allow for safe evaporation

Pour the liquid slowly on gravel or bare earth where it can evaporate without causing damage

Do not pour the LN2 on pavement

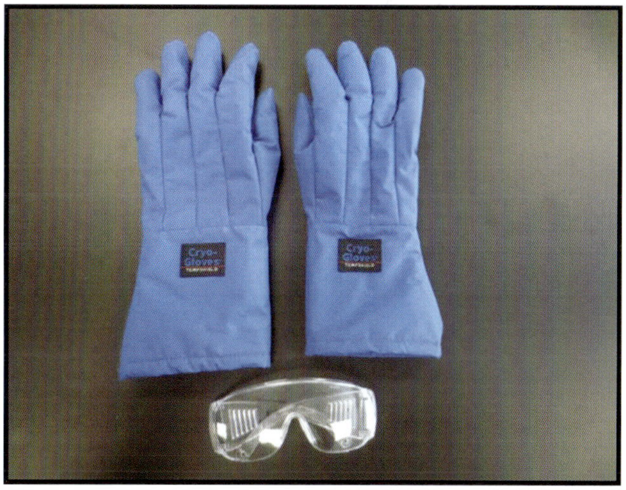